THE EUROPEAN CONVENTION
ON H

This book critically appra... Rights as it faces some daunting challenges. It argues that the Convention's core functions have subtly changed, particularly since the ending of the Cold War, and that these are now to articulate an 'abstract constitutional model' for the entire continent and to promote convergence in the operation of public institutions at every level of governance. The implications – from national compliance to European international relations, including the adjudication of disputes by the European Court of Human Rights – are fully explored. As the first book-length socio-legal examination of the Convention's principal achievements and failures, this study not only blends legal and social science scholarship around the theme of constitutionalization, but also offers a coherent set of policy proposals which both address the current case-management crisis and suggest ways forward neglected by recent reforms.

STEVEN GREER is Professor of Human Rights at the School of Law, University of Bristol. He has published widely and has also acted as consultant to various organizations, including the Council of Europe.

CAMBRIDGE STUDIES IN EUROPEAN LAW AND POLICY

This series aims to produce original works which contain a critical analysis of the state of the law in particular areas of European law and set out different perspectives and suggestions for its future development. It also aims to encourage a range of work on law, legal institutions and legal phenomena in Europe, including 'Law in context' approaches. The titles in the series will be of interest to academics; policymakers; policy formers who are interested in European legal, commercial, and political affairs; practising lawyers including the judiciary; and advanced law students and researchers.

Books in the series
EU Enlargement and the Constitutions of Central and Eastern Europe
Anneli Albi
Social Rights and Market Freedom in the European Economic Constitution
A Labour Law Perspective
Stefano Giubboni
The Constitution for Europe
A Legal Analysis
Jean-Claude Piris
The European Convention on Human Rights
Steven Greer

THE EUROPEAN CONVENTION ON HUMAN RIGHTS

Achievements, Problems and Prospects

STEVEN GREER

CAMBRIDGE UNIVERSITY PRESS
Cambridge, New York, Melbourne, Madrid, Cape Town, Singapore,
São Paulo, Delhi, Dubai, Tokyo, Mexico City

Cambridge University Press
The Edinburgh Building, Cambridge CB2 8RU, UK

Published in the United States of America by Cambridge University Press, New York

www.cambridge.org
Information on this title: www.cambridge.org/9780521608596

First published 2006
Reprinted 2008

A catalogue record for this publication is available from the British Library

Library of Congress Cataloguing in Publication Data

Greer, S. C. (Steven C.)
The European Convention on Human Rights: achievements, problems and prospects /
Steven Crawford Greer.
p. cm.
Includes bibliographical references and index.
ISBN-13: 978-0-521-84617-2 (hardback)
ISBN-10: 0-521-84617-X (hardback)
ISBN-13: 978-0-521-60859-6 (pbk.)
ISBN-13: 0-521-60859-7 (pbk.)
1. Convention for the Protection of Human Rights and Fundamental
Freedoms (1950) 2. Human rights Europe. I. Title.
KJC5132.G74 2006
342.4108'5–dc22 2006021254

ISBN 978-0-521-84617-2 Hardback
ISBN 978-0-521-60859-6 Paperback

To my parents, Crawford and Marie Greer

CONTENTS

LIST OF FIGURES

LIST OF TABLES

FOREWORD

The European Convention on Human Rights, the case law of the Strasbourg institutions and the degree of success with which, for all its problems, the Convention system has met in ensuring respect for fundamental rights in Council of Europe member states are subjects that have attracted much comment and analysis. To this great mass of scholarship, Professor Greer brings a work that stands out in several respects. This is neither a handbook nor a textbook. It is instead a thoroughgoing argument for the constitutionalization of the Convention and its Court, which the author portrays not as a transformation but rather as consolidation. This book comes at a particularly crucial moment for the Convention system. While its history is in fact one of continuous growth, adaptation and reform, the stakes for Europe and its human rights protection system have never been higher. In the matter of fundamental rights, the Strasbourg Court is positioned at the apex of all the national judicial systems in Europe with just one exception. Its ability to function effectively, i.e. to rule authoritatively on the Convention and to administer justice to those who come before it is vital not just to the Strasbourg strand, but to the whole web of institutions and procedures that uphold and enforce the substance of the Convention throughout the *espace juridique européen*. The year 2006 is one of anticipated and much-awaited change, with the expected entry into force of Protocol No. 14, which will effect certain valuable procedural reforms, giving the Court some additional breathing space. But the reflection process continues, steered by the Committee of Wise Persons, an eminent and expert group tasked with mapping the longer road to viability and effectiveness in the years ahead. Professor Greer's arguments and proposals will surely command much attention from all of the actors in this process: national authorities, the institutions of the Council of Europe, the Court itself, and civil society.

In keeping with the distinctive identity of the system, the author devotes much of this book to the evolving purpose and continuing effect of the Convention at national level. The impressive second chapter takes the reader into territory that is rarely visited by Convention scholars, where traditional legal analysis, however skilful, will not in itself suffice. Mindful of the difficulty of devising a methodologically sound and scientifically valid means of assessing national rates of compliance with the Convention, the author draws upon scholarship spanning several disciplines to present the reader with an assessment of and possible explanation for the degree to which Council of Europe states have successfully integrated the Convention into their national legal and political orders. In a nicely-turned phrase, the author observes that while the Convention was not the architect of the process of democratization in central and eastern Europe, it can play the role of interior designer. Although more comparative and cross-disciplinary inquiry will be required in this field, this book makes a major contribution to the endeavour.

The present state of the Convention system is described and analysed with great insight. In response to the near-crisis of the individual justice model, the author maps the way towards a more stable scenario by means of improved compliance at national level, modification of the current processes and fresh institutional innovation. Regarding each of these vectors, he advances arguments of considerable force and originality. Professor Greer writes as a friend of the Convention system, speaking with the candour that characterizes true friendship. His call to the Court to rearrange the 'primordial soup' of the principles of interpretation is delivered with the audacity of an ally who seeks to speed the institution towards its constitutional destiny.

I might add that since I have myself tried for some time to nudge the Court in the direction of a more constitutional future, it has given me great pleasure to encounter an ally who transcends by far the 'primordial soup' of those critics who either are content to advocate different outcomes of individual cases or else want to inflict ideologies on the Court that were never democratically discussed or approved.

I commend Professor Greer for this excellent book, and commend it to all those to whom the Convention's present and future are entrusted.

Luzius Wildhaber
President, European Court of Human Rights

PREFACE

This book critically appraises the European Convention on Human Rights at a time of considerable change. Unlike the many excellent textbooks now available it does not seek to offer a comprehensive description of relevant institutions, procedures and norms. Nor does it attempt to contribute to every issue-specific debate conducted in the periodical literature. Instead, it discusses both the key successes and a cluster of systemic problems which require resolution if the Convention is to be as successful as it could, and should, be in the twenty-first century. Some of the latter derive, ironically, from what is universally said to be its most notable achievement – the individual applications process – and others from the political, economic, constitutional, and legal environment in Europe, radically transformed by the post-1989 upheavals. Yet others stem from the way in which the European Court of Human Rights has interpreted both the Convention text and its own role. There is wide consensus on both the nature of some of these problems and how they should be resolved. Others provoke intense controversy and sharp differences of opinion. Yet others have been largely, and some even entirely, ignored.

Six core issues, organized around the theme of 'constitutionalization', are considered in the following pages. First, Chapter 1 argues that, at the close of the twentieth century, the original *raison d'être* for the Convention underwent subtle, yet fundamental, change. At its foundation the Convention provided both an expression of the identity of western European liberal democracy, self-consciously contrasted with the rival communist model of central and eastern Europe, and also a means by which states could seek to defend each other from the internal threat of authoritarianism by bringing complaints to an international judicial tribunal. However, at the beginning of the twenty-first century, the Convention's principal roles are to articulate an 'abstract constitutional model' for the entire continent – including and especially for the newly-admitted post-communist states – and to provide a device for promoting convergence in the deep structure and function of public institutions at all levels of governance in Europe.

The rest of the book is an attempt to discern what this might mean. Given that each member state, likely soon to be joined by the EU, bears the primary responsibility for the realization of Convention values within its jurisdiction, the second of the core issues, considered in Chapter 2, concerns how compliance might be measured and which factors most promote it. Chapter 3 addresses the third issue, the Court's case overload crisis, which is unlikely to be solved by the Protocol 14 reforms, scheduled to come into effect in late 2006 or early 2007. With an annual average of 45,000 individual applications, and only 800–1,000 judgments a year, the right of individual petition has become, contrary to the received wisdom, the Convention's biggest problem rather than its greatest success. Further changes are, therefore, urgently required, whether or not the existing institutional structure is altered. Two further difficulties concern the method of adjudication and the substantive case law. Chapter 4 argues that the coherence and impact of the Court's judgments could be improved if the former showed greater fidelity to the Convention's primary constitutional principles, while Chapter 5 pursues the logic of this analysis in the jurisprudence. Chapter 6 considers the sixth issue – the institutional changes which are required if Convention compliance is to be improved. It argues that, in addition to making all the Court's judgments binding on all member states, including their courts, a European Fair Trials Commission should be created. However, it also maintains that, in the final analysis, the best prospects for improving national compliance lie in the creation of National Human Rights Institutions, established according to a common model, which would provide the Court and the European Commissioner for Human Rights with reliable information about systemic national problems, and which could also be empowered to bring test cases to the Court, either through the Commissioner or on their own initiative. Finally, Chapter 7 seeks to weave the conclusions of the previous chapters into a coherent summary of the book's main themes, arguments, and proposals.

As with virtually all Convention scholarship, a key data source for this study has been the case law of the European Court of Human Rights, and, to a lesser extent, that of the European Commission of Human Rights (abolished in 1998). The *European Human Rights Reports* (EHRR), the Council of Europe's *Decisions and Reports* (DR) and the *Yearbooks of the European Convention on Human Rights* (YB) have provided particularly useful collections of the most significant decisions and judgments. However, for two reasons, no attempt has been made to cite this now substantial body of jurisprudence comprehensively, particularly in Chapters 4 and 5 where the temptation to do so was strongest. First, Convention case law typically takes the form of abstract principle applied to facts. Rarely, if ever, does it amount to what jurists in the common law tradition would recognize as an integrated system of judicially constructed 'legal rules'. This is an inevitable consequence not only of the highly abstract character of Convention rights and principles, but also of the fact that the concrete elements of any judgment will probably only apply to the specific respondent state because the precise legal and factual matters at issue are unlikely to be reproduced in all relevant particulars elsewhere. Unlike common law systems, where each judicial decision can plausibly be regarded as a component piece in a complex and integrated legal mosaic, judgments of the European Court of Human Rights tend, therefore, to illustrate how a relevant principle applies to certain facts. It follows that any one or more of several judgments can usually be cited for that purpose. Second, since the Court tends to restate its interpretation of a given principle verbatim in verdict after verdict, there is little need to refer to every occasion on which it has done so. For these reasons, and in keeping with the publisher's policy for this series, there is, therefore, no table of cases. Furthermore, in seeking answers to the questions raised by this research, the parameters have had to be cast much wider than is typical in most legal scholarship. Relevant contributions from philosophy, history, political science, international relations, and comparative law have also been consulted. My preliminary reflections on some of the core themes appeared in earlier publications, particularly in two short monographs published by the Council of Europe in the Human Rights Files series in 1997 and 2000, and in four articles in 2003, 2004, and 2005, in the *Oxford Journal of Legal Studies*, the *Cambridge Law Journal*, and *Public Law*. Further details can be found in the Bibliography. I am grateful to the respective publishers for allowing up-dated and revised versions of some of this material to be included here.

Without the assistance of a great many people and organizations this book would have been impossible or much more difficult to write. Needless to say, responsibility for the conclusions it contains remains mine alone. However, I would like to express my profound gratitude to the following for their contributions. The British Academy gave the project a flying start by awarding me the 'Thank-Offering' to Britain

Research Fellowship which I held at the University of Bristol in the academic year 2002–3, funds for which were generously provided by Jewish refugees who fled anti-semitism in continental Europe in the 1930s. I was also fortunate to receive a British Academy Small Research Grant which helped defray the costs of two visits to Strasbourg, in June 2003 and January 2004, when key players in the debate about the reform of the Convention system were interviewed. The University of Bristol not only contributed to the costs of these trips, and to a visit to London in 2004 when representatives of Amnesty International were interviewed, but also enabled me to accept the 'Thank Offering' Fellowship, and generously granted a further period of study leave in the academic year 2005–6 to hasten the project's completion. By commissioning the two monographs referred to in the previous paragraph, the Council of Europe helped inspire this study, provided and permitted the publication of some statistics otherwise not in the public domain, and also kindly facilitated three visits to Strasbourg where I was received with great courtesy and hospitality. David Crowe, of the Information and Publications Support Unit in the Council of Europe's Directorate General of Human Rights, not only expertly edited the Human Rights Files monographs, but also went to a great deal of trouble to arrange two of these visits, showed great kindness and friendship throughout my time there, and responded positively and promptly to various queries since. The Universities of Bristol, Ulster and Essex, and the Society of Legal Scholars and the Socio-Legal Studies Association, together provided no less than nine opportunities for embryonic versions of some of the ideas presented here to be exposed to probing questions and constructive criticism from colleagues in various staff seminars or conferences. Professor Colm Campbell of the University of Ulster, Professor David Feldman of the University of Cambridge, Professor Martin Lynn, formerly of Queens University Belfast (now sadly deceased), and Professor Malcolm Evans, Professor Rachel Murray, Dr Tonia Novitz, Dr Pat Capps, Dr Julian Rivers, Dr Phil Syrpis, Dr Achilles Skordas, and Chris Willimore of the University of Bristol, either referred me to sources I might otherwise have missed, commented on earlier drafts, enthusiastically debated the issues with me, or simply offered their encouragement and support. Mike Drew assisted with the graphics, Windy Hon and Esther Yee helped edit the Bibliography, and Esther also checked the figures. The Finnish delegation to the Council of Europe kindly invited me to attend a Symposium on the Reform of the European Court of Human Rights, held in Strasbourg on 17 November 2003 which provided an illuminating insight into the reform debate. Finola O'Sullivan and her colleagues at Cambridge University Press expertly piloted the project from submission of the initial proposal to publication. Finally, the love and support of Susan, my wife, and Cara, Lucy, and Hope, my daughters, helped, as always, to sustain me.

Steven Greer
Bristol
2006

1

The First Half Century

INTRODUCTION

The European Convention on Human Rights is an international treaty for the protection of fundamental (mostly) civil and political liberties in European democracies committed to the rule of law. It was created in 1950 by the ten Council of Europe states – an organization founded the previous year – as part of the process of reconstructing western Europe in the aftermath of the Second World War. Like the Council of Europe itself, it has since grown to embrace every state in Europe except Belarus, forty-six in total, with a land mass stretching from Iceland to Vladivostok and a combined population of nearly 800 million.

It is not, of course, the only international human rights treaty in the contemporary world. Several others are global in scope and there are also regional regimes in the Americas, Africa, in the Arab world, and between the former Soviet republics. But it is unique in providing, what is widely regarded as the most effective trans-national judicial process for complaints brought by individuals and organizations against their own governments, and, much less frequently, accusations of violation made by member states against each other. Nor is the Convention the only site for the institutionalization of the human rights ideal in post-war Europe. The profile of human rights has grown in other transnational European organizations, particularly and increasingly, the European Union, while national constitutional and legal processes have also converged around a single model characterized by the Convention ideals of constitutional democracy, human rights, and the rule of law.

The Convention's fiftieth birthday was marked, in 2000, by celebration of the fact that it had matured from uncertain infancy at the height of the Cold War into an institution now deeply entrenched in western Europe, and beginning to take root in the new democracies of the former Soviet-bloc. Yet, even before its birthday celebrations had begun, it was clear that it faced a crisis raising fundamental questions about its future and purpose. This study argues that the solution lies in a process of 'constitutionalization'. But, before considering what this might entail, the Convention's core achievements and difficulties first need to be identified. Two questions are particularly central: what was it originally for, and how, if at all, has this been changed by events over the past half century?

HUMAN RIGHTS, LIBERALISM AND INTERNATIONALISM

The modern western 'human rights ideal' can be summed up as follows: prima facie everyone has an equal legitimate claim to those tangible and intangible goods and benefits most essential for human well-being. Self-evident though this notion might seem in contemporary Europe, it did not gain serious political and social momentum until the collapse of feudalism in the early modern era accompanied by the rise of natural rights theory, liberalism, constitutionalism and internationalism.[1] The European Convention on Human Rights is one of the many products of this process.

Like many other pre-modern societies, European feudalism was based not upon rights as such, but upon obligations attached to tiers of a fixed social hierarchy considered 'natural' and God-given. But as feudalism succumbed to crisis in the late middle ages, new theories of legitimate social order and authority were required to fill the void. With the advance of secularism and rationalism, the 'naturalness' of divinely ordained, fixed social hierarchy became increasingly discredited, and the 'natural' needs of individual human beings was emphasized instead.[2] The natural rights theorists of the seventeenth and eighteenth centuries

[1] For useful accounts see, e.g. M. Freeman, *Human Rights: An Interdisciplinary Approach* (London: Polity Press, 2002), pp. 14–31; C. Douzinas, *The End of Human Rights: Critical Legal Thought at the Turn of the Century* (Oxford: Hart, 2000); R. J. Vincent, *Human Rights and International Relations* (Cambridge: Cambridge University Press, 1986), pp. 7–36; E. Kamenka, 'The Anatomy of an Idea' in E. Kamenka and A. Soon Tay (eds.), *Human Rights* (London: Edward Arnold, 1978), pp. 1–12.

[2] Although the ideas of 'rights' and of 'natural rights' gained currency in the early modern period, the roots of the debate can be traced to ancient Roman law. See, e.g. T. Honoré, *Ulpian: Pioneer of Human Rights* (Oxford: Oxford University Press, 2nd edn., 2002); Freeman, *Human Rights*, pp. 16–18.

argued that since nobody in the 'state of nature' – outside the social and political institutions associated with 'civilization' – has a stronger claim to survival than anybody else, everyone has an equal 'natural right to survive', the 'right to life'. The right to life implies a right to the means of survival – 'property' in a wide sense – plus the right to organize survival as each chooses – liberty and other derivative rights, for example the right freely to associate with others. According to this view, the political state and civil society can be conceived as a contract between rational, self-interested, formally equal individuals to secure their fundamental natural rights, with the social and political order this suggests retaining its legitimacy only in so far as these contractual commitments continue to be fulfilled.[3] Inherent in this idea was also the notion – deemed an essential condition for ending the religious wars which had scoured Europe since the Reformation – that the state should be neutral between competing conceptions of the meaning and purpose of life. Paradoxically for two of the three leading natural rights theorists – Hobbes and Rousseau – the social contract could legitimately produce authoritarianism of, respectively, the state and the community. But for Locke, and what became the liberal tradition, only the constitutional state – limited by constitutional rights and by the rule of law – could effectively protect natural rights.[4]

To gain ascendancy a political ideal not only needs a certain threshold level of coherence and plausibility, but also the support of powerful interest groups who see some benefit for themselves in its effective realization. This was also true of the Lockean idea of natural rights and the constitutional state which was carried to prominence in the early modern period by the economically powerful, though politically emasculated, mercantile (and later industrial) middle classes in Europe and America.[5] The identity and material interests of this social group were intimately connected both with the freedom they enjoyed from feudal obligation – a negative right from which a whole catalogue of other negative rights or freedoms could apparently be 'logically' derived – and with a commercial world in which contracts were central

[3] See Douzinas, *End of Human Rights*, pp. 69–107.

[4] See J. R. Milton and P. Philip Milton (eds.), *John Locke: An Essay Concerning Toleration and other Writings on Law and Politics, 1667–1683* (Oxford/New York: Clarendon Press, 2006); M. Goldie (ed.), *John Locke: Two Treatises of Government* (London: Everyman, 1993).

[5] See Kamenka, 'Anatomy of an Idea', p. 8.

to their own, and they assumed to everyone else's, legitimate prosperity and progress.

In the eighteenth century the liberal social contractarian vision, popularized by campaigners such as Tom Paine,[6] inspired two formal declarations of rights, which later provided models for numerous subsequent documents both national and international including, in the twentieth century, the European Convention on Human Rights. In 1776 the Preamble to the *American Declaration of Independence* famously claimed 'these truths to be self-evident, that all men are created equal, that they are endowed by their Creator with certain unalienable rights, that among these are life, liberty and the pursuit of happiness'. In 1791 the US Constitution was amended by a series of constitutional rights, known collectively as the US Bill of Rights, which include the rights to freedom of religion, assembly, speech and the press, and the rights to bear arms, to jury trial, to privacy, to public trial, and to security of property.[7] Meanwhile, in 1789, the Preamble to the *French Declaration of the Rights of Man and the Citizen* had declared that 'the Representatives of the people of France formed into a National Assembly, considering that ignorance, contempt, or neglect of human rights are the sole causes of public misfortune and corruptions of Government, have resolved to set forth, in a solemn declaration, these natural, imprescriptible, and inalienable rights'. Faithful to the social contractarian tradition, Article II states that 'the end of all political associations is the preservation of the natural and imprescriptible rights of man; and these rights are liberty, property, security, and resistance of oppression'. Other provisions contain familiar rights to freedom of thought, conscience and religion, fair trial according to the rule of law, freedom from arbitrary arrest and detention, and democratic participation. In spite of their similar content there are, however, various formal differences between the French Declaration and the US Bill of Rights. For example, the French document, unlike the American, was drafted before the constitution and, therefore, gave the latter

[6] See T. Paine, *The Rights of Man* (Harmondsworth: Penguin, 1984); F. Klug, *Values for a Godless Age: The Story of the United Kingdom's New Bill of Rights* (London: Penguin, 2000), pp. 79–82.

[7] For a discussion of the global legacy of the US Bill of Rights see A. Lester, 'The Overseas Trade in the American Bill of Rights', *Columbia Law Review* **88** (1988), 537–561. However, Ackerman argues that 'we must learn to look upon the American... (constitutional)... experience as a special case, not as the paradigmatic case', B. Ackerman, 'The Rise of World Constitutionalism', *Virginia Law Review* **83** (1997), 771–797 at 775.

its legitimacy,[8] and the rights enshrined in the US Bill of Rights are generally expressed in absolute terms while those in the French Declaration are more formally circumscribed.[9]

The doctrine of natural rights, and its implications for the structure of state and society have, however, been hotly disputed since first formally articulated in Europe in the seventeeth and eighteenth centuries. Conservative critics, such as Edmund Burke, argued against replacing the 'organic' bonds of personal fealty and mutual personal obligation, cultivated by tradition over the centuries, with the much more impersonal, universal, formal, rationalistic, legalistic – and also allegedly more volatile and antagonistic – ones derived from the doctrine of natural rights.[10] Jeremy Bentham also launched a scathing critique, arguing that there are no such things as natural rights, and that the promotion of the greatest happiness of the greatest number (the principle of utility), is the only rational and universal moral principle.[11] Arguing that the only genuine rights are legal rights, Bentham maintained that these should only exist if they are consistent with the principle of utility. The protection such rights offer minorities is, therefore, precarious and unstable since they can be dispensed with in an instant if the overall pain caused by the persecution of a troublesome minority would be less than the aggregate satisfaction it would give the majority. Addressing this much-criticized defect, John Stewart Mill modified utilitarianism in the mid-nineteenth century by acknowledging that the application of the principle of utility should

[8] L. Hunt, *The French Revolution and Human Rights: A Brief Documentary History* (Boston/New York: Bedford Books, 1996), p. 15.

[9] Compare, for example, the First Amendment to the US Constitution – 'Congress shall make no law respecting an establishment of religion, or prohibiting the free exercise thereof; or abridging the freedom of speech, or of the press; or the right of the people peaceably to assemble, and to petition the government for a redress of grievances' – with Art. 10 of the French Declaration of the Rights of Man and the Citizen – 'No one shall be disquieted on account of his opinions, including his religious views, provided their manifestation does not disturb the public order established by law'. See the discussion of differences between the European Convention on Human Rights and the US Bill of Rights in N. Bobbio, *The Age of Rights*, trans. by A. Cameron (Cambridge: Polity Press, 1996), Chs. 6–8; Klug, *Values for A Godless Age*, pp. 127–132.

[10] E. Burke, *Reflections on the Revolution in France* in T. O. McLoughlin and J. T. Boulton, *The Writings and Speeches of Edmund Burke* (Oxford: Clarendon Press, 1997); Douzinas, *End of Human Rights*, pp. 147–157.

[11] J. Bentham, *Anarchical Fallacies; Being an Examination of the Declaration of the Rights Issued During the French Revolution* in P. Schofield, C. Pease-Watkin and C. Blamires (eds.), *Jeremy Bentham – Rights, Representation, and Reform: Nonsense upon Stilts and other Writings on the French Revolution* (Oxford: Clarendon Press, 2002).

be grounded in an equal right to liberty,[12] a compromise which enthroned utilitarianism as the dominant political morality in England for a hundred years.[13] Darwinism also discredited the notion that society is the result of an historic association of once asocial individuals since, if the human race is descended from other primate species, it is, like them, social by nature.[14] In the late nineteenth and early twentieth centuries, under the influence of Marx, Weber, Durkheim, and others, interest in political and moral philosophy waned as social science grew. Within this paradigm the individual came to be seen as at least as much a product of society as the other way around, and the notion that moral or political entitlements can be derived from putative observations about universal characteristics of the 'human condition' or 'human nature', was either rejected or ignored.[15]

The liberal natural rights tradition also suffered from a double political weakness. Although some of its exponents, such as Kant, produced imaginative schemes for international peace and order, in the eighteenth century the social contract vision was generally limited to the constitutional protection of rights *within* the sovereign state. Therefore, if a state decided to violate the rights of its own subjects there was little other states, or their citizens, could do, or generally felt they were entitled to do, about it. Secondly, in the nineteenth century, nationalists ascribed to 'peoples' – defined by the allegedly 'natural' characteristics of kinship, language, and homeland – the 'natural rights' to statehood and self-determination in the 'state of nature' among nations, which earlier natural rights theorists had claimed for individuals. In western Europe in the nineteenth century this increasingly pitted state against state in a restless quest to incorporate scattered fragments of 'the nation' within the frontiers of the country to which they were deemed by kinship to belong, thus undermining the foundations of the large multi-ethnic Austro-Hungarian,

[12] J. S. Mill, *On Liberty* (London: Routledge, 1991); J. S. Mill, *Utilitarianism* (Oxford: Oxford University Press, 1991).

[13] See J. Rawls, *A Theory of Justice* (London/Oxford/New York: Oxford University Press, 1972) p. vii; R. Dworkin, *Taking Rights Seriously* (London: Duckworth, 1977), p. vii.

[14] Although Rousseau saw the social contract as an historical event, or series of events, for Hobbes and Locke it was less an historical claim about the origins of the state and civil society and more a heuristic device in a normative theory of political obligation. See R. Harrison, *Hobbes, Locke, and Confusion's Masterpiece: An Examination of Seventeenth-Century Political Philosophy* (Cambridge/New York: Cambridge University Press, 2003).

[15] Douzinas, *End of Human Rights*, pp. 109–114.

Russian and Ottoman empires which dominated the eastern and central regions of the continent.

However, as the nineteenth century progressed, international cooperation between states also became more routine, as problems demanding technical solutions increased, for example, with respect to travel and communications.[16] The growing humanitarian concern for needless human suffering also led to several significant developments. The drive against slavery, powerfully bolstered by the need for global labour mobility, resulted in an Anti-Slavery Act at the international Brussels Conference of 1890, which established enforcement procedures, including the right to search ships. In 1863 the Red Cross was founded, and in 1864 the Geneva Convention for the Amelioration of the Condition of the Wounded in Armies in the Field was promulgated. In the nineteenth century, a 'right to humanitarian intervention' – military interference in other states to prevent gross violations of human rights – was also claimed as a norm of customary international law by western powers seeking to protect Christian minorities in the Balkans and the Middle East from atrocities committed by the Ottoman Empire. However, this was to prove a double-edged sword as the same doctrine would later be used by Hitler as a pretext for the annexation of neighbouring countries in which German minorities were said to be suffering persecution.

Competitive nationalism in Europe climaxed in the First World War. Since no redrawing of Europe's national frontiers, whether by conquest or negotiation, would ensure that every state was homogenous in terms of language, ethnicity, religion and culture, one of the great challenges in its aftermath was to find ways of ensuring that minorities defined by these characteristics were not mistreated in whatever state they happened to find themselves. The victorious, and newly created, states signed special minority-protection treaties, chapters on minority rights were included in treaties with defeated powers, and some states made declarations before the Council of the League of Nations as a condition of membership.[17] The national minorities section of the League's secretariat supervised these arrangements by receiving petitions from any source which alleged violation of treaty commitments, and determined if they should be scheduled for a decision by the

[16] C. Archer, *International Organizations* (London/New York: Routledge, 2nd edn., 1992).
[17] See J. Jackson Preece, *National Minorities and the European Nation-States System* (Oxford: Clarendon Press, 1998), Ch. 5.

League Council. Although rarely used, a judicial procedure enabled advisory opinions to be sought from the Permanent Court of International Justice, which could also make a binding decision in a case referred to it by a Council member. However, Jackson Preece claims that the humanitarian conditions of minorities mattered less than the effect their mistreatment might have on relations within, and between, particular nation-states.[18] Indeed, human rights more generally had a low profile in the League's activities, making only a limited appearance in the League Covenant which enjoined members to work towards more humane working conditions, prohibited traffic in women and children, and encouraged the prevention and control of disease and the just treatment of native and colonial peoples. The post-war settlement, including the attempt to protect national minorities, was, however, to prove a dismal failure. A mere two decades later economic crises, rising tension between communism, fascism and liberalism, and the international competition produced by the still-robust nation-state system, doomed the League of Nations and set Europe on course for a war which would again engulf the world.

THE MERE SHADOW OF A UNION

When the Second World War ended in 1945 one question reverberated around the globe: how could such a catastrophe be prevented from recurring? It was clear that the constitutional, political, and legal systems of some European countries had not effectively curbed the ambitions of political movements offering authoritarian answers to economic problems and military solutions to territorial disputes. The way forward for many western democrats, therefore, seemed to lie in the firmer national entrenchment of constitutional democracy, human rights and the rule of law, and their better protection in much more effective international institutions. There was little enthusiasm for a return to the system devised by the League of Nations for the protection of minorities in Europe in the inter-war years. It had, after all, been a double failure. It had failed to protect minorities, which had become mere pawns in the territorial squabbles between 'kin-states' claiming to champion their interests, and the host-states in which they found themselves.[19]

[18] *Ibid.*, p. 94. [19] *Ibid.*, p. 91.

It had also failed to prevent war. Nor had the Second World War solved the minority question in Europe either. Indeed the displacement of millions had made it more complicated. The protection of individual rights seemed, therefore, to offer a simpler solution, and one which still offered the tantalizing prospect of success.

In 1941, when President Roosevelt enunciated the Four Freedoms, human rights became an official war aim, even before the US had officially entered the conflict.[20] Nevertheless, it was only as a result of successful lobbying by NGOs attending the San Francisco conference, which established the United Nations in the summer of 1945, that the UN Charter contained so many references to human rights. For example the Preamble reaffirms 'faith in fundamental human rights, in the dignity and worth of the human person, in the equal rights of men and women and of nations large and small'. Article 1 states that one of the purposes of the UN is to 'cooperate . . . in promoting respect for human rights and fundamental freedoms for all', Article 55 proclaims that the UN shall promote 'universal respect for, and observance of, human rights and fundamental freedoms for all without discrimination as to race, sex, language or religion,' and Article 56 provides that 'all members pledge themselves to take joint and separate action in co-operation with the Organization for the achievement of the purposes set forth in Article 55'. Other provisions, for example, Articles 13, 62, 68, and 76, enable UN organs to study, promote, and make recommendations about human rights.

But, in spite of these propitious developments, there was still a great deal of uncertainty about what the term 'human rights' meant. On the face of it, both 'human' and 'natural' rights share the same underlying assumption – that certain basic entitlements are universal, integral to being human, and are not merely the expression of the values of a particular culture at a particular stage in human history. But the upsurge of interest in human rights in the aftermath of the Second World War had less to do with the re-affirmation of natural rights theory than with the task of finding a normative language – and the national and international institutions and processes it suggests – which could effectively promote peaceful coexistence in an increasingly

[20] A. W. B. Simpson, *Human Rights and the End of Empire – Britain and the Genesis of the European Convention* (Oxford: Oxford University Press, 2001), pp. 172–173.

interdependent world.[21] The focus of the definitional debate, therefore, shifted from the attempt to derive a universal set of values from putative universals of the human condition, to finding a workable consensus between the core elements of the world's major value systems. The outcome was the proclamation of the *Universal Declaration of Human Rights* by the UN in 1948, the significance of which has divided commentators. Some regard it as a watershed in the history of human rights because, for the first time, representatives of western and non-western civilizations from around the world collaborated to produce a list of basic civil, political, social and economic rights going far beyond those the Enlightenment thinkers had regarded as 'natural'. For example, Mary Ann Glendon, a strong critic of the rights culture of the US, believes it to be 'on the whole, remarkably well-designed', not least because of the links it proclaims between freedom and solidarity.[22] On the other hand, the Declaration's aspirational character, and its lack of any enforcement machinery, have led others to regard it as virtually worthless. For example, according to Simpson, Hersch Lauterpacht, perhaps the leading scholar of human rights of the period, viewed the UN's adoption of it with 'something approaching contempt'.[23] Although the Universal Declaration has since inspired other rights documents at the national and international levels, the unwillingness of states to surrender sovereignty makes it, and subsequent UN human rights treaties, difficult to enforce.

However, in the latter half of the twentieth century, the new political momentum behind the international human rights ideal gave fresh impetus to the debate within the western intellectual tradition about the ontological and institutional status of human rights. But as time progressed it became increasingly clear that the centre of gravity of this debate had also shifted. While little interest has been expressed in resurrecting the old theories of natural rights, other attempts have been made to provide the human rights ideal with cogent theoretical foundations.[24] Although none of these has escaped criticism,

[21] *Ibid.*, p. 219.

[22] M. A. Glendon, 'Knowing the Universal Declaration of Human Rights', *Notre Dame Law Review* **73** (1998), 1153–1190 at 1176.

[23] A. W. B. Simpson, 'Hersch Lauterpacht and the Genesis of the Age of Human Rights', *Law Quarterly Review* **120** (2004), 49–80, at 74, 56, 62, 68, 72, 79.

[24] For example, J. Habermas, *Between Facts and Norms*, trans. W. Rehg (Cambridge: Cambridge University Press, 1996); A. Gewirth, *Human Rights: Essays on Justification and Applications* (Chicago/London: University of Chicago Press, 1982).

thorough-going intellectual antagonism towards the idea of human rights has become much more difficult to sustain in the west in the post-war era than it was in the heyday of the doctrine of natural rights. The paradoxical result is that, while no consensus has emerged in the west regarding the foundations of the human rights ideal, no politically or intellectually credible basis has been found for rejecting it either. The intellectual debate has, therefore, increasingly been conducted between 'rights affirmers', who believe that individual human rights are in some sense the top (though not the only) priority in national and international public policy, and 'rights sceptics' who maintain that, while human rights have some merit, they do not deserve a privileged status over the pursuit of the collective or public good.[25] Generally speaking, rights affirming theories suggest that human rights should be judicially entrenched against legislative encroachment, while rights scepticism suggests the converse, that democratic legislatures should be entrusted with the protection of human rights without strong judicial restraint.[26]

It may, therefore, still be possible, taking a robust Marxist view, to argue that human rights are nothing more than an expression of bourgeois ideology, or from a communitarian or cultural-relativist perspective to maintain that they have no universal characteristics transcending the points of view of particular communities, or to conclude from feminism that the very idea of rights (including human rights) is 'patriarchal', or to claim, as postmodernism suggests, that the human rights ideal is merely one of many illusory 'grand narratives', condemned by the irredeemable indeterminacies of language, never to attain an objective status. But the fact is that few scholars attempting to make a serious contribution to the human rights debate from any of these traditions would now expressly, and unequivocally, repudiate the human rights ideal in its entirety. Instead, most either avoid drawing such uncompromising conclusions, and simply leave it to the reader to discern where the analysis leads, while others, more honestly, openly

[25] This broadly corresponds to Dworkin's distinction between political theories which are right-based, duty-based and goal-based, with the former corresponding to 'rights-affirming' theories and the latter two to 'rights-sceptical' theories, Dworkin, *Taking Rights Seriously*, p. 171.

[26] For an influential contribution to the case against enshrining human rights in constitutional documents see J. Waldron, 'A Right-Based Critique of Constitutional Rights', *Oxford Journal of Legal Studies* **13** (1993), 18–51.

advocate some version of rights scepticism.[27] This is so for three principal reasons. First, it has become extremely difficult plausibly to condemn the human rights ideal, and the institutions it suggests, while simultaneously offering convincing reassurance that a recurrence of the inhumanities perpetrated by communism and fascism in the twentieth century could, nevertheless, be avoided in Europe in the twenty-first century. Second, it is difficult to see how the case against human rights can be advanced without relying on a self-contradiction, namely the assertion of the right to freedom of expression, unless (implausibly and for no obvious reason) this is the only genuine human right, and that it can coherently be exercised in order to reject the idea of human rights as a whole. Third, a viable normative language capable of replacing that of human rights, which is more suitable to the conditions of contemporary Europe, has proved at least as difficult to find as the ontological basis of the human rights ideal itself.

But, long before this intellectual debate had developed, interest in regional arrangements for human rights increased in the immediate aftermath of the Second World War.[28] Initially there was some concern that developments along these lines might undermine the authority of global institutions for peace and international order. But, as disillusionment rapidly grew with the slow rate of progress at the UN, particularly, but not only, on the human rights front, these concerns gave way to the view that European recovery, prosperity, and security required tailor-made arrangements, including a regional human rights regime. European states were not, however, to be the sole masters of their own

[27] For some contributions to the human rights debate from these perspectives see T. Campbell, *The Left and Rights: A Conceptual Analysis of the Idea of Socialist Rights* (London/Boston/Melbourne/Henley: Routledge & Kegan Paul, 1983); S. Lukes, *Marxism and Morality* (Oxford: Clarendon Press, 1985); C. Smart, *Feminism and the Power of Law* (London: Routledge, 1989) Ch. 7; E. Kingdom, *What's Wrong with Rights? Problems for Feminist Politics of Law* (Edinburgh: Edinburgh University Press, 1991); N. Lacey, 'Feminist Legal Theory and the Rights of Women', in K. Knop (ed.), *Gender and Human Rights* (Oxford: Oxford University Press, 2004); Douzinas, *End of Human Rights*; M. Salter, 'The Impossibility of Human Rights Within a Postmodern Account of Law and Justice', *Journal of Civil Liberties* **1** (1996) 29–66; M. Sandel, *Liberalism and the Limits of Justice* (Cambridge, Cambridge University Press, 2nd edn., 1982); A. MacIntyre, *After Virtue* (London: Duckworth, 1981); M. A. Glendon, *Rights Talk: The Impoverishment of Political Discourse* (New York: Free Press, 1991).

[28] According to Simpson the idea of a regional human rights treaty first appeared in a British Foreign Office minute of June 1948, A. W. B. Simpson, 'Britain and the European Convention', *Cornell International Law Journal* **34** (2001), 523–554 at 540.

destiny. The defeated European powers were obviously in no position to argue. But even the victors were constrained by the conflicting interests of the USA and the USSR. By 1948 it had become clear that Germany would be partitioned, that the USSR would dominate eastern and central Europe, and that the USA regarded an integrated western Europe, both as a bulwark against the spread of communism and the territorial expansion of the Soviet Union on the one hand, and as a constraint upon a resurgent German nationalism on the other.[29]

Various ideas about the form European collaboration should take, ranging from loose union to full-blooded federation, had been under discussion even in the inter-war years. However, although it was later to become central to the federalist agenda, the protection of rights was not emphasized at this stage.[30] Even as the Second World War raged, Churchill had argued that a United States of Europe should be constructed once hostilities ended, a view warmly endorsed by other Europeans, particularly those on the anti-communist centre-right of the political spectrum. But the post-war British Labour government preferred an anti-Soviet military alliance plus something more ideological and symbolic than integrationist. Other pressing foreign policy issues delayed the start of negotiations for several years. But in a key speech to the House of Commons on 22 January 1948 – misinterpreted on the continent as the UK assuming the leadership of the European integrationist movement – the British Foreign Secretary, Ernest Bevin, stated that a western European 'spiritual union' based on respect for human rights was now the prime aim of British foreign policy.[31] In fact, in 1948, the UK was the only European power capable

[29] See K. Sikkink, 'The Power of Principled Ideas: Human Rights Policies in the United States and Western Europe' in J. Goldstein and R. O. Keohane (eds.), *Ideas and Foreign Policy: Beliefs, Institutions and Political Change* (New York: Cornell University Press, 1993); A. H. Robertson, *The Council of Europe: Its Structure, Functions and Achievements* (London: Stevens & Sons, 2nd edn., 1961), p. 6. Lundestad identifies three other US motives in promoting the post-war integration of western Europe – spreading the American constitutional, political and economic model, cultivating European economic efficiency and rationalization, and reducing the American burden. But containing the USSR and Germany were 'particularly important and closely linked', G. Lundestad, *"Empire" by Integration: The United States and European Integration, 1945–1997* (Oxford: Oxford University Press, 1998), p. 13.

[30] Simpson, *Human Rights*, p. 215.

[31] *Ibid.*, pp. 574–579. These ideas had already been discussed with the US Secretary of State, George Marshall and the French Foreign Minister, George Bidault at secret meetings in the Foreign Office on 17–18 December, K. Morgan, *Labour in Power* (Oxford: Clarendon Press, 1984), pp. 273, 274.

of exercising significant leadership.[32] Bevin's vision, though vague on details, was to be implemented in three stages. First, the UK, France and the Benelux countries signed the *Brussels Treaty for Economic, Social and Cultural Collaboration and Collective Self-Defence* on 17 March 1948, which included a Consultative Council and which laid the foundations for what later became the Western European Union. Although this was seen as a pact for economic, social, cultural, and defence cooperation, respect for human rights was a condition of membership. According to Morgan, the Brussels Treaty 'marked a remarkable transformation' in UK foreign policy compared with the 'quiescence towards western Europe that had endured, largely unbroken, since the end of the Peninsular War in 1812'.[33] Second, a wider military alliance including the US and Canada – the *North Atlantic Treaty Organization* of 1949 – provided firmer military guarantees for these states. Third, it was envisaged that other European countries, including West Germany, would eventually sign the Brussels Treaty when they could comply with the membership requirements, particularly respect for human rights.

But there were other ideas in the air. A Congress of Europe, sponsored by the right-of-centre International Committee of the Movements for European Unity, and attended by some 660 delegates including 20 Prime Ministers and former Prime Ministers, met in the Hague in May 1948. In his keynote speech the Honorary President, Winston Churchill, argued that a European Charter of Human Rights should be at the centre of a new programme of European unification.[34] Delegates not only endorsed this idea but also proposed a judicial enforcement process at the instigation of individual petition and a European Parliamentary Assembly. The British government, which had not sent a delegation to the Congress, opposed both ideas on the grounds that an Assembly would provide an unwelcome platform for communists, while a court of human rights would create an equally unwelcome judicial authority superior to any British court.[35]

[32] Simpson, 'Britain and European Convention', 542.

[33] Morgan, *Labour in Power*, p. 274.

[34] Simpson, 'Britain and European Convention', 543, claims that it is unlikely that Churchill ever envisaged a federation which included the UK. Certainly, in spite of his tireless campaigning on behalf of this cause, Churchill remained vague about whether the UK should join and, in his last period as Prime Minister from 1951 to 1955, made little effort to involve the UK in less ambitious plans to establish a common market.

[35] Simpson, *Human Rights*, pp. 619, 612.

Leadership of the European movement then drifted to France, and, in October 1948, the various strands of European integrationism were woven into the single European Movement which continued to press for a European Assembly selected by national parliaments, which would discuss a wide range of issues, including human rights and further proposals for European integration.[36]

As 1948 drew to a close the governments of the UK, France and Belgium agreed to establish a Council of Europe and invited Ireland, Italy, Denmark, Norway, and Sweden to participate in the negotiations. Luxembourg and the Netherlands also later became founding members. The task of drafting the statute of the Council of Europe, and later the text of the European Convention on Human Rights, fell to the British Foreign Office.[37] This was ironic because the British government was committed to increased European cooperation rather than integration, the Foreign Office had little legal expertise, the British rights tradition emphasized the importance of effective concrete remedies for specific wrongs rather than lofty statements of general principle, and if the British governing class had a coherent shared political morality it was utilitarianism. Sir Gladwyn Jebb (later Lord Gladwyn), a British Foreign Office official at the heart of the negotiations, later described the Statute of the Council of Europe – signed on 5 May 1949 – as creating nothing more than the 'mere shadow of a union'.[38]

Six core principles underpinned the Council of Europe. Certain unspecified 'spiritual and moral values' – 'the cumulative influence of Greek philosophy, Roman law, the Western Christian Church, the humanism of the Renaissance and the French Revolution'[39] – are said to constitute the 'common heritage' of the signatory states (the 'common heritage' principle) and to be the true source of 'individual freedom, political liberty, and the rule of law' (the 'human rights' and 'rule of law' principles) which form the 'basis of all genuine democracy' (the 'democracy' principle). The promotion of these principles, and the interests of 'economic and social progress' (the principle of 'economic and social progress'), require closer unity

[36] *Ibid.*, p. 629.

[37] *Ibid.*, p. 642; Simpson, 'Britain and European Convention', 548–549.

[38] Lord Gladwyn, *The European Idea* (London: Weidenfeld & Nicolson, 1966), pp. 45–46, quoted in Simpson, *Human Rights*, p. 646.

[39] Robertson, *Council of Europe*, p. 2.

between like-minded European countries (the 'closer unity' priniciple). Similar ideas can be found in the Brussels and North Atlantic Treaties.[40] But while the Council of Europe is not unique in making adherence to the principles of human rights and the rule of law a condition of membership,[41] it is unique in defining what human rights mean in a further treaty (the European Convention on Human Rights), in providing means for their enforcement, and in promoting 'closer unity' among its members. But, as Robertson points out, the 'closer unity' principle is a less concrete commitment than the desire, expressed, for example, by the Hague Congress of 1948, for an economic and political union which would involve a merger of certain 'sovereign rights', and probably only refers to the kind of closer association which had already occurred as a result of the establishment of the Organization for European Economic Cooperation and the signing of the North Atlantic Treaty just months earlier. Moreover, Article 1 of the Statute of the Council of Europe also seems to envisage nothing more dramatic than the traditional methods of international cooperation for achieving it.[42]

While the exclusion of defence issues is deliberate, and understandable in view of the fact that these objectives were well covered by the Brussels and North Atlantic Treaties,[43] Article 1 of the Statute of the Council of Europe curiously says nothing specific about 'political' questions, possibly on the assumption that these are already entailed by the reference to social and economic issues.[44] Other provisions deal with membership (by invitation of the Committee of Ministers), the establishment of the various organs (the Committee of Ministers, the Secretariat, and the Consultative, later Parliamentary Assembly, composed of representatives from national parliaments), the official languages (French and English), the location (Strasbourg), financial matters, privileges and immunities (including those of representatives of member states), and arrangements for amendment, ratification, and other formalities.[45]

40 *Ibid.*, p. 13.
41 Art. 3 of Statute of Council of Europe.
42 Robertson, *Council of Europe*, pp. 14–15.
43 Art. 1(d). While this has prevented the Assembly from discussing the technical and military aspects of defence it has not precluded discussion of its political aspects, Robertson, *Council of Europe*, p. 17.
44 Robertson, *Council of Europe*, p. 16.
45 The Statute has since been amended, among other things transforming the Consultative Assembly into the Parliamentary Assembly.

In addition to the European Convention on Human Rights, its most celebrated achievement, the Council of Europe has, since its foundation, sponsored some 200 treaties, on matters as diverse as children, cybercrime, drugs, data protection, farming, terrorism, and torture, some of which also have a strong human rights element.[46] Among the most prominent are the European Social Charter 1961, the European Convention on the Prevention of Torture and Inhuman and Degrading Treatment or Punishment 1987, and the Framework Convention for the Protection of National Minorities 1995, which have their own distinctive monitoring mechanisms involving the submission of reports. But only the European Convention on Human Rights provides a judicial process for the adjudication of complaints by individuals or member states.[47]

A NOT UNSATISFACTORY AGREEMENT

According to Simpson, the European Convention on Human Rights was the product of 'conflicts, compromise and happenstance' and there are no simple explanations either for what it is or for why it came into being.[48] Although the discussions were inevitably influenced by the intellectual and political debates about rights which had been in progress since the early modern period, they were overwhelmingly driven by the urgent need to find workable institutions and procedures which all parties could accept, rather than by grand theories about the relationship between the individual, the state, and civil society.

[46] For a comprehensive study of the Council of Europe see F. Benoît and H. Klebes, *Council of Europe Law: Towards a Pan-European Legal Area* (Strasbourg: Council of Europe Publishing, 2005).

[47] A. Drezemczewski, 'The Prevention of Human Rights Violations: Monitoring Mechanisms of the Council of Europe', *International Studies in Human Rights* **67** (2001), 139–177 at 158–163; T. Novitz, 'Remedies for Violation of Social Rights within the Council of Europe: The Significant Absence of a Court' in C. Kilpatrick, T. Novitz and P. Skidmore (eds.), *The Future of Remedies in Europe* (Oxford: Hart, 2000), pp. 231–251.

[48] Simpson, *Human Rights*, p. ix. Other literature on the background to the Convention includes, G. Marston, 'The United Kingdom's Part in the Preparation of the European Convention on Human Rights 1950', *International and Comparative Law Quarterly* **42** (1993), 796–826; Simpson, 'Britain and European Convention'; E. Wicks, 'The United Kingdom Government's Perceptions of the European Convention on Human Rights at the Time of Entry', *Public Law* (2000), 438–455; D. Nicol, 'Original Intent and the European Convention on Human Rights', *Public Law* (2005), 152–172.

Things got off to a poor start with the Assembly anxious to press ahead, but a majority of the Committee of Ministers showing considerable reluctance.[49] In August 1949 three powerfully endorsed Assembly proposals compelled the Ministers to treat the matter with greater urgency.[50] By October the British government had reached the conclusion that a human rights convention was urgently required, partly to remedy the lack of global progress at the UN (for which the UK blamed the US), and also because it was now convinced that the Council of Europe had become 'one of the major weapons of the cold war'.[51] In November the Committee of Ministers approved the establishment of a Committee of Experts which met in January 1950 to consider five issues: content, including whether there should be a general limitation clause or separate clauses attached to each right; institutions and their functions; enforcement mechanisms; requiring member states to bring their domestic law into line with the Convention; and a provision regarding the safeguarding of democratic institutions. Having embarked on this course of action, the political pressure to avoid failure was enormous since it was unlikely that the Council of Europe itself would survive the acrimonious collapse of its first substantial project, and this, in its turn, would be seen by friend and foe alike as a huge defeat for the 'shared identity and common destiny' of post-war western Europe.[52]

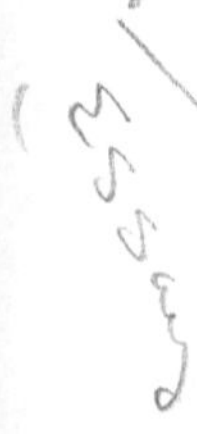

As with many treaties, and indeed with many written agreements of any kind, Convention negotiations were marked by sharply competing visions of what was required.[53] These differences were also, in their turn, reflected in disagreement on several substantive issues – which rights should be included (those to property, education, and free elections proved particularly controversial), how detailed their specification should be, and whether there should be a Court and a right of individual petition. Not only did the Committee of Ministers take a different view from the Consultative Assembly on these matters, but the position of some states differed from that of others, and some issues even divided

[49] Simpson, *Human Rights*, pp. 667–668.

[50] International figures as Churchill, De Valera, Teitgen, Bidault, Macmillan and Schumann, forced the pace of change, Simpson, *Human Rights*, p. 669.

[51] Simpson, *Human Rights*, p. 684.

[52] Marston, 'UK's Part in ECHR'; Simpson, *Human Rights*, p. 686; Wicks, 'UK's Perceptions of ECHR'.

[53] Nicol, 'Original Intent'.

delegates from the same state. Some of the differences of opinion stemmed from divergent assumptions about the appropriateness of judicial review of legislation, while others mirrored differences between the civilian and common law traditions. Those from the civil law tradition preferred to specify rights and limitations in very general terms, assuming that member states would be responsible for the provision of detailed legal mechanisms, and that effective protection would be provided by case law, anchored both in the Convention's own broad principles and in the 'general principles of law recognised by civilised nations', as gradually elaborated by a trans-national court. On the other hand, those who favoured the common law approach were distrustful both of catalogues of broadly defined rights and of a jurisprudence partly derived from the vague notion of 'the general principles of law'. They preferred, instead, the precise specification of rights and limitations together with the provision of effective remedies.[54] Strangely, virtually no attention was paid to the question of how the Convention text would be interpreted.[55] Some also considered the Convention merely as a first step, providing a collective guarantee of rights already well-protected in contracting states, to be followed by a second stage in which a fuller code would be elaborated.[56]

In spite of earlier reservations about the Convention being hijacked by communists, its impact on the Colonies, and the erosion of national sovereignty by a pan-European Court,[57] a Home Office official at the heart of the negotiations, Samuel Hoare, described the draft Convention, in June 1950, as 'not unsatisfactory' from the UK's point of view.[58] Yet, on 1 August 1950, a mere seven days before the Committee of Ministers of the Council of Europe approved the definitive text, the Labour cabinet 'expressed a violent if ill-defined dislike' of the form the Convention had taken. This was expressed particularly forcefully by the Lord Chancellor, Lord Jowitt, who, in spite of having failed to take earlier opportunities to make his hostility known, complained that 'it was wholly intolerable that the code of common law and statute law which had been built up in this country over many years should be made subject to review by an international

[54] Simpson, *Human Rights*, p. 713. [55] *Ibid.*, p. 737.
[56] Simpson, 'Britain and European Convention', 547; Nicol, 'Original Intent', 158–159.
[57] Marston, 'UK's Part in ECHR'. [58] Simpson, *Human Rights*, p. 722.

Court administering no defined system of law'. In September, only weeks before the Convention was signed, he was still denouncing it as 'an unqualified misfortune ... so vague and woolly that it may mean almost anything...'.[59]

Although the text of the Convention, which was eventually signed by the Committee of Ministers at the Barberini Palace in Rome on 4 November 1950, was inescapably an historic compromise it, nevertheless, represented a clear victory for the affirmation of certain human rights, as opposed to rights-scepticism, and for the non-integrationist conception of post-war Europe, and all that this entailed, over the integrationist alternative. The Convention's main functions were, therefore, to contribute to the prevention of another war between western European states, to provide a statement of common values contrasting sharply with Soviet-style communism (and nazism/fascism) capable of serving as a Cold War totem, to re-enforce a sense of common identity and purpose should the Cold War turn 'hot', and to establish an early warning device by which a drift towards authoritarianism in any member state could be addressed by an independent trans-national tribunal through complaints brought by states against each other.[60] Although enforcement followed the judicial model favoured by the Assembly and the European Movement, the final draft defined rights broadly subject to various limitations, largely based on the UK's proposals.[61] While there was to be a Court and a right of individual petition, neither would be compulsory for member states.[62] In any case the governments of the founding states regarded the Convention as merely a reflection of their own values and laws, and did not expect it ever to be used against them.[63] Nor could they have anticipated the recent debate about the extent to which the Convention has extra-territorial effect, i.e. whether or not it might apply in places, such as Serbia and Iraq, where the armed forces of member

[59] *Ibid.*, p. 742.

[60] P. Mahoney, 'An Insider's View of the Reform Debate', paper presented at the *Symposium on the Reform of the European Court of Human Rights*, Strasbourg, 17 November 2003, pp. 1–3.

[61] As Simpson points out, there is no obvious reason why these vary as they do between different rights, Simpson, *Human Rights*, p. 715.

[62] Only the UK and Greece had opposed the inclusion of a right to individual petition, *ibid.*, p. 721.

[63] Simpson, 'Britain and ECHR', 553.

states are, or have been, engaged in activities which raise compliance issues.[64]

The Convention's procedural and institutional structure is considered more carefully later in this chapter and in Chapter 3. Broadly speaking, until the changes introduced by Protocol 11 in 1998, individuals and states made their complaints to the European Commission of Human Rights, which considered whether or not the Convention had been violated, and then either forwarded the case to the European Court of Human Rights or reported to the Committee of Ministers, which initially had the quasi-judicial power to settle the dispute. Subject to various restrictions, considered in Chapters 4 and 5, the substantive provisions include from Articles 2 to 13 respectively: the right to life; the right not to be subjected to torture or to inhuman or degrading treatment or punishment; the right not to be held in slavery or servitude or to be required to perform forced or compulsory labour; the right to freedom from arbitrary arrest and detention; the right to a fair trial; the right not to be punished without law; the right to respect for private and family life, home, and correspondence; the right to freedom of thought, conscience, and religion; the right to freedom of expression; the right to freedom of assembly and association; the right to marry; and the right to an effective remedy before a national authority. Article 14 provides that the enjoyment of any Convention right shall be secured without discrimination on any ground such as sex, race, colour, language, religion, political or other opinion, national or social origin, association with a national minority, property, birth or other status. Article 15 provides for the suspension of all but a handful of rights 'in time of war or other public emergency threatening the life of the nation' provided such departures are 'strictly required by the exigencies of the situation' and not otherwise incompatible with international legal obligations. Article 16 states that nothing in Articles 10, 11, and 14 shall be regarded as preventing restrictions on the political activities of aliens.

[64] P. Leach, 'The British military in Iraq – The Applicability of the *Espace Juridique* Doctrine Under the European Convention on Human Rights', *Public Law* (2005), 448–458; N. Mole, '*Issa v Turkey*: Delineating the Extra-territorial Effect of the European Convention on Human Rights?', *European Human Rights Law Review* (2005), 86–91; A. Orakhelashvili, 'Restrictive Interpretation of Human Rights Treaties in the Recent Jurisprudence of the European Court of Human Rights', *European Journal of International Law* **14** (2003), 529–568; G. Ress, 'The Effect of Decisions and Judgments of the European Court of Human Rights in the Domestic Legal Order', *Texas International Law Journal* **40** (2005), 359–382, at 364–365.

Article 17 prohibits anything in the Convention from being interpreted as implying the right to engage in any activity, or to perform any act, aimed at the destruction of any Convention right or freedom, or its limitation to a greater extent than the Convention itself permits, and Article 18 limits restrictions upon rights to those purposes expressly provided in the Convention itself.

Since the Convention was promulgated a series of optional Protocols, some of which have not been signed by all states, have added further rights. Others, with universal effect in the Convention system, have addressed procedural problems. Protocol 1, for example, contains rights to the peaceful enjoyment of possessions, education, and to free elections, while Protocol 4 provides the right not to be imprisoned for debt, the right to freedom of movement, the right of nationals not to be expelled from the state to which they belong, and the right of aliens not to be collectively expelled. Protocol 6 abolishes the death penalty except in time of war, and Protocol 7 contains procedural safeguards regarding the expulsion of aliens, the right of appeal in criminal proceedings, the right to compensation for wrongful conviction, the right not to be tried or punished twice in the same state for the same offence, and the equal right of spouses under the law. Protocol 12 outlaws discrimination in relation to any right 'set forth by law' in contrast with Article 14 which prohibits discrimination only with respect to Convention rights, while Protocol 13 outlaws the death penalty even in time of war.

An appreciation of the dispute at the core of the negotiations which resulted in the Convention – the extent to which it should impinge upon national sovereignty – provides a key to understanding its character. Moravcsik argues that it can best be explained by reference to the differing national interests of the new (or re-established democracies) on the one hand – which favoured a much more intrusive regime – as compared with the long-established democracies, transitional states and dictatorships, on the other hand, which favoured much less intrusion. As he claims human rights treaties – and the European Convention in particular – pose a considerable challenge to the traditional 'realist' account of international relations which seeks to explain the activity of states in terms of the pursuit of national self-interest because, prima facie, they restrict the sovereignty of liberal democracies, which already have good human rights records, without apparently giving them anything tangible in return. However, realists maintain that, in entering an international human rights treaty, democratic states seek to further their interests by coercing other states to conform to their own standards and values and thus promote easier diplomatic and other relationships. 'Normative', or 'ideational' models, on the other hand, maintain that democratic states enter into international human rights treaties for the largely altruistic motive of persuading other less, or non-democratic, states to conform to what they take to be appropriate, or universal, values.

However, as Moravcsik points out, although various combinations of each approach are possible, they all rest on 'a remarkably thin empirical foundation'.[65] He argues that his study – the 'first systematic empirical test of competing theories of the establishment of formal international human rights regimes' – discredits realist and ideational approaches and their various hybrids. According to 'realist' theories, the primary advocates of a strong, sovereignty-limiting, regime would have been the great powers, while, for idealists, it would have been governments or trans-national groups in the long-standing European democracies. However, according to Moravcsik, established democracies only supported human rights declarations rhetorically, or when enforcement was optional. In fact they even allied themselves with dictatorships and transitional regimes in opposing effective enforcement, specifically over the enumeration of rights, the establishment of the Court, and the right of individual petition. The 'primary proponents of reciprocally binding human rights obligations' in Europe were, instead, the governments of 'newly established democracies' motivated by the desire to secure international support for their fledgling democratic institutions, a fact which neither realism nor idealism can adequately explain.[66] Contrary to what is often supposed, Moravcsik found that several other variables – the possession or absence of colonies, the strength of parliamentary sovereignty and domestic judicial review, support for European federalism, and experience of German occupation – do not correlate with either strong or weak support for the reciprocally binding human rights obligations in the Convention.[67]

65 A. Moravcsik, 'The Origins of Human Rights Regimes: Democratic Delegation in Postwar Europe', *International Organization* **54** (2000), 217–252, at 219.

66 'New democracies' are those which, although only established at some point between 1920 and 1950, were firmly democratic during Convention negotiations and remained so thereafter: Austria, France, Italy, Iceland, Ireland, and West Germany, 232. Moravcsik claims his conclusions remain sound even if France, which he admits is a marginal case, is not treated as a 'new democracy', 220.

67 *Ibid.*, pp. 232–233.

Moravcsik claims that his study supports a third explanation for the establishment of international human rights regimes, including the Convention. 'Republican liberalism' accepts the realist premise that states pursue self-interest in international relations, but maintains that the self-interest in question concerns domestic rather than foreign policy. The new (or re-established) democracies advocated a strong trans-national European human rights regime, not in order to facilitate trans-national interference in their own internal affairs, but in the hope that a strong international reaction to anti-democratic developments at the national level would trigger the appropriate response from their own domestic legislative and judicial institutions, and national public opinion. This is also consistent with the most common public justification offered for the Convention at the time – that it might help combat domestic threats from the totalitarian right and left, and thereby stabilize national democracy and prevent international aggression. Chapters 2 and 6 will argue that this observation continues to have significant implications for European policy in relation to Convention compliance.

INTER-STATE COMPLAINTS

As already indicated, the Council of Europe and the Convention were founded in an era dominated by the 'politics of ideology' when opinion in Europe was sharply divided over the merits of liberalism and the authoritarian alternatives of left and right. It was well understood by 'the founding fathers' that these differences not only split the continent geo-politically, but that they divided public opinion within states and could be expressed in violent civil conflict accompanied by serious systematic human rights abuses. But the inter-state applications process has proved to be less than a resounding success in addressing such problems for two reasons. First, making such complaints either requires a level of altruistic concern by governments towards the citizens of other states which is uncommon in international relations, or a degree of antagonism towards another European partner which is wholly at variance with the Council of Europe's underlying ethos of cooperation, interdependence, and the pursuit of greater unity. Second, while the inter-state applications process may have succeeded in drawing attention to some serious, systematic, Convention violations – and to have added some diplomatic pressure on the

states concerned – it would be very difficult to regard it as effectively remedying such problems.

Prior to Protocol 11, which came into effect in November 1998, any State Party to the Convention with a complaint against another first lodged an application with the European Commission of Human Rights. The Commission then attempted to ascertain the facts and considered if the admissibility requirements were satisfied, a test which was, and remains, less strict than that relating to individual applications.[68] 'Any alleged breach' of the Convention is included, and there is no requirement to exhaust domestic remedies, to establish 'victim-hood', to lodge a complaint within six months of the final decision of the relevant domestic tribunal, nor, usually, to produce evidence substantiating a prima facie case. Moreover, in inter-state cases the admissibility decision does not include a preliminary consideration of the merits, nor are such applications rendered inadmissible – as they would be in individual petitions – if they are substantially the same as a case already examined by the Strasbourg institutions.[69]

Until Protocol 11 came into force, if the admissibility requirements were satisfied, the Commission invited the parties to reach a friendly settlement. If this failed it then prepared a report which set out the facts and expressed a non-binding opinion about whether or not the Convention had been violated. The matter could then be referred to the European Court of Human Rights for a legally binding judgment, by the Commission or by any of the State Parties to the dispute, providing all State Parties involved accepted the Court's jurisdiction. If, after three months, the case was not referred to the Court, the matter was resolved by a legally binding decision of the Committee of Ministers, including representatives of both applicant and respondent states. As a result of Protocol 11, Article 33 of the Convention gives the Court compulsory jurisdiction over inter-state cases between any member state. But, since the Committee of Ministers remains

[68] S. C. Prebensen, 'Inter-State Complaints under Treaty Provisions – The Experience under the European Convention on Human Rights', *Human Rights Law Journal* **20** (1999), 446–455 at 448–449.

[69] The rules relating to exhaustion of domestic remedies, and applying within six months of the final decision by the relevant domestic tribunal, apply to inter-state complaints where the applicant state is acting on behalf of a specific individual or individuals affected by the alleged conduct of the respondent state, Prebensen, 'Inter-State Complaints', 448. Applicant states have to produce prima facie evidence at the admissibility stage when alleging a practice in violation of the Convention by the respondent state, *ibid.*, 449, note 24.

responsible for supervising the execution of Court judgments, the appropriate response from the respondent state remains a matter for negotiation between it and the Committee.

No application by any state under the inter-state procedure has ever fallen at the admissibility hurdle,[70] compared with, as this chapter will show later, around 98 per cent of individual complaints which are rejected as inadmissible. Yet, from the Convention's foundation until 1 January 2004, there had only been twenty inter-state applications.[71] Of the most celebrated, three were humanitarian, in that the applicant states had no particular political axe to grind with the respondents. In *Denmark, Norway, Sweden and the Netherlands* v. *Greece*,[72] the applicants complained about human rights abuses in the aftermath of the military coup in Greece in 1967. The Commission found Greece to be in violation of the Convention in November 1969, and, in December, Greece withdrew from the Council of Europe, denouncing the Convention before the Committee of Ministers could vote on a draft resolution calling for its suspension. *France, Norway, Denmark, Sweden and the Netherlands* v. *Turkey*,[73] which was resolved by friendly settlement, concerned widespread alleged Convention violations by the military government of Turkey in the early 1980s. However, more than a decade later, Kamminga reported that, in spite of this litigation, there had been 'no perceptible change in the widespread and systematic torture of detainees in Turkey and scores of people have continued to die as a result'.[74] The alleged mistreatment of a Danish national while in pre-trial detention was the subject of *Denmark* v. *Turkey*,[75] also resolved by friendly settlement.

70 Prebensen, 'Inter-State Complaints', 449.

71 According to Prebensen, 'Inter-State Complaints', 446, up until 1999 there had only been twenty-one inter-state applications in thirteen cases relating to seven kinds of situation, all but one of which occurred prior to Protocol 11. The Explanatory Report to Protocol 14 states: 'As at 1 January 2004, there have only been twenty interstate applications', *Protocol No. 14 to the Convention for the Protection of Human Rights and Fundamental Freedoms, amending the control system of the Convention, CETS No. 194, Explanatory Report as adopted by the Committee of Ministers at its 114th Session on 12 May 2004*, para. 11, footnote 3.

72 (1968) 11 Y.B.-II 691.

73 (1983) 35 D.R. 143.

74 See M. T. Kamminga, 'Is the European Convention on Human Rights Sufficiently Equipped to Cope with Gross and Systematic Violations?', *Netherlands Quarterly of Human Rights* **12** (1994), 153–164, at 159. The case of Turkey is considered more fully in the following chapter.

75 (2000) 29 EHRR CD35.

Other inter-state cases were motivated by political animosity between the states concerned. Greece brought the UK before the Commission in 1956 and 1957 over alleged mistreatment, by British forces in Cyprus, of those suspected of involvement with the armed nationalist movement, AOKA. However, in 1960, before the issue could be considered by the Committee of Ministers, Cyprus gained its independence.[76] Also in 1960, Austria complained against Italy about a breach of the right to fair trial in respect of a group of German speaking young men accused of killing a customs officer in the border region. But in 1963 the Commission found no violation, a decision endorsed by the Committee of Ministers.[77] In 1971 Ireland brought a case against the UK over the 'five techniques' of interrogation used against selected internees in Northern Ireland. The Commission found these amounted to torture. But, in a judgment delivered on 18 January 1978, the Court decided that, although they amounted to inhuman and degrading treatment, they did not constitute torture.[78] However, in March 1972, long before this verdict was reached, the British government announced the discontinuation of the practice, accepting the conclusions of the minority report of an official domestic inquiry that use of the 'five techniques' could not be justified.[79] It is impossible to determine if the impending litigation in Strasbourg acted as a further incentive. The Turkish invasion of Cyprus in 1974 also spawned three applications to the Commission by Cyprus against Turkey, the first two of which, in 1974 and 1975, were combined in a single report delivered on 10 July 1976, and the third, submitted in 1977, in a report of 4 October 1983.[80] Each found Turkey seriously to have breached a string of Convention provisions. But in 1979, responding to the first report, the Committee of Ministers merely called on the parties to resolve their differences through further dialogue under the auspices of the Secretary General of the UN, and, in 1992, almost a decade later, it simply made the Commission's second report public.[81] In a fourth application the Court held, on 10 May 2001, that Turkey remained in violation of the Convention on account of discrimination by the 'Turkish Republic

[76] *Greece* v. *United Kingdom* (1956–57) 2 Y.B. 174.
[77] *Austria* v. *Italy* (1961) 4 Y.B. 116, (1963) 6 Y.B. 740.
[78] *Ireland* v. *United Kingdom* (1980) 2 EHRR 25.
[79] *Hansard*, HC, vol. **832**, col. 743, 2 March 1972.
[80] *Cyprus* v. *Turkey* (1982) 4 EHRR 482.
[81] Kamminga, 'Is ECHR Sufficiently Equipped?', 157.

of Northern Cyprus' against the small Greek-Cypriot minority in the Karpas region, their refusal to allow some 211,000 displaced Greek-Cypriots access to their homes or to offer compensation, and their failure to conduct effective investigations into the disappearance of Greek-Cypriots in the aftermath of the invasion.[82] However, neither Turkey, nor the 'Turkish Republic of Northern Cyprus', have yet made an appropriate response to any of these judgments and the underlying problem – the Turkish occupation of northern Cyprus – remains unresolved.

Kamminga argues that the repeated failure of the Committee of Ministers effectively to address complaints about 'gross and systematic' abuse of human rights – by which he means 'officially inspired practices of torture, political killings or "disappearances"'[83] – in the various cases brought against Turkey, 'may actually serve to legitimize violations of human rights' because the lack of effective action can 'easily be invoked by the offending state as a vindication of its policies'.[84] Indeed, he claims that, 'the more serious and widespread the violations, the less adequate has been the response'.[85] Kamminga proposes that, in order to remedy the deficiencies of both the inter-state and the individual applications processes in relation to gross and systematic human rights abuses, NGOs should have the right to bring such allegations directly to the Court's attention.[86] A related proposal will be considered more carefully in Chapter 6.

ENLARGEMENT

The Council of Europe has been expanding since birth, incorporating western Europe's 'micro' states, other mature democracies, states with a recent history of right-wing dictatorship, and, most recently, the new republics which emerged from the collapse of the former Soviet Union

[82] (2002) 35 EHRR 731. L.G. Loucaides, 'The Judgment of the European Court of Human Rights in the *Case of Cyprus* v. *Turkey*', *Leiden Journal of International Law* **15** (2002), 225–236; F. Hoffmeister, 'Cyprus v. Turkey' App. No. 25781/94. *At* http://www.echr.coe.int/Eng/Judgments.htm. European Court of Human Rights, Grand Chamber, May 10, 2001', *American Journal of International Law* **96** (2002), 445–452.

[83] Kamminga, 'Is ECHR Sufficiently Equipped?', 154.

[84] *Ibid.*, 162. [85] *Ibid.*, 163. [86] *Ibid.*, 164.

and Balkan states.[87] Although, during the Cold War, over two thirds of the 130 or so treaties then sponsored by the Council of Europe were available for signature by non-members, no central or eastern European country, except Yugoslavia, took advantage of the opportunity.[88] In the 1980s some diplomatic connections had been made with Hungary and Poland, but relations with Romania, which looked promising throughout the 1970s and the early 1980s, subsequently 'went into inexorable decline, in spite of all the Parliamentary Assembly's efforts'.[89]

The next chapter will consider the role of the Council of Europe and the Convention in the processes of democratic transition and consolidation in central and eastern Europe. As Harmsen argues, the initial impact of expansion eastwards has been limited, with respect both to the functioning of the Court and to its jurisprudence. But, he maintains, that, in the longer term, it is likely to contribute towards recasting the Court as Constitutional Court for Europe, and to improving the integration between it and the Council of Europe's other human rights activities.[90] Simpson predicts that one consequence of the incorporation of the former communist states may be 'greater reliance upon inspection and reporting, and less on investigating and adjudicating upon individual complaints'.[91] Four particular challenges can be noted here. First, the disintegration of the 'iron curtain' ironically deprives both the Council of Europe and the Convention of one of their founding functions as vital weapons in the Cold War and raises deep questions about their current roles. Second, concerns have been raised that standards have been diluted, and the Convention's legitimacy compromised, by the unevenness of the processes by which the Council of Europe has monitored compliance with admissions criteria, and by which the former communist states have sought to make their

[87] Dates of accession can be found on the Council of Europe website, www.coe.int.

[88] In 1987 Yugoslavia signed the European Cultural Convention 1954, which in the 1980s the Council of Europe intended to be the main vehicle for encouraging East-West rapprochement, D. Huber, *A Decade Which Made History: The Council of Europe (1989–1999)*, trans. by V. Nash (Strasbourg: Council of Europe, 1999), p. 9.

[89] *Ibid.*, p. 10.

[90] R. Harmsen, 'The European Convention on Human Rights after Enlargement', *International Journal of Human Rights* (2001), 18–43, at 22–29 and 34–35.

[91] Simpson, *Human Rights*, p. 3. See also S. Swimelar, 'Approaches to Ethnic Conflict and the Protection of Human Rights in Post-Communist Europe: The Need for Preventive Diplomacy', *Nationalism and Ethnic Politics* **7** (2001), 98–126 at 115.

domestic laws and practices Convention-compliant.[92] The accession of the Russian Federation proved to be a particularly acute, and sharply debated, dilemma.[93] Third, from the end of the 1980s to the mid-2000s the number of State Parties to the Convention grew from 22 to 46, with the population over which the Court has jurisdiction almost doubling from 451 to 800 million. The huge implications for the effective processing of individual complaints are considered in Chapter 3. Fourth, while the Court is now the international institution with the most direct responsibility for the consolidation of constitutional democracy, and respect for Convention rights and the rule of law, in central and eastern Europe, it would be a mistake for it to be complacent about how secure these values are in the more mature democracies. In the 1990s the Council of Europe identified, for example, the protection of the rights of minorities and the rise of racism and xenophobia as particularly urgent problems in both east and west.[94]

MINORITY RIGHTS

There can be little doubt that, with the ending of the Cold War, the profile of the 'politics of ideology', which dominated the era in which the Convention was born, has diminished while the profile of the 'politics of identity' has increased. With both communism and fascism discredited, the sharpest conflicts in contemporary Europe are now over competing conceptions of the cultural, ethnic, linguistic, and religious identity of the state, rather than between competing visions of the relationship between the individual, society, the state, and the market. Few western European countries have no ethnic tensions and some of the most violent of these – particularly in Northern Ireland and in the Basque region of Spain – were unaffected by the post-Second World War settlement. In many of the former communist states the relaxation of authoritarian control has also re-opened historic disputes about the relationship between ethnicity and territory. As Swimelar points out,

[92] T. Meron and J. S. Sloan, 'Democracy, Rule of Law and Admission to the Council of Europe', *Israel Yearbook on Human Rights* **26** (1996), 137–156; Harmsen, 'ECHR After Enlargement'; A. Drzemczewski, 'Ensuring Compatibility of Domestic Law with the European Convention on Human Rights Prior to Ratification: The Hungarian Model', *Human Rights Law Journal* **16** (1995), 241–260 at 246.

[93] Meron and Sloan, 'Democracy', 151–155; Harmsen, 'ECHR After Enlargement', 20.

[94] See Huber, *Decade Which Made History*, pp. 60, 65–67, 85, 86, 88, 98–100, 113, 119.

ethnic conflict is 'currently the most important type of violent conflict in Europe'.[95] However, with the horrific exceptions of the Balkans and Chechnya, and the less dramatic but no less regrettable ethnic conflicts elsewhere in the Caucasus, the post-Cold War reconfiguration of Europe has involved remarkably little violence within states so far.

As already indicated, in the aftermath of the Second World War the prevailing view in western Europe was that strong formal minority rights are counter-productive, both for minorities and for the maintenance of international security because they tend to promote division within states along ethnic, linguistic, or religious lines, and, in a worst case, secessionism. The Convention and the Council of Europe were originally founded, therefore, on the alternative, individual rights, approach which accepts the existing borders of states and attempts to accommodate minority rights within a national framework of equal, non-discriminatory, individual rights, neutral on ethnic, religious, linguistic, cultural, and other identity criteria. According to Manas, the trouble with this, the 'republican' perspective, is that 'equality' can often be referenced to the cultural identity of the dominant majority in any given state.[96] Weller claims that, the 'shock of inter-ethnic violence that afflicted eastern Europe with the unfreezing of the Cold War' sparked a renewed interest in minority rights in Europe in the 1990s.[97] The Council of Europe sponsored a European Charter for Regional and Minority Languages in 1989. Notwithstanding the terrible ethnic conflict in the Balkans in the 1990s, which some attributed to Yugoslavia's multicultural foundations, this was followed by a proposed minority rights protocol to the European Convention on Human Rights, which was later superceded by the Framework

[95] Swimelar, 'Approaches to Ethnic Conflict', 104.

[96] J. E. Manas, 'The Council of Europe's Democracy Ideal and the Challenge of Ethno-National Strife' in A. Chayes and A. H. Chayes (eds.), *Preventing Conflict in the Post-Communist World – Mobilizing International and Regional Organizations* (Washington: The Brookings Institute, 1996) pp. 99–144 at p. 121.

[97] M. Weller (ed.), *The Rights of Minorities: A Commentary on the European Framework Convention for the Protection of National Minorities* (Oxford: Oxford University Press, 2005), p. vii; J. Jackson Preece, *Minority rights* (Cambridge: Polity Press, 2005), Ch. 7. Martínez-Torrón argues that it was not until 1993, and partly as a result of the incorporation of central and eastern European states into the Convention system, that the Strasbourg institutions began to take an interest in questions of religious freedom, J. Martínez-Torrón, 'The European Court of Human Rights and Religion', *Current Legal Issues* (2001), 185–204 at 188.

Convention for the Protection of National Minorities 1995.[98] Within the context of promoting toleration and mutual respect, the Framework Convention provides for the protection of a number of minority rights to such things as the manifestation of religion, access to the media, freedom to use minority languages, and education in – and the promotion of – minority culture, language, religion, and history. While it is not enforceable by any judicial process, states are nevertheless required, under the supervision of the Committee of Ministers, assisted by an advisory committee, to submit periodic reports to the Secretary General of the Council of Europe.

Manas argues that, as a result of these developments, the Council of Europe, therefore, currently embraces the mutually incompatible 'republican' (or individual) rights, approach, which underpins the European Convention on Human Rights, and the 'multicultural' approach, which underpins the 1995 Framework Convention. He also maintains that any of the solutions to the problem of conflict within European states ('republicanism', 'multiculturalism', or 'secessionism') tends to produce the problems associated with denying one or more of the other alternatives. While, as he argues, more 'flexible' arrangements may be required, it is not clear what this would entail. Preferring the concept of 'co-nation' to 'national minority', Malloy argues for 'a model of accommodation based on discursive justice', and concludes that the EU's politics of integration are more likely to provide the space for this than the 'legal approach of the politics of democratization of the Council of Europe'.[99] Trechsel, who also recognizes the differences between arrangements for the protection of individual and minority rights, advocates the creation of a European ombudsman for minority rights,[100] while Swimelar, who advocates a combination of legal and political approaches, praises the work of the High Commissioner on National Minorities of the Organization for Security and Cooperation in Europe as an exemplar of 'preventive diplomacy'.[101] However, Gilbert and Medda-Windischer have pointed out that the right of 'individual'

[98] For the most recent study see Weller (ed.), *Rights of Minorities.*

[99] T. E. Malloy, *National Minority Rights in Europe* (Oxford: Oxford University Press, 2005), p. 289.

[100] S. Trechsel, 'Human rights and minority rights – Two sides of the same coin? A sketch' in P. Mahoney, F. Matscher, H. Petzold and L. Wildhaber (eds.), *Protecting Human Rights: The European Perspective – Studies in Memory of Rolv Ryssdal* (Cologne/Berlin/Bonn/Munich: Carl Heymans, 2000) pp. 1443–1453 at 1452–1453.

[101] Swimelar, 'Approaches to Ethnic Conflict', 120–121.

application under Article 34 of the European Convention on Human Rights can be exercised by 'organizations or groups of individuals', provided they themselves have been victims of an alleged violation, and that, particularly from the late-1990s onwards, the Strasbourg institutions have responded positively to complaints from minority groups about Convention violation, especially those alleging discrimination, lack of official recognition, restrictions on effective participation in public and political life, interference with freedom of expression, and with religious life and institutions.[102] Harmsen predicts that cases alleging systematic discrimination against ethnic minorities may begin to appear on the Court's docket as a result of the post-communist accessions.[103]

INDIVIDUAL APPLICATIONS: 1955–2005

The mechanics of the individual applications process, initially optional for member states but now effectively the only way alleged violations can be brought to the Court's attention, are considered more fully in Chapter 3. The European Commission of Human Rights was able to receive individual applications from 5 July 1955, when the requisite number of states (at least six) had acceded to it, and the Court was open for business from 1959. However, things got off to a slow start. Broadly speaking, the process developed in three phases: dormancy – from the mid-1950s to the mid-1980s; activation – from the late-1980s to the late-1990s; and case overload – from the late-1990s to the mid-2000s. It is not yet clear if, or when, it will make the transition to a fourth phase – 'constitutionalization' – as this study argues it should. Figure 1 shows the dramatic increase in the individual application rate to the European Court of Human Rights from 1984 to 2004, while Figure 2 shows the increase in the number of cases ruled admissible and, following this trend by a few years as would be expected, in the number

[102] R. Medda-Windischer, 'The European Court of Human Rights and Minority Rights', *European Integration* (2003), pp. 249–271; G. Gilbert, 'The Burgeoning Minority Rights Jurisprudence of the European Court of Human Rights', *Human Rights Quarterly* **24** (2002), 736–780. Harvey and Livingstone also argue that, while the Court has been prepared to bring prisoners, immigrants and asylum seekers within the scope of the Convention, it can be criticized for having proceeded too cautiously, C. Harvey and S. Livingstone, 'Protecting the Marginalized: The Role of the European Convention on Human Rights', *Northern Ireland Legal Quarterly* **51** (2000), 445–465.

[103] Harmsen, 'ECHR After Enlargement', 28.

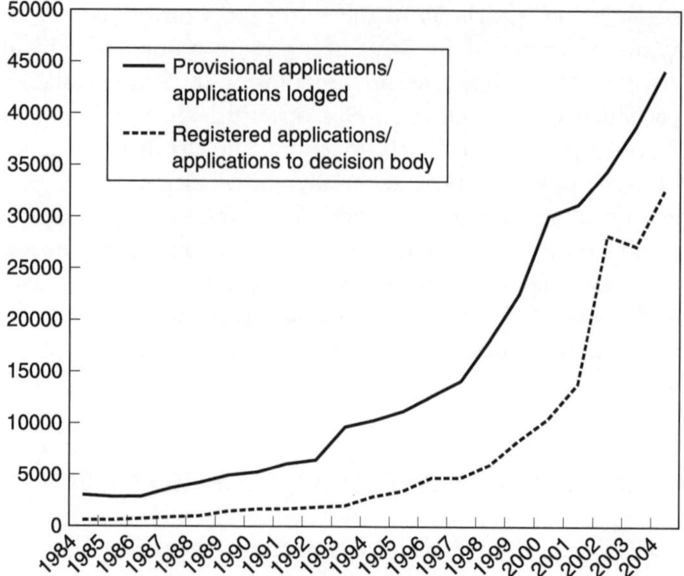

Figure 1. Applications to the European Court of Human Rights: – 1984–2004.[104]

of judgments of the Court and friendly settlements. The peak in applications ruled admissible in 2000, followed by the sharp decline, is probably connected with Protocol 11 discussed below.

Dormancy: mid-1950s–mid-1980s

Although modified in some minor details over this period, the broad characteristics of the individual applications procedure from 1950 until 1998 were as follows. Individual applicants first took their complaint to the European Commission of Human Rights at Strasbourg. Provided its competence had been accepted by the respondent state, the Commission

[104] Council of Europe, European Court of Human Rights, *Survey of Activities* (Strasbourg: Council of Europe, published annually, 1999–2004); European Court of Human Rights, 'Statistics – 2004'. The 'Survey of Activities – 1999' records, since 1983 the annual number of 'provisional applications' and 'registered applications'. In 2002 the categories were changed to 'applications lodged' and 'applications allocated to a decision body'. The annual figures in 'Survey of Activities – 2002' have been altered not only for this year but also, retrospectively, for every year since 1988. The figures reproduced here, up to and including 1987, are taken from 'Survey of Activities – 1999' and, therefore, refer to the old categories, while the figures for subsequent years are taken from 'Survey of Activities – 2004' and refer to the new classification.

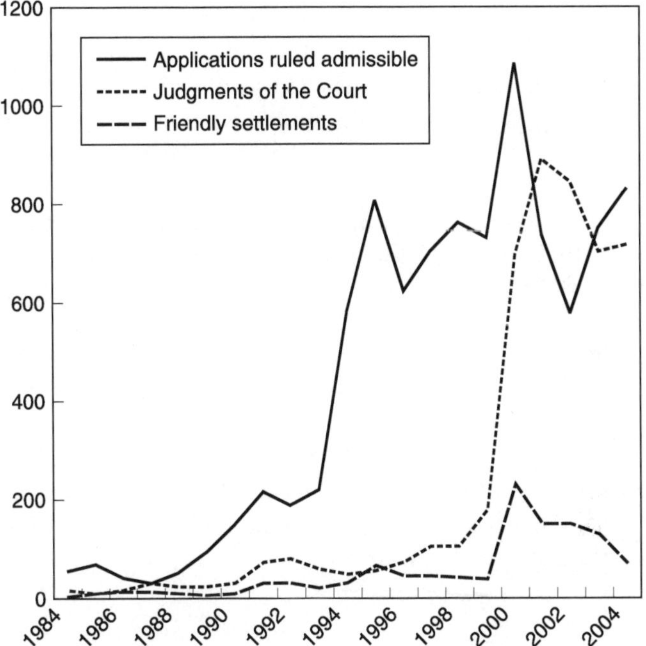

Figure 2. Resolution of Applications to the European Court of Human Rights: 1984–2004.[105]

began by ascertaining the facts and considered whether or not the application satisfied the admissibility criteria. If it did, the 'provisional application' was officially registered and the scope for a friendly settlement between the parties was explored. If no such settlement could be reached the Commission delivered a non-binding opinion concerning whether or not the Convention had been violated. Then, providing the Court's jurisdiction had been accepted by the state or states

[105] The figures for 'Applications ruled admissible' and 'Judgments of the Court' were obtained from ECtHR, *Survey of Activities* (1999–2004). Figures for 'Friendly Settlements' for 1999–2004 are from the same source, while those for 1984–1998 are from European Convention on Human Rights, *Yearbooks of the European Convention on Human Rights – Annuaire de la Convention Européenne des Droits de L'homme* (The Hague: Martinus Nijhoff, 1958–2004) and information provided by the Registry of the European Court of Human Rights. The annual figure for 'Judgments of the Court' includes the number of friendly settlements, plus the small number of judgments relating to applications struck out, just satisfaction, revision and preliminary objections. Any given judgment may relate to more than one application.

concerned, the case could be referred by the Commission, the respondent state, or the state of which the applicant was a national (but not by individual applicants themselves) to the European Court of Human Rights for a legally binding decision. The Committee of Ministers also decided cases over which the Court did not have jurisdiction and those which the Commission did not refer to the Court. Both the Commission and the Court were staffed by part-time judges.

Between 1955 and 1982 there were 22,158 provisional applications, an average of 791 per year.[106] Forty six per cent of these (10,210) were registered and, of these, 3 per cent (297) were declared admissible. By 1964 the Court had decided only two individual cases – *Lawless* v. *Ireland*[107] and *De Becker* v. *Belgium*[108] – and, a decade later, fourteen years after it had been in operation, this figure had risen to only seventeen.[109] However, by 1982 the Court had delivered sixty-one judgments, representing, since 1955, 0.27 per cent of provisional applications, 0.6 per cent of applications registered, and 21 per cent of applications declared admissible.[110]

Activation: mid-1980s–late-1990s

Things began to change significantly in the mid-1980s when the annual rate of provisional applications rose to nearly quadruple the average for 1955–82, around 3,000, dropping slightly from 3,150 in 1983 to 2,831 in 1985. From then onwards it increased in three, four-to-five year, bursts. Between 1987 and 1992 the number of provisional applications rose from 3,675 to 5,875. In 1993 the figure jumped further to 9,323, and increased yet again to 16,353 in 1998.[111]

The dramatic rise in individual applications in this period appears to be attributable to several factors. First, when the Convention came into force in 1953 only three of the then ten signatory states opted for the right of individual petition.[112] But, by 1960, only three out of thirteen

[106] ECtHR, *Survey of Activities 1999 – Development in the Number of Individual Applications Lodged with the Court (Formerly the Commission)*, p. 50.
[107] (1979) 1 EHRR 15. [108] (1979) 1 EHRR 43.
[109] Anon, 'Tribute to Rolv Ryssdal, Ground-Breaking Reformer', *Human Rights Information Bulletin No. 50: The European Convention at 50* (Strasbourg: Council of Europe, 2000), p. 6.
[110] ECtHR, *Survey of Activities* 1999, p. 50. [111] *Ibid.*
[112] Denmark, Ireland and Sweden.

withheld it, and by 1990 all twenty-two states had acceded to it.[113] In 1998 Protocol 11 made it compulsory. Second, as already indicated, the number of member states, and the population over which the Court has jurisdiction, have been increasing since the Convention came into force, although the effect of the biggest enlargement following the demise of communism did not begin to be felt until the late-1990s. Third, media interest in the Court's judgments, and in human rights generally, appears to have increased over the past two decades, raising the profile of these issues in public consciousness and making litigants more likely to consider pursuing their complaints at Strasbourg.[114] Employing sophisticated statistical techniques, Boyle and Thompson found that high application rates for the period 1976–93 correlate with the following national factors: 'constitutional openness' (civil society contributes effectively to policy formation), a low level of participation in a range of international governmental organizations, a high level of NGO activity, a large population, a high GDP per capita, the lack of formal incorporation of the Convention, the ratification of the Convention's Protocols, and a high level of reported human rights abuses.[115]

Responding to the rising application rate, the increasing complexity of cases and to enlargement, the Council of Europe approved Protocol 11 to simplify the system, to reduce the length of proceedings, and also to reinforce their judicial character.[116] The European Commission of Human Rights was abolished and the restructured Court became a full-time institution. It retained its original functions of delivering legally binding judgments on whether or not the Convention had been violated, and of providing advisory opinions upon request to the Committee of Ministers, while also assuming responsibility for all the Commission's previous tasks of registering applications, ascertaining the facts, deciding if the admissibility criteria were satisfied, and seeking friendly resolution. The Committee of Ministers was stripped of

[113] Prebensen, 'Inter-State Complaints', 449.

[114] *Report of the Evaluation Group to the Committee of Ministers on the European Court of Human Rights*, EG Court (2001)1, 27 September 2001, para. 35. See also 'Protocol No. 14 – Explanatory Report', para. 6.

[115] H. Boyle and M. Thompson, 'National Politics and Resort to the European Commission on Human Rights', *Law & Society Review* **35** (2001), 321–344 at 337–341.

[116] A. Drzemczewski, 'The European Human Rights Convention: A New Court of Human Rights in Strasbourg as of November 1, 1998', *Washington and Lee Law Review* **55** (1998), 697–736 at 716.

its power to settle cases and was confined to supervising the execution of judgments. In addition to the right of individual petition, the Court's jurisdiction also became compulsory, although, by this time, each had already been voluntarily accepted by all member states.[117]

Case Overload: late-1990s–mid-2000s

In spite of the reforms introduced by Protocol 11, by the early 2000s the volume of individual applications had reached pandemic proportions. In 1998 18,164 applications were lodged with the Court, but, by 2001, the figure had nearly doubled again to 31,228.[118] As already indicated, from 1 January 2002 the formal distinction between 'provisional' and 'registered' applications was abandoned. Since then all written contact between an applicant and the Registry is formally recorded as an 'application lodged with the Registry'. These are destroyed a year later if applicants have not, by then, submitted a written application on the correct form. Duly completed application forms are 'allocated to a decision body' for a decision about admissibility. The largest number of applications lodged in any year up to and including 2004 (44,100 in 2004)[119] is, in fact, just under twice as many as the total number of provisional applications received in the first 28 years of the Convention's entire history (22,158). One of the most serious consequences of case overload concerns the rising backlog of cases awaiting a decision about admissibility. The number of cases 'pending before a decision body' rose from 12,600 in 1999 to 50,000 in 2004,[120] and is expected to reach 250,000 by 2010.[121] It currently takes about five years between the lodging of a complaint with the Registry and the delivery of judgment on the merits by the Court.[122]

Two key questions about the individual applications process concern the chances of any given applicant having the merits of their complaint adjudicated by the Court, and, if this occurs, their chances of success. Unfortunately, the official statistics do not permit either to be calculated straightforwardly. Using the figure from 'Statistics – 2004' which have been rounded to the nearest 50, between 1999 and 2004 an annual

117 'Report of Evaluation Group', para. 10; Prebensen, 'Inter-State Complaints', 449.
118 ECtHR, 'Survey of Activities – 2004'.
119 ECtHR, 'Statistics – 2004', 2. 120 *Ibid.*, 9.
121 Lord Woolf, *Review of the Working Methods of the European Court of Human Rights* (Strasbourg: Council of Europe, 2005), p. 4.
122 Information supplied by the Council of Europe.

average of 33,583 applications was lodged with the Registry, 20,100 (60 per cent) of which were allocated to a decision body.[123] Of these, 800 applications on average a year were declared admissible (2.4 per cent of applications lodged and 4 per cent of applications scheduled for a decision about admissibility). Over the same period, 733 judgments were delivered on average per year (2.2 per cent of applications lodged and 3.6 per cent of applications allocated to a decision body).[124] However, as already indicated, any given judgment may include more than one application, and the figures for 'Judgments delivered by the Court' recorded annually since 1999 in both the annual 'Survey of Activities' and the Court's 'Statistics – 2004' combine, not only judgments of the merits, but also friendly settlements, applications struck off, and judgments regarding preliminary objections, revision, and just satisfaction. Other figures kindly provided by the Registry of the European Court of Human Rights indicate that 522 judgments on the merits were delivered on average between 1999 and 2004, in addition to an annual average of 147 other judgments.[125] Of the judgments on the merits 493 (94 per cent) resulted in a finding of at least one violation. Therefore, while just over 2 per cent of applications lodged with the Registry are ruled admissible, any applicant fortunate enough to have their application selected for adjudication, has a 94 per cent chance of receiving a judgment in their favour from the Court. The overall success rate is, in fact, even higher because all, or virtually all, friendly settlements can also be regarded as 'in the applicant's favour', although without any formal ruling by the Court that the Convention has been violated.

As the Explanatory Report on Protocol 14 notes, the Court's excessive workload derives not only from the need to process the 98 per cent or so of applications which are rejected without a hearing on the merits, but also from the fact that some 60 per cent of the Court's judgments concern the same systemic problem in the respondent state which has already been addressed in an earlier judgment ('repetitive' cases).[126] Furthermore, according to the former Registrar of the Court, Paul Mahoney, the vast majority of the Court's business – just under 60 per cent (3,129 out of 5,307) of applications declared admissible

[123] ECtHR, 'Statistics – 2004', 3, 4. [124] *Ibid.*, 3, 4, 6.
[125] 'Violations by Article and by Country 1999–2004'.
[126] 'Protocol No. 14 – Explanatory Report', paras. 7, 68.

between 1955 and 1999 and just under 70 per cent of the Court's judgments (485 out of 695) in 2000 – concerned allegations of breach of fair trial on account of unreasonable delays in the administration of justice.[127] In 2000, 81 verdicts (12 per cent) applied standard case law, and fewer than 20 per cent of the Court's judgments raised a new or serious issue under the Convention.[128] Of the total number of judgments delivered between 1999 and 2004 only an annual average of 86 out of 670 (13 per cent) were of 'high importance'.[129]

According to Rolv Ryssdal, the former President of the Court, people turned 'to the Strasbourg institutions to seek redress for their grievances in sometimes very ordinary situations, far removed from the concern to defeat totalitarian dictatorship and genocide that motivated the Convention system's founders'. The individual applications process, therefore, came to be applied to 'relatively minor, sometimes highly technical issues'.[130] But, as Mahoney argues, this is 'not an unnatural development' because the Convention has developed to offer two levels of protection: 'firstly, against bad-faith abuse of governmental power and, secondly, against good-faith limitations on liberty which nevertheless go beyond what is "necessary in a democratic society" to use the terminology of Articles 8 to 11 of the ECHR.'[131] Mahoney claims that, in its first forty years or so, the Convention predominantly fulfilled this second function, protecting individuals and groups from the excesses of majoritarianism in healthy democracies. In other words, the Strasbourg enforcement system can be seen as judicially controlling, on the international plane, the exercise of democratic discretion by domestic legislative, executive, and judicial authorities at national level.

Mahoney claims that the nature of complaints has also changed in five other ways in the first half century or so the Convention has been in force, and uses the case of Turkey as an example.[132] First, there have been more allegations of serious and systematic abuses of human rights – for example, destruction of villages, torture of detainees

[127] P. Mahoney, 'New Challenges for the European Court of Human Rights Resulting from the Expanding Case Load and Membership', *Penn State International Law Review* **21** (2002), 101–114 at 110–111.

[128] *Ibid.* [129] ECtHR, 'Statistics – 2004', 7.

[130] R. Ryssdal, 'The Coming of Age of the European Convention on Human Rights', *European Human Rights Law Review* (1996), 18–29 at 22.

[131] P. Mahoney, 'Speculating on the Future of the Reformed European Court of Human Rights', *Human Rights Law Journal* **20** (1999), 1–4 at 2.

[132] *Ibid.*, 3.

and prohibition of political parties. It could be added that neither the inter-state, nor the individual, applications processes is very effective in addressing such problems. While the experience of the former has already been considered, the principal problem with the latter is that individual applications tend to focus on the specific complaint of a particular victim rather than upon underlying patterns of official conduct which have resulted in the violation of the Convention rights of many.[133] Second, the primary facts have increasingly been contested, necessitating difficult and costly fact-finding missions by the Strasbourg institutions.[134] Third, and partly in response, the Court has held in several cases that the existence of special circumstances – for example the lack of investigation of allegations by national authorities and a state of strife between local populations and the state – absolves the applicant of the obligation to exhaust domestic remedies. This has effectively turned the European Court of Human Rights into the court of first instance with respect to complaints arising out of the civil unrest in these areas. Fourth, in circumstances such as these, the respondent state has been accused of hindering, and even of obstructing, the application to Strasbourg. Finally, the cases in question have been politically controversial in their country of origin. As Mahoney adds: 'this phenomenon may well be reproduced, to a greater or lesser degree, in relation to some of the new and expected participating States from the former Soviet bloc' which may require the Court to engage in more protection of the kind envisaged by the first of the two levels he distinguishes.[135] According to this analysis, the primary objectives of the Convention system at the beginning of the twenty-first century, therefore, are to ensure that each member state effectively secures Convention rights in its own legal processes (the 'subsidiary facet'), that repetitive violations are avoided (the 'preventive facet') and that a 'human rights community of nations with shared values' is welded together from the mosaic of post-1989 Europe.[136]

[133] P. Sardaro, '*Jus Non Dicere* for Allegations of Serious Violations of Human Rights: Questionable Trends in the Recent Case Law of the Strasbourg Court', *European Human Rights Law Review* (2003), 601–630; A. Reidy, F. Hampson and K. Boyle, 'Gross Violations of Human Rights: Invoking the European Convention on Human Rights in the Case of Turkey', *Netherlands Quarterly of Human Rights* **15** (1997), 161–173; Kamminga, 'Is ECHR Sufficiently Equipped?'.

[134] See also Harmsen, 'ECHR After Enlargement', 29; Drezemczewski, 'Prevention of Human Rights Violations', 157.

[135] Mahoney, 'Speculating on Future', 4.

[136] P. Mahoney, 'New Challenges', 105.

Protocol 14 – Towards the Delivery of Constitutional Justice?

Within eight months of Protocol 11 coming into effect on 1 November 1998, the President of the Court, Luzius Wildhaber, admitted that the system was 'under pressure'. A year later he urged states to appoint a committee to consider further major reforms in order to avert 'asphyxiation' by the ever-increasing back log of applications.[137] A European Ministerial Conference on Human Rights in Rome, from 3–4 November 2000, marking the fiftieth anniversary of the Convention's first signatures, provided a convenient opportunity for stock-taking. Concern was expressed about the implications of case overload and a Resolution was passed calling upon the Committee of Ministers to 'identify without delay the most urgent measures to be taken to assist the Court in fulfilling its functions' and 'to initiate as soon as possible a thorough study of the different possibilities and options with a view to ensuring the effectiveness of the Court in the light of this new situation'.[138]

Over the next three and a half years several Strasbourg committees debated nearly a dozen central issues, including financial and other resources, improving Convention compliance at national level, streamlining the filtering of applications and the criteria for admissibility, providing different procedures for different kinds of case (for example, 'clone' or 'repeat' applications involving violations the Court has already condemned in the respondent state concerned, 'straightforward' cases, and those meriting a 'fast track'), encouraging friendly settlement, providing another instrument to deal with administrative and procedural matters capable of being amended more easily than the Convention itself, improving the enforcement and supervision of judgments, the possible accession of the European Union to the Convention, and the number and terms of office of judges

[137] Press releases of 21 June 1999 and 8 June 2000 respectively quoted in A. Mowbray, 'Proposals for reform of the European Court of Human Rights', *Public Law* (2002), 252–264 at 252. See also (2000) 21 *Human Rights Law Journal*, 90. It is also widely expected that the recent Protocol 12, which provides a general right of non-discrimination in respect of any legal right and not just Convention rights as is the case with Article 14, will 'generate a substantial volume of business when the time comes', 'Report of Evaluation Group', para. 36.

[138] Resolutions I.16 and I.18 (i) and (ii) of the Ministerial Conference on Human Rights, *The European Convention on Human Rights at 50* (Strasbourg: Council of Europe, Human Rights Information Bulletin No. 50, December 2000), pp. 35, 37.

of the European Court of Human Rights.[139] Contributions were also made by the Parliamentary Assembly, the European Commissioner for Human Rights, NGOs, governments, experts, and other interested parties.[140] The Report of the Evaluation Group, published on 27 September 2001, was welcomed by the Committee of Ministers at its 109th Session on 8 November 2001, and the Council of Europe's Steering Committee on Human Rights (Comité Directeur pour les Droits de l'Homme, the 'CDDH') was instructed to carry out a feasibility study on the most appropriate way to conduct the preliminary examination of applications, particularly by reinforcing filtering, and to consider proposals for the amendment of the Convention on the basis of the recommendations of the Evaluation Group. The CDDH produced separate reports in October and December 2002 respectively,[141] and its Final Report, published in April 2003,[142] was welcomed at the 112th Session of the Committee of Ministers on 14–15 May that year. Throughout this period the Court improved its working methods,[143] and, also made formal and informal contributions to the debate.

The draft Protocol 14 was published, together with an Explanatory Report provided by the CDDH, on 7 April 2004, and approved by the

[139] The principal ones are: 'Report of Evaluation Group'; Steering Committee for Human Rights (CDDH), *Guaranteeing the Long-Term Effectiveness of the European Court of Human Rights – Addendum to the Final Report Containing CDDH Proposals (Long Version)*, CDDH(2003)006 Addendum Final, 9 April 2003; Steering Committee for Human Rights (CDDH), *Guaranteeing the Long-Term Effectiveness of the European Court of Human Rights – Implementation of the Declaration Adopted by the Committee of Ministers at its 112th Session (14–15 May 2003) Interim Activity Report*, CDDH(2003)026 Addendum I Final, 26 November 2003; see Mowbray, 'Proposals'; S. Greer, 'Reforming the European Convention on Human Rights: Towards Protocol 14', *Public Law* (1993), 663–673; S. Greer, 'Protocol 14 and the Future of the European Court of Human Rights', *Public Law* (2005), 83–106.

[140] *(Updated) Joint Response to Proposals to Ensure the Future Effectiveness of the European Court of Human Rights*, signed by 114 NGOs, April 2004; *Amnesty International's Comments on the Interim Activity Report: Guaranteeing the Long-Term Effectiveness of the European Court of Human Rights*, AI Index: IOR 61/005/2004, February 2004.

[141] Steering Committee for Human Rights (CDDH), *Interim Report of the CDDH to be Submitted to the Committee of Ministers – 'Guaranteeing the Long-Term Effectiveness of the European Court of Human Rights'*, CDDH(2002)016 *Addendum*, 14 October 2002; Steering Committee for Human Rights (CDDH), *Report of the Reflection Group on the Reinforcement of the Human Rights Protection Mechanism*, CDDH-GDR(2002)012, 12 December 2002.

[142] CDDH(2003)006 Addendum Final. See Greer, 'Reforming ECHR'.

[143] *Three Years Work for the Future. Final Report of the Working Party on the Working Methods of the European Court of Human Rights* (Strasbourg: Council of Europe, 2002).

Committee of Ministers at its 114th session on 12–13 May that year. Having reviewed the scale of the case overload problem the Explanatory Report repeats two well-rehearsed assumptions. First, reforming the Convention should 'in no way affect what are rightly considered the principal and unique features of the Convention system. These are the judicial character of European supervision, and the principle that any person claiming to be the victim of a breach of the rights and freedoms protected by the Convention may refer the matter to the Court (the right of individual petition)'.[144] Second, the Court's role is subsidiary to that of member states, which have the primary responsibility of ensuring respect for Convention rights.[145] But, unlike Protocol 11, Protocol 14: 'makes no radical changes to the control system established by the Convention. The changes it does make relate more to the functioning than to the structure of the system. Their main purpose is to improve it, giving the Court the procedural means and flexibility it needs to process all applications in a timely fashion, while allowing it to concentrate on the most important cases which require in-depth examination'.[146]

The principal changes introduced by Protocol 14, which is likely to come into effect towards the end of 2006 or early 2007, are to the applications process, judicial terms of office, and the composition of the Court's constituent units. The European Commissioner for Human Rights has been empowered to submit written comments and to take part in Chamber and Grand Chamber hearings (although not to initiate litigation), while the Committee of Ministers has been empowered to enlist the Court's support in the enforcement of judgments and in the supervision of the implementation of friendly settlements (subsequently also available at any stage of the proceedings and not just post-admissibility as under the former arrangements). The EU has also been permitted to accede to the Convention. A new summary procedure for the more rapid disposal of 'manifestly well-founded' complaints has also been provided which should contribute to the improvement of productivity. The CDDH decided that an earlier proposal, which would have enabled the Committee of Ministers to invite the Court to identify systemic Convention compliance problems in its judgments and to provide for applications covered by 'pilot judgments' to be diverted

[144] 'Protocol No. 14 – Explanatory Report', at para. 10.
[145] *Ibid.*, para. 12. [146] *Ibid.*, para. 35.

back to states, should not be included in the protocol. It was suggested instead that the Committee of Ministers should make appropriate recommendations.[147] This is surprising because the CDDH's Final Report in April 2003 claimed that 'a very significant contribution to reducing the case load of the Court could be achieved if a domestic remedy was available to other individuals who are also affected by the systemic problem exposed in the pilot judgment', and that this could potentially be substantial for both adjudicative and managerial resources.[148]

The Explanatory Report also mentions several other proposals raised in the preceding debate which it chose not to endorse.[149] The Committee of Ministers was not empowered to increase the number of judges at the request of the Court's Plenary Assembly. States will not be liable to financial penalties for failure to comply with judgments. No new quasi-judicial institution for the filtering of applications has been created. 'Regional human rights courts' will not be established because of the associated costs and the risk that divergent case law might develop as a result. Empowering the Court to give preliminary rulings at the request of national courts, or expanding the scope of the existing power to give advisory opinions, were also excluded due to possible interference with the contentious jurisdiction of the European Court of Human Rights and the risk of compounding the workload crisis, at least in the short term. Two other proposals were rejected on the grounds that they would restrict the right of individual petition – giving the Court a wide discretion over the selection of cases for judgment similar to that enjoyed by many national constitutional courts and requiring all applicants to be legally represented from the moment they submit their application. Some wider constitutional problems in the relationship between the Court and the Council of Europe were also ignored.[150]

147 CDDH, (2003)026, Addendum I Final', 26 November 2003, paras. 8 and 20 and Appendix IV. This was duly accomplished in recommendations Rec(2004)5, and Rec(2004)6, adopted at the 114th session of the Committee of Ministers on 12 May 2004.

148 CDDH, (2003)006 Addendum Final, 9 April 2003, p. 9.

149 'Protocol No. 14 – Explanatory Report', para. 34.

150 Mahoney argues that there should be a more formal acknowledgment by the Council of Europe that the Registry is 'hierarchically accountable' to the Court and not to any other Council of Europe institution, P. Mahoney, 'Separation of powers in the Council of Europe: the Status of the European Court of Human Rights vis-à-vis the Authorities of the Council of Europe', *Human Rights Law Journal* **24** (2003), 152–161 at 159.

The details of Protocol 14 are considered more fully in Chapter 3, but three preliminary observations can be made about it here. First, although it may have bought extra time, it is unlikely to solve the current case management crisis. In April 2004 the President of the European Court of Human Rights, Luzius Wildhaber, announced that although 'a step in the right direction', he believed that '(e)ven with the new reform, the Court will continue to have an excessive workload'.[151] However, speaking at his annual press conference in January 2006, even before the new protocol came into effect, the President saw grounds for optimism in the productivity figures for 2005 which showed a 54 per cent increase in the number of judgments as compared with the previous year (718 in 2004 and 1,105 in 2005) and a 36 per cent increase in cases terminated by judicial decision, i.e. struck off or rejected as inadmissible (20,350 in 2004 and 27,612 in 2005).[152] Only time will tell if this improvement is sustained. But even if it is, the percentage of applications reaching judgment is unlikely to rise because the application rate is itself likely to continue to increase. Second, Protocol 14 fails to address the core issue underlying this crisis – the debate over whether the Court's mission should be to deliver individual or constitutional justice. Third, the Council of Europe appears already to have realized that the case-overload crisis has not been solved. At a summit in Warsaw on 16–17 May 2005, the Heads of State and Government of Member States not only declared their commitment 'in the short term' to implement Protocol 14, but also decided to establish a 'group of wise persons to draw up a comprehensive strategy to secure the effectiveness of the system in the longer term, taking into account the initial effects of Protocol 14 and the other decisions taken in May 2004' while 'preserving the basic philosophy underlying the ECHR'.[153] However, since it is likely to take at least a year to gauge even the preliminary impact of the new

[151] Interview with President Luzius Wildhaber, 'The reform is an absolute necessity', 21 April 2004. This view is shared by Georg Ress, a former judge of the European Court of Human Rights, 'Effect of Decisions and Judgments', 367.

[152] Annual Press Conference of the President of the European Court of Human Rights, 'Brighter Prospects for the European Court of Human Rights', European Court of Human Rights Press Release – 034(2006), 23 January 2006.

[153] *Declaration of the Heads of State and Government of the Member States of the Council of Europe Gathered for their Third Summit in Warsaw on 16–17 May 2005*, para. 2. *Action Plan of the Ministers' Deputies Approved by the Heads of State and Government of the Member States of the Council of Europe Gathered for their Third Summit in Warsaw on 16–17 May 2005*, CM(2005)80 final 17 May 2005, para. 1.

provisions, the post-Protocol 14 debate is unlikely to be initiated until 2007–8 at the earliest. Nor, given the precedents of Protocols 11 and 14, is it likely to be concluded until the beginning of the next decade. In December 2005 a review, conducted at the instigation of the Secretary General of the Council of Europe and the President of the European Court of Human Rights by a team led by one of the 'group of wise persons', Lord Woolf, made a series of recommendations about how the Court's working methods could be improved without amending the Convention. In addition to a number of suggestions about detailed managerial issues, the main proposals are that satellite offices of the Registry should be established in countries producing high application rates, that greater use be made of national ombudsmen and other methods of Alternative Dispute Resolution, and that the Court should make more use of pilot judgments.[154]

THE CONVENTION AND THE EUROPEAN UNION

For much of the past half century the European Convention on Human Rights on the one hand, and the European Economic Community/European Union on the other, had little to do with each other. Only in the past few years has it become apparent that the futures of each are likely to be increasingly intertwined. For European integrationists the Council of Europe was a missed opportunity and a bitter disappointment. Jean Monnet, the French Planning Commissioner, regarded it as 'entirely valueless', and de Gaulle found it 'simply ridiculous'.[155] The French Foreign Minister, Robert Schumann therefore decided that France should proceed with more substantial proposals for European integration without British participation.[156] Schumann's plan laid the foundations for the six-member European Coal and Steel Community of 1951, the primary goal of which was to integrate the French and German coal and steel industries in order to prevent another Franco-German war. In 1957 the European Economic Community emerged from these humble, but imaginative and hugely significant beginnings, with the objective of establishing a common market among member states. The amalgamation of the EEC with the European Coal and Steel

[154] Woolf, 'Review', 67–70.

[155] Simpson, *Human Rights*, p. 646. [156] *Ibid.*, p. 648.

Community and the European Atomic Energy Community in 1965 created the European Communities. Further developments in 1992 transformed the European Communities into the twelve-member European Union. Retaining the distinctive identity of the European Communities as the 'First Pillar' this further re-organization added a 'Second Pillar' (a Common Foreign and Security Policy) and a 'Third Pillar' (Justice and Home Affairs) which includes such issues as asylum and immigration, drugs, judicial cooperation on civil and criminal justice, and police cooperation on terrorism and international crime. In 2002 twelve of the fifteen members of the EU exchanged their national currencies for the Euro, and by the mid-2000s ten new states had joined the EU (most from the former communist bloc), bringing the number of member states to twenty-five, over half that of the Council of Europe.

For much of its forty-year history the EEC/EC showed little overt interest in human rights.[157] This was largely for two reasons. First, while the EEC/EC always regarded the ideals of democracy, human rights and the rule of law as important and desirable, human rights were not initially seen as integral to the project of European integration. Second, it was, in any case, assumed that they were adequately covered by the Council of Europe and the European Convention on Human Rights – to which all members of the EEC/EC also belonged – and by the fact that the European Court of Justice (ECJ) in Luxembourg, the principal judicial organ of the EEC/EC, generally interpreted Community law as it applied to member states (although not as it applied to the institutions of the Union itself) in accordance with the Convention and the jurisprudence of the Strasbourg institutions.[158] However, towards the end of the twentieth century the profile of human rights increased in the EC/EU for several reasons. First, it became clear

[157] The extensive literature on human rights and the EC/EU includes: A. Williams, *EU Human Rights Policies: A Study in Irony* (Oxford: Oxford University Press, 2004); G. Quinn, 'The European Union and the Council of Europe on the Issue of Human Rights: Twins Separated at Birth?', *McGill Law Journal* **46** (2001), 849–874; P. Alston with M. Bustelo and J. Heenan (eds.), *The EU and Human Rights* (Oxford: Oxford University Press, 1999).

[158] H. C. Krüger and J. Polakiewicz, 'Proposals for a Coherent Human Rights Protection System in Europe: the European Convention on Human Rights and the EU Charter of Fundamental Rights', *Human Rights Law Journal* **22** (2001), 1–13 at 3 and 6–7; D. Spielmann, 'Human Rights Case Law in the Strasbourg and Luxembourg Courts: Conflicts, Inconsistencies and Complementarities' in Alston, 'EU and Human Rights', pp. 757–780; P. Lemmens, 'The Relation between the Charter of Fundamental Rights of the European Union and the European Convention on Human Rights – Substantive Aspects', *Maastricht Journal of European and Comparative Law* **8** (2001), 49–67;

that the success of European integration hinged upon the supremacy of community law. But a rebellion against supremacy, led by national constitutional courts fearing the risks that it posed to national constitutional rights, compelled the ECJ, from the 1970s onwards, to articulate its own fundamental rights jurisprudence.[159] Second, the EU began to require respect for human rights as a condition of non-EU states entering into formal trading and other relationships with it. As a result, it became increasingly difficult for the EU to justify not having a developed human rights policy for its own internal affairs. Third, Third Pillar issues have an inescapable human rights dimension, and finally, in the late 1990s the provision of a formal human rights document and more effective human rights monitoring arrangements were seen as offering a solution to the 'legitimation crisis' caused by the realization that the project of European integration had lost touch with the needs and aspirations of Europe's citizens.

The Treaty of Nice 2001, therefore, provided the EU with its first formal statement of rights, the Charter of Fundamental Rights, which collects together, in a single document, rights which the EU already provides in various other sources.[160] The Treaty of Nice also

S. Peers, 'The European Court of Justice and the European Court of Human Rights: Comparative Approaches', *United Kingdom Comparative Law Series* **22** (2003), 107–128.

159 A. Stone Sweet, *The Judicial Construction of Europe* (Oxford: Oxford University Press, 2004), pp. 87–91.

160 Lord Goldsmith, 'The Charter of Rights – A Brake Not an Accelerator', *European Human Rights Law Review* (2004), 473–478 at 478. In addition to this article, the extensive literature on the Charter includes: S. Peers and A. Ward (eds.), *The EU Charter of Fundamental Rights: Politics, Law and Policy* (Oxford: Hart Publishing, 2004); S. Carruthers, 'Beware of Lawyers Bearing Gifts: A Critical Evaluation of the Proposals on Fundamental Rights in the EU Constitutional Treaty', *European Human Rights Law Review* (2004), 424–435; S. Douglas-Scott, 'The Charter of Fundamental Rights as a Constitutional Document', *European Human Rights Law Review* (2004), 37–50; D. Ashiagbor, 'Economic and Social Rights in the European Charter of Fundamental Rights', *European Human Rights Law Review* (2004), 62–72; A. Arnull, 'From Charter to Constitution and Beyond: Fundamental Rights in the New European Union', *Public Law* (2003), 774–793; K. Kańska, 'Towards Administrative Human Rights in the EU. Impact of the Charter of Fundamental Rights', *European Law Journal* **10** (2004), 296–326; P. Drzemczewski, 'The Council of Europe's Position with Respect to the EU Charter of Fundamental Rights', *Human Rights Law Journal* **22** (2001), 14–31; C. E. Ergun, 'The EU Charter of Fundamental Rights: An Alternative to the European Convention on Human Rights?', *Mediterranean Journal of Human Rights* (2004), 91–105; R. Bellamy and J. Schönlau, 'The Normality of Constitutional Politics: An Analysis of the Drafting of the EU Charter of Fundamental Rights', *Constellations* **11** (2004), 412–433; V. D. Bojkov, 'National Identity, Political Interest and Human Rights in Europe: The Charter of Fundamental Rights of the European Union', *Nationalities Papers* **32** (2004), 323–355.

inaugurated the process of providing the Union with more formal constitutional foundations.[161] The Charter differs from the Convention in five fundamental ways. First, while the former includes the rights contained in the latter it does not do so in precisely the same terms. For example, Article 6 of the Charter expresses the right to liberty and security of the person in a single clause – 'everyone has the right to liberty and security of the person' – while Article 5 of the Convention has no less than five clauses, one of which has six further sub-clauses, twelve elements in total, for the same right. Article 52(3) of the Charter requires the meaning and scope of rights found in both Charter and Convention to be interpreted in the same way as those found in the Convention. But, as the Council of Europe's Steering Group puts it: 'experience tends to show that it is difficult to avoid contradictions where two differently worded texts on the same subject-matter are interpreted by two different courts'.[162] Second, the Convention is largely confined to civil and political rights, but the Charter includes a wide range of social, economic, cultural, and citizenship rights, which curiously do not correspond with any competences the EU already possesses.[163] Third, the Convention provides different restriction clauses for each right, while the Charter provides a single general limitation clause.[164] Fourth, the Convention binds member states, in any and all of their activities, but Article 51(7) of the Charter indicates that it is addressed to the institutions of the EU and to its member states only as far as the formulation and implementation of EU law are concerned. Finally, the Charter does not provide a right of individual petition to the ECJ. Were it ever to become legally binding and enforceable, the only

161 The extensive literature on the attempt to provide the EU with a more formal constitution includes: P. Birkinshaw, 'A Constitution for the European Union? – A Letter from Home', *European Public Law* **10** (2004), 57–84; G. de Burca, 'The Drafting of a Constitution for the European Union: Europe's Madisonian Moment or a Moment of Madness?', *Washington and Lee Law Review* **61** (2004), 555–586; M. Dougan, 'The Convention's Draft Constitutional Treaty: Bringing Europe Closer to its Lawyers?', *European Law Review* **28** (2003), 763–793.

162 Steering Committee for Human Rights (CDDH), *Study of Technical and Legal Issues of a Possible EC/EU Accession to the European Convention on Human Rights, Report adopted by the Steering Committee for Human Rights (CDDH) at its 53rd meeting (25–28 June 2002)*, Council of Europe DG-II(2002)006[CDDH(2002)010 Addendum 2] at para. 80.

163 Quinn, 'Twins Separated at Birth', 872.

164 P. Mahoney, 'The Charter of Fundamental Rights of the European Union and the European Convention on Human Rights from the Perspective of the European Convention', *Human Rights Law Journal* **23** (2002), 300–303.

recourse to Luxembourg open to litigants for a breach of a Charter right would, therefore, be through the preliminary reference procedure which enables domestic courts to consult the ECJ for rulings on points of Community law.

The Charter of Fundamental Rights has added grist to the mill of those who maintain that the range of rights provided by the Convention is outdated and restricted and that it should be expanded to include social, economic, and cultural ones as well.[165] But there are three compelling arguments for not going down this road. First, as already indicated, the Convention was never intended to promote human flourishing as such, but rather to defend the character of democratic institutions in Europe and, in spite of the momentous developments over the past half century, this remains its primary role. Second, including even the minimum corpus of social and economic rights is likely to compound the current case overload crisis. Adjudication on whole new species of rights would, therefore, not only further diminish the chances of any given applicant receiving adjudication on any of the current Convention rights, it would also greatly increase the risk of the entire system grinding to a terminal standstill. Third, in spite of the ubiquity of welfare rights in contemporary constitutional documents and international human rights treaties, requiring courts, particularly trans-national ones, to settle disputes about whether or not they have been violated, is controversial. There are two main difficulties.[166] In the first place, there is no direct correlation between the constitutionalization of welfare rights and high levels of welfare provision. The average citizen is much worse off in some states which have constitutionalized welfare rights, such as India, than the average citizen in others, such as the Scandinavian countries, Australia, and New Zealand, which have not. Clearly many other social, political, and economic factors – including national prosperity and wealth distribution – play much more important roles than the adjudication of such rights. Second, the constitutionalization of welfare rights tends to transfer decisions about the allocation of public funds raised through taxation,

[165] For example, E. Møse, 'New rights for the new Court?', in Mahoney, 'Protecting Human Rights', 943–956; Lord Steyn, 'Laying the Foundations of Human Rights Law in the United Kingdom', *European Human Rights Law Review* (2005), 349–362 at 352.

[166] For a review of the debate in central and eastern Europe see W. Sadurski, *Rights Before Courts: A Study of Constitutional Courts in Postcommunist States of Central and Eastern Europe* (Dordrecht: Springer, 2005), Ch. 7.

from democratically accountable legislative and executive institutions to non-accountable judicial ones, a feature less prominent in the adjudication of civil and political rights.

The negative votes in the referendums on the EU constitution in France and the Netherlands in the summer of 2005 not only ended, at least for the time being, the attempt to provide the EU with clearer and deeper constitutional foundations; they also deprived the Charter of Fundamental Rights of the formal legal character it would otherwise have had. The Charter, therefore, remains an unenforceable and non-binding set of guidelines with no real legal status. Nevertheless, it continues to be used as a point of reference by national courts and by EU institutions.[167] The Commission, for example, still regards the Charter as an essential vehicle for the promotion of an authentic EU rights culture, for strengthening the rights of its citizens, and for raising the level of protection across the Union,[168] and has stated that EU legislative proposals will be 'systematically and rigorously' checked for Charter compliance.[169] While for its part the ECJ has yet to cite the Charter expressly, preferring to refer to the Convention instead,[170] there is nothing to prevent the Charter from being used by it as a guide to the interpretation of Community law, thereby 'conferring on it legal status of sorts through the back door'.[171]

Another EU human rights initiative, independent of the constitutionalization debacle, considered more fully in Chapter 6, also deserves mention here. Developing an idea first approved in 2003, the EU formally proposed in June 2005 to expand the remit of the European Centre on Racism and Xenophobia to create a Fundamental Rights Agency expected to be operational from 1 January 2007.[172] Using the Charter as its main point of reference, attempting to avoid overlap with the Council of Europe, and networking with national institutions, the FRA is intended to be 'an independent centre of expertise on fundamental rights issues through data collection, analysis and networking', to provide 'relevant institutions and authorities of the Community and its Member States when implementing the Community

[167] Justice, *Annual Report 2005*, p. 15; M. Goldberg, 'EU Charter – the baby in the bathwater?' *Justice Bulletin* **6** (2005).

[168] Goldberg, 'EU Charter'. [169] *Ibid.* [170] *Ibid.*

[171] Quinn, 'Twins Separated at Birth', 872.

[172] P. Alston and O. De Schutter (eds.), *Monitoring Fundamental Rights in the EU: The Contribution of the Fundamental Rights Agency* (Oxford/Portland: Hart, 2005).

law with assistance and expertise relating to fundamental rights', and to 'advise the Union institutions and the Member States on how best to prepare or implement fundamental rights related Union legislation'.[173] The FRA will, however, have no powers to examine individual complaints, to issue regulations, or to carry out 'normative monitoring' for the purposes of Article 7 of the Treaty of European Union.[174]

In the long term, the on going development of human rights activity by the EU, and the prospect of the further enlargement of the Union, conceivably to a point where only ten or so European states will not be members, will make two overlapping, though not identical, trans-national systems for the protection of human rights in Europe difficult, if not impossible, to justify. Some commentators predict that the EU might even eclipse the Strasbourg institutions as the pre-eminent European guardian of human rights.[175] But this is on the distant horizon. The short-to-medium term priority is the more modest, but nonetheless challenging, task of improving coordination between the two systems. Resolving 'to create a new framework for enhanced cooperation and interaction' in 'areas of common concern, in particular human rights, democracy and the rule of law', the Council of Europe has commissioned a report, from Jean-Claude Juncker, Prime Minister of Luxembourg, on the relationship between the two organizations.[176] Of most immediate concern, is the possible accession of the EU to the Convention. Among other things this has been prompted by the fact that applicants are increasingly turning to Strasbourg with complaints about Community law,[177] by the lack of adequate processes by which

173 http://europa.eu.int/comm/justice_home/fsj/rights/fsj_rights_agency_en.htm.

174 This authorizes the Council of Ministers, on a reasoned proposal by one third of the Member States, by the European Parliament or by the Commission, to address appropriate recommendations to a Member State suspected of a serious breach of the principles of liberty, democracy, respect for human rights, and fundamental freedoms, including those found in the European Convention on Human Rights and the rule of law principles common to the Member States.

175 Sudre, quoted in Harmsen, 'ECHR After Enlargement', 20.

176 'Warsaw summit', para. 10.

177 The case of *Matthews* v. *United Kingdom* (1999) 28 EHRR 361, which involved a complaint to the Strasbourg Court about the UK's failure to organize elections in Gibraltar for the European Parliament (an EU institution), has excited particular interest. See, e.g. R. Harmsen, 'National Responsibility for European Community Acts Under the European Convention on Human Rights: Recasting the Accession Debate', *European Public Law* **7** (2001), 625–649; I. Canor, 'Primus Inter Pares: Who is the Ultimate Guardian of Human Rights in Europe', *European Law Review* **25** (2000) 3–21; Krüger and J. Polakiewicz, 'Proposals', 5.

individuals can litigate alleged violations of fundamental rights by EU institutions themselves, and by the risk of an increasing divergence between the Luxembourg and Strasbourg Courts over how the Convention should be interpreted.[178]

The new Article 59(2) to the Convention, provided by Article 17 of Protocol 14, revises the Convention to facilitate accession. But several technical problems have first to be resolved. These include: whether the EU or merely the EC should join; the precise form and terms of accession, for example whether it should be by way of a Protocol or a separate accession treaty; the amendment of various 'state-specific' aspects of the Convention, for example references to 'State Parties', 'inter-state' cases, and to 'national security', the 'economic well-being of the country' etc. in restriction clauses; possible accession to Convention Protocols which some EC/EU states may have signed but others not; whether there should be a 'preliminary reference' procedure enabling the ECJ to seek the opinion of the Strasbourg Court on matters of Convention interpretation before delivering judgment; the participation of the EC/EU as a third party or co-defendant in proceedings before the Strasbourg Court; the pros and cons of setting up a joint panel of the Luxembourg and Strasbourg Courts for certain purposes; the status and participation of the judge elected to the Strasbourg Court in respect of the EC/EU; the EC/EU's political representation on the Committee of Ministers; and the EC/EU's contribution to the budgets of the Council of Europe and the European Court of Human Rights.[179] However, none of these presents an insurmountable obstacle. But assuming, as most commentators do, that accession will take place, more significant problems may emerge later. Not the least of these is the risk that, by adding a whole new dimension of possible complaints, the case load of the European Court of Human Rights could increase still further, especially on the fair trial front. Tricky constitutional questions could also arise from the need to reconcile the autonomy and complementary nature of the EU and Convention legal orders with ensuring coherence

[178] Harmsen, 'National Responsibility', pp. 641–649; Krüger and J. Polakiewicz, 'Proposals'; C. Turner, 'Human Rights Protection in the European Community: Resolving Conflict and Overlap Between the European Court of Justice and the European Court of Human Rights', *European Public Law* **3** (1999), 453–470; J. M. Sera, 'The Case for Accession by the European Union to the European Convention for the Protection of Human Rights', *Boston University International Law Journal* **14** (1996), 151–186; Arnull, 'Charter to Constitution', 785–790.

[179] CDDH, 'Study of Legal and Technical Issues'; Krüger and J. Polakiewicz, 'Proposals'.

and harmony in the interpretation and application of common human rights standards.[180]

CONCLUSION

The Council of Europe's most obvious achievement is that it has not only survived the challenges of the past half century, but has flourished when it might just as easily have been marginalized by another European war, abolished as a result of the successful annexation of all, or part, of western Europe by the Soviet Union, rendered redundant by a resurgence of indigenous illiberal regimes in core states, ignored by prospective applicants, or simply wound up by common consent of its members. The most tangible expression of this success are the buildings, staff and bureaucracies of its various institutions in Strasbourg, their call upon the diplomatic and financial resources of member states, and the Court's management of a prodigious annual average of nearly 45,000 individual applications and the delivery of an average of between 700 and 800 judgments a year, until 2005 when the figure rose to 1,105. But, of itself, mere bureaucratic activity of this kind would satisfy only the most blinkered bureaucrat, jurist, or textbook writer. Indeed, if the 'juridification' and 'bureaucratization' of human rights at the European level were all that had occurred, it would be more a cause for regret than celebration.

Fortunately, there are other successes. But any attempt to identify what they might be, and what problems and challenges lie ahead, must begin with a clear understanding of how developments in the past fifty or so years may have altered the Convention's core objectives. Several things are clear about its creation. First, as a result of British reservations about anything more ambitious, the Council of Europe emerged from the negotiations of the late 1940s as a forum for intergovernmental cooperation rather than – as some would have preferred – a vehicle for structural integration. Second, although the result of compromise and political horse-trading, with little explicit intellectual coherence, the European Convention on Human Rights, was undeniably the product of a 'rights-affirming' rather than a 'rights-sceptical' political morality, the implications of which will be considered more fully in Chapter 4. It was, thirdly, intended to serve

180 Krüger and J. Polakiewicz, 'Proposals', 8–10.

four main objectives. It was, first and foremost, a symbolic statement of the identity signatory states had of themselves, designed to contrast sharply with Soviet-style communism and, less prominently, with the discredited right-wing European dictatorships of the then recent past, two of which still lingered in Spain and Portugal. The Convention articulates, in other words, an 'abstract constitutional identity' prescribing limits, in terms of human rights, to the exercise of public power in European liberal democracies committed to the rule of law. The model is 'abstract' in two main senses. First, it frames relevant standards at a high level of generality, leaving plenty of scope for equally Convention-compliant, though different, institutional, procedural, and normative interpretations at the national level. Second, as a 'partial polity', with judicial and executive but no legislative institutions, neither the Council of Europe nor the Convention system could have 'constitutions' in a more substantial sense.

Although generally said to have been inspired by the UN's Universal Declaration of Human Rights, the fact that the Convention focuses almost entirely on civil and political rights rather than upon the much wider rights catalogue provided by the Universal Declaration, indicates a much stronger debt to the liberal rights tradition expressed, in particular, by the French Declaration of the Rights of Man and the Citizen, and many subsequent national bills of rights. But this does not mean that it presupposes the theory of natural rights or that it is locked in the constitutional, political, and legal theory of classical liberalism. Criticizing it as a flawed, incomplete, or out moded attempt to provide the citizens of Europe with a pan-continental judicial process which should offer remedies for alleged breaches of the full panoply of fundamental rights – including social, economic, and other rights – also misunderstands its true character.

The second purpose the Convention was intended to serve was more instrumental – to provide an early warning device by which a drift towards authoritarianism, particularly in weak democracies, could be detected and dealt with through complaints by another member state, or states, to pan-European judicial and political institutions. Each of these two objectives, one symbolic and the other instrumental, was also fundamentally connected with war. The Convention was not only intended to contribute to the prevention of war in western Europe (its third purpose) – on the largely correct assumption that authoritarian regimes are more belligerent than democracies – but also to assist its effective prosecution by making western Europe a more cohesive unit in the Cold War and by giving it a clearer sense of collective purpose should this turn 'hot' (its fourth objective). It is, however, impossible to assess the role it, and the Council of Europe may have played in preserving international peace and security in Europe since this contribution cannot now be disentangled from that made by the EC and the European Union.

The ending of the Cold War in the 1990s has, however, deprived the Convention of its war-related founding objectives and has subtly transformed those which remain. States whose ideology was once the Convention's *bête noire*, including Russia, have been brought into the fold. As a result, the risk of international war has greatly diminished in Europe, while the risk of civil conflict, with the attendant risks of gross and systematic human rights abuses, may have increased – particularly in the former communist states – a prospect which could not have been foreseen in the late 1940s. Although the Convention has expanded geographically before, the enlargement of the 1990s was on a wholly different scale and brought a critical mass of states, some with chronically weak democratic traditions, into its judicial system. Simpson claims that, as a result, the Convention has departed from its original function to become 'a mechanism for changing the political character' of these states.[181] But this puts it too strongly. As the following chapter will seek to show, the Convention was, and remains, at best an instrument for gently encouraging, rather than for instigating, change. And, in spite of the developments of the past fifty or so years, its original purposes of providing an abstract European constitutional identity, and of sounding the 'alarm bell', remain, although the dominant risk is now the institutionalization of intolerance by ethnic majorities, and the risk of civil conflict and further human rights violations this portends, than it is of 'ideological' authoritarianism of the old fashioned left and right. From these another objective has emerged: promoting convergence in national public institutions, processes, and norms around Convention principles, particularly in those states, and not all in the former communist zone, where they are not yet very deeply institutionalized. But the principal mechanisms for attaining all these goals is no longer the inter-state complaint which is based on the self-contradictory assumption that antagonism between states can contribute towards their greater interdependence and unity. Instead it must lie with the individual application or some other alternative.

[181] Simpson, *Human Rights*, p. 3.

How effective the individual applications process is in protecting minority rights, in tackling the kind of gross and systematic human rights abuses which may arise out of ethnic tensions in member states, and in promoting convergence in European public institutions and processes around a common abstract constitutional model including those of the EU, is in considerable doubt at the beginning of the twenty-first century, not least because the process suffers from two critical internal problems, one procedural and the other conceptual. First, the rate of applications, likely to reach at least 80,000 a year by the end of the decade, is now so high that in spite of Protocol 14 it threatens to paralyse the Convention's judicial process. Second, this phenomenon has led to the development of the 'myth of individual justice', which maintains that, whatever the original intentions of the Convention's founders, the Court's primary objective is now to resolve each legitimate complaint about Convention violation for the benefit of the particular applicant making it. While this may be a laudable aim, it is one which the Court is wholly incapable of fulfilling. With jurisdiction over more than 800 million people, and an adjudicative capacity of around 800 cases a year, any given citizen of a Council of Europe state has, on the bare statistics, around one in a million chance of having a complaint heard at Strasbourg. Even though many fewer were likely to have been the victim of a breach of the Convention in the first place, only 2 per cent or so of the 40,000 or so now applying to the Court every year are likely to receive judgment. The extent to which the summary procedure provided by Protocol 14, discussed more fully in Chapter 3, may increase the rate of decisions in favour of applicants remains to be seen. Traditionally, even fully reasoned judgments were limited to declaring whether or not the Convention had been violated rather than granting applicants specific remedies. As Chapter 3 indicates, this is beginning to change as the Court shows a greater willingness to specify the kind of remedial action required. However, it is not yet clear how much impact this will have both on case load and on levels of national compliance.

All this tends to suggest that the Convention may have become a hugely flawed and cost-inefficient exercise, incapable, due to the inadequacies of both the inter-state and individual applications processes, of addressing big structural problems and gross violations in member states and, notwithstanding the Protocol 14 changes, capable instead of delivering individual justice to only a tiny fraction of complainants. These charges would be difficult to refute if the delivery of individual justice had indeed become the Convention's real objective.

However, the primary purpose of the judicial process is not to benefit individual applicants at all, but remains, as it always has been, to enable the Court to address the most serious defects with Convention compliance in member states – 'constitutional justice'. The key problem currently facing the Convention system is, therefore, to determine how its scarce judicial resources can be targeted effectively on the most serious alleged violations in Europe, and how the tiny annual cluster of cases it is capable of subjecting to fully reasoned judgments can be settled with maximum authority and impact. The purpose of the remainder of this study is to consider how this might be achieved.

2

Convention Compliance

INTRODUCTION

One of the key challenges which has always faced the Council of Europe, but which has arguably become even more acute at the beginning of the twenty-first century, concerns what more can be done to improve Convention compliance by member states.[1] Two kinds of non-compliance can be distinguished. 'Contingent' breaches – occasioned by specific conduct or decisions occurring within institutions or processes operating in a largely Convention-compliant manner – are likely to lead only to a single or to comparatively few applications to Strasbourg. But, as widely recognized in recent debates, a more serious problem concerns 'structural' or 'systemic' violations stemming from the character or design of public institutions or processes.

Chapter 6 will consider how these problems might be tackled as a matter of Council of Europe policy. Since this will inevitably involve seeking to encourage those national factors most likely to produce high levels of Convention compliance, it is necessary to begin by seeking, in this chapter, to identify what these might be. First, an attempt needs to be made to determine how Convention compliance could be measured. Second, since this study argues that the scarce resources of the European Court of Human Rights should be targeted more strategically on the least Convention-compliant states, some empirically-grounded picture must, therefore, be obtained as to which countries are in this category. Third, some hypotheses will be framed which offer preliminary explanations, open to verification or falsification by more detailed empirical study than is possible here, for, respectively, differential rates of official Convention violation in western Europe and the varying human rights records of the post-communist states of central and eastern Europe.

[1] R. Harmsen, 'The European Convention on Human Rights after Enlargement', *International Journal of Human Rights* **5** (2001), 18–43 at 34.

Finally, some conclusions will be drawn which offer at least a tentative empirical basis for policy formation.

ASSESSING NATIONAL CONVENTION COMPLIANCE

One of the earliest attempts to record statistical information about human rights abuses was the publication, by *New York World*, of periodic data starting in 1885, about lynchings in the United States.[2] However, a more concerted effort did not begin until the 1970s when social scientists and campaigning organizations began not only to document specific violations such as this, but also to find ways of expressing numerically the extent to which different countries effectively protect specific human rights, or human rights in general. States have then also been ranked accordingly. In the 1980s, the Carter administration in the US used such measures to help guide its decisions about granting or withholding aid and trade and, in the 1990s, the World Bank and the United Nations Development Programme followed suit in the belief that higher levels of 'freedom' strengthen economic growth.[3] The tide of indicators, indices, and benchmarks has continued to grow,[4] with the Freedom House Democracy Index, the Human Freedoms Index of the UN Development Programme, the Humana Index, and the Physical Quality of Life Index, among the most well-known.[5] The collection and dissemination of compatible information about human rights violations was also enhanced by the establishment, in 1982, of the Human Rights Information and Documentation System International (HURIDOCS).[6]

[2] R. P. Claude and T. B. Jabine, 'Exploring Human Rights Issues with Statistics' in T. B. Jabine and R. P. Claude (eds.), *Human Rights and Statistics: Getting the Record Straight* (Philadelphia: University of Pennsylvania Press, 1992), pp. 5–34 at 5.

[3] R. L. Barsh, 'Measuring Human Rights: Problems of Methodology and Purpose', *Human Rights Quarterly* **15** (1993), 87–121 at 87 and 98.

[4] Human rights 'indicators' are quantitative or qualitative measures which serve as proxies or metaphors for rates of violation or protection which cannot be directly observed. Human rights 'indices' are comparative rankings of states according to the information provided by indicators. Human rights 'benchmarks' are specific human rights goals or targets, usually national, see M. Green, 'What We Talk About When We Talk About Indicators: Current Approaches to Human Rights Measurement', *Human Rights Quarterly* **23** (2001), 1062–1097 at 1076–1084.

[5] Barsh, 'Measuring Human Rights', 91; Green, 'What We Talk About', 1082.

[6] J. Dueck, 'HURIDOCS Standard Formats as a Tool in the Documentation of Human Rights Violations' in Jabine and Claude (eds.), *Human Rights and Statistics*, pp. 127–158.

The range of measures has also expanded to include 'coding country participation in regional and international human rights regimes, coding national constitutions according to their rights provisions, qualitative reporting of rights violations, survey data on perceptions of rights conditions, quantitative summaries of rights violations, abstract scales of rights protection based on normative standards, and individual and aggregate measures that map the outcomes of government policies that have consequences for the enjoyment of rights'.[7] More recently state compliance/non-compliance with human rights treaties have also been subjected to empirical assessment.

Methodological Problems in the Measurement of Human Rights Violations

Many commentators are, however, sceptical about the use of statistical methods to measure human rights abuses,[8] with particular concern being raised about the reliability, and hence utility, of national numerical scoring.[9] For example, writing in 1993, Barsh, although not hostile to measurement in principle, maintained that no instrument free from problems with reliability, validity, and equivalence had then been produced.[10] As a result, he argued that there was no credible empirical basis for the accurate measurement of human rights protection in given states, nor for understanding scientifically, the relationship between human rights and other variables such as development and prosperity.[11] Barsh maintained that summated scores are often arrived at prematurely, that numerical indicators typically suffer from a lack of conceptual clarity, including a lack of specificity and consensus about what the values or rights in question mean, and that data collection problems also tend to affect primary sources. By relying on formal sources such as particular legal provisions, or on secondary sources such as newspaper reports, indicator-based studies tend simply to reproduce

[7] T. Landman, 'Measuring Human Rights: Principle, Practice and Policy', *Human Rights Quarterly* **26** (2004), 906–931 at 911.

[8] R. J. Goldstein, 'The Limitations of Using Quantitative Data in Studying Human Rights Abuses' in Jabine and Claude (eds.), *Human Rights and Statistics*, pp. 35–61; G. A. Lopez and M. Stohl, 'Problems of Concept and Measurement in the Study of Human Rights' in Jabine and Claude (eds.), *Human Rights and Statistics*, pp. 216–234.

[9] Barsh, 'Measuring Human Rights'. [10] *Ibid.*, p. 121.

[11] *Ibid.*; Green, 'What We Talk About'.

what are likely to be distorted pictures of the frequency and type of violations at the grass roots. And as Goldstein, who endorses most of Barsh's observations adds: 'Even if one avoids trying to create overall "indexes" of repression ... instead sticking to raw accounts of human rights abuses, numerous problems of comparability, context and interpretation remain that statistical data alone cannot resolve.'[12] For Lopez and Stohl the way forward lies in 'more nuanced information collection and the use of a multidimensional approach to assessing the meaning of that information – with each activity informed by political judgement'.[13] Although some progress has been made on these fronts over the past decade or so, it is not clear that the fundamental problems have yet been fully solved. Writing in 2001, Raworth, for example, argues that lack of clarity about what is to be assessed and how it is to be measured continue to compromise attempts to develop human rights indicators, and that time should be devoted instead to more reliable case studies focusing, in a context-sensitive way, on state obligations under international human rights law.[14] However, in contrast, Landman, has also recently argued that, while the information upon which it is based may be 'lumpy and incomplete',[15] the measurement of human rights is 'nonetheless useful for mapping human rights developments in the world, examining the plausible explanations for the continued global variation in their protection and providing policy solutions for improving that protection in the future'.[16]

Measuring Compliance with Human Rights Treaties and Other Trans-National Legal Regimes

Until recently, the lack of rigorous referencing to the specific provisions of international human rights law had been a particular weakness of the social scientific attempt to measure national levels of human rights protection, a defect Hathaway set out to remedy in a pioneering study[17] which rejects 'rational actor' and 'normative' accounts of state

[12] Goldstein, 'Limitations of Quantitative Data', 51.
[13] Lopez and Stohl, 'Problems of Concept and Measurement', 217.
[14] K. Raworth, 'Measuring Human Rights', *Ethics and International Affairs* **15** (2001), 111–131.
[15] Landman, 'Measuring Human Rights', 917. [16] *Ibid.*, p. 931.
[17] O. A. Hathaway, 'Do Human Rights Treaties Make a Difference?', *Yale Law Journal* **111** (2002), 1935–2042.

treaty-related behaviour and argues instead that treaties operate on symbolic and instrumental levels simultaneously.[18] According to 'rational actor' models, states only adhere to the provisions of a treaty when they judge it to be in their interests to do so. Hathaway distinguishes three different versions. The 'realists', of which there are also various kinds, argue that treaty compliance is the result of a mere coincidence between treaty obligations and what states take to be in their best interests. 'Institutionalists' argue that states comply with international regimes in pursuit of a reputation for good international citizenship which can facilitate the realization of long-term strategic goals. 'Liberalists' maintain that liberal democracies are more likely to comply with international obligations than other kinds of state, and that they do so in order to minimize the domestic political costs of non-compliance.

'Normative' models, on the other hand, maintain that the persuasive power of legitimate obligations not only constrains what states might otherwise be tempted to do, but also contributes to the construction of what they take to be in their own interests in the first place. According to Hathaway there are also three versions of this approach. The 'managerial model' argues that states comply with treaties because they have been socialized to do so as a result of the persuasive power of a network of international norms, international processes, and mutual expectations, and that compliance failures are more likely to be the result of insufficient information than a cynical cost-benefit calculation. The 'fairness' model maintains that states comply with treaties when they regard them as legitimate and fair. Finally, the 'trans-national legal process' model claims that states observe treaty obligations when treaty norms have been effectively internalized in their domestic political and legal systems.

Using four comprehensive human rights databases,[19] and five subject areas from a broad spectrum of human rights treaties – genocide, torture, civil liberty, fair and public trials, and the political representation of women – Hathaway seeks to discover how rates of reported human

[18] The rich, and expanding, theoretical literature on the question of why states obey international law is helpfully reviewed in H. H. Koh, 'Review Essay: Why Do Nations Obey International Law?', *Yale Law Journal* **106** (1997), 2599–2659. As Kingsbury argues, in international law 'compliance' cannot simply be equated with 'correspondence of behaviour with legal rules' but depends critically upon which conception of international law is adopted, B. Kingsbury, 'The Concept of Compliance as a Function of Competing Conceptions of International Law', *Michigan Journal of International Law* **19** (1998), 345–372.

[19] Hathaway, 'Human Rights Treaties', 1967.

rights violation (the dependent variable) correlate with treaty ratification (the independent variable). Several other studies have concluded that, although the impact which international human rights law may have on state conduct may be difficult to detect, this does not mean it has no influence at all.[20] However, Hathaway's main, counterintuitive, conclusions are that, apart from full democracies, ratification of a human rights treaty tends to be associated with (although Hathaway does not suggest it causes) *worse*, rather than better, human rights practices, and that countries with poor human rights records appear to ratify treaties at a higher rate than those with good records.[21] While treaties may create formal legal obligations with specific implications for state practice, they also allow states to present a particular image of themselves in international society whether or not this accords with reality. In fact, Hathaway maintains that states often have little intention of altering their conduct to conform with their treaty obligations and that they tend to ratify human rights treaties in order to reduce, in a virtually cost-free way, the scrutiny of other states. This in its turn can contribute to a deterioration in the protection of human rights in any given state rather than its improvement. And the position is worse for regional regimes since ratification of regional human rights treaties appears to be more likely than ratification of universal treaties to be associated with high rates of non-compliance, and with worse human rights records than would be expected, even for full democracies.[22] Hathaway suggests that this is because greater regional interdependence increases pressures on states to ratify treaties whether or not they intend to adhere to them, notwithstanding the fact that regional enforcement mechanisms tend to be stronger than their global counterparts.[23] Indeed a 'statistically significant' relationship was found between ratification of the European Convention on Human Rights and less fair trials,[24] although not with lower levels of protection for civil liberty.[25]

[20] T. Risse, S. C. Ropp and K. Sikkink (eds.), *The Power of Human Rights: International Norms and Domestic Change* (Cambridge: Cambridge University Press, 1999); D. Cassel, 'Does International Human Rights Law Make a Difference?', *Chicago Journal of International Law* **2** (2001), 121–135; L. C. Keith, 'The United Nations International Covenant on Civil and Political Rights: Does it Make a Difference in Human Rights Behavior?', *Journal of Peace Research* **36** (1999), 95–118; R. Schwartz, 'The Paradox of Sovereignty, Regime Type and Human Rights Compliance', *International Journal of Human Rights Research* **8** (2004), 199–215.

[21] Hathaway, 'Human Rights Treaties', 1978.

[22] *Ibid.*, pp. 1980, 1981, 1995, 2000. [23] *Ibid.*, pp. 2016–2017.

[24] *Ibid.*, p. 1996. [25] *Ibid.*, p. 1997.

The solution to the problem of poor compliance with human rights treaties, Hathaway maintains, is for the international community to make treaty ratification more costly to states by improving the monitoring and enforcement of obligations in order to prevent the expressive, or symbolic, dimension dominating the instrumental. She suggests that membership of treaty regimes could also be tiered, with probationary periods followed by comprehensive reviews of country practices and with recalcitrant states facing more serious risks of expulsion.

Goodman and Jinks regard Hathaway's research as 'the most well-conceived empirical study' of treaty compliance in the literature, which is likely to 'influence empirical debates in the legal academy for some time to come'.[26] Nevertheless, they maintain that the empirical analysis, the theoretical explanations, and the policy implications are fatally flawed with the central weakness being a failure adequately to account for the ways, and the conditions under which, international human rights norms are incorporated into national practice. On the empirical front three main problems are identified with the dependent variable, reported human rights violations. First, there are serious problems in taking reported human rights violations as an indicator of the rate of actual violations since it is well-recognized in social science research that reported instances of any social phenomenon rarely tally with its true incidence. Second, a misleading picture will emerge if a deterioration in official respect for any given human right is not linked with an improvement in the protection of other human rights. For example, in the 1970s levels of torture, political imprisonment, and unfair trials appear to have declined in Latin America as governments opted for an even more serious human rights violation – disappearances – in their struggle against internal dissent. Any study of these states which was confined only to torture, political imprisonment, and fair trials but not disappearances would, therefore wrongly, conclude that the human rights position had improved when in fact it had seriously deteriorated. Third, the rate of reported violations of any human right is likely to increase where repressive regimes become less repressive and where greater access to official information is permitted in consequence. Reported violations may, therefore, rise as a result of increased visibility,

[26] R. Goodman and D. Jinks, 'Measuring the Effects of Human Rights Treaties', *European Journal* of *International Law* **14** (2003), 171–183 at 172.

while the rate of actual violations declines. As Goodman and Jinks point out, Hathaway's model cannot account for effects such as these.

Moreover, Goodman and Jinks argue that ratification is not only a problematic variable in itself, it also *exacerbates* problems inherent in the dependent variable (the rate of reported violations). Treaty ratification is, in the first place, only one point on a continuum of national adjustment to treaty obligations which includes, among other things, pledging to join a treaty regime, signature, incorporating treaty provisions in domestic law, and effecting changes in official conduct. As Goodman and Jinks argue, the central empirical task is not merely to discover the relationship between reported human rights violations and ratification, but to identify the conditions under which the entire process of fulfilling treaty obligations moves forward, and those under which it stalls. Secondly, for many governments, the decision to ratify a human rights treaty indicates a willingness to permit greater access to information about its human rights practices, and to increased national and international scrutiny of its record, which could lead to an increase in reported violations, at least in the short term, a phenomenon particularly true of regional regimes.

Goodman and Jinks identify four main problems with Hathaway's theoretical model. First, the quantitative analysis is not designed to test the validity of the theory, which amounts merely to 'a post-hoc causal explanation (arguably) consistent with, but neither confirmed nor assessed by, the empirical findings'.[27] Hathaway suggests, for example, that, post-ratification, the US government reduces pressure on states to improve their human rights record by, among other things, under-reporting violations. Yet she uses these very reports as independent indicators of the objective human rights position in given states. Second, the complexity of state treaty practice – including non-ratification and the varied forms of qualified participation such as ratification-with-reservation or formal notification of derogation – is not adequately accommodated. Third, Hathaway's theory underestimates the sovereignty costs of ratification and claims, self-contradictorily, that states ratify human rights treaties with little or no intention of honouring them in order to reduce the pressure from other states who, themselves, naively fail to realize that ratification can often be an empty gesture. Fourth, Hathaway not only fails to make the theoretical assumptions of her model explicit, but, having rejected the rational actor approach, implicitly

[27] *Ibid.*, 179.

assumes a rationalist theory of social action by claiming that, while persuasion generally fails, international political pressure works. Regrettably, according to Goodman and Jinks, she 'neither identifies a causal mechanism by which international norms are incorporated into national practice, nor the deeper incentives that form or guide state choices', thereby failing to deliver on her promise of addressing the defects of the rational actor and normative traditions.[28]

Finally, Goodman and Jinks argue that the main policy implication of Hathaway's analysis is 'unpersuasive and ultimately counterproductive' because her proposal to increase the costs of ratification would jeopardize the role ratification plays in the gradual construction of both national, and trans-national, human rights cultures.[29] Moreover, her model is incapable of detecting the effect this would have even in countries which do not participate in a particular international human rights regime. As Goodman and Jinks argue, given the lack of a fully scientific measurement of the impact of human rights treaties on state conduct, the best assumption is the conventional one that they advance rather than inhibit the cause they seek to promote.

Among other attempts to measure compliance with trans-national legal regimes, those relating to the EU are, prima facie, of particular relevance. The results of a recent study, edited by Zürn and Joerges, challenge the received wisdom that the EU suffers from significant compliance problems.[30] In fact, the level of compliance with regulations on the control of subsidies, food, and redistribution, was found to be higher in the EU than in either Germany or the World Trade Organization. Zürn and Neyer[31] attribute this to the interaction between four main factors: 'rational instrumentalism' – the effective monitoring and institutionalization of enforcement (which need not be coercive), particularly when these two functions are assumed by centralized institutions which make full use of trans-national non-governmental actors, and when more than one institution or actor has an interest in enforcing compliance;[32] 'legalization' – the establishment of a framework of genuine legal norms and hierarchically organized, independent

[28] *Ibid.*, 180. [29] *Ibid.*, 181.

[30] M. Zürn and C. Joerges (eds.), *Law and Governance in Postnational Europe: Compliance Beyond the Nation-State* (Cambridge: Cambridge University Press, 2005).

[31] M. Zürn and J. Neyer, 'Conclusions – the conditions of compliance' in Zürn and Joerges (eds.), *Law and Governance*, pp. 183–217.

[32] This is similar to the claim made by Helfer and Slaughter, in a comparative study of the European Court of Justice and the European Court of Human Rights, that

adjudicatory bodies using formal legal reasoning rather than, for example, bargaining to resolve disputes; 'legitimacy' – the involvement of all relevant parties, including non-state ones, in will-formation and decision-making, especially the acceptance of a strong compliance and enforcement system by the general public; and 'management' – sufficient capacity for implementation and the flexible ('reflexive') application of rules.

Methodological Problems in the Measurement of Compliance with the European Convention on Human Rights

Commentators frequently lavish praise on the Council of Europe and on the Convention for their role in promoting human rights, democracy and the rule of law in Europe. Drezemczewski, Head of the Monitoring Department of the Directorate of Strategic Planning of the Council of Europe, for example, states: 'That individuals can successfully plead their cases before the European Court of Human Rights, that war between France and Germany is no longer possible and that democracy is well-embedded – since the late 1970s – on the Iberian Peninsula and, more recently, in a number of countries in Central and Eastern Europe, are surely clear indicators of the historical role the Council of Europe has played in *preventing* human rights violations and in consolidating pluralistic democracy and respect for the Rule of Law.'[33] He adds that it would be difficult to deny that the ECHR and its case law have had a 'profound effect in preventing many human rights violations'.[34] Such claims are, however, easy to make, yet enormously difficult to prove. In fact, the available evidence is, at best, equivocal.

A number of conclusions can be drawn from the discussion in the earlier part of this chapter for the assessment of national Convention compliance. First, although most scholars have not ruled it out in principle, there is, as yet, no universally accepted means by which the

supranational adjudication is likely to be more effective the more the tribunal in question is able to penetrate the surface of states and provide points of reference of use to various state and non-state institutions in exerting domestic pressure for change, L. R. Helfer and A.-M. Slaughter, 'Towards a Theory of Effective Supranational Adjudication', *Yale Law Journal* **107** (1997), 273–391 at 387–388.

[33] A. Drezemczewski, 'The Prevention of Human Rights Violations: Monitoring Mechanisms of the Council of Europe', *International Studies in Human Rights* **67** (2001), 139–177 at 1139, italics in original.

[34] *Ibid.*, 155.

human rights record of any state can be reliably scored numerically. Second, and more specifically, since there is, as yet, no scientifically reliable way of measuring state compliance with human rights treaties either, their full effects, as Goodman and Jinks point out, are unknown.[35] Hathaway's conclusions, therefore, remain open to question. Third, the debates about measuring the human rights records of states and about their compliance with human rights treaties can, nevertheless, contribute to the refinement of the debate about national Convention compliance in several ways. As Hathaway points out, it should be recognized that 'compliance' can mean several different things – including conforming with procedural obligations such as reporting, honouring substantive obligations, and fulfilling the spirit of the treaty – and that states can comply, in any of these senses, to varying degrees. Writing about the EU, Zürn also distinguishes 'compliance' (behaviour in conformity with that which is prescribed) from the 'implementation' of rules or regulations (the extent to which they are actually put into practice) and 'effectiveness' (the capacity of a regulatory regime to solve commonly perceived problems).[36] As he says, assessing compliance is inevitably indeterminate because of the ambiguity of rules and the irresolvability of debates over what constitutes their 'correct' interpretation. In the Convention context a further distinction could be drawn between 'compliance with adverse judgments of the Court' and 'compliance with Convention standards even where the Court's judgment has not been sought'. As Hathaway also points out, there are several competing explanations for state compliance/non-compliance with international human rights regimes. Jordan, for example, argues in a study of the impact of the Council of Europe on the post-Soviet transition explored more fully below, that 'constructivist approaches best inform the process of norm diffusion in countries of high compliance (Latvia), while neoliberal and neorealist approaches better explain why norm diffusion is less successful in medium (Croatia) and low compliance (Russia) countries'.[37]

[35] Goodman and Jinks, 'Measuring Effects', 183.

[36] M. Zürn, 'Introduction: Law and Compliance at different levels' in Zürn and Joerges (eds.), *Law and Governance*, pp. 1–39 at 8–9.

[37] P. A. Jordan, 'Does Membership Have Its Privileges?: Entrance into the Council of Europe and Compliance with Human Rights Norms', *Human Rights Quarterly* **25** (2003), 660–688 at 660.

These distinctions and discussions throw considerable light on what is, otherwise, a paradox in the limited Convention literature which concerns compliance.[38] Until recently, the largely unchallenged orthodoxy was that states readily and fully comply with adverse decisions of the Strasbourg institutions.[39] For example, as the then President of the European Court of Human Rights, Rolv Ryssdal, stated in 1996: 'To date judgments of the European Court of Human Rights have, I would say, not only generally but always been complied with by the Contracting States concerned. There have been delays, perhaps even some examples of what one might call minimal compliance, but no instances of non-compliance.'[40] The following chapter considers in more detail the process by which the execution of the Court's judgments is supervised. But, as Judge Martens, expressing a more sceptical view, points out, the Committee of Ministers 'does not make any ruling on the compliance of remedial legislation with the requirements of the Convention as interpreted by the Court'. It, therefore, restricts itself to what may be called '*prima facie* control'.[41] For Judge Martens: 'What is at stake is . . . not only whether remedial legislation is passed at all, but also whether, if passed, it is adequate and meets the requirements implied in the relevant judgment.' As he adds, this 'cannot be ascertained without careful research and such research is scarce' although some studies indicate that it is not uncommon for states to fail to pass the kind of legislation required.[42] The orthodox view is also undermined, and Judge Marten's scepticism confirmed, by the fact, revealed in the Protocol 14 debate, that some 60 per cent of the Court's judgments condemn violations by the specific respondent state which have already been condemned in previous cases ('repeat' applications). It should also be noted, however,

38 For a useful review see M. W. Janis, 'The Efficacy of Strasbourg Law', *Connecticut Journal of International Law* **15** (2000), 39–46.

39 See the citations in Janis, 'Efficacy', notes 6, 16 and 27.

40 R. Ryssdal, 'The Enforcement System set up under the European Convention on Human Rights' in M. K. Bulterman and M. Kuijer (eds.), *Compliance With Judgments of International Courts: Proceedings of the Symposium organized in honour of Professor Henry G. Schermers by Mordenate College and the Department of International Public Law of Leiden University* (The Hague/Boston/London: Martinus Nijhoff, 1996) pp. 49–69 at 67.

41 S. K. Martens, 'Commentary', in Bulterman and Kuijer (eds.), *Compliance With Judgments* at p. 77.

42 Martens, 'Commentary', 73. See also R. R. Churchill and J. R. Young, 'Compliance with Judgments of the European Court of Human Rights and Decisions of the Committee of Ministers: the Experience of the United Kingdom, 1975–1987', *British Yearbook of International Law* **62** (1991), 283–346.

that some confusion remains over how similar any application needs to be in order to be regarded as repetitive.[43]

Although, crucially, the Convention system lacks the EU's legislative dimension, the Convention scores very well on one of Zürn and Neyer's four criteria for successful compliance, 'legalization', and fairly well on another two, 'legitimacy' and 'management'.[44] While the Council of Europe is highly 'legitimate' because of its fundamentally consensual nature, this is less true of the Convention system itself, although it may be incapable of achieving full legitimacy in the sense Zürn and Neyer mean because of its essentially judicial, rather than public policy, character. The Protocol 14 debate, for example, had little national public resonance beyond lawyers and NGOs, although it is difficult to imagine how public interest in member states could have been more successfully ignited. The extent to which the Convention could be said to fulfil the 'management' criterion is also in doubt because, although the application of its constituent norms is reflexive, many states seem to have genuine difficulty in fulfilling the fair trial requirement that national legal systems deliver justice promptly. But of all Zürn and Neyer's criteria, 'rational instrumentalism' is the one which the Convention most obviously lacks, particularly because the individual applications process entrusts enforcement to only one kind of trans-national non-governmental actor, 'victims' of violation.

Finally, while it is difficult, if not impossible, objectively to measure a state's Convention compliance, it can, nevertheless, be assessed in other ways. Although the rate of violation as determined by the Strasbourg institutions invites explanation for both eastern and western Europe, for five main reasons this is not an unproblematic surrogate for national Convention compliance. First, the road to judgment at Strasbourg is long and arduous. As indicated in the previous chapter, any applicant currently has only a 2 per cent chance of having their complaint heard by the Court, and many more may be deterred from even making an application by lack of awareness that it is possible to do so, by inadequate legal advice, or by lack of cooperation – or even, in extreme cases, obstruction – on the part of state authorities.[45]

43 See Chapter 3. 44 Zürn and Neyer, 'Conclusions'.

45 Contributions to R. Blackburn and J. Polakiewicz (eds.), *Fundamental Rights in Europe: The European Convention on Human Rights and its Member States, 1950–2000* (Oxford: Oxford University Press, 2001) suggest that the Convention is better known to litigants and lawyers in Austria, Belgium, Denmark, Finland, Greece, Switzerland, Italy, and the

Some national cultures are also more litigious than others. Second, because of the lapse in time between the events giving rise to complaints and the delivery of judgment, the human rights record in any given state on any given date may either be better or worse than the pattern of officially designated violation on that date. Third, a finding that a Convention right has been violated often involves a finely balanced, and often not a unanimous, legal judgment, involving technical issues such as the scope of formal limitations upon rights and the respondent state's 'margin of appreciation'. Fourth, the bald violation statistics give no indication of the seriousness of any given violation. Finally, any given official finding of a violation may represent either the breach of the Convention rights of a single applicant, or a systemic problem suffered by thousands of others. While these problems apply to both eastern and western Europe, there are two particular difficulties in seeking to establish conclusively, according to the information currently available, how effectively Convention rights are protected in the former communist states. First, these states have not been subject to the jurisdiction of the European Court of Human Rights long enough for clear official violation patterns to emerge across the entire region. Second, although a useful source of hypotheses, the social scientific literature is not nearly systematic enough to permit sound social scientific conclusions.[46]

The view taken here is that Convention compliance cannot be objectively measured, not only because the statistical techniques which are available are not sophisticated enough, but because the question of what constitutes compliance/non-compliance involves, in many instances, the exercise of judgment and evaluation which cannot by its nature be objectively settled. But where the conclusions of several

Netherlands, than it is in Ireland, France, and Portugal, each of these two categories including both low and high violation states. See H. Tretter, 'Austria', pp. 103–165 at 129; S. Marcus-Helmons and P. Marcus-Helmons, 'Belgium', pp. 167–190 at 167–168; P. Germer, 'Denmark', pp. 259–276 at 275; A. Rosas, 'Finland', pp. 289–312 at 304; K. Ioannou, 'Greece', pp. 355–381 at 371 and 381; M. Borghi, 'Switzerland', pp. 855–878 at 856; E. Meriggiola, 'Italy', pp. 475–501 at 475; L. F. Zwaak, 'Netherlands', pp. 595–624 at 622–3; D. O'Connell, 'Ireland', pp. 423–473 at 468; C. Dupré, 'France', pp. 313–333 at 332; J. Madureira, 'Portugal', pp. 681–709 at 683.

46 For example, the best available, and most recent, collection of country-specific studies, Blackburn and Polakiewicz (eds.), *Fundamental Rights*, lacks contributions for Albania, Armenia, Azerbaijan, Bosnia and Herzegovina, Croatia, Georgia, Serbia and Montenegro, Latvia, Macedonia, and Moldova.

independent, professionally conducted, and reliable quantitative and qualitative studies converge, there is a good chance that the picture they present is accurate. However, although a great deal of human rights 'monitoring' is being conducted in contemporary Europe – by NGOs, various agencies of the Council of Europe, and other international organizations – its reliability is often difficult to determine on account of queries about sources and its often vague, subjective and impressionistic, character.[47]

Subject to all these qualifications and reservations the official violation rate invites explanation. Table 1 shows 'Violations by Article as Found by the European Court of Human Rights: 1999–2005', while Figure 3 represents them in the form of a bar chart.

According to these figures, 58 per cent of Convention violations concern the right to fair trial under Article 6, while 37 per cent relate to unreasonable delays in the administration of justice, a specific Article 6 violation. Violations of Article 1 of Protocol No. 1 follow next at 14 per cent, with violations of Article 5, the right to freedom from arbitrary arrest and detention, at 7.5 per cent. However, according to the former Registrar of the European Court of Human Rights, Mr Paul Mahoney, of a total of 695 judgments delivered by the Court in 2000, 485 (69.78 per cent) were 'straightforward cases exclusively or principally concerning alleged excessive length of proceedings . . .', a higher figure than the number of violations for excessive length of proceedings (303) recorded for 2000 in Table 1.[48] In an exchange of emails with the author which does not wholly resolve the issue, the Registry of the Court explained that there is a difference between the absolute number of violations of any given Convention provision and the number of judgments in which it was the 'exclusive or principal' violation, because any given judgment of the Court may include more than one application and several violations. However, of the two figures, Mr Mahoney's is

[47] A. Bloed, L. Leicht, M. Nowak and A. Rosas, 'Introduction', p. xiv, and 'General conclusions and recommendations' at p. 319 (para. 3), in A. Bloed, L. Leicht, M. Nowak and A. Rosas, (eds.), *Monitoring Human Rights in Europe: Comparing International Procedures and Mechanisms* (Dordrecht/Boston/London: Martinus Nijhoff, 1993); V. Dimitrijević, 'The Monitoring of Human Rights and the Prevention of Human Rights Violations through Reporting Procedures', in Bloed, Leicht, Nowak and Rosas (eds.), *Monitoring Human Rights*, at 17–19.

[48] P. Mahoney, 'New Challenges for the European Court of Human Rights Resulting from the Expanding Case Load and Membership', *Penn State International Law Review* **21** (2002), 101–114 at 110–111.

Table 1. *Violations by Article as Found by the European Court of Human Rights: 1999–2005* [49]

Year	2	3	4	5	6*	6**	7	8	9	10	11	12	13	14	P1–1	P1–2	P1–3	P7–4	Other
1999	5	2	0	12	37	62	1	4	2	18	2	0	5	4	6	0	1	0	1
2000	20	16	0	4	68	303	0	18	1	10	0	0	18	3	14	0	1	0	5
2001	14	17	0	36	72	444	1	20	2	8	3	0	19	3	143	1	0	1	6
2002	14	7	0	43	149	410	1	28	1	13	3	2	22	3	96	0	2	2	3
2003	4	35	0	56	234	210	2	48	2	14	2	0	29	8	137	0	0	0	8
2004	29	46	0	101	192	253	3	32	1	30	3	0	54	10	97	0	5	0	12
2005	54	56	1	153	382	311	1	41	0	50	11	1	138	12	265	1	1	0	21
Total	140	179	1	405	1134	1993	9	191	9	143	24	3	285	43	758	2	10	3	56

[49] Figures compiled from annual 'Violations by Article and by Country' tables, 1999–2005, kindly supplied by the Registry of the European Court of Human Rights. '2–14' refers to Articles 2–14 of the Convention, '6*' to violations of the right to fair trial under Article 6, '6**' to length of procedure cases (also violations of Article 6), 'P1–1' to Article 1 of Protocol No. 1 (the right to peaceful enjoyment of possessions), 'P1–2' to Article 2 of Protocol No. 1 (the right to education), 'P1–3' to Article 3 of Protocol No. 1 (the right to free elections), 'P7–4' to Article 4 of Protocol No. 7 (the right not to be tried or punished twice for the same offence), and 'other' to other Convention provisions.

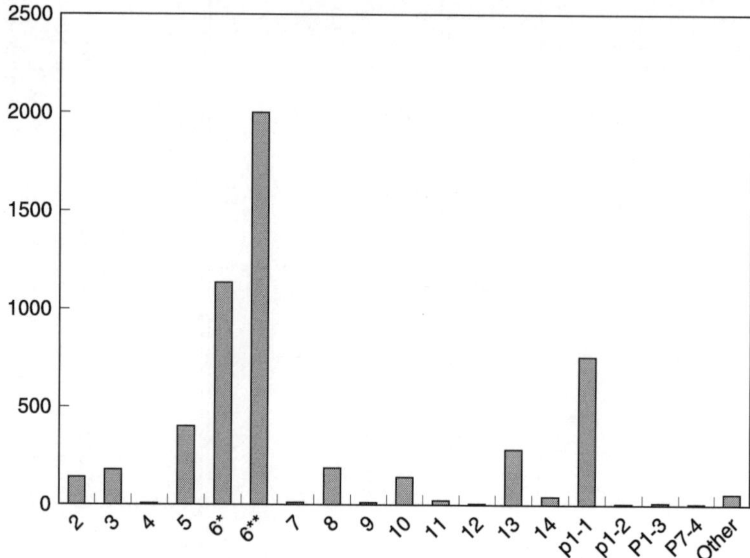

Figure 3. Violations by Article as Found by the European Court of Human Rights:1999–2005.

probably the most telling. Nevertheless, whichever way the issue is approached, the violation figures are dominated by violations which stem from breaches of Article 6, particularly those occasioned by excessive length of legal proceedings.

Table 2 shows 'National Violation Rates as Found by the European Court of Human Rights:1999–2005', with countries ranked in order of highest number of judgments finding at least one violation. This is a useful time frame, since it runs from the first full year of the full-time Court to the last for which figures were available at the time this study was completed, and includes all 46 parties to the Convention, although not all of these were members for the entire period. However, it is not perfect, for the simple reason that seven years is not long enough for stable patterns to have emerged, particularly for states which joined most recently. Although the table shows western and former communist bloc countries distributed fairly evenly at all violation levels, the implications of this information are discussed below in separate sections for each of these two zones.

Table 2. *National Violation Rates as Found by the European Court of Human Rights:1999–2005* [50]

	1999	2000	2001	2002	2003	2004	2005	Total	Average
Italy	44	231	359	325	106	36	67	1168	166.86
Turkey	18	23	169	54	76	154	270	764	109.14
France	16	49	32	61	76	59	51	344	49.14
Poland	1	12	17	20	43	74	44	211	30.14
Greece	5	15	14	16	23	32	100	205	29.29
Ukraine	0	0	0	1	6	13	119	139	19.86
United Kingdom	12	16	19	30	20	19	15	131	18.71
Russia	0	0	0	2	5	13	81	101	14.43
Austria	3	13	14	14	16	13	18	91	13.00
Romania	2	3	0	26	24	12	21	88	12.57
Portugal	8	11	10	14	16	5	6	70	10.00
Czech Republic	0	4	1	4	5	27	28	69	9.86
Slovak Republic	1	3	5	4	17	11	28	69	9.86
Bulgaria	1	3	2	2	10	25	23	66	9.43
Hungary	0	1	1	1	13	20	17	53	7.57
Croatia	0	0	4	6	6	11	24	51	7.29
Germany	0	2	13	6	10	6	10	47	6.71
Belgium	1	1	2	12	7	11	12	46	6.57
Finland	0	5	4	5	3	8	10	35	5.00
Netherlands	0	3	2	6	6	6	7	30	4.29
Moldova	0	0	1	0	0	10	13	24	3.43
Spain	1	3	1	1	8	5	0	19	2.71
Switzerland	0	5	6	2	0	0	5	18	2.57
Lithuania	0	4	2	4	3	1	3	17	2.43
Cyprus	1	3	1	5	1	2	1	14	2.00
Sweden	0	0	0	4	2	0	4	10	1.43
Luxembourg	0	1	2	0	4	1	1	9	1.29
Estonia	0	0	0	1	2	1	4	8	1.14
San Marino	1	2	0	0	3	2	0	8	1.14
Ireland	0	2	0	1	1	2	1	7	1.00
Latvia	0	0	0	2	1	3	1	7	1.00
Norway	2	1	0	0	4	0	0	7	1.00

(*continued*)

[50] Figures compiled from 'Judgments finding at least one violation' from annual 'Violations by Article and by Country' tables, 1999–2005, kindly supplied by the Registry of the European Court of Human Rights. No violations were recorded against Armenia, Azerbaijan, Bosnia and Herzegovina, Monaco or Serbia and Montenegro where the Convention entered into force only recently.

Table 2. (*cont.*)

	1999	2000	2001	2002	2003	2004	2005	Total	Average
Malta	2	1	0	0	1	1	1	6	0.86
Georgia		0	0	0	0	1	3	4	0.57
Iceland		0	0	0	2	2	0	4	0.57
The FYRO Macedonia		0	0	0	0	0	4	4	0.57
Denmark		1	0	1	1	0	0	3	0.43
Liechtenstein	1	0	0	0	0	1	1	3	0.43
Slovenia		2	0	0	0	0	1	3	0.43
Albania		0	0	0	0	1	0	1	0.14
Andorra		0	0	0	0	1	0	1	0.14

EXPLAINING PATTERNS OF CONVENTION VIOLATION IN WESTERN EUROPE

Before considering the information in Table 2 as it applies to western European states, figures are presented in Table 3 which show the annual average number of Convention violations between 1960 and 2000 as found by the Court and the Committee of Ministers.

Using the data from Tables 2 and 3, Table 4 ranks western European states in order of the highest number of violations for both the 1960–2000 and 1999–2005 periods.

Several conclusions can be drawn from this information. First, in both Tables 4(a) and 4(b), states fall into one of three, or four broad Convention-violation categories. However, these are not hermetically sealed and the boundaries could just as plausibly be drawn at slightly different points. For the 1960–2000 period the states with the highest violation rates (annual average) were Italy (84.94) and France (18.55). Those in the medium category were Turkey (5.36), Portugal (4.29), Greece (4.02), the United Kingdom (3.91), and Austria (3.52), while those in the low category were the Netherlands (1.48), Switzerland (1.30), Finland (1.03), Belgium (0.95), Sweden (0.92), Spain (0.87), Germany (0.70), Cyprus (0.58), Malta (0.29), San Marino (0.25), Ireland (0.22), Norway (0.16), Denmark (0.11), Liechtenstein (0.05), Luxembourg (0.05), Iceland (0.04), and Andorra (0). States in Table 4(b) fall into four broad categories with Italy (166.86), Turkey (109.14), and France (49.14) in the 'high violation' group.

Table 3. *Official Violation Rates for Western European States:1960–2000*[51]

Country	Date of IA	No. of violations	No. of years of IA	Annual average no. of violations
Andorra	22.1.96	0	5.00	0
Austria	3.9.58	149	42.33	3.52
Belgium	5.7.55	43	45.50	0.95
Cyprus	1.1.89	7	12.00	0.58
Denmark	5.7.55	5	45.50	0.11
Finland	10.5.90	11	10.67	1.03
France	2.10.81	357	19.25	18.55
Germany	5.7.55	32	45.50	0.70
Greece	10.11.85	61	15.17	4.02
Iceland	5.7.55	2	45.50	0.04
Ireland	5.7.55	10	45.50	0.22
Italy	1.8.73	2,329	27.42	84.94
Liechtenstein	8.9.82	1	18.33	0.05
Luxembourg	28.4.58	2	42.75	0.05
Malta	1.5.87	4	13.67	0.29
Netherlands	28.6.60	60	40.58	1.48
Norway	10.12.55	7	45.08	0.16
Portugal	9.11.78	95	22.17	4.29
San Marino	22.3.89	3	11.83	0.25
Spain	1.7.81	17	19.50	0.87
Sweden	5.7.55	42	45.50	0.92
Switzerland	28.11.74	34	26.17	1.30
Turkey	28.1.87	75	14.00	5.36
UK	14.1.66	137	35.00	3.91

[51] Information derived from Blackburn and Polakiewicz (eds.), *Fundamental Rights*, Table 1.4, pp. 26–27. Date of IA = 'Date of acceptance of the right of individual application'. Although Denmark, Iceland, Ireland, and Sweden accepted the right of individual petition at earlier dates than the ones indicated here, the European Commission of Human Rights was not able to accept individual petitions from any state until at least six states had done so, which did not happen until 5 July 1955. 'No. of violations', is an amalgamation of violations found by the Court (to 31.12.00) and those found by the Committee of Ministers (to 31.12.99). No adjustment needs to be made for population sizes as there appears to be no correlation between these variables. Germany, for example, with a population of over 82,000,000 has an annual violation rate of 0.72, while Greece, with a population an eighth this size has an annual

Greece (29.29), the UK (18.71), Austria (13.00) and Portugal (10.00) are in the 'upper medium' category, while Germany (6.71), Belgium (6.57), Finland (5.00), and the Netherlands (4.29) are in the 'lower medium' band. In the 'low violation' category are Spain (2.71), Switzerland (2.57), Cyprus (2.00), Sweden (1.43), Luxembourg (1.29), San Marino (1.14), Ireland (1.00), Norway (1.00), Malta (0.86), Iceland (0.57), Denmark (0.43), Liechtenstein (0.43), and Andorra (0.14).

Second, the annual average violation rate for 1999–2005 is higher for all states than their 1960–2000 score, even for those countries whose position in the later table is lower than the one they held in the earlier one. For example, although Portugal moved down from fourth place in the 1960–2000 table to seventh in 1999–2005, its annual average rate of violation nevertheless increased from 4.29 to 10.00. It would be premature, however, to conclude from this that respect for Convention rights is deteriorating throughout western Europe. It may well be that long-standing structural or systemic compliance problems are simply becoming more visible. Third, although the position of some states changes between the two tables, the rankings are nevertheless remarkably similar with the same states – Italy, Turkey, and France – showing the highest violation rates in both. Fourth, the rate of increase in national violation rates varies substantially, with the most significant being Turkey's massive twenty-fold increase from 1960–2000 to 1999–2005.

The fact that Italy comes top of Tables 4(a) and (b) is no surprise. Its problems with breaches of the right to fair trial under Article 6, stemming from unreasonable delays in the judicial process, are well known and are discussed further below. Nor is there any great surprise in finding Turkey, long regarded as having the worst human rights record in western Europe, in third and second places respectively. This is also considered more fully below. But it is much less clear why France should come so close to the top of both violation tables, given its long

average violation rate nearly six times as large. In the absence of any evidence to the contrary, it can also be assumed that applications have not been systematically selected in any way which would result in the over or under-representation of any particular state. On a slightly different, but related matter, Bruinsma and de Blois found, on the basis of a quantitative study of voting patterns from 1991–95, that although national background had no impact on the Court's collective judgments, there were some 'striking examples of national bias in separate opinions', F. J. Bruinsma and M. de Blois, 'Rules of Law from Westport to Wladiwostok. Separate Opinions in the European Court of Human Rights', *Netherlands Quarterly of Human Rights* **15** (1997), 175–186 at 175.

Table 4. *Western European States Ranked by Annual Average Violation Rates: 1960–2000 and 1999–2005*

(a) 1960–2000	(b) 1999–2005
1. Italy (84.94)	1. Italy (166.86)
2. France (18.55)	2. Turkey (109.14)
3. Turkey (5.36)	3. France (49.14)
4. Portugal (4.29)	4. Greece (29.29)
5. Greece (4.02)	5. UK (18.71)
6. UK (3.91)	6. Austria (13.00)
7. Austria (3.52)	7. Portugal (10.00)
8. Netherlands(1.48)	8. Germany (6.71)
9. Switzerland (1.30)	9. Belgium (6.57)
10. Finland (1.03)	10. Finland (5.00)
11. Belgium (0.95)	11. Netherlands (4.29)
12. Sweden (0.92)	12. Spain (2.71)
13. Spain (0.87)	13. Switzerland (2.57)
14. Germany (0.70)	14. Cyprus (2.00)
15. Cyprus (0.58)	15. Sweden (1.43)
16. Malta (0.29)	16. Luxembourg (1.29)
17. San Marino (0.25)	17. San Mario (1.14)
18. Ireland (0.22)	18= Ireland (1.00)
19. Norway (0.16)	18= Norway (1.00)
20. Denmark (0.11)	20. Malta (0.86)
21= Liechtenstein (0.05)	21. Iceland (0.57)
21= Luxembourg (0.05)	22= Denmark (0.43)
23. Iceland (0.04)	22= Liechtenstein (0.43)
24. Andorra (0)	24. Andorra (0.14)

historical record of championing the human rights cause. The lack of effective domestication of the Convention by judicial institutions, also considered more fully below, seems most to blame. There are few surprises about the low-violation states in both Tables 4(a) and (b). Andorra, Cyprus, Liechtenstein, Luxembourg, Iceland, Malta, and San Marino belong in a special category because the scope for Convention violation is reduced by the close connection between rulers and ruled facilitated by their small populations. Each of these states has less than a million inhabitants, with the populations of Andorra, Liechtenstein, and San Marino not even reaching 100,000. However, this is not an entirely consistent trend as tiny San Marino, with a population of only 26,000, has a higher violation rate on both tables (0.25 in Table 4(a) and 1.14 in Table 4(b)) than, for example, Denmark (0.11 in Table 4(a) and 0.43 in Table 4(b)) whose population, at over five million, is over two hundred times as large. In view of the fact that relevant information about these states is sparse – only Cyprus, Iceland, Luxembourg and Malta are covered, for example, in the collection of essays edited by Blackburn and Polakiewicz – and in order to simplify the analysis they will not be considered further in what follows. The Scandinavian countries, the low countries, and Switzerland, also have long-standing reputations as stable, rights-sensitive, democracies. However, the difference in violation rates between Portugal and Spain (respectively fourth and thirteenth in Table 4(a) and seventh and twelfth in Table 4(b)) is more difficult to explain given their historical, cultural, and geo-political similarities, not least their parallel transitions from dictatorship to democracy in the 1970s.

Detailed systematic data of the kind necessary to justify sound conclusions about the factors most likely to contribute to differential official national violation rates are not yet available. However, there is sufficient published literature to permit the framing of some tentative hypotheses. The Blackburn and Polakiewicz collection[52] provides a useful source of information, not least because most of the contributors to the thirty-two substantive chapters discuss the impact of the Convention on a particular state according to a common template featuring the status of the Convention both in national law and in parliamentary proceedings, leading human rights cases decided by national courts, cases brought before the Strasbourg institutions, remedial action taken by governments in response to findings of violation, plus assessments of achievements and future prospects.[53]

However, for several reasons this mammoth study is not a wholly satisfactory source for present purposes. First, while many of the contributions are very clear, sharply focused, and thoughtful, others are, unfortunately, opaque and lacking in depth. Some are even, regrettably, self-contradictory. Second, while most contributors provide some information about the responsiveness of national judicial and legislative

[52] Blackburn and Polakiewicz (eds.), *Fundamental Rights.*
[53] *Ibid.*

processes to official findings of violation, this varies greatly in insight and sophistication. Some discussions of this issue are so brief that they offer virtually no information at all while others confine their attention to the narrow question of the execution of judgments. The net effect is a lack of systematic data on the critical question of how *effective* these processes are in ensuring low rates of Convention violation. Third, although there is some speculation about which national factors affect 'the manner and degree of the Convention's influence' in member states, there is no attempt to identify systematically which are most strongly linked with high and low violation rates.[54] The following factors are examined here: the Convention's formal incorporation, the routine 'Convention-proofing' of draft legislation, the availability of effective domestic judicial remedies (and in particular the 'French paradox'), the problem of 'authoritarian democracy' in Turkey, and structural impediments to full compliance presented by the Italian legal system.

Formal Incorporation

The Convention formally operates in any national legal system according to whether the member state in question subscribes to the 'monist' or 'dualist' tradition.[55] Under the former, rules of international law become part of the domestic legal order without any further legal formality, whereas under the 'dualist' tradition this does not happen until national legislation to this effect has been enacted. Although in both cases some national legislation is, in fact, required, in monist states the act of ratification is a mere procedural formality confirming that the treaty has been duly entered into by the state. In dualist states, on the other hand, a more significant legislative exercise is needed, and one which may include debate about the merits of incorporation and about the possibility of choosing which provisions of a given treaty should be incorporated and which not. The received wisdom among jurists and lawyers is that formal incorporation of the Convention in national law is essential to improve Convention compliance. For example, while accepting that the Court has consistently taken the view that, as long as

[54] *Ibid.*, p. x.

[55] J. Polakiewicz, 'The Status of the Convention in National Law', in Blackburn and Polakiewicz (eds.), *Fundamental Rights*, pp. 31–53.

Convention rights are effectively protected in both domestic law and practice, states have a wide discretion concerning the manner in which this result is achieved,[56] Polakiewicz argues that '(i)ncorporation is the most faithful way of implementing the Convention into domestic law' and that 'an obligation to incorporate the Convention's substantive provisions can be derived from the special character of the Convention, and in particular from Articles 1, 41 and 46'.[57] Blackburn also claims that 'the strong prevailing opinion at Strasbourg has always been that the most effective way of both enforcing the Convention's principles and minimizing the work of the Court of Human Rights is through incorporation'.[58]

Although Boyle and Thompson found that formal incorporation of the Convention tends to lower the application rate,[59] incorporation is not significantly associated with low national violation rates, nor the absence of incorporation with high violation rates. Although some have done so only recently, all western European states have now incorporated the Convention in their domestic law, generally by granting it superiority over conflicting domestic legislation – as in Belgium, Denmark, Finland, France, Germany, Greece, Italy, Norway, Portugal, Spain, Sweden, Switzerland, Turkey, and the UK – although without, necessarily, a judicial power of annulment.[60] Only in Austria does the Convention rank as a domestic bill of rights, and only in the

[56] *Ibid.*, pp. 32–33.

[57] *Ibid.*, pp. 35–36. This appears to be a retreat from an earlier view that the Court has consistently held that the Convention does not create any obligation regarding the precise manner for ensuring effective implementation of Convention rights, J. Polakiewicz, 'The Application of the European Convention on Human Rights in Domestic Law', *Human Rights Law Journal* **17** (1996), 405–411 at 405.

[58] R. Blackburn, 'The Institutions and Processes of the Convention' in Blackburn and Polakiewicz (eds.), *Fundamental Rights*, pp. 3–29 at 27.

[59] Boyle, H. and Thompson, M., 'National Politics and Resort to the European Commission on Human Rights', *Law & Society Review* **35** (2001), 321–344.

[60] Incorporated by judicial decision in Belgium in 1971, Marcus-Helmons and Marcus-Helmons, 'Belgium', 168–169. Incorporated as ordinary legislation in Denmark in 1992, Germer, 'Denmark', 260–261. Incorporated as ordinary legislation in Finland in 1990, Rosas, 'Finland', 294–295. Technically incorporated in French domestic law when the Convention was ratified in May 1974, a position the French courts have, however, been reluctant to accept, Dupré, 'France', 315–319. Incorporated with the status of federal law in Germany, but subordinate to the Basic Law, by Art. 59(2) of the Basic Law of 1949, A. Zimmermann, 'Germany' in Blackburn and Polakiewicz, *Fundamental Rights* pp. 335–354 at 337–343. Incorporated by Art. 28(1) of the Greek Constitution of 1975, superior to domestic statute but subordinate to the Constitution

Netherlands does it take precedence over the constitution itself.[61] However, leaving the micro-states aside, nearly half the remaining states in the 1960–2000 low-violation category – Denmark, Norway, Ireland, and Sweden – permitted individual applications for forty or more years before they incorporated the Convention into their domestic law, while the Convention was formally incorporated into the national law of the two states with the highest annual average violation rates – Italy and France – throughout the entire period they were exposed to individual applications. And in France it has had a formal status higher than that of domestic statute. Nor is there any evidence to support another common assumption – that indigenous bills of rights, binding on domestic courts, are likely to promote low Convention violation rates. Such bills of rights have been available throughout the relevant period of individual application in the high violation states of France and Italy, and also in low violation ones such as Ireland, Spain, and Germany.

Routine Screening of Draft Legislation

Contrary to what might be supposed, the available evidence suggests that routine Convention-proofing of draft legislation is not strongly linked to low annual average violation rates either. As Polakiewicz

itself, Ioannou, 'Greece', 357–361. Incorporated in Italy with the same status as ordinary law upon ratification in October 1955, Meriggiola, 'Italy', 475 and 479. In spite of not being formally incorporated into domestic law in Norway until 1999, the Convention had a significant profile before, E. Møse, 'Norway', in Blackburn and Polakiewicz (eds.), *Fundamental Rights*, pp. 625–655 at 628. Formally incorporated by the Portuguese Constitution of 1976 between ordinary law and the Constitution upon ratification in November 1978, Madureira, 'Portugal', 682. According to Art. 94(1)(e) of the Spanish Constitution of 1978 the Convention is part of 'national regulations' subordinate to the Constitution but superior to other laws, G. Escobar Roca, 'Spain', in Blackburn and Polakiewicz (eds.), *Fundamental Rights*, pp. 809–831 at 812–813. Incorporated as ordinary law in Sweden with effect from 1995, I. Cameron, 'Sweden' in Blackburn and Polakiewicz (eds.), *Fundamental Rights*, pp. 833–853 at 838. The precise status of the Convention in the Swiss national legal system remains controversial although it appears to have had superiority 'over the whole Swiss legal system' since ratification in November 1974, Borghi, 'Switzerland', 858. Polakiewicz, 'Status of Convention', 36–46. In Turkey, Law No. 5170 of 22 May 2004 gives the Convention clear precedence over conflicting domestic law, E. Örücü, 'Seven Packages towards Harmonization with the European Union', *European Public Law* **10** (2004), 603–621 at 621. The Convention was incorporated into the domestic law of the UK with effect from October 2000 by the Human Rights Act 1998, S. Greer, 'A Guide to the Human Rights Act 1998', *European Law Review* **24** (1999), 3–21.

61 Tretter, 'Austria', 105; Zwaak, 'Netherlands', 597.

points out, in most states 'the Convention is only referred to sporadically during parliamentary debates, mainly in order to confirm that proposed legislation is in full harmony with its requirements'.[62] While many low-violation states from the 1960–2000 period – Belgium, Denmark, Finland, Ireland, the Netherlands, and Switzerland[63] – routinely Convention-proof draft legislation, others – such as Germany, Spain, Sweden, and Norway[64] – do not, or have begun to do so only recently. While the Convention is not frequently referred to in debates in the Greek legislature, draft legislation is routinely screened by the Scientific Service of Parliament,[65] and although affected by the Convention, it cannot be said that Austrian legislation has been 'profoundly influenced' by it.[66] In Portugal there is no apparent routine screening of draft legislation while this has only happened systematically in the UK since 1999.[67]

Regrettably, the chapter on Italy in the Blackburn and Polakiewicz collection contains no information whatever about this matter. While the French Conseil Constitutionnel 'steadily refuses to check the constitutionality of a bill against the ECHR' it seems, however, 'to integrate, indirectly and implicitly, some elements of the Convention and its case law'.[68] The Convention is not considered systematically by French MPs, nor mentioned in the preamble to legislation (*exposé des motifs*), although ministers occasionally refer to it. It is, therefore, 'difficult to appreciate the extent of its influence on French legislation'.[69]

[62] Polakiewicz, 'Status of Convention', 50. Ironically, Convention-oriented legislative review is strongest in the newly acceded former communist states, not least because it was a vital component of the accession requirements, *ibid.*

[63] Marcus-Helmons and Marcus-Helmons, 'Belgium', 170; Germer, 'Denmark', 261; Rosas, 'Finland', 297–298; O'Connell, 'Ireland', 436; Zwaak, 'The Netherlands', 600; Borghi, 'Switzerland', 859 and 874.

[64] Zimmerman, 'Germany', 344, reports that, in Germany, parliamentary references to the ECHR are most likely in criminal cases. Although the Convention has influenced the Spanish constitution it has not had much direct influence on the routine legislative process, Escobar Roca, 'Spain', 814. Although there is no routine formal legislative scrutiny, the Swedish legislative process is very open to input from interest groups, Cameron, 'Sweden', 841. In Norway routine legislative screening is comparatively recent, Møse, 'Norway', 639 and 641.

[65] Iaonnou, 'Greece', 361.

[66] Tretter, 'Austria', 107, quoting Polakiewicz and Jacob-Foltzer, 'The European Human Rights Convention in Domestic Law', *Human Rights Law Journal* **12** (1991), 65 at 67.

[67] Madureira, 'Portugal', 684; R. Blackburn, 'The United Kingdom' in Blackburn and Polakiewicz (eds.), *Fundamental Rights*, pp. 935–1008 at 991–998.

[68] Dupré, 'France', 315. [69] *Ibid.*, 319.

Although influential in the Turkish civilian constitutions, particularly of 1982, and in the constitutional amendment of 1995[70] references to the Convention in Turkish parliamentary proceedings have been increasing, particularly since the right of individual petition was permitted in 1987. However, no formal arrangements for the routine Convention-proofing of legislation appear to have been provided.[71] Őzdek and Karacaoğlu claim that the profile of human rights issues in parliamentary debates derives more from a concern to improve Turkey's international image than an attempt to raise standards of effective protection.[72]

Effective Domestic Judicial Remedies: the 'French Paradox'

Prima facie, two critical elements in the successful integration of Convention standards into national legal processes are the provision of institutional mechanisms by which individual applicants can effectively litigate alleged violations before national courts and the development of an appropriate rights jurisprudence. Article 13 of the Convention requires that those whose Convention rights and freedoms are violated 'shall have an effective remedy before a national authority'. However, there are several problems with this provision. First, '(u)ntil comparatively recently Article 13 occupied something of a twilight zone in the case law of the Convention organs'.[73] Second, there is no obligation to provide a *judicial* remedy. Third, the Strasbourg institutions have, arguably, permitted states too much discretion in determining how this obligation should be formally discharged and have not been too exacting over the substantive issue of what constitutes 'effectiveness'. Finally, there are grounds for believing that judicial remedies which permit Convention standards to be effectively litigated in national legal processes provide the best means by which such standards can be effectively integrated into national public decision-making.

Broadly speaking the mode of constitutional rights litigation in western Europe depends on whether the state in question conforms to

[70] Y. Őzdek and E. Karacaoğlu, 'Turkey', in Blackburn and Polakiewicz (eds.), *Fundamental Rights*, pp. 879–914 at 889 and 906–907.

[71] *Ibid.*, pp. 884–890. [72] *Ibid.*, pp. 885, 890

[73] C. Ovey and R. C. A. White, *Jacobs and White, The European Convention on Human Rights* (Oxford: Oxford University Press, 3rd edn., 2002), p. 386.

the US, to the Austrian, or to a mixed model of constitutional review.[74] Under the US model – which applies in Denmark, Ireland, Norway, and Sweden – constitutional issues can be raised, usually a posteriori, by any party, individual or otherwise, in any ordinary court, under regular legal procedures, subject to final review by the national supreme or constitutional court. Although not conforming to this model in all particulars, constitutional rights issues can also be addressed by ordinary courts in the Netherlands, Finland, and the UK. However, the available evidence suggests that very few cases before regular courts concern human rights.[75] Under the Austrian model – which also applies in Belgium, Germany, Iceland, Liechtenstein, Italy, Luxembourg, Malta, Monaco, Spain, and Turkey – constitutional matters can only be addressed by constitutional or supreme courts in special proceedings which may include a priori, in addition to a posteriori, review. However, these do not all permit a right of individual constitutional complaint. A mixed model, with both ordinary courts and specialized constitutional or supreme courts empowered to address constitutional issues, applies in Greece, Portugal, and Switzerland. There is no obvious correlation between type of constitutional review and low levels of Convention violation because, as Cameron states: 'The principle that national law be interpreted in accordance with treaty commitment can be either a real safeguard or a mere formality depending, first, on how much time and effort the courts devote to investigating what the Convention really requires in a given case, and second, the status such

[74] See 'Constitutional Courts', http://www.concourts.net/tab/intonet.htlm. For a comparative study of the arrangements for constitutional complaint in Europe see A. Alen and M. Melchior in collaboration with B. Renauld, F. Meersschaut and C. Courtoy, 'The Relations Between the Constitutional Courts and the Other National Courts, Including the Interference in this Area of the Action of the European Courts – XIIth Conference of the European Constitutional Courts, Brussels, 14–16 May 2002: General Report', *Human Rights Law Journal* **23** (2002), 304–330 at 317–321. See also P. Pasquino, 'Constitutional Adjudication and Democracy. Comparative Perspectives: USA, France, Italy', *Ratio Juris* **11** (1998), 38–50.

[75] For example, between 1980 and 1986, less than 2 per cent of the decisions of the Dutch Supreme Court dealt with human rights treaties, but more than 70 per cent of these concerned the Convention. The court upheld the applicant's complaint about a human rights violation in less than 7 per cent of cases, 95 per cent of which related to the Convention, M. Nowak and H. von Hoebel, 'A Statistical Analysis of Dutch Human Rights Case Law' in Jabine and Claude (eds.), *Human Rights and Statistics*, pp. 313–327 at 324. However, while the Convention is virtually invisible in the routine legal process of the UK, its profile is much greater in the higher courts and is currently referred to in about 30 per cent of decisions of the Judicial Committee of the House of

a principle is given by the courts compared to other principles of interpretation.'[76]

The low-violation states in the 1960–2000 period exhibit a strong judicial constitutional rights tradition responsive to Convention standards. For example, although taking the Convention seriously with a 'grudging manner and reserve', the Belgian courts have used it to enrich the long-standing national constitutional rights tradition.[77] While the Danish courts have only begun to take the Convention seriously recently, similar rights are available under the Constitution of 1953.[78] The same seems to be largely true of Ireland, the Netherlands, and Sweden.[79] Nowak and von Hoebel argue that in spite of the fact that the Dutch constitution of 1983 contained a comprehensive modern Bill of Rights, as the 1980s progressed, 'it was more and more the International Bill of Rights adopted by the United Nations and the Council of Europe which determined the human rights position of the Dutch people'.[80] Although, in Finland, the direct application of the Convention has not become 'standard procedure', references to it are 'fairly common' in national court decisions.[81] In Germany, where most Convention rights are also enshrined in the Basic Law, Convention provisions are binding on national courts except the Federal Constitutional Court. However, although the German courts were at first reluctant to take account of the Convention, the number of court decisions referring to it greatly increased in the 1980s, particularly in decisions of the Federal Constitutional Court.[82] The Norwegian courts have taken the Convention seriously since before its formal incorporation, with references to it in Supreme Court decisions growing

Lords, the highest court in the land. The website of the Human Rights Act Research Project, based at the University of London and Doughty Street Chambers http:/ www.doughtystreet.co.uk/ records a total of 428 cases featuring the Human Rights Act in the 19 months between 2 October 2000 and 30 April 2002, an average of 270 per year, derived from the LAWTEL Human Rights and Butterworths Human Rights Direct databases. Butterworths Lexis-Nexis database http://www.butterworths.com reports an annual average of around 100 House of Lords cases a year about 30 of which cite the Act.

76 Cameron, 'Sweden', 844.

77 Marcus-Helmons and Marcus-Helmons, 'Belgium', 170.

78 Germer, 'Denmark', 275.

79 O'Connell, 'Ireland', 438–443, 469; Zwaak, 'The Netherlands', 596, 622–623; Cameron, 'Sweden', 835, 843, 844.

80 Nowak and von Hoebel, 'Statistical Analysis', 313.

81 Rosas, 'Finland', 300, 301, 303.

82 Zimmermann, 'Germany', 342–343, 346, 354.

from only one case in the 1970s, to an annual average of twenty to thirty in the 1990s, between 13 and 19 per cent of its total annual decision-rate.[83] All Swiss courts are bound to comply with the Convention, a demand they have met 'rigorously', at least since 1983.[84] The influence of the Convention and the Strasbourg case law on the Spanish courts 'has been particularly strong' with the Constitutional Court having referred to the Convention, or to the Strasbourg jurisprudence, in about 200 cases.[85]

As far as states in the 1960–2000 medium violation category are concerned, Őzdek and Karacaoğlu report that, while until the 1990s, Turkish courts referred to the Convention 'in only a few decisions', it is increasingly being taken into account, particularly by the Constitutional Court, although ironically in some cases in order to justify restrictions upon rights, for example, to dissolve political parties for advocating a federal solution to the Kurdish question, which has been condemned by the European Court of Human Rights.[86] According to Hicks: 'Many prosecutors and judges still believe, and are willing to state as much to representatives of international human rights organizations, that their first priority is to support the security forces in maintaining national security. If the security forces break Turkish law and violate international instruments in pursuit of this goal, then they are willing to overlook it and even to condone it.'[87] The Convention was fully incorporated in Austrian law in 1958, and, according to Tretter, since then the Austrian Constitutional Court has 'developed a rich jurisdiction' regarding Convention rights and freedoms. However, it has not been sufficiently proactive in 'screening the national legal order according to the requirements of the Convention', and has insisted that no Convention right can have greater scope than a similar national fundamental right. Tretter also argues that the Convention is still 'inadequately established' in the criminal justice system.[88] In Portugal while references to the Convention by the Portuguese Constitutional Court are 'not rare' there is a lack of awareness of Strasbourg case law on the part of lower courts.[89] In Greece, although the Convention is rarely

[83] Møse, 'Norway', 628, 633 and 642. In 1998 the Supreme Court dealt with 94 civil appeals and 61 criminal appeals http://odin.dep.no/jd/norsk/dok/andre_dok/utredninger/012005-020026/hov015-bn.html.

[84] Borghi, 'Switzerland', 864.

[85] Escobar Roca, 'Spain', 815.

[86] Őzdek and Karacaoğlu, 'Turkey', 890–895, 910. See following section.

[87] N. Hicks, 'Legislative Reform in Turkey and European Human Rights Mechanisms', *Human Rights Review* **3** (2001), 78–85 at 83.

[88] Tretter, 'Austria', 106, 163, 164.

[89] Madureira, 'Portugal', 685–6.

applied by the domestic courts to correct defects in domestic law, it is often invoked to show that it does not apply. Between 1974 and 1994 Greek judges were reluctant to accept that any international instrument could grant wider rights protection than the Greek constitution, the legal reasoning in such cases was usually very poor, and the Convention had little impact on everyday legal practice.[90] Although the UK has long prided itself on a strong judicial rights tradition, the principle of parliamentary sovereignty excluded the prospect of any rights-based challenges to legislation in the domestic legal system until the Human Rights Act 1998 came into effect in October 2000.[91] As argued below, Italy's high annual average violation rate is attributable more to systemic problems with its legal system than to judicial attitudes towards the Convention or towards constitutional rights.

However, the position in France is unique. Since French is one of the two official languages of the Council of Europe, French courts suffer from none of the translation difficulties cited by some commentators as the main reason why domestic courts in other countries have not been able to refer effectively to Convention case law.[92] The 'French paradox' is best explained by the lack of an individual right of constitutional complaint, together with an historic reluctance – albeit currently undergoing rapid change – on the part of ordinary French courts to apply Convention standards as rigorously or as consistently as they might.[93] Since 1958 constitutional review has been accepted in France only under very limited conditions. Because it can only be initiated by designated political authorities in respect of certain types of legislation prior to promulgation, the constitutionality of

90 Ioannou, 'Greece', 364–367, 380–381.

91 Blackburn, 'UK', 946–947, 960–971.

92 See, e.g., Zimmerman, 'Germany', 354.

93 L. Heuschling, 'Comparative Law and the European Convention on Human Rights in French Human Rights Cases', *United Kingdom Comparative Law Series* **22** (2003), 23–47. In his report on the condition of human rights in France, the European Commissioner for Human Rights recommended, among other things: better provision for courts and prisons; compulsory legal advice for suspects in police custody; improvements in tackling domestic violence, xenophobia, anti-Semitism, racism, and misconduct by law enforcers; and better treatment for those with mental health problems, victims of human trafficking, minors, Travellers, Roma, and foreigners, A. Gil-Robles, *Report by Mr Alvaro Gil-Robles Commissioner for Human Rights on the Effective Respect for Human Rights in France Following his Visit from 5–21 September 2005*, CommDH(2006)2 (Strasbourg: Council of Europe, Office of the Commissioner for Human Rights, 15 February 2006), at para. 374.

some statutes can never be challenged. Individuals cannot apply to the Conseil constitutionnel and may not plead the unconstitutionality of a statute as applied to them in a trial. Only since 1971 has the Conseil constitutionnel even agreed to check the compliance of legislation with the Declaration of 1789 or the preamble to the 1946 constitution, and it refuses, officially, to use the ECHR as a guide to interpretation.[94]

Due to their historic commitment to legislative sovereignty, and in spite of the fact that Article 55 of the French constitution provides that ratified treaties have 'an authority superior to legislation', ordinary French courts have traditionally been reluctant to call into question the validity of legislation, much less refuse to apply it, on the grounds that it violates the constitution or fundamental human rights.[95] The Conseil constitutionnel has given confusing signals by holding, in 1975, that 'control of conventionality' (reviewing compliance of domestic legislation with international treaties) was beyond its jurisdiction because, unlike the constitution, treaties require reciprocity between signatory states. Yet it also encouraged ordinary courts to consider the compatibility of domestic law with the ECHR.[96] Nevertheless, 'it took judges, especially administrative judges, a long time to accept that a provision of the ECHR should prevail over a subsequent domestic statute', and, although the Cour de Cassation has regularly mentioned the Convention since 1975, it was not until 1990 that the Conseil d'État also came to this conclusion.[97] According to Dupré the approaches of the French courts to the ECHR have 'varied greatly', and the use of ECHR provisions in French judicial reasoning is 'very meagre', not least because the French tradition favours brief and schematic reports of judicial decisions. Although the Convention is often cited in judgments, this is frequently to sustain the unexplained conclusion that French law is Convention-compliant.[98] In other cases French judges integrate the substance of the Convention without mentioning it openly, often preferring instead to cite general principles of domestic law

[94] Heuschling, 'French Human Rights Cases', 28.

[95] A. West, Y. Desdevises, A. Fenet, D. Gaurier, M.-C. Heussaff and B. Lévy, *The French Legal System*, 2nd edn. (London/Edinburgh/Dublin: Butterworths, 1998) p. 159; Pasquino, 'Constitutional Adjudication', 46–47. Challenges may be made, in administrative courts in France, to administrative decisions which allegedly violate the European Convention on Human Rights, L. N. Brown and J. S. Bell, *French Administrative Law*, 5th edn. (Oxford: Clarendon Press, 1998), pp. 225–227.

[96] Brown and Bell, *French Administrative Law*, p. 316.

[97] *Ibid.*, pp. 317–318.

[98] Dupré, 'France', 315 and 321.

including the French Declaration of the Rights of Man and the Citizen of 1789. Concurring with this analysis, Heuschling also describes the attitude of the French courts towards the ECHR and the European Court of Human Rights as being disconcertingly varied and incoherent, and underpinned by incompatible strategies of 'openness' or 'containment' adopted for no obvious reason. Negative judicial attitudes towards the ECHR can be explained, he maintains, in terms of misunderstanding, ignorance, conservatism, national pride, and a distrust of foreign judges.[99]

Although there is evidence that these traditional judicial attitudes are changing in France, resistance can still be encountered.[100] For example, despite the fact that the European Court of Human Rights has unequivocally established that it is a violation of Article 3 to deport aliens to countries where they risk being tortured or inhumanly/degradingly treated or punished, the Conseil d'État 'still seems very cautious about following this trend'.[101] Similarly, after a long period of ignorance followed by a series of adverse judgments and decisions against France by the Strasbourg institutions in relation to the right of aliens to respect for family life in expulsion cases under Article 8, the Conseil d'État departed from its previous case law only to refer to the Convention in 'a very restrictive manner'.[102] In spite of the fact that the fair trial provisions of Article 6 of the Convention have often been used by litigants in France to challenge the lack of a public hearing in professional disciplinary procedures, for a long time the administrative courts 'openly denied' that the Convention had any relevance to such proceedings, although the Cour de Cassation held in 1984 that disciplinary proceedings against avocats should be heard publicly.[103] It was not until the mid-1990s that the attitude of the Conseil d'État towards Article 6 began to change following an adverse decision of the European Court of Human Rights in the Diennet case.[104] The European Court of Human Rights has also found the French institutions of Avocat general and commissaire du gouvernement to be only partially compliant with the fair trial provisions of Article 6 of the ECHR.[105]

99 Heuschling, 'French Human Rights Cases', 32–37.
100 Dupré, 'France', 313 and 332; Heuschling, 'French Human Rights Cases', 47.
101 Dupré, 'France', 323.
102 *Ibid.*, 322. 103 *Ibid.*, 324.
104 *Diennet* v. *France* (1996) 21 EHRR 554.
105 *Reinhardt and Slimane Kaïd* v. *France* (1998) 28 EHRR 59; *Kress* v. *France*, judgment of 7 June 2001; Heuschling, 'French Human Rights Cases', 37 and 47.

Authoritarian Democracy: the Turkish Problem

A critical, if largely self-evident, explanation for any state's low annual average Convention violation rate is the extent to which a culture of respect for rights is embraced by political elites and by officials in key executive institutions such as police forces and prison services. Sensitivity towards rights may either stem from a long historical tradition – as in the low countries, the Scandinavian democracies and Switzerland – or from a decisive break with an anti-democratic past, as in Germany and Spain. The more pervasive a rights-culture, the more likely Convention violation will be avoided in the first place. Where such a culture is not so deeply entrenched, the responsiveness of national authorities to having been found in breach of the Convention by the Strasbourg institutions becomes a key consideration.

There is very little systematic, comparative, information about how effectively the governments of different states respond to adverse decisions at Strasbourg. Although this is a sub-heading in the country studies assembled in the Blackburn and Polakiewicz collection, the quality of the information they contain is uneven.[106] Not surprisingly commentators tend to report good responses on the part of low-violation states, even, in some cases, to judgments against other states.[107] However, the position is much less clear with respect to states in the medium and high-violation categories. According to Tretter, in Austria, a minimalist approach aimed at the avoidance of repetitive applications is preferred to a more thorough re-evaluation of the offending element of the domestic legal order, with few re-trials of cases in which the right to fair trial has been breached.[108] The position in France and Italy is unclear, and in Turkey not many remedies have been provided in response to violations.[109]

[106] Blackburn and Polakiewicz (eds.), *Fundamental Rights.*

[107] See, e.g., Marcus-Helmons and Marcus-Helmons, 'Belgium', 185 and 187; Zimmerman, 'Germany', 353; O'Connell, 'Ireland', 466; Zwaak, 'The Netherlands', 623; Møse, 'Norway', 652, Cameron, 'Sweden', 849–852; Borghi, 'Switzerland', 874–77. Dupré claims that, although 'in some cases, French courts have tended to comply "spontaneously" with the European Convention by following its case law' this 'is not a quick and easy process and a specific ruling against France is usually needed', 'France', 331.

[108] Tretter, 'Austria', 161–163.

[109] Őzdek and Karacaoğlu, 'Turkey', 902.

Of all the 'western' European member states of the Council of Europe, Turkey has had the most serious systemic problems with a lack of respect for human rights on the part of executive institutions, a result of its uniquely authoritarian, centralist, and militaristic process of modernization and democratization. Following the dismemberment of the Ottoman Empire in the aftermath of the First World War, Turkey embarked on a bold, though tortuous, process of modernization and self-redefinition from oriental despotism to European constitutional democracy. At its inception in 1924 the Turkish constitutional vision was expressed in terms of the 'six arrows of Kemalism' – nationalism, secularism, republicanism, populism, statism, and reformism.[110] In the 1920s the Turkish constitution and legal codes were copied, in some cases almost verbatim, from European models and, in 1949, Turkey became one of the founding members of the Council of Europe, though the right of individual petition to the European Commission of Human Rights was not permitted until 1987, nor to the Court until 1990. The current constitution – which dates from 1982, and which was substantially amended in November 2001 as a result of negotiations to join the EU – declares Turkey to be a unitary 'democratic, secular, and social state governed by the rule of law', with a multi-party parliament, a president, a government, and an independent judicial system.[111] Subject to several significant exceptions, including decisions of the Supreme Military Council, legislation and administration are subject to judicial review.[112]

However, the attitude of the Turkish authorities to human rights was both appalling and impervious to significant improvement until the early twenty-first century. According to Gündüz, '(h)ardly any country in the world has been so criticized for its human rights record, nor is the future of any other country so dependent on the promotion of human

[110] M. Koçak and E. Örücü, 'Dissolution of Political Parties in the Name of Democracy: Cases from Turkey and the European Court of Human Rights', *European Public Law* **9** (2003), 399–423 at 407; C. Rumford, 'Resisting Globalization? Turkey-EU Relations and Human and Political Rights in the Context of Cosmopolitan Democratization', *International Sociology* **18** (2003), 279–394 at 381–383.

[111] Hakyemez and Akgun argue that the 1982 constitution is more restrictive of human rights and individual freedoms than previous Turkish constitutions, Y. S. Hakyemez and B. Akgun, 'Limitations on the Freedom of Political Parties in Turkey and the Jurisdiction of the European Court of Human Rights', *Mediterranean Politics* **7** (2002), 54–78 at 56 and 67.

[112] A. Gündüz, 'Human Rights and Turkey's Future in Europe', *Orbis-Philadelphia* **45** (2001), 15–30 at 21.

rights'.[113] In 2000 the ending of the bitter conflict over Kurdish autonomy which claimed over 30,000 lives – together with pressure to fulfil human rights targets derived from the Copenhagen Political Criteria for membership of the EU – initiated an unprecedented period of both constitutional and legislative change.[114] Four particular areas of reform were highlighted in the Political Criteria section of the Turkey 2000 Accession Partnership Document – improvements in freedom of thought and expression, progress towards abolition of the death penalty, cultural rights for all Turkish citizens, and reducing the influence of the military in politics by curbing the role of the military-dominated National Security Council.[115] While emphasizing that it is too early to assess how much impact the changes produced by the accession process will have in practice, and that much still remains to be done, most commentators welcome them as genuine improvements.[116]

Pervasive though it may be in the current debate about the accession of Turkey to the EU, it is, however, a misconception to attribute Turkey's long-standing human rights problem to the fact that it has an Islamic culture unreceptive to the secular human rights ideal. The problem stems instead from the attempt by the modernizing Kemalist political movement – which has dominated Turkish national life since the 1920s – to identify the state with an uncompromising conception of secularism and 'Turkishness', and from an authoritarian law

113 *Ibid.*, 15.

114 *Ibid.*, 16; E. Örücü, 'The Turkish Constitution Revamped?', *European Public Law* **8** (2002), 201–218; Örücü, 'Seven Packages'.

115 Hicks, 'Legislative Reform in Turkey', 83–84. Arikan argues that the EU's view of progress on meeting the political conditions for membership hinge more upon 'a general assessment of the basic quality of political life in the applicant countries, rather than on a detailed examination of their political structure', H. Arikan, 'A Lost Opportunity? A Critique of the EU's Human Rights Policy Towards Turkey', *Mediterranean Politics* **7** (2002), 19–50 at 22.

116 Amnesty International's Annual Report 2005, 'Turkey', claims that, although legal and other reforms have been introduced, implementation has been 'patchy' and broad legal restrictions on the exercise of fundamental rights remain. http://web.amnesty.org/report2005/tur-summary-eng. The European Commissioner for Human Rights concludes that, although 'Turkey is only at the start of its path of applying substantial and courageous reforms' constitutional and legislative changes in 2001 and 2002 are 'of major importance' and are to be 'welcomed and encouraged', although there are 'problems as to their full and complete application,' A. Gil-Robles, *Report by Mr Alvaro Gil-Robles, Commissioner for Human Rights on His Visit to Turkey, 11–12 June 2003*, CommDH(2003)15 (Strasbourg: Office of the Commissioner for Human Rights, Council of Europe, 19 December 2003) at paras. 242, 243 and 252; Örücü, 'Turkish Constitution Revamped?', 202; Örücü, 'Seven Packages', 619.

enforcement tradition. This has led to difficulties in three main areas, not all of which have yet been resolved by the EU harmonization process.[117]

First, in spite of the 2001 constitutional amendments and the Harmonization Laws, Turkey continues to have a uniquely strong constitutional commitment to a secular, unitary state, not wholly consistent with the European notion of political pluralism and the rights of minorities.[118] In *Şahin* v. *Turkey* the European Court of Human Rights rejected the applicant's complaint, that the ban on the Islamic headscarf in Turkish institutions of higher education violated Articles 8, 9, 10, and 14 of the Convention and Article 2 of Protocol No. 1, on the grounds that, given the unique characteristics of the principle of secularism in Turkey, it could be justified to protect the rights and freedoms of others and to preserve public order.[119] However, the Court has been less tolerant of restrictions on political activity. Article 14 of the Turkish constitution, as revised, states: 'None of the rights and freedoms embodied in the Constitution can be exercised in activities with the aim of violating the indivisible integrity of the state with its territory and nation or to eliminate the democratic and secular Republic based on human rights'.[120] Protecting the 'unity' or 'indivisible integrity' of the state 'with its territory and nation' also provide constitutional grounds for restricting freedom of expression.[121] Political parties can also be dissolved where, among other things, they have become 'a centre' for activities in 'conflict' with this objective, as well as where they threaten the 'principles of the democratic and secular republic'.[122] Limitations short of dissolution, for example withdrawing official financial

[117] Other human rights problems concern trade union rights, the property of religious organizations, and the plight of vulnerable groups such as refugees, asylum seekers, women and children. See, e.g. Gil-Robles, 'Visit to Turkey', paras. 94–107, 178–214.

[118] Örücü, 'Seven Packages', 604 and Gil-Robles, 'Visit to Turkey', paras. 11–93 and 235, trace how this constitutional commitment plays out in various substantive laws and policies.

[119] (2005) 41 EHRR 109.

[120] Örücü, 'Turkish Constitution Revamped?', 210.

[121] This, among other things – including the violation of the fundamental tenets (or character) of the Republic – provides a legal justification for the confiscation, by court order, of printed material, printing presses and printing material following sentence for offences of this kind, and for banning television programmes and private courses in languages other than Turkish, Örücü, 'Seven Packages,' 611 and 615.

[122] *Ibid.*, 610–613. For further details on the relevant substantive law see Gil-Robles, 'Visit to Turkey', paras. 80–93.

assistance, are also possible.[123] No association can lawfully be established which violates the 'fundamental tenets of the Republic', including its unitary state structure.[124] Since the founding of modern Turkey more than twenty 'Islamist' or 'separatist' parties have been outlawed, mostly by the Constitutional Court.[125] Cases brought by six of these have been heard by the European Court of Human Rights.[126] In all but the *Refah Partisi* case, the European Court of Human Rights decided that the ban violated the right to freedom of association under Article 11 of the Convention.

The verdict in the *Refah Partisi* case rested on the view of a majority of a Chamber of the European Court of Human Rights, unanimously endorsed by the Grand Chamber, that the decision by the Turkish Constitutional Court to ban Refah were, notwithstanding the narrow national margin of appreciation, proportionate to the pressing social need to protect democracy. This was justified, it was held, because the party proposed the introduction of a plurality of legal systems organized according to religious adherence (deemed contrary to the Convention principle of non-discrimination), it intended to establish a regime of Sharia law at variance with Convention principles, it had not taken adequate steps to distance itself from statements made by some of its members endorsing the use of violence to achieve its goals, and its electoral success created a real prospect that its programme would be implemented.[127] The judgments in both the *Şahin* and *Refah Partisi* cases could be criticized for having too readily endorsed Turkish fears about Islamic fundamentalism gaining a toe-hold in national public institutions. However, it would also be a serious mistake to underestimate the vulnerability of the Turkish republic, not only to militant

123 Örücü, 'Seven Packages', 613.

124 *Ibid.*, 612. For further information on the relevant substantive law see Gil-Robles, 'Visit to Turkey', paras. 48–93.

125 Gündüz, 'Human Rights', 23; Hakyemez and Akgun, 'Limitations on Freedom'.

126 *United Communist Party of Turkey* v. *Turkey* (1998) 26 EHRR 121; *Socialist Party of Turkey* v. *Turkey* (1999) 27 EHRR 51; *ÖZDEP* v. *Turkey* (2001) 27 EHRR 674; *Democratic Party* v. *Turkey*, judgment of 10 December 2002; *People's Labour Party* v. *Turkey*, judgment of 9 April 2002; *Refah Partisi (The Welfare Party)* v. *Turkey* (2002) 35 EHRR 3.

127 (2002) 35 EHRR 3 at paras 119, 123, 131–134. While the judgment does not directly link dissolution with a specific legitimate aim in Article 11(2), it appears to be based on 'the rights and freedoms of others' to live in a democratic society. In the general election of December 1995, Refah obtained 22 per cent of the vote, emerging as the largest political party in the Grand National Assembly. Its chairman, Necmettin Erbakan, became Prime Minister in a coalition government with the True Path Party.

Islam, but also to military intervention prompted by the perception that civil processes are not robust enough to protect it from precisely this threat.

This brings us to the second area of difficulty. The army has occupied a position in the modern Turkish state, unique by comparison with other western democracies. Not only did it play the pivotal role in founding the modern republic, it has also governed three times in the past forty years, the coup of 1980 enabling it to draft the 1982 constitution which continues to give it a privileged political function. As Gündüz puts it: 'Therein lies another irony of the Turkish human rights imbroglio: the military elite is the most pro-Western force in the country.'[128] A particular problem with the political role of the military is that the National Security Council, which has a mixed military-civilian membership, exercises 'a disproportionate influence in the running of the state'.[129] While some have argued that the NSC should be abolished altogether, the 2001 constitutional amendments and the Harmonization Laws instead increase the civilian representation from five to nine, with the number of generals remaining at five, and restrict the NSC's remit to advising the Council of Ministers solely on national security issues. The constitutionality of legislation passed by the NSC between 1980 and 1982, when it acted on behalf of the Turkish Grand National Assembly, can also now be judicially challenged.[130]

Third, Turkish law enforcement agencies have a reputation for taking an excessively forceful approach to public protest and political unrest, and for torturing and ill-treating detainees with impunity. Systematic and serious abuses of human rights by the state occurred in the counter-terrorist climate of the 1970s and 1980s, and the conflict over Kurdish autonomy in the 1990s involved extra-judicial killings, torture, disappearances, breaches of the right to fair trial, destruction of property, and forcible emptying of villages on a significant scale, in addition to the restrictions upon freedom of association and expression already mentioned.[131] In a series of cases the

See B. Olbourne, 'Case Analysis: Refah Partisi (The Welfare Party) v. Turkey', *European Human Rights Law Review* (2003), 437–444; Koçak and Örücü, 'Dissolution of Political Parties', 415.

128 Gündüz, 'Human Rights', 21. 129 *Ibid.*

130 *Ibid.*, 22; Örücü, 'Turkish Constitution Revamped?', 214; Örücü, 'Seven Packages', 616.

131 A. Reidy, F. Hampson and K. Boyle, 'Gross Violations of Human Rights: Invoking the European Convention on Human Rights in the Case of Turkey', *Netherlands Quarterly of Human Rights* **15** (1997), 161–173.

Strasbourg institutions strongly criticized the Turkish authorities for failing to provide adequate domestic remedies and for failing to investigate thoroughly, or even at all, complaints about unjustified conduct, including killings and destruction of property, by security forces.[132] While this problem is no longer prevalent, Amnesty International continues to express concern about the use of disproportionate violence in the policing of demonstrations, and the lack of legal accountability in relation to those who resort to it.[133] As noted in Chapter 1, the Turkish invasion of Cyprus in 1974 also spawned three applications against Turkey by Cyprus to the European Commission of Human Rights, the first two of which were combined in a single report delivered on 10 July 1976, and the third in a report of 4 October 1983.[134] Each found Turkey to have seriously breached a string of Convention provisions. In a fourth application the Court held, on 10 May 2001, that Turkey remained in violation of the Convention on account of discrimination by the 'Turkish Republic of Northern Cyprus' against the small Greek-Cypriot minority in the Karpas region, their refusal to allow some 211,000 displaced Greek-Cypriots access to their homes or to offer compensation, and their failure to conduct effective investigations into the disappearance of Greek-Cypriots in the aftermath of the invasion.[135] However, in December 2005 the European Court of Human Rights held Turkey liable to compensate, not only the applicant who had lost her land and home during the 1974 invasion, but all others with similar complaints pending before the Court.[136]

The systematic torture and ill-treatment of prisoners and detainees, whether political or otherwise, has been the subject of numerous individual applications to Strasbourg, and two inter-state cases brought against Turkey in the 1980s and 1990s, which, in spite of a negotiated settlement, as Chapter 1 also noted, did not result in the effective

[132] *Ibid.*; V. Burskey, 'Times of Change – Can Turkey Make the Necessary Changes in its Human Rights Policies to be Admitted to the European Union?', *North Carolina Journal of International Law and Commercial Regulation* **29** (2004), 713–735 at 714–724.

[133] Amnesty International, 'Turkey'.

[134] *Cyprus* v. *Turkey* (1982) 4 EHRR 482.

[135] (2002) 35 EHRR 731. L. G. Loucaides, 'The Judgment of the European Court of Human Rights in the Case of *Cyprus* v. *Turkey*', *Leiden Journal of International Law* **15** (2002), 225–236; F. Hoffmeister, 'Cyprus v. Turkey. App. No. 25781/94', *American Journal of International Law* **96** (2002), 445–452.

[136] *Xenides-Arestis* v. *Turkey*, judgment of 22 December 2005.

resolution of the problem.[137] Notwithstanding the recently declared official policy of 'zero tolerance of torture', this remains a matter of concern to Amnesty International.[138] As a result of the constitutional amendments of 2001 and the Harmonization Laws, the death penalty and the State Security Courts (which tried terrorist cases with reduced due process standards) have each been abolished, a process of integrating 'repentant terrorists' back into society has been established, the period of detention prior to appearance before a judge has been limited to 48 hours (except for states of emergency, under martial law or in time of war), there is a right of access to a lawyer after forty-eight hours detention, detainees' next-of-kin must be informed of their detention, and improvements have been made to the fairness of legal proceedings which, in common with nearly every other European country, suffer from excessive delays.[139]

However, the impact of the Strasbourg institutions on Turkish law and practice are matters of dispute. While Gündüz claims that the European Court of Human Rights 'exercises a decisive, if indirect, influence on the Turkish legal and political system',[140] Őzdek and Karacaoğlu State, more convincingly, that as far as the prevention of human rights violations is concerned it cannot be said that the Convention has had a 'notable function', although they also point out that the 1982 Turkish Constitution was based upon it.[141] Őzdek and Karacaoğlu also claim that prior to the EU accession negotiations, and in spite of increasing references to human rights in Turkish political and legal debates and attempts by the government to establish human rights institutions (including a State Ministry for Human Rights), Turkey had still not taken effective steps to prevent systematic abuses from occurring in practice.[142] As a result of the accession negotiations several other human rights institutions have also since been established – including a Supreme Council for Human Rights, an

[137] *France, Norway, Denmark, Sweden and Netherlands* v. *Turkey* (1983) 35 D.R. 143; *Denmark* v. *Turkey* (2000) 29 EHRR CD35.

[138] Amnesty International, 'Turkey'. See also Gil-Robles, 'Visit to Turkey', paras. 108–159.

[139] Gil-Robles, 'Visit to Turkey', paras. 114, 118–120, 170–173; Örücü, 'Turkish Constitution Revamped', 211–212; Örücü, 'Seven Packages', 618 and 621.

[140] Gündüz, 'Human Rights', 18.

[141] Őzdek and Karacaoğlu, 'Turkey', 889 and 905.

[142] *Ibid.*, 881. See also Gündüz, 'Human Rights', 24–25 on the flourishing of human rights NGOs. Human Rights Commissions have also been set up in provinces and districts as part of the EU harmonization process, Örücü, 'Seven Packages', 618.

Investigative Council responsible for investigating allegations of human rights violations, an Advisory Council to assist the Minister for Human Rights and Foundations, a National Human Rights Commission, local Human Rights Councils, and the National Assembly's Human Rights Committee.[143] Although individual applications filed in Strasbourg in recent years may have brought violations to international attention and may also have led to some improvements in domestic legal arrangements, according to Őzdek and Karacaoğlu, these improvements were mostly 'too little and ineffective' and were aimed more at changing the state's image rather than genuinely seeking to address real human rights needs.[144] In recent years Turkey has also acceded to a raft of other international human rights treaties including the European Convention for the Prevention of Torture.[145]

It is, therefore, hard to deny that the EU has had a much greater impact than the Council of Europe on the position of human rights in Turkey. Rumford claims that the prospect of accession to the EU has created a sharp dilemma for Turkey's Kemalist political elites who traditionally have regarded cosmopolitan or trans-national processes of democratization as contrary to the interests of domestic harmony and a threat to national integrity, but who now realize that the national interest, not least economically, depends upon them succeeding.[146] The fact that the military leadership has accepted the need for the human rights reforms required by the EU has also removed a potentially insurmountable obstacle in the path of their realization.[147] Arikan maintains that, compared with other applicant states, the EU has imposed higher human rights conditions for membership, and has offered less concrete assistance in an attempt to increase European influence over Turkey's internal affairs, while delaying, though not rejecting, Turkish membership.[148] However, the strongly centralist and secular vision of the Turkish republic, which persists notwithstanding recent positive developments, is still not yet in complete harmony with the more pluralist western European conception of democracy. It therefore remains to be seen if Turkey will make further adjustments in order to bridge the gap, or if, on the other hand, the rest of

[143] Gil-Robles, 'Visit to Turkey', paras. 236–241.
[144] Őzdek and Karacaoğlu, 'Turkey', 906. [145] Gündüz, 'Human Rights', 15.
[146] Rumford, 'Resisting Globalization?'.
[147] Hicks, 'Legislative Reform in Turkey', 84.
[148] Arikan, 'Lost Opportunity', 38–40.

Europe shows a greater willingness to tolerate the unique Turkish model.

Structural Defects in National Legal Processes: the Italian Problem

As already indicated, the most pervasive Convention compliance problems throughout Europe, both east and west, concern fair trials and, in particular, delays in the administration of justice. However, these problems have reached epic proportions in Italy where, for example, a civil case at first instance can take between twenty-six and forty-six months, compared with four and a half to six and a half months in Germany, seven and a half months in France, and nineteen months in the UK, and, for criminal trials, nine to thirteen months in Italy, seven to nine months in France, and two months in the UK.[149] Over 10 per cent (2,211) of the 21,128 applications registered with the European Court of Human Rights between 1 November 1998 and 31 January 2001, were against Italy, 68.6 per cent of which (1,516) related to length of legal proceedings. Of a total of 1,085 applications from all states declared admissible in 2000, Italy accounted for 486, almost all of which (428) concerned the problem of delay in the administration of justice. By July 2001 approximately 10,000 further Italian 'length of proceedings' complaints had accumulated, of which 3,177 were ready for registration but which could not proceed due to lack of human resources at the Registry.[150]

Until the 1990s there was confusion about the relationship between the Italian legal system and the Convention. For example, according to Meriggiola, the Convention became 'an integral part of the Italian legal system' in 1955, prompting a mushrooming of interest in human rights among Italian lawyers and jurists.[151] However, there was also some dispute about whether because of its vague and, some claimed, inconsistent nature, the Convention was capable of being directly applied in the Italian legal system at all.[152] Meriggiola also claims that

[149] S. Wolf, 'Trial Within a Reasonable Time: The Recent Reforms of the Italian Justice System in Response to the Conflict with Article 6(1) of the ECHR', *European Public Law* **9** (2003), 189–209 at 194.

[150] *Report of the Evaluation Group to the Committee of Ministers on the European Court of Human Rights*, EG Court (2001) 1, 27 September 2001 at para. 27.

[151] Meriggiola, 'Italy', 475–477.

[152] *Ibid.*, 481.

the Convention had little impact in the 1960s and 1970s because lawyers were reluctant to use it and because the Italian legal system was largely Convention-compliant in any case.[153] The latter is a staggering claim not only because it is unclear how such a conclusion can be reached when the question of Convention compliance was incapable of being effectively tested domestically, but also because of Italy's unrivalled position at the top of the Convention violation league tables discussed earlier in this chapter. It is clear, however, that, until the 1990s, Italian courts regarded the Convention as having only the status of ordinary law and therefore that its provisions could be overridden by subsequent national legislation. But in 1993, following two judgments of the Supreme Court of Appeal in 1988 and 1990, the Italian Constitutional Court recognized that Convention rights and freedoms constitute 'inviolable human rights', in the sense of Article 2 of the Italian constitution, and are therefore incapable of being abrogated by ordinary legislation.[154]

There are five main reasons for the unique scale of the Italian problem.[155] First, although the Italian civil justice process is less complex than the criminal justice process – the latter of which was reformed in 1988 to make it more consistently accusatorial and to enhance the rights of the accused – each includes cumbersome and frequently changing procedures and unclear or contradictory legal provisions. Second, the Italian legal system is unusually generous with appeals, which can often take the form of a re-trial rather than merely a review of the original verdict, and which are permitted against any substantially conclusive and definite judicial decision. The Corte di Cassazione is 'flooded with thousands of applications every year' as a result.[156] In 1999, for example, the criminal section alone delivered 46,920 judgments compared with 7,335 decisions of the Cour de Cassation, and 3,249 of the Bundesgerichtshof, its French and German counterparts respectively. Moreover, the rate of appeal continues to rise, with 23,986 in 1999 compared with 13,663 in 1995 and 4,291 in 1950, creating delays and a rising backlog of unresolved litigation. Third, there are not enough judges and, with some notable exceptions, a poor work ethic and inadequate training have led to inefficient productivity. Fourth, lawyers compound delays by seeking frequent adjournments in

[153] *Ibid.*, 483.
[154] *Ibid.*, 482; Polakiewicz, 'Status of Convention', 43–44.
[155] Wolf, 'Trial Within Reasonable Time'. [156] *Ibid.*, 193.

order to facilitate overlapping engagements and by resisting the introduction of more efficient working practices. Finally, since Italian citizens cannot directly appeal to the Constitutional Court claiming a violation of their fundamental rights, they must take the 'collateral route' of an individual application to the European Court of Human Rights.[157] According to Wolf, the embarrassment caused by a series of adverse judgments at Strasbourg led to a series of constitutional and legal changes, including, in November 1999, the insertion of a right to fair trial into Article 111 of the Constitution, and Law No. 89 of 24 March 2001 (the 'Pinto Law') which enables anyone who has suffered pecuniary or non-pecuniary damage as a result of unreasonable delays in the legal process to lodge a claim for 'just satisfaction' with the Court of Appeal.[158] But, in spite of the fact that the European Court of Human Rights regards the Pinto Law as 'sufficient',[159] there is little sign so far that the problem with the administration of justice in Italy has been effectively addressed.[160]

THE CONVENTION IN CENTRAL AND EASTERN EUROPE

Prima facie, the same factors which appear to promote good Convention compliance for western European member states should also be influential in the former communist states which joined the Council of Europe in the 1990s. But the unique recent history of these countries raises some specific issues and difficulties. Over the period which has elapsed since the collapse of the Berlin wall in 1989, the focus of social scientific analysis has shifted from charting the post-communist transition – now an undeniable and apparently irreversible fact – to describing and analysing 'democratic consolidation' – the process by, and the degree to which, democratic institutions and values have been, or are being, both successfully institutionalized in state and

[157] *Ibid.*, 194. In Italy only the courts can refer matters to the Constitutional Court, Pasquino, 'Constitutional Adjudication', 47–48.

[158] Wolf, 'Trial Within Reasonable Time', 198–203.

[159] G. Ress, 'The Effect of Decisions and Judgments of the European Court of Human Rights in the Domestic Legal Order', *Texas International Law Journal* **40** (2005), 359–382 at 381.

[160] Wolf, 'Trial Within Reasonable Time', 203.

civil society and effectively disseminated by and through them.[161] According to Pridham, the consolidation of democracy is 'very largely on track in central and eastern Europe' and, although there is 'significant cross-national variation', regimes are 'now mostly recognizable as liberal democratic, at least in their construction and potential if not actual achievement so far'. As a result, the 'prospects for democratic consolidation across the region look better than a decade and a half ago'.[162] The only post-Soviet state to which this does not apply, Belarus, remains the sole surviving European autocracy and the only European country not yet a member of the Council of Europe. There are, however, increasing concerns that Russia, and some of the trans-Caucasian republics, may not make a full transition to democracy and may remain 'democratic-authoritarian' hybrids.

As with Spain and Portugal a decade and a half earlier, the transition in the eastern bloc was precipitated largely by internal factors. According to Lanham and Forsythe, '(t)here is little reason to doubt the conventional wisdom that the key to rights behaviour is found mostly within the state' and that, although in some circumstances, international factors generated 'a moderate degree of influence', they were largely 'secondary rather than primary for the fate of human rights' in the post-communist transition.[163] And as Brett points out, the non-binding Helsinki Final Act of 1975 – in which NATO and the Warsaw Pact states agreed common principles as the basis of future cooperation – was much more influential in strengthening human rights and dissident groups in eastern Europe and in the USSR than the UN's legally binding International Covenant on Civil and Political Rights.[164] The governments of the new democracies of central and eastern Europe were eager

[161] S. Berglund, J. Ekman and F. H. Aarebrot (eds.), *The Handbook of Political Change in Eastern Europe*, 2nd edn. (Cheltenham, UK/Northampton, USA: E. Elgar, 2004), at 1; G. Pridham, 'Democratization in Central and Eastern Europe: A Comparative Perspective' in S. White, J. Batt, and P. G. Lewis (eds.), *Central and East European Politics* **3** (Basingstoke/New York: Palgrave MacMillan, 2003), pp. 269–289 at 272.

[162] Pridham, 'Democratization', 287–288. See also P. A. Ulram and F. Plasser, 'Political Culture in East-Central Europe: Empirical Findings 1990–2001' in D. Pollack, J. Jacobs, O. Müller, and G. Pickel (eds.), *Political Culture in Post-Communist Europe: Attitudes in new democracies* (Aldershot: Ashgate Publishing Ltd, 2003), pp. 31–46.

[163] H. R. Lanham and D. P. Forsythe, 'Human Rights in the New Europe: A Balance Sheet' in D. P. Forsythe (ed.), *Human Rights in the New Europe – Problems and Progress* (Lincoln/London: University of Nebraska Press, 1994), pp. 241–259 at 242 and 250.

[164] R. Brett, 'Human Rights and the OSCE', *Human Rights Quarterly* **18** (1996), 668–693 at 676.

to join the Council of Europe mainly to symbolize their break from Russian domination, to silence domestic and foreign critics of the transition process, to consolidate democracy and human rights, to boost their international legitimacy, and to fulfil some of the minimum requirements for membership of the EU.[165]

Although secondary to domestic processes, the Council of Europe nevertheless played several important roles in the transition process. First, it offered the 'first point of institutionalized contact' with democratic Europe, and a 'privileged structure for dialogue'.[166] Second, it provided moral and diplomatic support. Third, in addition to its largely rhetorical debates and declarations, the Parliamentary Assembly organized fact-finding missions, monitored elections, and instituted round table discussions for the various parties involved.[167] Fourth, the Council of Europe made expertise and advice about the creation and management of democratic political and legal institutions available through a number of specialized programmes, including those found in treaties other than the Convention, such as the Framework Convention for the Protection of Minorities 1995. In addition to seminars, conferences, ad hoc training programmes, translation services and the provision of information, this was delivered mainly through the European Commission for Democracy through Law (the 'Venice Commission'), and the Demosthenes, Lode, Demo-droit, and Themis programmes which provided assistance with, respectively, democratization, local government, legal and judicial systems, and training for law enforcement and related officials.[168] The advice offered by the Venice Commission has undoubtedly been influential, particularly with respect to the creation of over-powerful executive presidencies (as in Ukraine, Belarus, Slovenia, and Moldova), the death penalty (as in Albania and Ukraine where the respective constitutional courts eventually held it to

165 J. E. Manas, 'The Council of Europe's Democracy Ideal and the Challenge of Ethno-National Strife' in A. Chayes and A. H. Chayes (eds.), *Preventing Conflict in the Post-Communist World – Mobilizing International and Regional Organizations* (Washington: Brookings Occasional Papers, Brookings Institution, 1996), pp. 99–144 at 111.

166 D. Huber, *A Decade Which Made History: The Council of Europe 1989–1999* (Strasbourg: Council of Europe Publishing, 1999), pp. 26 and 46–47.

167 *Ibid.*, pp. 31 and 152.

168 A. Drzemczewski, 'The Council of Europe's Cooperation and Assistance Programmes with Central and Eastern Europe in the Human Rights Field: 1990 to September 1993', *Human Rights Law Journal* **14** (1993), 229–248; Manas, 'CE's Democracy Ideal', 114–118; Huber, *Decade Which Made History*, pp. 22 and 27.

be unconstitutional), and on several constitutional issues in Bosnia and Herzegovina. Moldova has also received advice about the status of minorities and central-local relations, while Azerbaijan, Armenia, Bulgaria, Croatia, Slovenia, Kosovo, Georgia, and Macedonia, have been advised about their constitutions or electoral laws.[169] However, the Demosthenes, Lode, Demo-droit, and Themis programmes have been criticized for being under-funded and 'extremely limited in scope'.[170]

Fifth, and most importantly, the Council of Europe provided each new democracy with specific, tailor-made accession requirements.[171] Membership applications from states in the former communist zone, particularly that of the Russian Federation, have posed acute and sharply-debated dilemmas for the Council of Europe – how strict should it be in interpreting and applying its membership requirements, and would tailor-made ones result in some states being admitted with poorer human rights records than others?[172] According to Manas, the Parliamentary Assembly – the institution with the most extensive role in the admissions process – adopted a flexible approach, loosening the membership criteria while tightening the post-admission monitoring processes and creating 'special guest status' for non-member states with their own, alternative, human rights monitoring arrangements.[173] To take just two from the many accession agreements as examples, Moldova was required, among other things, to adopt a new criminal code and a new code of criminal procedure complying with Council of Europe standards within a year of joining, to amend its constitution to ensure judicial independence (also within a year), to guarantee complete freedom of worship for all citizens without discrimination, and to find a peaceful solution to the dispute between the Moldovan and the Bessarabian Orthodox Churches. Albania, on the other hand, undertook to ensure that no religious community would effectively be deprived of the opportunity to flourish, to encourage and protect the independence of broadcasters and the print media, to guarantee even-handedness in

[169] J. Jowell QC, 'The Venice Commission: disseminating democracy through law', *Public Law* (2001), 675–683,

[170] Manas, 'CE's Democracy Ideal', 114–115.

[171] See *ibid.*, 106–114; see Manas, 'CE's Democracy Ideal' and T. Meron and J. S. Sloan, 'Democracy, Rule of Law and Admission to the Council of Europe', *Israel Yearbook on Human Rights* **26** (1997), 137–156 for accounts of the admissions process.

[172] Meron and Sloan, 'Democracy, Rule of Law'; R. Harmsen, 'ECHR after Enlargement', 21.

[173] Manas, 'CE's Democracy Ideal', 113.

taxation, to change the role of the Prosecutor's Office making it more consistent with the rule of law and with Council of Europe standards, to ensure judicial independence, and to set up a commission (including experts from the Council of Europe) in order to draft a new constitution.[174] The accession of Belarus was suspended following a constitutional coup in 1996.[175] However, the processes by which the Council of Europe has monitored compliance with admissions criteria, and by which applicant states have sought to make their domestic laws and practices Convention-compliant, have been uneven at best.[176]

Democratization and Constitutionalization

The Convention has had a limited impact on the processes of democratization and constitutionalization in the former communist zone for two main reasons. First, democratization and constitutionalization raise a whole series of issues beyond its remit. Second, even within what might be considered the Convention's own domain, it has had to compete with some enduring features of the 'communist', or at least 'socialist', constitutional tradition. Take democratization first. As Pridham points out, while 'democratic consolidation' requires the framing of a genuinely democratic constitution, 'democratic progress' – in the sense of, for example, the stabilization of party and electoral systems, the smooth transfer of executive power following an electoral defeat, and the re-fashioning of an authoritarian political culture – can, at least begin, without it.[177] Poland, for example, made significant progress at the beginning of the 1990s in spite of not receiving a new constitution until 1997, while Albania and Macedonia made less progress notwithstanding the inauguration of democratic constitutions in 1992.[178]

The pattern of democratization has, to some extent, differed between sub-regional categories – Poland, Hungary, the Czech Republic, and

[174] Huber, *Decade Which Made History*, pp. 129–130. Information about the accession requirements of some other former Soviet and Yugoslav states can be found in *ibid.*, pp. 95, 121, 142–143, and 180–182.

[175] *Ibid.*, p. 151.

[176] Meron and Sloan, 'Democracy, Rule of Law', 155–156; A. Drzemczewski, 'Ensuring Compatibility of Domestic Law with the European Convention on Human Rights Prior to Ratification: The Hungarian Model', *Human Rights Law Journal* **16** (1995), 241–260 at 246.

[177] Pridham, 'Democratization', 274, 278–281. [178] *Ibid.*, 272–274.

Slovakia, the Visegrad states of East-Central Europe ('ECE'); the Balkan states of South-East Europe ('SEE'); the Baltic states of Estonia, Latvia and Lithuania, and the remaining 'outsider' states, for example Russia, Belarus, Ukraine, and Moldova – largely determined by national and sub-regional factors.[179] According to Pridham 'regime change has faced more arduous problems in the SEE than in the ECE countries', while, in the 'outsider zone', democratic procedures are at best fragile and the rule of law is weak.[180] Having undergone forms of liberalization even under communism, Slovenia, Hungary, and Poland had a head-start. But by 1992 nearly all central and eastern European countries had achieved the first stages of democratization. Party stabilization and the construction of a post-authoritarian political culture have been slow in most cases, although survey research indicates that some ECE states compare favourably with west European democracies in levels of diffuse support for democracy.[181] The fact that Poland, the Czech Republic, Estonia, Latvia, Lithuania, and Slovenia joined the EU in May 2004, is also an important indicator of the degree to which their political, economic, and legal institutions are already effectively consolidated and in conformity with the western European model.

Although broadly in agreement about the states in which democratization is most securely established, commentators disagree over the countries where this is least the case. Pridham singles out Bosnia and Herzegovina as 'undoubtedly weak especially at the civil society level', and Ukraine as having 'serious difficulties which may or may not prove systematically problematic in the future'.[182] Von Beyme, on the other hand, regards Russia, most CIS states,[183] Slovakia, Albania, Bulgaria, Yugoslavia, and Romania, as 'illiberal', or 'defective democracies', rather than full-blown 'liberal democracies', on account of significant flaws – for example, an emphasis on political participation over civil rights, a failure to guarantee basic democratic rights, and/or the holding of free, but not fair, elections – with Estonia and Latvia labelled

[179] *Ibid.*, 275–281. Although members of the Council of Europe, the trans-Caucasian states of Georgia, Azerbaijan, and Armenia, are not usually included in studies of Central and East European politics.

[180] *Ibid.*, 277–278. [181] *Ibid.*, 281. [182] *Ibid.*, 288.

[183] The 'Commonwealth of Independent States' was founded in 1991 as a loose association of the former Soviet states of Azerbaijan, Armenia, Belarus, Georgia, Kazakhstan, Kyrgyzstan, Moldova, Russia, Tajikistan, Turkmenistan, Uzbekistan, and Ukraine.

'exclusive democracies' because of the poor treatment of their Russian minorities.[184] Closely linked to democratization, although admittedly not entirely the same, is Berglund, Ekman, and Aarebrot's 'freedom league', according to which Slovenia, Bulgaria, the Czech Republic, Estonia, Hungary, Latvia, Lithuania, Poland, Slovakia, Croatia, Romania, and Serbia and Montenegro are 'free', Albania, Macedonia, Moldova, Armenia, Bosnia and Herzegovina, Georgia, Ukraine, Russia, and Azerbaijan, are 'partly free', and Belarus (plus five former Soviet Central Asian Republics – Kazakhstan, the Kyrgyz Republic, Tajikistan, Uzbekistan, Turkmenistan), are 'not free'.[185] However, as the twenty-first century has unfolded, significant progress with democratization has been made in Georgia, Ukraine, Romania, Slovakia, and Bulgaria.

According to von Beyme, there were two routes to constitutional change in eastern and central Europe, 'pluralist bargaining or the imposition of ideas by a dominant group', and two outcomes, the reform of the existing constitution or the introduction of an entirely new one. However, little correlation can be detected between routes and results and in neither was the European Convention on Human Rights particularly influential.[186] For example, pluralist bargaining in Hungary, Albania, and Poland led merely to the reform of existing constitutions, while in the Czech Republic[187] and Russia it created new ones. Similarly, the influence of dominant groups in Lithuania, Yugoslavia (Serbia and Montenegro), Romania, Croatia, Bulgaria, Slovenia, and Slovakia, produced new constitutions, but in many CIS states it led merely to the reform of those already in existence. Pridham notes that some country-specific controversy over constitutional change in the 1990s has 'evaporated' in recent years, except in Romania where some constitutional amendments have been required as a condition of EU membership.[188] The impetus to create new constitutions was stronger where states had emerged from the disintegration of multi-ethnic communist regimes, particularly in the Baltic and Balkans.

[184] K. von Beyme, 'Constitutional Engineering in Central and Eastern Europe' in White, Batt, and Lewis (eds.), *Central & East European Politics* **3**, at 209.

[185] Berglund, Ekman and Aarebrot (eds.), *Handbook of Political Change*, Table 1.1, p. 4.

[186] Von Beyme, 'Constitutional Engineering', 190 and 192.

[187] See D. Hendrych, 'Constitutionalism in the Czech Republic' in J. Přibáň and J. Young (eds.), *The Rule of Law in Central Europe: The Reconstruction of Legality, Constitutionalism and Civil Society in the Post-Communist Countries* (Aldershot/Brookfield/Singapore/Sydney, 1999), pp. 13–28.

[188] Pridham, 'Democratization', 286.

Furthermore, the liberal democratic constitutional model was itself only one among several influences in the constitutionalization processes which were 'full of internal tensions and contradictions, "ontological", conceptual and epistemological', some of which reflected global constitutional change and uncertainty, others being peculiar to the post-communist zone.[189] As Přibáň and Young point out, '(o)ne of the most striking legal facts in post-1989 legal and constitutional development was ... the continuing existence of socialist constitutions',[190] and, according to Pogany, '(t)o a significant extent, the countries of the region have been preoccupied with re-establishing important elements of their past rather than with forging innovative structures, often prompted by an idealized and romanticized picture of their former, pre-Communist selves'.[191] Sadurski adds that the legislatures and constitutional courts have been 'from the outset, dispensing a complex mix of continuity and discontinuity' with respect to previous constitutional regimes.[192]

Some states, such as Poland, followed the 'strong elected presidency model', while others, like Hungary and Czechoslovakia, chose 'pure parliamentarism'. However, according to von Beyme, each of these two models tended to converge into a hybrid – 'rationalized parliamentarism' – with both recognizably liberal democratic and 'socialist' characteristics such as: formal recognition of the 'constitutionally legalized state'; a commitment to the market (or 'social market') economy, albeit with in some cases the preservation of some state ownership; protection of private property; the separation of Church and State; forbidding enumerated 'abuses of communist systems' such as forced labour, the death penalty, and censorship; a popularly elected

[189] G. Skąpska, 'Between "Civil Society" and "Europe": Post-Classical Constitutionalism after the Collapse of Communism in a Socio-Legal Perspective' in Přibáň and Young (eds.), *Rule of Law*, pp. 204–222 at 205–206.

[190] J. Přibáň and J. Young, 'Central Europe in Transition: An Introduction', in Přibáň and Young (eds.), *Rule of Law*, pp. 1–10 at 6. See also P. Paczolay, 'Traditional Elements in the Constitutions of Central and East European Democracies' in M. Krygier and A. Czarnota (eds.), *The Rule of Law after Communism: Problems and Prospects in East-Central Europe* (Aldershot/Brookfield/Singapore/Sidney: Ashgate/Dartmouth, 1999); G. Skąpska, 'Paradigm Lost? The Constitutional Process in Poland and the Hope of a "Grass Roots Constitutionalism"' in Krygier and Czarnota (eds.), *Rule of Law*, pp. 149–175 at 151.

[191] I. Pogany, *Righting Wrongs in Eastern Europe* (Manchester: Manchester University Press, 1997), p. 213.

[192] W. Sadurski, *Rights Before Courts – A Study of Constitutional Courts in Postcommunist States of Central and Eastern Europe* (Dordrecht: Springer, 2005), p. 262.

president; representative legislatures; collective responsibility of ministers; fair multi-party elections, party systems, and electoral processes; the establishment of constitutional courts and an independent judiciary; and provisions concerning citizenship, ethnic minorities, environmental rights/obligations, human rights, and social duties.[193] The distinction drawn in post-communist constitutions between public and private spheres is also less sharp than in the west and greater emphasis is also placed on social rights. Citizenship also tends to be linked with duties, including many familiar under communism, and is often based on ethnic criteria with insufficient protection for minority rights.[194] According to Sós, in Hungary, 'constitutionalism has become the strongest legitimizing force of political transition',[195] but, Paczolay claims, 'the phenomena that mostly jeopardize constitutionalism throughout the central-east European area are nationalist hostilities and the violations of ethnic minority rights' which can lead to violent conflict.[196]

The establishment of independent constitutional courts, faithful to the rule of law and liberal democratic values, has been one of the central achievements of the constitutionalization process in central and eastern Europe. But, as Schwartz points out, constitutional courts can only make a significant contribution to the transition to liberal constitutional democracy if, and only if, the 'nation has already made a good start in that direction'.[197] Sadurski observes that, with some marginal variations, all central and eastern European states have centralized processes of constitutional review of 'considerable homogeneity'.[198] In spite of its incompatibility with the 'hegemonic claims of the party', the principle of judicial review by constitutional courts had already been introduced in some central and east European states even before the fall of communism.[199] Final, ex post facto, and abstract review by constitutional courts is now virtually universal, although as von Beyme points

[193] Von Beyme, 'Constitutional Engineering', 197–208.

[194] *Ibid.*, 201–205; Sadurski, *Rights Before Courts*, pp. 284–285; Skąpska, 'Civil Society and Europe', 205; Paczolay, 'Traditional Elements', 111.

[195] V. Sós, 'The Paradigm of Constitutionalism: The Hungarian Experience', in Krygier and Czarnota (eds.), *Rule of Law*, pp. 131–148 at 135.

[196] Paczolay, 'Traditional Elements', 111.

[197] H. Schwartz, *The Struggle for Constitutional Justice in Post-Communist Europe* (Chicago/London: University of Chicago Press, 2000), p. 226. Schwartz's study covers Poland, Hungary, Russia, Bulgaria and Slovakia.

[198] Sadurski, *Rights Before Courts*, p. 25.

[199] Von Beyme, 'Constitutional Engineering', 206.

out only half the constitutions in question provide an individual right of constitutional complaint.[200] Some central and eastern European constitutions also enable draft legislation to be reviewed. According to Sadurski, this institutional design has led to a 'concentration of the power to interpret, articulate and apply the meaning of constitutional norms in a prominent body of high public visibility, setting it quite evidently apart from the judicial system'.[201] In its turn this has often led to friction between constitutional courts and majorities in national legislatures over controversial legislation, raising the familiar dilemma of discerning when a powerful constitutional court has overstepped the line separating legitimate from illegitimate contribution to the legislative process.[202] Sadurski concludes that a 'robust power of constitutional review' is not necessarily a threat to, nor an important ingredient in, the protection of human rights.[203] But Schwartz argues that it is desirable for ordinary courts to have the power to refer substantial constitutional issues to the constitutional court, and for individuals and third parties such as NGOs to have a right of constitutional complaint, with constitutional courts having a discretionary power to reject minor infringements of constitutional rights in order to control what might otherwise be an overwhelming case load.[204] Although constitutional courts in the region enjoy high public esteem, arguably attributable to the fact that the judges who staff them tend to be distinguished legal scholars, ordinary courts are not very sensitive to constitutional issues and often take little notice of judgments in constitutional cases.[205] There is also a need, according to Schwartz, for constitutional courts to deliver more substantially reasoned judgments.[206]

Human Rights

It is clear, however, that a key component in the processes of democratic transition and consolidation in central and eastern Europe has been the universal attempt to provide constitutional protection for civil and political, and usually also social and economic rights, with particular

[200] *Ibid.*, 207. For fuller details about the arrangements in Poland, Hungary, Russia, Bulgaria, and Slovakia see Schwartz, *Struggle for Constitutional Justice*, pp. 34–35.
[201] Sadurski, *Rights Before Courts*, p. 26.
[202] *Ibid.*, pp. 104 and 289–299; Schwartz, *Struggle for Constitutional Justice*, pp. 240–242.
[203] Sadurski, *Rights Before Courts*, p. 125.
[204] Schwartz, *Struggle for Constitutional Justice*, pp. 243–244.
[205] *Ibid.*, pp. 236, 237, 239–240. [206] *Ibid.*, p. 246.

responsibility falling on national constitutional courts.[207] In most if not all cases, the European Convention on Human Rights also takes precedence over conflicting national law, except for the national constitutions themselves.[208] But, as the experience of western Europe reveals, this formal arrangement does not guarantee that a high official Convention violation rate will be avoided. However, it does not follow that because constitutional bills of rights in the new democracies of central and eastern Europe embody, in various forms, civil and political rights similar to those found in the Convention, that these have been directly derived from the Convention itself, because the Convention is after all merely one among many formulations of the liberal civil and political rights tradition. It is a moot point, therefore, whether the Convention or the wider liberal tradition, was the more influential.

Sadurksi concludes that, in post-communist central and eastern Europe, socio-economic rights are the most hotly contested of constitutional rights. In the equality field constitutional jurisprudence has not radically shifted from the values and principles of the ancien regime, and constitutional courts have made only a 'modest' contribution to the protection of minority rights and to the promotion of ethnic relations.[209] Nevertheless, with few exceptions, constitutional courts have faithfully applied liberal-democratic standards in the process of interpreting personal, civil, and political constitutional rights, although according to Schwartz there have been very few cases in this area.[210] But Sadurski does not attribute this to deliberate and self-conscious referencing by constitutional courts to the European Convention on

[207] J.-M. Henckaerts and S. Van der Jeught, 'Human Rights Protection Under the New Constitutions of Central Europe', *Loyola of Los Angeles International and Comparative Law Journal* **20** (1998), 475–506.

[208] See the following contributions to Blackburn and Polakiewicz (eds.), *Fundamental Rights*: A. Arabadjiev, 'Bulgaria', pp. 191–215 at 195; D. Jílek and M. Hofmann, 'Czech Republic', pp. 241–258 at 242, 249–51; R. Maruste, 'Estonia', pp. 277–287 at 281; V. Vadapalas, 'Lithuania', pp. 503–529 at 508; A. Drzemczewski and M. A. Nowicki, 'Poland', pp. 657–679 at 660, 667; R. Weber, 'Romania', pp. 711–730 at 715; M. Ferschtman, 'Russia', pp. 731–754 at 736; M. Blaško, 'Slovakia', pp. 755–779 at 756 and 760; A. Mavčič, 'Slovenia', pp. 781–808 at 785; V. Potapenko and P. Pushkar, 'Ukraine', pp. 915–934 at 918–919.

[209] Sadurski, *Rights Before Courts*, pp. 191 and 222; Schwartz, *Struggle for Constitutional Justice*, pp. 228 and 233.

[210] Sadurski, *Rights Before Courts*, pp. 169–170; Schwartz, *Struggle for Constitutional Justice*, p. 231.

Human Rights nor to decisions of the European Court of Human Rights. As Schwartz points out, although the Convention has been cited by the constitutional courts of Hungary, Poland, and Bulgaria, there is 'usually very little analysis or discussion of the relevant case law, but merely passing references to the relevant provisions'.[211] In other words, while national constitutional courts in central and eastern Europe may be said generally to uphold *Convention standards*, they do so without much direct reference to the Convention itself.[212] Therefore, the provisions of the Convention itself have mattered less in the initial phase of democratic and constitutional change in the region than the precise terms of specific national constitutional provisions – some of which may be in a similar form to their Convention or EU counterparts – and the culture of given constitutional courts, in particular, their grasp of and determination to apply liberal-democratic values.[213] While this tends to indicate that neither the European Convention on Human Rights nor the European Court of Human Rights have, so far, had much influence in central and eastern Europe, it does not mean that neither can, should, nor will, have the same relatively marginal role in future. Schwartz, for example, predicts that the civil and political rights jurisprudence of these countries may soon be determined not so much by how their constitutional courts interpret and apply their own constitutions, but by how the European Court of Human Rights in Strasbourg interprets the European Convention of Human Rights.[214] Finding effective ways to enhance the contribution made by constitutional courts as democracy and the rule of law are consolidated in the region is, therefore, one of the primary challenges facing the Council of Europe and the European Court of Human Rights as the twenty-first century progresses.

According to Harmsen, the short-term impact of enlargement on the case law of the Strasbourg institutions has been 'relatively small', with the initial influx of cases dominated by doomed attempts by applicants to obtain redress for the wrongs of the communist past.[215] The rest show little difference from the western European pattern with

[211] Schwartz, *Struggle for Constitutional Justice*, p. 234.
[212] Sadurski, *Rights Before Courts*, Ch. 6.
[213] According to Sadurski, the constitutional texts, in what were then the CEE candidate countries for entry to the EU, show 'very similar patterns of thinking about constitutional rights to those revealed by the EU Charter', *ibid.*, p. XVIII.
[214] Schwartz, *Struggle for Constitutional Justice*, p. 234.
[215] Harmsen, 'ECHR after Enlargement', 24–29.

a preponderance of applications raising fair trial issues, particularly the all-too-familiar complaint about delays in the administration of justice, often the length of pre-trial detention.[216] Harmsen also reports that, 'the enlargement of the Court has not had a notable effect on either its functioning or its jurisprudence'.[217]

The figures for the former communist states taken from Table 2 are reproduced in Table 5 below. However, as the following discussion will seek to show, information from other sources indicates that this seven-year time frame is not long enough for stable violation patterns to have emerged. Georgia (in fourteenth place), for example, has, according to other information, a worse human rights record than the Czech Republic (in fifth place), and, as discussed further below, the high score for Poland, which tops the table, may be as much due to its litigious culture and to the Convention's high public profile there as it is to genuinely poor protection for Convention rights.

The position of human rights in the post-communist zone can, however, be fleshed out with information from other sources. Commentators report the following problems, though not all are equally prevalent in all states: demands from victims that the many abuses of the communist era be remedied;[218] a weak official commitment to the rule of law;[219] a lack of popular confidence in administrative, and in some cases

[216] *Ibid.*; Arabadjiev, 'Bulgaria', 207–212; Jílek & Hofmann, 'Czech Republic', 257–258; H. Bokor-Szegö and M. Weller, 'Hungary', in Blackburn and Polakiewicz (eds.), *Fundamental Rights*, pp. 383–398 at 393–398; Vadapalas, 'Lithuania', 522–527; Drezemczewski and Nowicki, 'Poland', 672–675; Weber, 'Romania', 722–727; Ferschman, 'Russia', 742–752; Blaško, 'Slovakia', 767–776; Mavčič, 'Slovenia', 805–806.

[217] Harmsen, 'ECHR after Enlargement', 23.

[218] Pogany, *Righting Wrongs*. The judicial process provided by the Convention offers no relief to applicants complaining about the expropriation of property during the communist era because Convention obligations only bind states from the moment they join the Convention system. However, the compatibility of any process of restitution with Convention rights is, in principle, justiciable at Strasbourg. A. M. Gross, 'Reinforcing the New Democracies: The European Convention on Human Rights and the Former Communist Countries – A Study of the Case Law', *European Journal of International Law* **7** (1996), 89–102 at 96; M.-B. Dembour and M. Krzyżanowska-Mierzewska, 'Ten Years On: The Voluminous and Interesting Polish Case Law', *European Human Rights Law Review* (2004), 517–543 at 529–530.

[219] M. Krygier and A. Czarnota, 'The Rule of Law after Communism: An Introduction' in Krygier and Czarnota (eds.), *Rule of Law*, pp. 1–18 at 2; J. Kurczewski, 'The Rule of Law in Poland' in Přibáň and Young (eds.), *Rule of Law*, pp. 181–203; L. E. Wolchover, 'What is the Rule of Law? Perspectives from Central Europe and the American Academy', *Washington Law Review* **78** (2003), 515–524.

Table 5. *Annual National Violation Rates for the Former Communist States as Found by the European Court of Human Rights: 1999–2005*[220]

	1999	2000	2001	2002	2003	2004	2005	Total	Average
Poland	1	12	17	20	43	74	44	211	30.14
Ukraine	0	0	0	1	6	13	119	139	19.86
Russia	0	0	0	2	5	13	81	101	14.43
Romania	2	3	0	26	24	12	21	88	12.57
Czech Republic	0	4	1	4	5	27	28	69	9.86
Slovak Republic	1	3	5	4	17	11	28	69	9.86
Bulgaria	1	3	2	2	10	25	23	66	9.43
Hungary	0	1	1	1	13	20	17	53	7.57
Croatia	0	0	4	6	6	11	24	51	7.29
Moldova	0	0	1	0	0	10	13	24	3.43
Lithuania	0	4	2	4	3	1	3	17	2.43
Estonia	0	0	0	1	2	1	4	8	1.14
Latvia	0	0	0	2	1	3	1	7	1.00
Georgia	0	0	0	0	0	1	3	4	0.57
The FYRO Macedonia	0	0	0	0	0	0	4	4	0.57
Slovenia	0	2	0	0	0	0	1	3	0.43
Albania	0	0	0	0	0	1	0	1	0.14

judicial and law enforcement, institutions;[221] problems stemming from the association of judges with the ancien regime, a lack of a proper understanding of judicial independence on the part of both judges and other public officials, and an excessive judicial commitment to legal formalism;[222] limited respect for rights and for the rule of law on the part of law enforcement agencies;[223] corrupt, or undemocratic, public processes;[224] harsh conditions and ill-treatment in prison and other

[220] Same source as Table 2. Armenia, Azerbaijan, Bosnia and Herzegovina, and Serbia and Montenegro had no violations recorded against them over this period.

[221] Ulram and Plasser, 'Political Culture', 37.

[222] A. Fijalkowski, 'The Judiciary's Struggle towards the Rule of Law in Poland' in Přibáň and Young (eds.), *Rule of Law*, pp. 242–253; F. Emmert, 'Editorial: The Independence of Judges – A Concept Often Misunderstood in Central and Eastern Europe', *European Journal of Law Reform* **3** (2002), 405–409.

[223] N. Uildriks and P. van Reenen (eds.), *Policing Post-Communist Societies: Police-Public Violence, Democratic Policing and Human Rights* (Antwerp: Intersentia, 2003).

[224] Schwartz, *Struggle for Constitutional Justice*, p. 236.

places of detention including psychiatric hospitals;[225] trafficking in women and children;[226] and problems with respect for minorities, particularly the Roma, the largest and arguably the most systematically disadvantaged ethnic group in the region.[227] However, over the past decade or so several central and east European states have either solved some of these problems entirely or have begun to tackle them with greater success, thereby entrenching respect for human rights in their national public processes at least as effectively as some of their western neighbours.[228]

Although, therefore, the official violation rate is an even more problematic surrogate for compliance for the post-communist states that it is for their western European counterparts, a rough-and-ready distinction can nevertheless be made between states with 'good', 'satisfactory', and 'poor' human rights records more generally. Jordan, for example, claims that, as of April 2003, the states of central and eastern Europe fell into three categories as far as compliance with their tailor-made accession obligations for membership of the Council of Europe were concerned.[229] Those in the high compliance group – the Czech Republic, Estonia, Hungary, Latvia, Lithuania, Poland, and Slovenia – were not under investigation by the Parliamentary Assembly,

[225] Harmsen, 'ECHR after Enlargement', 28. Some of the new member states now have proportionately more than twenty times as many prisoners as other states, and those with the highest incarceration rates are typically those least financially well-equipped to afford decent prison conditions, R. Morgan and M. Evans, *Combating Torture in Europe: the Work and Standards of the European Committee for the Prevention of Torture* (Strasbourg: Council of Europe, 2001), p. 164.

[226] See, for example, Amnesty International's *Annual Reports*, http://web.amnesty.org/.

[227] P. Danchin and E. Cole (eds.), *Protecting the Human Rights of Religious Minorities in Eastern Europe* (New York: Columbia University Press, 2002); F. de Varennes, 'The Protection of Linguistic Minorities in Europe and Human Rights: Possible Solutions to Ethnic Conflicts?', *Columbia Journal of European Law* **2** (1996), 107–143; I. Pogany, '(Re)Building the Rule of Law in Hungary: Jewish and Gypsy Perspectives' in Přibáň and Young (eds.), *Rule of Law*, pp. 141–159; I. Pogany, 'Post-Communist Legal Orders and the Roma: Some Implications for EU Enlargement', in W. Sadurski, A. Czarnota and M. Krygier (eds.), *Spreading Democracy And The Rule Of Law?* (New York: Springer Science, 2005), Ch. 15; I. Pogany, 'Minority Rights and the Roma of Central and Eastern Europe', forthcoming in *International Journal of Human Rights* **11** (2007). According to von Beyme, 'Constitutional Engineering', 203, the treatment of ethnic minorities, and in particular minority languages, provides '(t)he most important test of the democratic convictions of the constitution-makers in the new regimes'.

[228] For discussions of the position of human rights in post-communist Europe in the early 1990s see Forsythe (ed.), *Human Rights*.

[229] Jordan, 'Membership Privileges?'.

nor by the Committee of Ministers, for failure to fulfil their accession commitments, they had generally complied with the Council's non-binding recommendations, and they appeared to be actively and successfully promoting democratic practices such as free elections, judicial independence, and the protection of minorities. States in the medium category – Bulgaria, Croatia, Romania, Slovakia, and Macedonia – generally fulfilled the first two of these criteria but, although having made an 'effort in good faith', had not progressed far enough on the third to justify being placed in the 'high compliance' group. Those in the low compliance group, among the last to join the Council of Europe – Albania, Armenia, Azerbaijan, Bosnia and Herzegovina, Georgia, Moldova, the Russian Federation, Serbia and Montenegro, and Ukraine – were under investigation for failing to fulfil key accession obligations, had not complied with specific Council of Europe recommendations, and exhibited some serious systemic human rights problems including electoral malpractice, a lack of judicial independence, and inadequate protection for minorities. While this picture is not corroborated in every particular by other commentators, its broad contours are. Pridham, for example, claims, that, at the beginning of the twenty-first century across the Central and East European region, Hungary, Slovenia, and Poland had the most positive human rights record in spite of problems in Hungary and Slovenia concerning the Roma.[230] The states with the best human rights records also tend to be those with the best 'democracy' and 'freedom' ratings such as that offered by Berglund, Ekman and Aarebrot.[231]

Broadly speaking, five factors seem most likely to determine whether a post-communist Council of Europe state has a 'good', 'satisfactory', or 'poor' human rights record: a successfully revived pre-Communist experience of democracy and the rule of law; an identification, on the part of both the political elite and the general public, with contemporary European political and economic institutions and values; significant progress with the establishment of effective legal remedies, particularly an individual complaints process to a constitutional court; an independent, rights-aware judiciary; and the lack of significant ethnic tensions, particularly violent ones.[232]

230 Pridham, 'Democratization', 284.

231 Berglund, Ekman and Aarebrot (eds.), *Handbook of Political Change*, Table 1.1, p. 4.

232 In a statistically sophisticated study of 28 post-communist states, including the former Soviet Asian republics, Horowitz found that, while economic development had a relatively weak positive influence on human rights and war a relatively strong negative

States with 'Good' Human Rights Records

In spite of half a century of Soviet occupation, the Czech Republic, Poland, Hungary, and the three Baltic states, have quickly resurrected their pre-Soviet democratic political culture, and traditions, while Slovenia's history, culture and geography, coupled with its much easier secession from Yugoslavia than that of its sister republics, facilitated rapid assimilation with its other western European neighbours. According to Pridham, by 2001 'very significant progress' in creating an independent judiciary had occurred in Hungary and Poland, Slovenia had made 'significant progress', and the Baltic states had made 'important progress'.[233] Ulram and Plasser report that '(i)n East-Central Europe, including Slovenia, democratic attitudes are shared by a stable majority of the population'.[234] However, court reform, the main problem following the partition of Czechoslovakia in 1997, remained a problem for Slovakia four years later.

The determination of the judiciary in these countries to apply constitutional rights effectively, particularly where there is a constitutional complaints process, seems to have been a particularly important factor in producing their good human rights records. Indeed, it appears to be a more important factor than direct judicial reference to either the European Convention on Human Rights or to the jurisprudence of the European Court of Human Rights. While, as already indicated, Sadurski makes little mention of any role played either by the Convention or by the European Court of Human Rights in constitutional adjudication in these states,[235] other commentators claim that it has had a considerable impact – particularly in Slovenia, the Czech Republic, Hungary, and Lithuania. Mavčič states that, in Slovenia, where there is a strong Constitutional Court, '... it has become normal that domestic courts are influenced by the case law of the European Court of Human Rights

influence, 'frustrated national identities' had by far the strongest and most consistent positive impact on democratization and the effective protection of human rights, S. Horowitz, 'Human Rights in the Post-Communist World: The Roles of National Identity, Economic Development and Ethnic Conflict', *International Journal of Human Rights* **8** (2004), 325–343. 'Frustrated national identities' were defined as: 'widely held beliefs that the communist system frustrated pre-communist national potential, particularly in the areas of political autonomy and greatness, economic development and cultural autonomy and expression' (at 330).

233 Pridham, 'Democratization', 283–284.

234 Ulram and Plasser, 'Political Culture', 42.

235 Sadurski, *Rights Before Courts*, Ch. 6.

thus raising the level of human rights protection'.[236] Jílek and Hofman claim that in the Czech Republic both the Convention and the jurisprudence of the European Court of Human Rights are 'frequently referred to and applied in the practice of the Constitutional Court'.[237] Similarly, Bokor-Szegö and Weller maintain that in Hungary the Convention has already had a 'considerable impact' on the legal order, while Krygier and Czarnota claim that the Hungarian Constitutional Court 'has more prestige and its judgments more legitimacy than virtually any other institution, or than comparable institutions have in virtually any other country' even though in Hungary, as in most post-communist societies, public institutions are 'rarely trusted'.[238] Vadapalas states that, although 'Lithuanian courts are more reticent to apply the ECHR than Polish courts . . . the Constitutional Court of Lithuania has on many occasions based its decisions on the provisions of the ECHR'.[239]

The impact of the Convention in Poland is disputed. Poland has a set of constitutional rights, a constitutional complaints process, and the jurisdiction of the Constitutional Tribunal expressly includes assessing conformity with international agreements.[240] Some commentators claim that the Polish courts had begun to apply the Convention even before its formal incorporation,[241] but others point out that, although the Supreme Court and the Constitutional Tribunal are aware of the Convention, it plays only a modest role in the daily practice of the lower courts.[242] The Convention is, however, very popular with the public. Poland now has the second highest rate of applications registered with

[236] Mavčič, 'Slovenia', 807–808.

[237] Jílek and Hofman, 'Czech Republic', 252; V. Sládeček, 'The Protection of Human Rights in the Czech Republic' in Přibáň and Young (eds.), *Rule of Law*, pp. 82–98 at 88.

[238] Bokor-Szegö and Weller, 'Hungary', 397; Krygier and Czarnota, 'Rule of Law After Communism', 7. See also Sós, 'Paradigm of Constitutionalism', 137–139. The public respect in Hungary for the Constitutional Court contrasts with the 'lack of respect Poles show the courts', Dembour and Krzyżanowska-Mierzewska, 'Voluminous and Interesting', 535.

[239] Vadapalas, 'Lithuania', 512.

[240] W. Sadurski, 'Rights and Freedoms Under the New Polish Constitution', in Krygier and Czarnota (eds.), *Rule of Law*, pp. 176–193; Drzemczewski and Nowicki, 'Poland', 668.

[241] Drzemczewski and Nowicki, 'Poland', 660.

[242] M.-B. Dembour and M. Krzyżanowska-Mierzewska, 'Ten Years On: The Popularity of the Convention in Poland', *European Human Rights Law Review* (2004), 400–423 at 419–420.

the European Court of Human Rights – over 90 per cent of which are submitted without legal representation – and generates a tenth of the Court's caseload.[243] According to Dembour and Krzyżanowska-Mierzewska this can be attributed to a lack of popular faith in the domestic courts, 'a persistent "victim mentality" ', and the reluctance of the judiciary in the lower courts and the legal profession to take the Convention seriously.[244] In common with most other member states, the bulk of the Polish cases litigated at Strasbourg concern length of judicial proceedings.[245] Poland has also found that the ombudsman has been able to exert pressure on the domestic courts to apply human rights standards enunciated by the European Court of Human Rights.[246] However, in Estonia the Convention is not used by the administrative law courts as the basis of its decisions in judicial review cases, and the national courts are generally reluctant to apply it, believing it to be 'foreign law'.[247] Formal Convention-proofing of draft legislation is part of the legislative process in Bulgaria, Lithuania, and Slovakia, but not in Poland or Romania.[248]

However, notwithstanding these generally positive developments, some of these states have faced considerable challenges regarding the treatment of their ethnic minorities. Pridham notes that both the Czech Republic and Slovakia had been criticized in 1997 for the lack of active human rights policies and, in the case of the former, for persistent latent racism. By 2001, although significant progress had been made in Slovakia, the EU's European Commission was not convinced that these problems had been adequately tackled in the Czech Republic.[249]

States with 'Satisfactory' Human Rights Records

Also for cultural, historical, and geographical reasons, Bulgaria, Croatia, Romania, Slovakia, and Macedonia – with neither the best nor the worst human rights records in the post-communist zone – have a

[243] *Ibid.*, 401–404, 415.
[244] *Ibid.*, 401–402, 409, 413, 417–419 and 419–422.
[245] Dembour and M. Krzyżanowska-Mierzewska, 'Voluminous and Interesting', 517–521.
[246] Von Beyme, 'Constitutional Engineering', 206.
[247] Maruste, 'Estonia', 283–284 and 287.
[248] Arabadjiev, 'Bulgaria', 198; Vadapalas, 'Lithuania', 510; Blaško, 'Slovakia', 764; Drezemzcewski and Nowicki, 'Poland', 660; Weber, 'Romania', 718.
[249] Pridham, 'Democratization', 284–285.

weaker sense of European identity and other difficulties. As a province of the Ottoman empire for centuries before the Soviet occupation, Bulgaria had much more experience of 'oriental despotism' than of western liberal democracy. Although influenced by the Convention, the Bulgarian constitution is an 'overambitious mixture of liberal and social and economic rights' with inadequate review mechanisms, insufficient protection for minorities, no individual right of complaint nor any effective alternative review process.[250] The Convention is considered to have a largely declarative, rather than instrumental, character in the Bulgarian legal system, although its importance is increasing, particularly in the interpretation of constitutional provisions by the Constitutional Court.[251] While the Convention takes formal precedence over domestic legislation, this is not readily accepted by the Bulgarian judiciary.[252] Articles 36.2 and 36.3 of the Bulgarian constitution are widely regarded as illiberal in stipulating that 'the study and use of the Bulgarian language is a right and obligation of every Bulgarian citizen', with its sole use a legal requirement in certain circumstances.[253] Pridham claims that in Bulgaria, although the Turkish minority has been quite well integrated, other human rights problems remained, including police violence, 'people-trafficking', and problems concerning the enforcement of minority legislation especially to protect the Roma.[254] The need for significant institutional and constitutional reform in Bulgaria remains, especially the provision of effective national remedies.[255] Demitrova claims, however, that, '(i)f the level of discussion in the public sphere is any indicator', by comparison with the EU, 'the Council of Europe's methods have been more successful in reaching Bulgarian actors and socializing them in democratic norms'.[256] She adds:

> On the whole the Council of Europe's role in the consolidation and even sometimes the day-to-day workings of Bulgarian democracy is considerable. It complements in important ways the weak judiciary and creates

[250] Arabadjiev, 'Bulgaria', 193 and 203.
[251] *Ibid.*, 194–198, 202, 214. [252] *Ibid.*, 195, 214.
[253] Von Beyme, 'Constitutional Engineering', 203; Sadurski, *Rights Before Courts*, p. 285.
[254] Pridham, 'Democratization', 285.
[255] Von Beyme, 'Constitutional Engineering', 215.
[256] A. L. Demitrova, 'The Council of Europe and the European Union and Their Roles in Democratization in Central and Eastern Europe: The Case of Bulgaria', paper for the *Conference of JPSA/ECPR Project on Measuring Democratic Consolidation Through Inter-Regional Comparisons – Europe and East Asia*, 11–13 November 2001 at 25.

> a constraint for institutions and actors, as well as forcing change in the behaviour of parts of the criminal justice system which are still not up to European standards. The activities and opinions of the Council have a high profile in the media and the public sphere in general, making this organization an important factor for democratization in Bulgaria.[257]

In Romania, where the 1989 revolution was at least in the first instance as much about the overthrow of Ceaucescu's personal tyranny as it was about the demolition of communism, the Convention was also influential in the drafting of the constitution and although it formally takes precedence over conflicting domestic law, the vast majority of Romanian courts , apart from the Constitutional Court do not take it seriously.[258] The Romanian courts are even split over whether decisions of their own Constitutional Court are binding upon them.[259] Neither Parliament nor the media seem to know or understand the significance of adverse decisions of the European Court of Human Rights and there was even some Parliamentary hostility to the Convention in the early 1990s in spite of it having been incorporated in domestic law.[260] Although Romania has also had problems with respect to minorities and in developing an independent judiciary, the Convention is now said to be slowly finding its way into public life.[261]

Decisions of the Slovakian Constitutional Court, which contain some references to the Convention, are declaratory only, and the decisions of the ordinary Slovakian courts refer to the Convention only sporadically.[262] The Council of Europe intervened in Slovakia, where Article 34.2 of the constitution provides a 'right of ethnic minorities to learn the official language', in order to mitigate the tension caused by the aggressive 'Slovakization' of names, particularly with respect to the Hungarian minority.[263] Croatia and Macedonia emerged from the Balkan wars of the 1990s much more tarnished by ethnic nationalism and intolerance than Slovenia. Yet, as Jordan points out, Croatia made internationally recognized progress in the late 1990s towards democratic governance, the introduction of fair and open elections, and the strengthening of the rule of law, as well as cooperating with

257 *Ibid.*, 17.
258 Weber, 'Romania', 711, 713, 715, 718, 719.
259 *Ibid.*, 722.
260 *Ibid.*, 717, 728. 261 *Ibid.*, 728. Pridham, 'Democratization', 284–285.
262 Blaško, 'Slovakia', 764–765.
263 Von Beyme, 'Constitutional Engineering', 203.

the Criminal Tribunal for the former Yugoslavia and ratifying the statute of the International Criminal Court. However, problems remained, especially with judicial independence, the enforcement of court decisions, and with the treatment of ethnic minorities. For example, in spite of having worked with the Venice Commission, the preamble to the Croatian constitution differentiated between national minorities by listing some but omitting others, voting registers continued to identify voters by their ethnicity, displaced ethnic Serbs and Croats had unequal voting rights, some ethnic Serbs and Roma were treated in a discriminatory fashion by Croatian officials, and displaced ethnic Serbs faced problems obtaining jobs, housing, and education.[264]

States with 'Poor' Human Rights Records

Former communist states with the poorest human rights records, according to Jordan, are either ex-constituents of the USSR – Armenia, Azerbaijan, Moldova, the Russian Federation, Georgia, and Ukraine – with at best very ambivalent senses of their European identity and with no domestic experience of the western liberal democratic tradition at all, or states which emerged from the Balkan wars – as did Albania, Serbia and Montenegro, and Bosnia and Herzegovina[265] – more damaged in institutional and other ways than any of the other former Yugoslav republics. A particular problem with these countries is their comparatively slow progress in establishing independent judicial processes and appropriate democratic and legal cultures.[266] Most of the senior judiciary were compromised by their association with the ancien regime, the legal process has often been dominated by the Procuracy (a judicial-administrative hybrid), and the prevailing legal culture has been largely passive with respect to officialdom.[267] Although the Convention takes formal precedence over conflicting domestic law in Ukraine, with the Constitutional and Supreme Courts guided by it, the Ukrainian judicial system is 'far from perfect' and 'is not yet free

[264] Jordan, 'Membership Privileges?', 675–680.

[265] J. Simor, 'Tackling Human Rights Abuses in Bosnia and Herzegovina: The Convention is Up To It, Are its Institutions?', *European Human Rights Law Review* **6** (1997), 644–662.

[266] Ulram and Plasser, 'Political Culture', 40–44.

[267] Von Beyme, 'Constitutional Engineering', 207.

from the traditions of the totalitarian past'.[268] Potapenko and Pushkar argue that there is a need for a system of administrative courts, for the Supreme Court to pass a resolution on the application of the Convention in the Ukrainian legal system, and for the norms of European law to be much more thoroughly studied, promoted and disseminated.[269] However, following the political revolutions of 2003 and 2005 the prospects for human rights may have improved in Georgia and Ukraine.

Of all the former communist Council of Europe states, Russia presents the greatest human rights challenges. A centuries-old tradition of centralized autocracy in state and official ideology has inhibited the development of a culture of respect for democracy and constitutional rights. The rule of law made little impact before the Bolshevik revolution, and in the communist era there was scant respect for formal legal rules with judges 'firmly under the control of the local party organization, which could appoint or remove them at will'.[270] Certain features of the transition process – in particular the 'shock therapy' of marketization without effective legal and regulatory frameworks – have also weakened the post-communist state, enabling organized crime and official corruption to flourish on an epic scale, causing massive impoverishment and social dislocation, and marginalizing vulnerable social groups such as women, prisoners, orphans, and ethnic minorities.[271] An insecure ethnic nationalism, favourably disposed to the quick fix of what President Putin calls

[268] Potapenko and Pushkar, 'Ukraine', 918–919, 928, 930.

[269] *Ibid.*, 930 and 932.

[270] B. Bowring, 'Politics, the Rule of Law and the Judiciary' in N. Robinson (ed.), *Institutions and Political Change in Russia* (Basingstoke: Macmillan, 2000), pp. 69–84 at 73.

[271] A. Brown, 'Political Culture and Democratization: The Russian Case in Comparative Perspective' in Pollack *et al.* (eds.), *Political Culture*, pp. 17–27; J. Weiler, *Human Rights in Russia: A Darker Side of Reform* (Boulder/London: Lynne Rienner, 2004); E. Gilligan, *Defending Human Rights in Russia: Sergei Kovalyov, Dissident and Human Rights Commissioner, 1969–2003* (London/New York: Routledge Curzon, 2004); D. Satter, *Darkness at Dawn: The Rise of the Russian Criminal State* (New Haven/London: Yale University Press, 2003), pp. 2–3, 249–256; R. Service, *Russia – Experimenting With a People* (London: Macmillan, 2002), Chs. 6 and 10; F. Feldbrugge, 'Human Rights in Russian Legal History' in F. Feldbrugge and W. B. Simons (eds.), *Human Rights in Russia and Eastern Europe: Essays in Honor of Ger P. van den Berg* (The Hague/London/New York: Martinus Nijhoff, 2002), pp. 65–90; O. Orlov, 'Status of Human Rights in the Chechen Republic, Autumn 2000', *Russian Politics and Law* **39** (2001), 25–33.

'dictatorship through law',[272] has emerged in response to these developments and also to the disappearance of the USSR, the war in Chechnya and the perceived vulnerability of a weak Russian state to western interference manifesting itself in, among other ways, universal human rights promoted by the 'Trojan horses' of western-funded NGOs.[273] Most commentators agree that a future in which democracy and a culture of respect for human rights and the rule of law flourish, cannot be taken for granted in Russia.[274] Indeed, most predict the further entrenchment of the current unique mix of the western economic model, old Soviet habits of statecraft including tight control of the media, plus newly acquired skills in electoral manipulation. However, Morozov, among others, argues that because of the strong, though not unchallenged, Russian fear of isolation from contemporary Europe, all is not yet lost.[275] But the difficulty lies in finding effective ways of nourishing the incipient sense of European identity to the point where Russia becomes less of a wayward sibling and begins more closely to resemble the rest of the family of European nations.

As already indicated in Chapter 1, Russia's prospects as an authentic and committed member of the Council of Europe were matters of concern even when its application for membership was under

[272] Open letter from Vladimir Putin to Russian voters, 25 February 2000: http://putin2000.ru/07/05.html, quoted in J. Kahn, 'Russian Compliance with Articles 5 and 6 of the European Convention on Human Rights as a Barometer of Legal Reform and Human Rights in Russia', *University of Michigan Journal of Law Reform* **35** (2002), 642–693 at 652 note 46.

[273] Brown, 'Political Culture', 23–24; Ulram and Plasser, 'Political Culture', 40; V. Morozov, 'Human Rights and Foreign Policy Discourse in Today's Russia: Romantic Realism and Securitization of Identity', *East European Human Rights Review* **8** (2002), 143–198; V. Morozov, 'Resisting Entropy, Discarding Human Rights – Romantic Realism and Securitization of Identity in Russia', *Cooperation and Conflict* **37** (2002), 409–430; S. Zassorin, 'Human and Ethnic Minority Rights in the Context of an Emerging Political Culture in Russia', *Javnost-Ljubljana* **7** (2000), 41–54.

[274] Brown, 'Political Culture', 24–25; Ulram and Plasser, 'Political Culture', 44; Bowring, 'Politics, Rule of Law and Judiciary', 84.

[275] See, e.g. Morozov, 'Human Rights', 174–181, 188–189; Morozov 'Resisting Entropy', 410, 422–423, 426; R.A. Jordan, 'Russia's Accession to the Council of Europe and Compliance with European Human Rights Norms', *Demokratizatsiya-Washington* **11** (2003), 281–296 at 286.

consideration in the mid-1990s.[276] Although many of these worries remain, Russia has nevertheless fulfilled a number of formal key accession requirements, including the ratification of the European Convention for the Prevention of Torture and the Framework Convention for the Protection of Minorities. Attempts to provide more judicial independence, and greater adherence to formal legal standards, began under Gorbachev in the 1980s before the fall of communism, and continued, turbulently, in the 1990s, when among other things the Constitutional Court was abolished and reconstituted, and the Communist Party of the Soviet Union was put on trial. In July 2002 a new criminal code – which includes many of the guarantees found in Articles 5 and 6 of the European Convention on Human Rights – came into force.[277] In Russia the Convention takes precedence over conflicting domestic law apart from the constitution.[278] However, although the Constitutional and Supreme Courts have made some reference to it, there is no mechanism for enforcing Constitutional Court judgments.[279] In spite of the fact that 'at the highest judicial level considerable efforts are being made to ensure proper judicial human rights protection in accordance with both national and international law', some significant compliance problems with Articles 5 and 6 remain, particularly regarding the lack of judicial control over the powers of prosecutors in pre-trial matters.[280] Bowring claims that the Russian judicial system is threatened by structural tensions from three sources: the position of the Procuracy; jurisdictional conflicts between the Supreme Court and the Constitutional Court; and, ironically, unprecedented independence on the part of the regional judiciary which threatens to undermine the coherence of the national legal order.[281]

In 2003 the Council of Europe was still monitoring Russia on two fronts: its refusal to ratify Protocol No. 6 of the Convention which

[276] B. Bowring, 'Russia's Accession to the Council of Europe and Human Rights: Compliance or Cross-Purposes?', *European Human Rights Law Review* (1997), 628–643; B. Bowring, 'Russia's Accession to the Council of Europe and Human Rights: Four Years On', *European Human Rights Law Review* (2000), 362–379; Jordan, 'Russia's Accession'.

[277] Kahn, 'Russian Compliance', 667. [278] Ferschtman, 'Russia', 736.

[279] *Ibid.*, 742, 749 and 753.

[280] *Ibid.*, 740–1, 749 and 753. Kahn, 'Russian Compliance', 663–690.

[281] Bowring, 'Politics, Rule of Law and Judiciary', 77–84.

abolishes the death penalty, except in time of war, and the human rights implications of the Chechen wars.[282] Although President Putin has since expressed his opposition to capital punishment, Jordan claims that execution remains popular, not only with the Russian public, but also with many prisoners who would prefer it to a slow death in the country's notoriously harsh prisons.[283] The Chechen wars have already resulted in an estimated 100,000 deaths, atrocities on all sides, and the virtual demolition by Russian forces of the region's capital city, Grozny, home to some 490,000 inhabitants. Misconduct by its forces deprived Russia of voting rights in the Parliamentary Assembly in April 2000, and, on 24 February 2005, the European Court of Human Rights found Russia in breach of Article 2 of the Convention in respect of an anti-insurgent operation in October 1999 which resulted in a number of civilian deaths which were not adequately investigated.[284] The Chechen conflict has presented the Council of Europe with another dilemma: would the interests of European peace and security – and the protection of democracy, human rights, and the rule of law – be better served in the long term by expelling Russia for such gross and flagrant violations, or by retaining it in spite of them? While expulsion has the short-term merit of signifying profound condemnation, it also raises the much more troubling question of how the rest of Europe can collectively exert any further influence over a neighbour which has been shunned.

While acknowledging that there have been 'profound' changes in Russia over the past fifteen years, the European Commissioner for Human Rights, in a lengthy report based on visits in July and September 2004, identified the following as among the country's most pressing human rights challenges: legal reform, judicial training and independence, conditions of detention, police violence, official corruption, the protection of minorities, the situation in the Chechen Republic, conditions in the armed forces, freedom of expression in the current anti-terrorist climate, the powers of regional Ombudsmen, and the plight of vulnerable groups including women

[282] Jordan, 'Membership Privileges?', 682–683; Jordan, 'Russia's Accession', 287–293.

[283] Jordan, 'Membership Privileges?', 682; D. Barry, 'Capital Punishment in Russia', in Feldbrugge and Simons (eds.), *Human Rights*, pp. 3–14; T. Abdel-Monem, 'The European Court of Human Rights: Chechnya's Last Chance?', *Vermont Law Review* **28** (2004), 237–297.

[284] *Isayeva, Yusupova and Bazayeva* v. *Russia* (2005) 41 EHRR 347.

and children.[285] Other commentators regard judicial problems, linked to difficulties with the effective institutionalization of the rule of law, as among the most potent structural impediments to the development of a proper culture of respect for human rights, while rule by presidential decree, authoritarianism, and the prospect of economic collapse also present considerable challenges for the future.[286]

CONCLUSION

Although made in relation to the European Union, Stone Sweet's conclusion is no less apt with respect to the Convention: 'We still desperately need comparative, contextually rich case studies that blend the lawyer's concern with doctrinal evolution, and the social scientist's concern with explanation, in a sustained way.'[287] There are two reasons why a much more comprehensive, systematic, and scientific attempt should be made to determine which Council of Europe states comply most, and which least, effectively with the Convention than has yet been attempted. First, it makes more sense, in spite of the political problems it is likely to cause, for the Council of Europe's scarce resources to be targeted upon low-compliance states than on all states equally. Second, in order to develop an appropriate pan-European policy to boost national levels of Convention compliance the factors most likely to produce them need to be identified. However, there is unfortunately as yet no objective, scientifically valid way of measuring the extent to which Convention rights are protected at the national level. But this does not, however, mean that guesswork is the only viable alternative.

285 A. Alvaro-Robles, *Report by Mr Alvaro Gil-Robles, Commissioner for Human Rights, on His Visits to the Russian Federation, 15 to 30 July 2004, 19 to 29 September 2004*, CommDH(2005)2 (Strasbourg: Council of Europe, Office of the Commissioner for Human Rights, 20 April 2005), para. 564.

286 K. Hendley, 'Rewriting the Rules of the Game in Russia: The Neglected Issue of the Demand for Law' in A. Brown (ed.), *Contemporary Russian Politics* (Oxford: Oxford University Press, 2001), pp. 131–138; Kahn, 'Russian Compliance', 642–643, 645–654; B. Bowring, 'Politics versus the Rule of Law in the Work of the Russian Constitutional Court' in Přibáň and Young (eds.), *Rule of Law*, pp. 257–277 at 277; B. Bowring, 'Politics, Rule of Law and Judiciary'; Brown, 'Political Culture', 24; Satter, *Darkness at Dawn*, pp. 249–256.

287 A. Stone Sweet, *The Judicial Construction of Europe* (Oxford: Oxford University Press, 2004), p. 241.

Plausible hypotheses, open to verification or falsification by much more systematic and comprehensive country-specific data, are clearly required. One of the main purposes of this chapter has been to attempt to provide some.

Although official national violation rates are not unproblematic surrogates for compliance, they nevertheless invite explanation. The available data suggest that the two most influential factors in producing low levels of Convention violation in western Europe are that the relevant standards are taken seriously by executive agencies and by domestic courts, and that effective domestic legal procedures – particularly, in some form, a right of individual constitutional complaint – are available for challenging violations of fundamental rights, whether these are directly referenced to the Convention itself or are found in a comparable domestic constitutional bill of rights. Contrary to the received wisdom among jurists, the fact that the Convention has a privileged formal status in national constitutional and legal systems is largely irrelevant, as is routine Convention-proofing of draft legislation. This enables some light to be shed on differential annual average rates of official violation between, on the one hand, Italy, Turkey, and France with the highest and on the other hand Denmark, Norway, and Ireland with the lowest, leaving aside the low-violation but very small or micro-states of Andorra, Cyprus, Liechtenstein, Luxembourg, Iceland, Malta, and San Marino. There are few surprises in finding Italy top of the league, since its judicial problems are legendary, nor in discovering which states are in the low violation group, since these all have good reputations as stable, rights-sensitive, democracies. The Turkish problem is best explained by a difficult transition from oriental despotism to modern European democracy, and, in particular, by the strongly secularist and unitary concept of the state expressed by successive constitutions. However, the fact that France is third in the 1999–2005 league table and second in the 1960–2000 one is much less expected. Since the seminal Declaration of the Rights of Man and the Citizen of 1789, France has not only had a series of rights-affirming liberal constitutions, French statesmen were among the most determined of those from the founding nations that the Council of Europe should have an effective, binding, judicial system for the protection of human rights accessible to individual applicants. France was also the birthplace of the post-war idea of European integration expressed in what has since become the European Union. There is no obvious answer to these paradoxes. But the lack of an individual constitutional complaints procedure, plus certain flaws in the attitude of the French courts to legally enforceable rights, appear to be most to blame.

As for the former communist block of central and eastern Europe, Convention compliance is even more difficult to assess because none of these states has belonged to the system for long enough for clear patterns to emerge. Although the Convention may have had some influence on the design of post-communist constitutions, the available evidence suggests that neither it nor the Council of Europe as such played a central role in the process of democratic transition, although the wider liberal democratic tradition did. However, both the broader liberal tradition – and the Convention in particular – could, and should, play a much more central role in the ongoing process of democratic consolidation. It is, therefore, too much to claim as Blackburn does that the European Court of Human Rights has been 'an architect of the fledgling democracies of Europe'.[288] But it is poised and well-equipped to become a very effective interior designer. However, it cannot fully realize this role unless it is taken more seriously by all national institutions, particularly national courts, a process which is at best uneven both in central and eastern Europe and also in the west. The available data also broadly tends to suggest a significant variation between, on the one hand, the Baltic and central European states (including Slovenia) – where human rights are increasingly well-protected – and, on the other, the former Soviet republics where a lot of progress still has to be made. In the Balkans between these two categories, Croatia and Macedonia appear to be doing better than Albania, Bosnia, and Herzegovina, and Serbia and Montenegro. It should come as no surprise that, in addition to some regional variations, broadly the same factors appear to produce good human rights records in the eastern half of Europe as in the west. The most significant of these include: a commitment to the European conception of democracy, human rights, the rule of law and the socially regulated market, shared by populace and political elites; the establishment of modern legal processes fully committed to the rule of law; a well-trained, independent, and rights-aware judiciary; and the lack of significant ethnic

[288] R. Blackburn, 'Current Developments, Assessment, and Prospects' in Blackburn and Polakiewicz (eds.), *Fundamental Rights*, pp. 77–100 at 84.

conflict or systematic official discrimination against minorities. Two particularly key factors, derived from these broader ones, appear to be: effective constitutional complaints mechanisms to enable applications about violations of Convention or constitutional rights to be litigated, including from interested third parties such as NGOs, with a wide discretion to reject minor complaints however well-founded; and a willingness by national executive institutions to abide by the decisions which emerge from such litigation. With Georgia and Ukraine more convincingly (though not yet entirely securely) on the road to liberal democracy as a result of their revolutions in 2003 and 2005, Russia is now the Council of Europe state which presents the greatest human rights challenges.

The material presented in this chapter also enables some hypotheses to be framed about how the various treaty compliance theories distinguished by Hathaway might explain differential patterns of human rights protection throughout Europe. 'Normative' models, particularly the 'fairness' version which maintains that states adhere to international human rights treaties when they regard them as legitimate and fair, offer the best explanation for the conduct of those low-violation western European states with a long indigenous constitutional rights tradition, as in the case of Ireland and the low, and Scandinavian, countries. And perhaps yet another version of this model could be distinguished, the 'mirror model', according to which low rates of Convention violation in such states are best explained by the fact that the Convention 'mirrors' the deepest values in national political and legal cultures. However, an 'institutionalist' version of the 'rational actor' model – which maintains that states comply with international treaties in order to cultivate a good reputation as a means to realize other longer-term goals – offers the best explanation for the behaviour of Turkey and European states which have made a more decisive break with a discredited anti-democratic recent past, such as Germany, Spain, the Czech Republic, Poland, Hungary, and the Baltic states. The long-term goal in each of these cases has been to secure the political, economic, strategic, security, and other benefits, of asserting a convincing European constitutional, political and economic identity, and of obtaining the benefits of full participation in European integration in both its strong (EU) and weak (Council of Europe) forms.

The next three chapters depart significantly from these themes in order to consider the processes by which applications are lodged with the European Court of Human Rights, how its judgments are reached and their execution supervised, and the degree to which the case law is adequate for the purpose of promoting the best future for the Convention system. However, Chapter 6 picks up the threads of this chapter again by discussing, in the light of the information presented here and in the remainder of this study, what more the Council of Europe might do, in particular by altering the institutional framework, to improve Convention compliance at the national level.

3

The Applications and Enforcement of Judgment Processes

INTRODUCTION

As already indicated in Chapter 1, given the effective demise of inter-state complaints, individual applications have become the life-blood of the Convention system. A separate process enables the Committee of Ministers of the Council of Europe to consider whether or not judgments in an applicant's favour are properly observed by the state concerned. The purpose of this chapter is to consider how both these processes operate, paying particular attention to the modifications contained in Protocol 14, which are likely to come into operation in late 2006 or early 2007. As already indicated, according to the President of the Court, Professor Luzius Wildhaber, although it constitutes 'a step in the right direction ... (e)ven with the new reform, the Court will continue to have an excessive workload'.[1] Assuming, as this study does, that this verdict is correct, two key questions now need to be addressed. The first, the subject of this chapter, is: what further changes are required within the existing institutional structure in order, simultaneously, to enable the Court's burgeoning case load to be dealt with more effectively, and for the Court to contribute more strategically to raising the level of Convention compliance throughout Europe? In seeking answers, relevant documentary sources have been supplemented by interviews with judges and officials in Strasbourg and with representatives of Amnesty International in London (hereafter the 'Strasbourg' and 'London' interviews respectively).[2] The second

[1] Interview with President Luzius Wildhaber, 'The reform is an absolute necessity', 21 April 2004, http://www.coe.int/t/e/com/files/interviews/20040421_interv_wildhabber (misspelling in original).

[2] Questionnaires were used in both the London and Strasbourg interviews as informal guides to the issues rather than as formal survey instruments. Since it was impossible to construct a 'representative sample', respondents were simply those who were available and willing to participate at the times concerned. Although conducted before the

question, which will be considered in Chapter 6, is what institutional innovations might also be required.

THE INDIVIDUAL APPLICATIONS PROCESS

Budget and Personnel

Of all the committees which contributed to the Protocol 14 debate, only the Evaluation Group considered resource issues in any depth.[3] The Court's budget derives from the Council of Europe's general budget, decided annually by the Committee of Ministers. This not only increased from €7 million in 1989 (including that attributed to the European Commission of Human Rights) to €41.7 million, in 2005, but has also accounted for a continuously increasing proportion of the Council of Europe's total budget, rising from 10 per cent in 1989 to 16.2 per cent in the draft budget for 2002. The budget for 2005 represents 'a growth of 4.8 per cent compared to 2004, and 64 per cent since the creation of the single Court on 1 November 1998'.[4] The bulk of the Court's funds are spent on staffing. Other costs include information technology, legal aid to applicants, and, occasionally, fact-finding missions to respondent states where particular applications require it. The proportion of the Council of Europe's staff employed by Convention institutions increased from 8.6 per cent in 1989 to 17 per cent in 2001 and the number of permanent officials at the Registry of the Court grew from 74 in 1989 to 185 in 1 February 2001, not including 95 temporary personnel and 15 trainees.[5] By the early 2000s 196 staff – including 62 permanent and 31 temporary lawyers – were assigned to case processing and were responsible for dealing

authoritative version of Protocol 14 was published, the Strasbourg interviews nevertheless considered most of the issues eventually incorporated, including the pros and cons of filtering panels which the CDDH did not endorse until its report of November 2003, Steering Committee on Human Rights (CDDH), *Guaranteeing the Long-Term Effectiveness of the European Court of Human Rights – Implementation of the Declaration Adopted by the Committee of Ministers at its 112th Session (14–15 May 2003): Interim Activity Report*, CDDH(2003)026 Addendum I Final, 26 November 2003 at paras. 12–19.

[3] *Report of the Evaluation Group to the Committee of Ministers on the European Court of Human Rights*, EG Court (2001)1, 27 September 2001 at paras. 17–21.

[4] *Ibid.*, paras. 16–17; http://press.coe.int/cp/2004/637a(2004).htm

[5] 'Report of Evaluation Group', para. 18.

with correspondence, examining applications and preparing paper work for the attention of judges. The remainder were engaged in managerial, administrative, translation, and support duties.[6] As of 1 January 2005, the Registry employed 458 people.[7] In his review of the Court's working methods, published in December 2005, Lord Woolf recommends that satellite offices of the Registry be established in states with high application rates and that, within the Registry at Strasbourg, several new units be created to deal with friendly settlements, compensation, the training of lawyers, and the backlog of applications.[8]

However, in spite of increases in recent years, the Court's staffing levels contrast unfavourably with those of comparable institutions, such as the Registry of the European Court of Justice at Luxembourg – which has 800 full-time staff – and the International Criminal Court for the former Yugoslavia which has 650 permanent employees.[9] Nevertheless, while a case can be made for increasing the Court's resources,[10] for two main reasons money alone cannot be relied upon to solve the current case management crisis. First, the sum required would be so great that member states would not be prepared to pay it and, secondly, there are in any case persuasive policy reasons for seeking to address the problem in other ways. For example, while doubling the number of judges on the Court would improve its case-processing capacity, it would become a much more unwieldy body, deprived of collegiality and at risk of producing an increasingly incoherent case law.[11]

[6] *Ibid.*, para. 55.

[7] European Court of Human Rights, 'Statistics – 2004', 2.

[8] The Right Honourable The Lord Woolf, *Review of the Working Methods of the European Court of Human Rights – December 2005* (Strasbourg: Council of Europe, 2005), pp. 68–69.

[9] A. Drzemczewski, 'The Internal Organization of the European Court of Human Rights: the Composition of Chambers and the Grand Chamber', *European Human Rights Law Review* (2000) 233 at 242.

[10] *(Updated) Joint Response to Proposals to Ensure the Future Effectiveness of the European Court of Human Rights*, signed by 114 NGOs, April 2004 at paras. 6, 15 and 37, claims that the budget for the European Court of Justice in Luxembourg is five times that of the European Court of Human Rights; M.-A. Beernaert, 'Protocol 14 and New Strasbourg Procedures: Towards Greater Efficiency? And At What Price?', *European Human Rights Law Review* **5** (2005), 544–557 at 555.

[11] P. Mahoney, 'New Challenges for the European Court of Human Rights Resulting from the Expanding Case Load and Membership', *Penn State International Law Review* **21** (2002), 101–114 at 106.

Judges

The forty-six judges of the European Court of Human Rights discharge case management and adjudicative responsibilities.[12] They must be persons of high moral character and either possess the qualifications required for 'appointment to high judicial office or be jurisconsults of recognized competence'.[13] During their tenure they sit on the Court in their individual capacities and are not permitted to engage in any activity incompatible with their independence, impartiality, or with the demands of their full-time office.[14] One judge is elected by majority vote of the Parliamentary Assembly of the Council of Europe from each list of three candidates nominated per member state. As a result of Protocol 14 each member state is now also required to compile a reserve list of ad hoc judges upon whose services the President can call in any case in which the judge elected in respect of the respondent state is unable to sit.[15] Hitherto ad hoc judges were nominated by respondent states after the proceedings in question had begun. While member states are encouraged 'to do everything possible to ensure that their lists contain both male and female candidates', Protocol 14 does not make this obligatory since, according to the Explanatory Report, a requirement to do so 'might have interfered with the primary consideration to be given to the merits of potential candidates'.[16]

Intending to promote judicial independence and impartiality, Protocol 14 also alters the term of judicial office from six to a maximum of nine years, prohibits re-election, requires retirement at seventy, and provides that judges shall hold office until replaced and that they shall not be dismissed except by decision that they have ceased to fulfil the required conditions taken by a two-thirds majority of the other judges on the Court.[17] The system whereby the tenure of large groups

[12] For a review of the judicial appointments process prior to Protocol 14, and for recommendations regarding the standardization of national nomination processes and the improvement of appointments procedures at Strasbourg, see A. Coomber, 'Judicial Independence: Law and Practice of Appointments to the European Court of Human Rights', *European Human Rights Law Review* (2003), 486–500.

[13] Art. 21(1).

[14] Art. 21(2) and (3).

[15] New Art. 26(4) (Protocol 14, Art. 6); *Protocol No. 14 to the Convention for the Protection of Human Rights and Fundamental Freedoms, Amending the Control System of the Convention, CETS No. 194, Explanatory Report as adopted by the Committee of Ministers at its 114th Session on 12 May 2004*, para. 64.

[16] 'Protocol No. 14 to Convention', para. 49.

[17] Art. 2 of Protocol 14 amending Art. 23 of the Convention.

of judges was renewed at three-year intervals, and where appointments could be made for the residue of a judicial term, has therefore been abolished.[18] Candidates for judicial office who would be over sixty-one years of age at the time of their appointment can, however, still be recommended, although member states are encouraged not to do so in the case of those who would reach the age of seventy before the expiry of half the nine-year term.[19] Member states concerned are also encouraged to submit their lists of three candidates at least six months before a particular judge is due to retire.[20] Judges currently serving their first term of office at the date Protocol 14 comes into effect, including those completing their predecessor's term of office, shall have their term extended to a total of nine years, while the other judges shall complete their term of office extended by two years.[21] The Council of Europe's Steering Committee for Human Rights, the 'CDDH', which was responsible for drafting Protocol 14, decided not to recommend that the Committee of Ministers be empowered to increase the number of judges on the Court at the request of the Court's Plenary Assembly.

Procedure

Broadly speaking there are three stages to the individual applications process: the lodging of files with the Registry, the decision regarding admissibility, and the resolution of applications ruled admissible. Cases can also be struck off the list. As already indicated in Chapter 1, since the Court judges some 94 per cent of admissible applications in the applicant's favour, from the applicant's point of view, the decision about admissibility is the critical stage in the process. New filtering arrangements, a new admissibility test in addition to those already available, and a new summary procedure for the resolution of 'manifestly well-founded' Convention violations are introduced to the applications process by Protocol 14.

[18] 'Protocol No. 14 to Convention', para. 51. Art. 22(2) of the Convention, which requires that the standard election procedure provided in Art. 22(1) shall apply to complete the Court in the event of the accession of new member states and in filling casual vacancies, has also been deleted because the standard election procedure now applies to every situation where there is a need to proceed to the election of a judge, 'Protocol No. 14 to Convention', para. 48.

[19] *Ibid.*, para. 53. [20] *Ibid.*, para. 54. [21] Article 21 of Protocol 14.

Lodging Applications with the Registry

In order to lodge their complaint applicants need to write an introductory letter to the Registry of the Court. The Registry's key functions are to manage applications including corresponding with applicants, to prepare cases for admissibility decisions by the Court, to explore the possibility of friendly settlement, and to schedule admissible applications for adjudication. Until 1 January 2002 a formal distinction was drawn between 'provisional' and 'registered' applications, the former referring to all applications the Registry received, and the latter referring to those which, following correspondence with applicants, were subsequently registered for an admissibility decision. However, from this date a different distinction has applied. All written contact between an applicant and the Registry generates a file. Those 'applications lodged with the Registry' are destroyed a year later if applicants have not within this time submitted a written application on the correct forms which require such things as personal particulars, identification of the respondent state, an outline of the grievance including an indication of which Convention rights have allegedly been violated, a statement concerning the object of the application (including any claim for compensation), that domestic remedies have been exhausted, the decisions of domestic courts, and that no more than six months have elapsed since the last decision on the matter by the domestic legal system.[22] Applications submitted on the proper application form are 'allocated to a decision body or judicial formation' to determine their admissibility. The CDDH decided against including a provision in Protocol 14 requiring applicants to be legally represented because it would restrict the right of individual petition. This is sensible because, while requiring applicants to be legally represented may offer the prospect of reducing the number of unmeritorious claims,[23] it would not relieve the Registry of the task of advising those applicants who were not legally represented to re-submit their complaint when they had consulted a lawyer. As indicated in Chapter 1, the annual number of registered applications increased from 1,013 in 1988 to 10,486 in 2000, a rise of 935 per cent.[24] Between 1999 and 2004 an

[22] Lord Woolf recommends adherence to more rigorous formalities about what constitutes an application, Woolf, 'Review', 21–23.

[23] Beernaert, 'Protocol 14', 556–557.

[24] 'Report of Evaluation Group', para. 25.

annual average of 33,583 applications were lodged with the Court, and 20,100 (60 per cent) were allocated to a decision body.[25]

Admissibility – Procedure

Under the pre-Protocol 14 arrangements, once an application had been registered Phase I, 'first examination', began. The management of registered applications was the responsibility of a Judge Rapporteur, appointed by the President of one of the four Sections of the Court, assisted by a case-processing lawyer.[26] The Judge Rapporteur examined and prepared the case, including requiring documents and further particulars from the parties, and channelled it for an admissibility decision – together with proposals about its disposal – either to one of twelve three-judge Committees, if it appeared to be clearly inadmissible, or to a Chamber of seven judges if its inadmissibility was not so clear. A Committee could, and can still,[27] by unanimous and final decision, declare an application inadmissible or strike it off the list, 'where such a decision can be taken without further examination',[28] a fate which, according to the pre-Protocol 14 figures, befell between 80 and 90 per cent of the 98 per cent or so of applications rejected as inadmissible or struck off each year.[29]

Cases which could not be settled unanimously were referred to a seven-judge Chamber at Phase II ('second examination') together with a report from the Judge Rapporteur summarizing the facts, indicating the issues raised, and making a proposal as to what should happen next – for example, a decision against admissibility or further correspondence with the parties. While some cases were declared

[25] ECtHR, 'Statistics – 2004', 3 and 4.

[26] For useful guides to the processing of individual applications see: 'Report of Evaluation Group', para. 30; Drzemczewski, 'Internal Organization'; A. Drzemczewski, 'The European Human Rights Convention: Protocol No. 11 – Entry into Force and First Year of Application', *Human Rights Law Journal* **21** (2000), 1–17; L. Clements, 'Striking the Right Balance: the New Rules of Procedure for the European Court of Human Rights', *European Human Rights Law Review* (1999) 266–272; A. Mowbray, 'The Composition and Operation of the New European Court of Human Rights', *Public Law* (1999), 219–231; P. Mahoney, 'Short Commentary on the Rules of Court: Some of the Main Points', *Human Rights Law Journal* **19** (1998) 267–269.

[27] Preserved by Art. 28(1)(a) and (2) (Protocol 14, Art. 8).

[28] Where, for example, the respondent state had shown that domestic remedies had not, in fact, been exhausted, 'Protocol No. 14 to Convention', para. 69.

[29] 'Report of Evaluation Group', para. 28; 'Protocol No. 14 to Convention', para. 7.

inadmissible at the outset, Chambers usually solicited observations from the respondent state, together with comments from the applicant, and could decide to hold a hearing on the merits simultaneously with the admissibility hearing in order to save time. If the application was ruled inadmissible there was no reason to deliver a judgment. But if, on the other hand, it was declared admissible the hearing on the merits could proceed immediately. Although admissibility decisions by Chambers were reasoned and made public, there was no right of appeal. Between 1999 and 2004 an annual average of 800 applications were declared admissible (2.4 per cent of applications lodged and 4 per cent of applications allocated to a decision body).[30] The depth of the crisis produced by the rising tide of applications is revealed by the growing backlog of cases, currently 82,100, but projected to rise to 250,000 by 2010.[31]

Various alternatives for filtering inadmissible applications out of the Court's docket were canvassed in the debate which led to Protocol 14, including the creation of a separate filtering institution staffed by a new corps of judicial, or quasi-judicial, officials and Registry staff.[32] While stopping short of providing such a body, the new protocol nevertheless creates single-judge 'formations', staffed by a judge and Registry rapporteur, for the preliminary processing of applications.[33] The judge has sole formal responsibility,[34] and can by final decision reject the application as inadmissible or strike it out of the list, where this can be done 'without further examination',[35] i.e. where its inadmissibility is 'manifest from the outset'.[36] Where this is not the case

[30] ECtHR, 'Statistics – 2004', 3, 4 and 6.

[31] Lord Woolf, 'Review', 4.

[32] This option was strongly favoured by the NGOs – '(Updated) Joint Response', para. 17 – by the Court itself – Steering Committee for Human Rights (CDDH), *Drafting Group on the Reinforcement of the Human Rights Protection Mechanism (CDDH-GDR) – Response of the European Court of Human Rights to the CDDH Interim Activity Report Prepared following the 46th Plenary Administrative Section* (CDDH-GDR(2004)001, 10 February 2004 at para. 7 – and by the former Registrar of the Court, Mr Paul Mahoney, writing in a personal capacity, P. Mahoney, 'An Insider's View of the Reform Debate', paper presented at the *Symposium on the Reform of the European Court of Human Rights*, Strasbourg, 17 November 2003 at 12–16; Mahoney, 'New Challenges', 108–109.

[33] New Art. 24(2) (Art. 4, Protocol 14), new Art. 26(1) (Art. 6, Protocol 14).

[34] 'Protocol No. 14 to Convention', para. 67.

[35] New Art. 27(1) and (2) (Art. 7, Protocol 14).

[36] 'Protocol No. 14 to Convention', para. 67.

the application must be forwarded to a three-judge committee or seven-judge Chamber.[37] Registry rapporteurs, with, in principle, some knowledge of the language and legal system of the respondent state, will assume the functions formerly discharged by Judge Rapporteur and case-processing lawyer.[38] Single judges cannot sit in cases where the member state in respect of which they have been elected is the respondent.[39] The main difference between the pre- and post-Protocol 14 arrangements, therefore, is that under Protocol 14 the preliminary decision about admissibility is now taken by single-judges and a Registry lawyer, rather than, as hitherto, by committees of three judges advised by a Judge Rapporteur and Registry lawyer. Apart from claiming that it will lead to 'a significant increase in the Court's filtering capacity', the Explanatory Report to Protocol 14 gives no indication of the productivity gains this is likely to produce.[40] In fact, as Amnesty International has pointed out, no official information has yet been provided to indicate how much time judges used to spend on committee work under the previous arrangements, and how much is, therefore, likely to be saved by entrusting these responsibilities to single judges.[41] Some respondents in the Strasbourg interviews cautioned against overestimation on the grounds that most judicial time committed to the pre-Protocol 14 admissibility process involved the activities of Judge Rapporteurs, a responsibility which is largely retained by judges in the new single-judge formations.[42]

Admissibility Criteria

Under the pre-Protocol 14 admissibility tests a registered application could be declared inadmissible on one or more of five largely

[37] New Art. 27(3) (Art. 7, Protocol 14). Neither Protocol 14 nor the Explanatory Report indicate when applications not declared inadmissible or struck off by single-judge formations should be referred to a committee, and when to a Chamber.

[38] 'Protocol No. 14 to Convention', paras. 58 and 62. The Explanatory Report also recommends seconding lawyers from member states to the Registry to work as rapporteurs for fixed periods, *ibid.*, para. 59.

[39] New Art. 26(3) (Art. 6 of Protocol 14).

[40] 'Protocol No. 14 to Convention', para. 62.

[41] *Amnesty International's Comments on the Interim Activity Report: Guaranteeing the Long-Term Effectiveness of the European Court of Human Rights*, AI Index: IOR 61/005/2004, February 2004, para. 46.

[42] See also Beernaert, 'Protocol 14', 549.

formal grounds – the complaint was anonymous,[43] it had not been pursued as far as possible in the legal system of the respondent state,[44] more than six months had elapsed since the final decision on the matter by the domestic legal system,[45] it was incompatible with the Convention,[46] or it was an abuse of process.[47] There were also three further 'substantive' grounds more directly linked to issues of policy or principle – the applicant was not a victim of a Convention violation,[48] the complaint was substantially the same as a matter already examined by the Court or another international process, or it was 'manifestly ill-founded'.

Protocol 14 retains all of these and adds a new ground of inadmissibility. The controversy surrounding this, the most contentious

[43] While Article 35(2) of the Convention treats anonymity as a ground of inadmissibility, anonymous applications are unlikely to be registered in the first place. But having identified themselves, applicants may request that their identities are not disclosed, Rules of Court, December 2005, Rule 47(3).

[44] The Court has held that this requirement should be applied 'with some degree of flexibility and without excessive formalism', *Cardot* v. *France* (1991) 13 EHRLR 853 at para. 34.

[45] The Court has discretion to be flexible about the six-month deadline, but, according to Simor and Emmerson, this is rarely exercised in the applicant's favour, J. Simor and B. Emmerson Q. C. (eds.), *Human Rights Practice* (London: Sweet & Maxwell, 2000), para. 20.031.

[46] An application may be 'incompatible' with the Convention in one of four ways: the right was not binding on the respondent state at the time of the events concerned (ratione temporis); the Convention did not apply to the place where the alleged events occurred (ratione loci); the complaint was against persons not bound by the Convention or over whom Convention institutions had no jurisdiction (ratione personae); and the complaint did not relate to a right provided by the Convention (ratione materiae). See Simor and Emmerson (eds.), *Human Rights Practice*, para. 20.034–20.038.

[47] By, for example, arising from misconduct such as forgery or misrepresentation, or uses offensive or provocative language, or is vexatious, *ibid.*, para. 20.040.

[48] Article 34 provides that the Court 'may receive applications from any person, non-governmental organization or group of individuals claiming to be the victim of a violation by one of the High Contracting Parties of the rights set forth in the Convention or the protocols thereto.' However, being a 'victim' does not necessarily mean having been directly harmed by a violation. The Court has held, for example, that laws which criminalize homosexual conduct between consenting adults in private, or which permit secret surveillance without adequate safeguards, violate the right to respect for the private lives of those concerned even though they might not have suffered personally as a result. See respectively, *Norris* v. *Ireland* (1991) 13 EHRR 186 at para. 31, *Klass* v. *Germany* (1980) 2 EHRR 214 at para. 33. Similarly exposure to a real risk of torture, inhuman and degrading treatment or punishment may, in itself, be a violation of Article 3, *Soering* v. *United Kingdom* (1989) 11 EHRR 439 at para. 111.

issue in the entire debate which divided even the Court itself, is considered more fully below.[49] The new Article 35(3)(b), one of several compromises considered by the CDDH,[50] which applies only to applications lodged after Protocol 14 comes into effect,[51] enables both single-judge 'formations' and committees to declare applications inadmissible if 'the applicant has not suffered a significant disadvantage, unless respect for human rights as defined in the Convention and the Protocols thereto requires an examination of the application on the merits and provided that no case may be rejected on this ground which has not been duly considered by a domestic tribunal'.[52] However, in order to allow time for an adequate case law to be developed, neither single-judge formations nor committees will be able to apply this new criterion until two years after the new protocol comes into effect.[53]

Since the Court does not keep statistics on the number of applications rejected under each head of inadmissibility it is impossible to determine which are the most critical. The victim test, although prima facie sensible as a limit upon merely speculative applications which could greatly compound the Court's workload problems, also prevents cases being brought by third parties, for example NGOs or National Human Rights Institutions, which might be more indicative of systemic compliance problems in member states than those brought by aggrieved victims or their next of kin acting on their own initiative. The 'substantially the same as' criterion refers to other applications by the same applicants on substantially the same facts, or applications by different applicants alleging the same violations.[54] While similar applications by different applicants can either be joined together or, if they have not been submitted simultaneously,

[49] CDDH, 'Response of ECtHR', paras. 18–24.

[50] See, e.g. the alternatives set out in CDDH, 'Interim Activity Report', November 2003, paras. 32–40.

[51] Art. 20(2), Protocol 14.

[52] New Art. 35(3)(b) (Art. 12, Protocol 14). The second clause is intentionally drawn from existing Art. 37(1)(c) where it fulfills a similar function in relation to striking out decisions, 'Protocol No. 14 to Convention', para. 81.

[53] Art. 20(2), Protocol 14; 'Protocol No. 14 to Convention', paras. 84 and 105.

[54] 'The Court shall not deal with any application submitted under Article 34 that is ... substantially the same as a matter that has already been examined by the Court or has already been submitted to another procedure of international investigation or settlement and contains no relevant new information', Art. 35(2)(b).

dealt with by summary procedure,[55] the use of the adjectives 'substantially' and 'relevant' make the exercise of some discretion inevitable. But the fact that 60 per cent of the Court's judgments concern 'repetitive' cases where the alleged violation has already been condemned in the respondent state, suggests this criterion has not been effectively applied.[56] The 'manifestly ill-founded' test is also arguably the most important criterion of admissibility of all because it permits the greatest discretion on the part of the Court. As one textbook puts it: 'In principle it applies to cases where the evidence submitted fails to substantiate the complaint, where the facts do not disclose an interference with a protected right, where the interference is plainly justified, or where the applicant has ceased to be a victim. In practice, however, the Court has used this ground of inadmissibility as a means of controlling its case load, and has often conducted a quite detailed examination of the merits of a complaint before declaring it to be "manifestly" ill-founded.'[57]

According to the Explanatory Report, the purpose of the new Article 35(3)(b) test is to provide the Court with an 'additional tool', necessary in order to give the Court 'some degree of flexibility', for filtering applications in order to allow more time for cases which warrant examination on the merits, either from the applicant's perspective, from that of the Convention, or with respect to the wider 'European public order'.[58] It admits that, as a result, some cases may now be ruled inadmissible which would not have been rejected before, and it anticipates that the main effect will be to promote the more rapid disposal of unmeritorious cases once the Court has established clearer interpretive guidelines. But the Explanatory Report does not repeat the estimate made by the CDDH in its report of April 2003 which claimed that only some 5 per cent of cases admissible under the pre-Protocol 14 criteria were likely to be affected by an earlier version of the new admissibility test, which differed only in the absence of the 'duly

55 P. Van Dijk and G. J. H. van Hoof, *Theory and Practice of the European Convention on Human Rights*, 3rd edn. (The Hague/London/Boston: Kluwer Law International), p. 115.

56 'Protocol No. 14 to Convention', para. 68.

57 Simor and Emmerson (eds.), *Human Rights Practice*, para. 20.039.

58 'Protocol No. 14 to Convention', paras. 77 and 78.

considered by a domestic tribunal' requirement.[59] Nor does it repeat the CDDH's earlier inexplicable conclusion that the new test would, nevertheless, 'turn out to be an indispensable tool to preserve the Convention system in the longer term'.[60] Opinion among respondents in the Strasbourg interviews was divided over the earlier version. While some thought it wrong in principle, others pointed out that, as considered below, the German Federal Constitutional Court also applies a 'significant disadvantage' criterion. It was generally agreed, however, that such a test would have little impact upon the Court's case management problems.

Admissibility and Resolution by Committees – the New Summary Procedure

A key issue in the pre-Protocol 14 debate concerned the problem of repetitive applications complaining of violations the Court has already condemned in the state concerned. It has been convincingly argued that such cases are essentially problems in the execution of judgments and should, therefore, be referred back to national authorities and to a special process of the Committee of Ministers.[61] However, the new Article 28(1)(b) introduced by Protocol 14 provides a new summary process enabling committees of three judges, by unanimous and final vote, to rule on all aspects (admissibility, merits, and just satisfaction) in a single judgment where 'the underlying question in the case, concerning the interpretation or the application of the Convention or the Protocols thereto, is already the subject of well-established case law of the Court'.[62] The Explanatory Report states that, while this is both 'simplified and accelerated', it 'preserves the adversarial character of

[59] Steering Committee for Human Rights (CDDH), *Guaranteeing the Long-Term Effectiveness of the Control System of the European Convention on Human Rights – Addendum to the Final Report Containing CDDH Proposals (Long Version)*, 9 April 2003, para. 17, p. 6. The Parliamentary Assembly claims it would 'exclude only 1.6 per cent of existing cases', Opinion No. 251 (2004), para. 11.

[60] CDDH, 'Guaranteeing Long-Term Effectiveness', April 2003, para. 18.

[61] Mahoney, 'New Challenges', 111–113.

[62] New Art. 28(1) and (2) (Art. 8, Protocol 14). The term 'manifestly well-founded' was used in earlier CDDH documents to describe such cases, see, for example, CDDH, 'Guaranteeing long-term effectiveness', April 2003, p. 17. But it does not appear in 'Protocol No. 14 to Convention'.

proceedings and the principle of judicial and collegiate decision-making on the merits'.[63] 'Well-established case law' will normally mean 'case law which has been consistently applied by a Chamber', but it might, exceptionally, refer to a single judgment, particularly if rendered by the Grand Chamber.[64] While the Explanatory Report indicates that this provision is targeted particularly on 'repetitive' applications, the operative criterion is not necessarily an adverse finding against the specific respondent state but a judgment against any state condemning the conduct in question.[65] Parties may dispute whether or not the relevant case law is, in fact, 'well established'.[66] It is also open to respondent states to contest resort to the procedure, for example when they consider that domestic remedies have not been exhausted or that the case at issue differs from those found in the well-established case law. But they cannot veto it.[67] This provision is similar to an amendment to Article 104(3) of the Rules of Procedure of the European Court of Justice introduced in July 2000 to enable the ECJ to dispose of references by order without giving judgment in three circumstances: (a) where the question referred is identical to a question on which the Court has already ruled; (b) where the answer may be clearly deduced from the existing case law; or (c) where the answer admits of no reasonable doubt. As Tridimas argues, although on its face Article 104(3) 'appears to be an uncontroversial house-keeping measure, conceivably, it has considerable potential to operate as a quasi-filtering mechanism since it enables the Court to decide which precedents to revisit.'[68]

Judges elected in respect of the respondent state are not entitled to sit on committees applying the new summary procedure ex officio, as they can when the Court is judging the merits. However, if the judge elected in respect of the respondent state is not a member of the committee, he or she may be invited, at any stage of the proceedings, to take the place of one of its members, having regard to all relevant factors including whether or not the respondent state has contested resort to the

[63] 'Protocol No. 14 to Convention', para. 69.

[64] *Ibid.*, para. 68. [65] *Ibid.*, paras. 40 and 68.

[66] *Ibid.*, para. 68. [67] *Ibid.*, para. 69.

[68] T. Tridimas, 'Knocking on Heaven's Door: Fragmentation, Efficiency and Defiance in the Preliminary Reference Procedure', *Common Market Law Review* **40** (2003), 9–50 at 18.

summary procedure.[69] NGOs have criticized this provision claiming that it raises 'serious issues about the appearance of independence of the Court and has no place in a human rights treaty'.[70] The Explanatory Report defends it on the grounds that expertise in the law of the respondent state may be useful, particularly on the question of the exhaustion of domestic remedies.[71] However, Amnesty International maintains that it is difficult to see how such expertise would be relevant since the expedited procedure would only apply to manifestly well-founded repetitive complaints.[72] Chambers can also settle cases which cannot be resolved by single-judge formations or committees, usually by jointly deciding admissibility and merits, although separate decisions will still be possible.[73] Under the new summary procedure provided by Article 28(1)(b), decisions and judgments are final and cannot, therefore, be referred to the Grand Chamber.[74]

In April 2003 the CDDH predicted that the new summary procedure would affect more than 50 per cent of cases currently entrusted to Chambers[75] and would represent 'a significant increase' in the Court's decision-making capacity, permitting further time for the adjudication of more important cases.[76] It also admitted that, while 'significant productivity gains will certainly be achieved in this way, they will probably not be sufficient, especially in the longer term'.[77] However, this assessment was made before the new filtering process was devised. By contrast, the Explanatory Report makes the more modest claim that the new summary procedure 'will increase substantially the Court's decision-making capacity and effectiveness, since many cases can be decided by three judges, instead of the seven currently required when judgments or decisions are given by a Chamber'.[78] Respondents in the Strasbourg interviews generally welcomed the new summary procedure

[69] New Art. 28(3) (Art. 8, Protocol 14).
[70] '(Updated) Joint Response', para. 23.
[71] 'Protocol No. 14 to Convention', para. 71.
[72] Amnesty International, 'Comments', para. 23.
[73] New Art. 29(1) (Art. 9, Protocol 14). As before, decisions on admissibility and merits in inter-state cases will remain separate in all but exceptional cases, new Art. 29(2) (Art. 9, Protocol 14).
[74] New Art. 28(2) (Art. 8, Protocol 14).
[75] CDDH, 'Guaranteeing Long-Term Effectiveness', April 2003, p. 20.
[76] *Ibid.*, p. 18. [77] *Ibid.*, p. 4, para. 10.
[78] *Ibid.*, para. 70.

and thought it was likely to make a substantial contribution to alleviating the Court's workload.

Striking Off

The Court may strike an application off its list where the applicant does not intend to pursue it, where the matter has been resolved, for example, by friendly settlement between the parties, or where for any other reason it considers it no longer justified to continue to examine it. But it must continue to consider any application 'if respect for human rights as defined in the Convention and the protocols thereto so requires',[79] an indication that individual applications may have importance above and beyond the vindication of the Convention rights of the particular alleged victim.[80] Only very small numbers of applications – for example fifteen in 2000 – are struck off after the admissibility decision.[81]

Resolution by Friendly Settlement or by Judgment of a Chamber

Between 1984 and 2004 there was an annual average of 55 friendly settlements, although the figure peaked at 230 in 2000 and remained between 125 and 155 until 2004 when it dropped to 68.[82] Under the pre-Protocol 14 process, once an application had been ruled admissible, the Registry, acting on instructions from the Chamber or its President at Phase III ('post-admissibility'), contacted the parties in an attempt to arrive at a friendly settlement based on respect for Convention rights. However, Protocol 14 empowers the Court to place itself at the disposal of the parties to secure a friendly settlement at any stage in the proceedings, and enables the Committee of Ministers to supervise the execution of the Court's judgments endorsing such outcomes.[83] The Explanatory Report states that friendly settlement may prove 'particularly useful in repetitive cases, and other cases where questions of principle or changes in domestic law are not involved'.[84] But this conclusion is open to dispute since, by virtue of their individualistic

[79] Art. 37(1).
[80] Simor and Emmerson (eds.), *Human Rights Practice*, para. 20.045.
[81] 'Report of Evaluation Group', para. 28.
[82] See Figure 2, Chapter 1.
[83] New Art. 39(1) and (4); 'Protocol No. 14 to Convention', para. 94.
[84] 'Protocol No. 14 to Convention', para. 93.

nature, friendly settlements are unlikely to resolve the underlying structural problem which has produced the sequence of repetitive applications.

Between 1999 and 2004, an annual average of 733 cases were disposed of by final judgment (including friendly settlement), 2.2 per cent of the annual average number of cases lodged with the Registry (33,583) and 3.6 per cent of the cases allocated for a decision (20,100).[85] There was an annual average of 153 friendly settlements over this period resulting in an annual average of 580 other cases judged by the Court. However, as Chapter 1 discussed, judgments on the merits cannot easily be extracted from this figure. But, assuming that the vast majority fell into this category, somewhere between 1 and 2 per cent of cases lodged with the Registry, and 2 to 3 per cent of cases allocated for a decision, eventually receive judgement on the merits.

The Committee of Ministers is also now permitted, by unanimous decision at the request of the plenary Court and for a fixed period, to reduce the number of judges on all Chambers to five.[86] The judge from the respondent state sits in Chamber (and Grand Chamber) hearings ex officio, ostensibly, as already indicated, to ensure a proper understanding of the legal system in question, but may be replaced for logistical reasons by a judge from the respondent state's reserve list. However, no two judges elected in respect of the same member state may sit in the same committee, Chamber, or Grand Chamber.[87] The Rules of Court require the composition of Chambers to 'be geographically and gender balanced' and to 'reflect the different legal systems among the Contracting Parties', requirements which generally seem to be observed.[88] At any stage of the proceedings a Chamber can also, subject to the consent of the parties, relinquish jurisdiction in favour of a Grand Chamber if the case raises 'a serious question affecting the interpretation of the Convention or the protocols thereto, or where the resolution of a question before the Chamber might have a result inconsistent with a judgment previously delivered by the Court . . .'.[89]

[85] ECtHR, 'Statistics – 2004', 3, 4 and 6.
[86] New Art. 26(2) replacing former Art. 27 of the Convention (Art. 6, Protocol 14).
[87] New Art. 26(4).
[88] Rules of Court, Rule 25 (2); Drzemczewski, 'Internal Organization', 237.
[89] Art. 30.

Following a decision in favour of admissibility the Chamber may invite the parties to submit further evidence and written observations, including any claim for 'just satisfaction', and to attend a hearing.[90] In the interests of the proper administration of justice, the President of the Chamber may invite or grant leave to any member state not a party to the proceedings – or any other person concerned apart from the applicant – to submit written comments and, in exceptional cases, to make representations.[91] At the request of the European Commissioner for Human Rights and the Parliamentary Assembly, Protocol 14 gives the Commissioner the right to intervene as third party in all cases brought before a Chamber or the Grand Chamber by making written submissions or by taking part in hearings.[92] The Explanatory Report states that the Commissioner's experience 'may help enlighten the Court on certain questions, particularly in cases which highlight structural or systemic weaknesses' in the respondent state or in other member states.[93]

The judgment of the Court is drafted by the Judge Rapporteur, assisted by the judge elected in respect of the respondent state, or in some cases by a drafting committee, and put to a vote.[94] Judgments, which are usually concise, contain summaries of the assumed facts, the history of the dispute including a review of domestic law, the arguments presented by both parties, relevant provisions of the Convention, and short dissenting opinions, if any. Because of the wide-ranging nature of the subject matter of disputes under many Convention provisions, and the lack of a formal doctrine of precedent, few areas of Convention jurisprudence, with the possible exception of the case law under Article 6, resemble the kind of ordered rule system familiar in domestic law. Instead most amount to little more than a series of 'decisions on the facts' where the precise circumstances of the dispute have been held to constitute, or not to constitute, a violation.[95]

[90] Rules of Court, Rules 59 and 60.

[91] Art. 36. A member state whose national is an applicant in the case is entitled to intervene as of right. 'Protocol No. 14 to Convention', para. 19, recommends more frequent third party intervention in cases raising issues of general importance.

[92] New Art. 36(3), Art. 13, Protocol 14.

[93] 'Protocol No. 14 to Convention', para. 87. The Explanatory Report states that it was decided not to provide for third party intervention in the new summary committee procedure under Art. 28(1)(b) given the straightforward nature of these cases, *ibid.*, para. 89.

[94] 'Report of Evaluation Group', para 30(d).

[95] CDDH, 'Guaranteeing Long-Term Effectiveness', April 2003, p. 34, para. 2(vi).

A Chamber's majority verdict usually disposes of the matter. However, 'exceptional cases'[96] may be referred by one or more of the parties to a Grand Chamber of seventeen judges within three months of the decision of a Chamber.[97] Technically, a referral to the Grand Chamber is not an 'appeal' but a 're-hearing' and is conditional upon the approval of the Grand Chamber's five-judge 'admissibility' panel which considers references by the parties from Chambers, and is obliged to accede to them where the case in question raises 'a serious question affecting the interpretation or application of the Convention or the protocols thereto, or a serious issue of general importance'.[98] Chamber judgments become final when the parties declare that they will not request a reference to a Grand Chamber, three months after the date of judgment if a reference to a Grand Chamber has not been made, or where a reference to a Grand Chamber has been made but the five-judge panel has rejected it.[99]

According to Article 41 of the Convention, the Court should grant just satisfaction 'if necessary'. The award of compensation is, therefore, discretionary and not automatic, with the result that many successful applicants have not received any compensation at all, and the amounts have tended to be smaller than those awarded by British courts.[100] The Court's judgments also give little guidance as to how this discretion is exercised. Relevant factors appear to include the extent to which applicants' Convention rights have been breached and their conduct, including any criminal offences they may have committed. Awards can be made to the applicant, or to his or her heirs or estate, for pecuniary damage – such as loss of past and future earnings, fines, or a reduction in the value of property – and to the applicant personally for non-pecuniary damage – such as anxiety, distress, loss of employment prospects, a sense of injustice, deterioration of a way of life, and for

[96] Art. 43 (1). The Explanatory Report to Protocol 11, para. 100, indicates that 'exceptional cases' are those which raise a 'question of importance not yet decided by the Court, ... or when the decision is of importance for future cases and for the development of the Court's case law,' Drzemczewski, 'ECHR Protocol No. 11', 3.

[97] The process of empanelling sittings of the Grand Chamber is set out by Drzemczewski, 'Internal Organization', 241–2.

[98] Art. 43(2). [99] Art. 44(2).

[100] F. Klug (with R. Singh and M. Hunt), *Rights Brought Home: A Briefing on the Human Rights Bill*, Human Rights Incorporation Project, School of Law, King's College London, 1998, p. 4.

other varieties of less tangible harm and suffering. Aggravated or exemplary damages are not awarded.[101]

Traditionally, judgments by the Court are declaratory only. The reluctance to be more prescriptive stemmed from the principles of subsidiarity and 'limited expertise', which were taken to mean that the Court was less well-placed, constitutionally and professionally, than national authorities to determine what precisely should be done to correct the violation.[102] This means that, where the respondent state is found in breach of the Convention, the Court will generally refrain from specifying what action needs to be taken to restore the applicant to the position they would have been in had their rights not been violated (the principle of restitutio in integrum). However, in a number of recent cases the Court has been more willing to indicate the kind of remedial action required, particularly those involving claims for the restitution of property expropriated by the state, unlawful detention, the effectiveness of criminal investigations, the sustainability of convictions where the trial has been unfair, or where the complaint is the result of systemic compliance problems in the state concerned.[103]

SUPERVISING EXECUTION OF JUDGMENTS

As the April 2003 Report of the CDDH states: 'The acid test of any judicial system is how promptly and effectively judgments are implemented'.[104] And as President Wildhaber notes, the Court's credibility is undermined if its repeated findings of violation have no obvious effect in the state concerned.[105] And yet this is the Achilles heel of the entire Convention system because there is very little the Council of Europe can do with a state persistently in violation, short of suspending its voting rights on the Committee of Ministers or expelling it from the Council altogether, each of which is likely in all but the most

[101] Simor and Emmerson (eds.), *Human Rights Practice*, paras. 19.063–19.075.

[102] E. Lambert-Abdelgawad, *The Execution of Judgments of the European Court of Human Rights* (Strasbourg: Council of Europe Publishing, Human Rights Files No. 19, 2002), p. 7.

[103] P. Leach, 'Beyond the Bug River – A New Dawn for Redress Before the European Court of Human Rights', *European Human Rights Law Review* (2005), 148–164.

[104] CDDH, 'Guaranteeing Long-Term Effectiveness', April 2003, p. 34, para. 1.

[105] L. Wildhaber, 'The Role of the European Court of Human Rights: An Evaluation', *Mediterranean Journal of Human Rights*, **8** (2004) 9–32 at 27.

extreme circumstances to prove counterproductive.[106] Traditionally, respondent states were left to choose the means to fulfil the obligation under Article 46(1) to 'abide by the final judgment of the Court in any case to which they are parties'.[107] Therefore, once the Court's judgment was delivered, supervision of its execution passed entirely to the Committee of Ministers which negotiated what this might entail with respondent states which, therefore, participated in supervising the enforcement of judgments against themselves. Although this process remains essentially one of political negotiation, the 'traditional model', has, however, recently undergone some modification.

The 'Traditional Model'

States have three distinct obligations following an adverse judgment from the Court: to put an end to the violation, to avoid repeating it, and to make reparation to the affected parties.[108] Judgments, including those involving friendly settlement, are referred to the Committee by the Secretariat of the Human Rights Directorate (one of six Directorates General of the Secretariat of the Council of Europe) as soon as they are received and are entered on the agendas of special human rights meetings of the Committee, which the Directorate also drafts and makes public. The Committee of Ministers usually meets only twice a year at ministerial level and for several days each month at the level of Deputies (the Permanent Representatives of Member States of the Council of Europe). Virtually all the Committee of Ministers' responsibilities with respect to the supervision of the execution of judgments are discharged by Deputies and the ministers themselves are likely to intervene only in particularly sensitive inter-state cases.[109] While the Committee of Ministers' responsibility for supervising the judgments of the Court is found in Article 46(2) of the Convention, the procedure is contained

[106] 'Protocol No. 14 to Convention', para. 100.

[107] Lambert-Abdelgawad, *Execution of Judgments*, pp. 6–7.

[108] *Ibid.*, p. 10.

[109] Y. S. Klerk, 'Supervision of the execution of the judgments of the European Court of Human Rights – The Committee of Ministers' role under Article 54 of the European Convention on Human Rights', *Netherlands International Law Review* **45** (1998), 65–86 at 67.

in Rules adopted by the Committee itself.[110] At its human rights meetings the Committee first invites the respondent state to provide it with information about the remedial measures taken to ensure compliance.[111] Applicants are not represented at these meetings, but are entitled to communicate with the Committee about the implementation of individual measures, including the payment of just satisfaction.[112]

Although, as indicated above, the award of compensation by the Court is discretionary, the Committee of Ministers has recommended that states should restore successful applicants, as far as possible, to the position they would have been in had the violation not occurred.[113] However, notwithstanding the developments noted in the previous section, the re-opening of domestic legal proceedings is regarded as 'exceptional',[114] possibly in order to avoid harming third parties.[115] By December 2000 domestic proceedings had been re-opened in fewer than fifteen cases, half of which were criminal, and in some of these the original penalty was confirmed.[116] Lambert-Abdelgawad concludes that the system for the adoption of individual non-pecuniary measures is 'rather ineffective'.[117] 'General measures', on the other hand, may range from changes to administrative practice, for example in prison regimes or in judicial organization, or alterations to domestic case law brought about by a refusal of domestic courts to apply the offending legal provisions or re-interpreting them in a more

[110] These were introduced first in 1976, and have been periodically up-dated since, A. Tomkins, 'The Committee of Ministers: Its Roles under the European Convention on Human Rights', *European Human Rights Law Review* (1995), 49–62 at 58. The current version is *Rules adopted by the Committee of Ministers for the application of Article 46, paragraph 2, of the European Convention on Human Rights* (text approved by the Committee of Ministers on 10 January 2001 at the 736th meeting of the Ministers' Deputies).

[111] *Ibid.*, Rule 3. [112] *Ibid.*, Rule 6(a).

[113] *Recommendation No. R (2000) of the Committee of Ministers to Member States on the Re-examination or Re-opening of Certain Cases at Domestic Level Following Judgments of the European Court of Human Rights*, adopted at the 694th meeting of the Ministers' Deputies on 19 January 2000, Lambert-Abdelgawad, *Execution of Judgments*, Appendix II.

[114] 'Recommendation No. R (2000)', Preamble.

[115] Lambert-Abdelgawad, *Execution of Judgments*, p. 15. Others, such as the Parliamentary Assembly, have argued that the re-opening of domestic proceedings should be more commonplace, Parliamentary Assembly of the Council of Europe, 'Execution of judgments of the European Court of Human Rights', Resolution 1226 (2000) adopted on 28 September 2000, para. 10.iii.

[116] Lambert-Abdelgawad, *Execution of Judgments*, pp. 16–17.

[117] *Ibid.*, p. 20.

Convention-compliant manner.[118] However, Lambert-Abdelgawad's conclusion that, as 'a general observation, the European system is more effective in terms of general measures than in terms of individual reparation, with the exception of just satisfaction, ordered by the Court',[119] is difficult to square with the fact that 60 per cent of the Court's judgments concern violations it has already condemned in the respondent state.[120] This may be because general measures will usually involve the issuing of new regulations, the passage of fresh legislation, or even constitutional change, which may require endorsement by national referendum. According to the CDDH's April 2003 report, correcting systemic compliance problems may also be adversely affected by eight other difficulties: political problems, the daunting scale of the reforms required, legislative procedures, budgetary issues, public opinion, casuistic or unclear judgments of the Court, the possible impact of compliance on obligations deriving from other institutions, and bureaucratic inertia.[121]

Cases are listed for consideration at six-monthly intervals until the Committee of Ministers is satisfied that the violation has been properly addressed. The Committee requires respondent states to provide evidence that it has adopted all general measures necessary to avoid further violations of the kind in question and the Directorate of Human Rights has the unenviable task of pointing out shortcomings in their responses to the Committee. But what the Committee regards as sufficient evidence that the violation has been remedied, varies from case to case with little apparent rationale. For example, sometimes the following have been accepted: an undertaking by the respondent state that the offending practice will not happen again; the fact that the government has brought the Court's judgment to the attention of domestic public authorities leaving them to decide what to do about it; or the laying of a bill before the national legislature aimed at correcting the source of the violation.[122] However, on other occasions the Committee has regarded draft legislation as merely a step in the right direction and has awaited enactment itself before accepting that the Court's judgment has been fully executed.[123] In spite of the fact

[118] *Ibid.*, pp. 21–22. [119] *Ibid.*, p. 30.
[120] 'Protocol No. 14 to Convention', para. 68.
[121] CDDH, 'Guaranteeing Long-Term Effectiveness', p. 34, para. 2.
[122] Tomkins, 'Committee of Ministers', 59–60; Klerk, 'Supervision of Execution', 77–78.
[123] Klerk, 'Supervision of Execution', 74–75.

that the Committee may prefer a legislative solution, it will usually settle for a judicial one providing it considers this an appropriate response to the violation.[124] In accordance with Article 21 of the Statute of the Council of Europe, the Committee's deliberations remain secret. While awaiting final execution of judgments, the Committee of Ministers can issue interim resolutions which may simply note that execution has not yet occurred, report progress and encourage completion, or threaten the respondent state with more serious measures if full compliance is not forthcoming. Commentators disagree over whether interim measures delay or promote prompt execution of judgment. Tomkins argues that they tend to insulate respondent states from repeated embarrassment in the Committee of Ministers stemming from slow progress in complying.[125] Klerk, on the other hand, regards them as indicators that the Committee of Ministers is not going to be easily satisfied with an incomplete response.[126] When it is satisfied that any compensation has been paid, and that any other necessary measures have been introduced, the Committee of Ministers publicly certifies that its responsibilities under Article 46(2) have been exercised.[127] This can take years, for example, over eight-and-a-half in the notoriously protracted case of *Marcks* v. *Belgium*.[128] The Court's work load problems are mirrored in the enforcement process. Cases raising similar problems are examined by the Committee of Ministers en bloc, with the number considered at each meeting increasing, from a mere 24 in February 1992, to 2,300 in October 2001.[129]

Protocol 14 and Other Recent Modifications

In recent years the traditional model has changed in three respects, with Protocol 14 altering it in two further ways. First, as already indicated, since the mid-1990s, notwithstanding the principle of subsidiarity and doubts about its country-specific expertise, the Court has become increasingly willing to identify the specific structural shortcomings in domestic law which need to be changed in order to ensure compliance

[124] Lambert-Abdelgawad, *Execution of Judgments*, p. 35.
[125] Tomkins, 'Committee of Ministers', 60–61.
[126] Klerk, 'Supervision of Execution', 76.
[127] 'Committee of Ministers' Rules', Rule 8.
[128] Tomkins, 'Committee of Ministers', 61.
[129] 'Report of Evaluation Group', para. 34.

and to avoid repetitive applications.[130] The case of *Broniowski* v. *Poland* has attracted particular interest.[131] The Court held that expropriation by the government, of property belonging to the applicant east of the Bug River which Poland ceded to the Soviet Union after the Second World War, constituted a violation of Article 1 of Protocol No. 1 because inadequate compensation had been paid. Although similar verdicts have been reached in a number of other expropriation cases over the years, in *Broniowski* the Court expressly stated that the violation of the applicant's right 'originated in a widespread problem which resulted from a malfunctioning of Polish legislation and administrative practice and which has affected and remains capable of affecting a large number of persons'.[132] It therefore required Poland to adopt appropriate measures to secure an adequate right of compensation or redress, not just for this particular applicant, but for all similar claimants.[133]

There are three particular advantages to the Court being more specific about the kind of systemic action required by national authorities: compliance with the judgment is less open to political negotiation in the Committee of Ministers, it is easier to monitor objectively both by the Committee and by other bodies such as NGOs and other domestic human rights agencies, and a failure by relevant domestic public authorities to comply effectively is, in principle, easier to enforce by both the original litigant, and others, through the national legal process as an authoritatively confirmed Convention violation. The CDDH suggested, in its April 2003 report, that in order to assist a respondent state to identify what needs to be done to avoid repetitive applications, the Committee of Ministers should invite the Court to identify in its judgment as a matter of routine what it considers to be an underlying

130 Lambert-Abdelgawad, *Execution of Judgments*, pp. 26–28. This has been encouraged by the Parliamentary Assembly, Resolution 1226, paras. 11.B.ii and 12.i.e and by former Judge Martens, S. F. Martens, 'Individual Complaints under Article 53 of the European Convention on Human Rights' in R. Lawson and M. de Bois (eds.), *The Dynamics of the Protection of Human Rights in Europe: Essays in Honour of Henry G. Schermers*, Vol. **III** (Dordrecht: Martinus Nijhoff, 1994), p. 253 at 271–273. See also G. Ress, 'The Effect of Decisions and Judgments of the European Court of Human Rights in the Domestic Legal Order', *Texas International Law Journal* **40** (2005), 359–382 at 372–373.

131 R. Harmsen, 'The European Court of Human Rights as a "Constitutional Court": Definitional Debates and the Dynamics of Reform', draft contribution to collection of essays kindly supplied by author; Leach, 'Beyond Bug River'; Woolf, 'Review', 39–40.

132 (2005) 40 EHRR 495 at para. 189.

133 *Ibid.*, at para. 200.

structural or systemic problem and its source.[134] It also proposed that judgments indicating a structural problem should be notified not only to the respondent state but also to the Parliamentary Assembly, the Secretary General of the Council of Europe, and the European Commissioner for Human Rights.[135] The report also suggests that measures which might alleviate a systemic problem could be discussed in, for example, the Court's annual activity report.[136] But it was decided instead of including these proposals in Protocol 14 that the Committee of Ministers should make appropriate, though non-binding, recommendations.[137] Reports from the European Fair Trials Commission and National Human Rights Institutions, as proposed in Chapter 6, could also significantly add to the independent, country-specific expertise upon which the Court could draw in delivering more customised judgments.

The second change to the traditional model is the emergence of a doctrine that a violation of Article 6(1) in respect of undue length of proceedings entails a failure to provide an effective remedy, a breach of Article 13.[138] As Harmsen points out, this may mean that Article 13, 'long confined to the relative margins of Strasbourg jurisprudence' is 'set to assume a more prominent place as an embodiment of a wider principle of subsidiarity'. Although this shifts attention to the issue of national Convention compliance, Harmsen maintains the effects could be counterproductive and may put further strain on the Court's already overburdened docket.[139]

The third change to the traditional model is the increasing interest, particularly since the mid-1990s, the Parliamentary Assembly has shown in the supervision of the execution of judgments. This has taken several forms. In 1993 the Parliamentary Assembly's Committee for Legal Matters and Human Rights was instructed to report to the Assembly 'when problems arise on the situation of human rights in member States including their compliance with judgments of the European Court of

[134] CDDH, 'Guaranteeing Long-Term Effectiveness', April 2003, pp. 35–36.
[135] *Ibid.*, pp. 43–44. [136] *Ibid.*, p. 36.
[137] CDDH, 'Guaranteeing Long-Term Effectiveness', November 2003, paras. 8 and 20 and Appendix IV. Recommendations of the Committee of Ministers on the verification of the compatibility of draft laws, existing laws and administrative practice with the standards laid down in the European Convention on Human Rights (Rec(2004)5), and on the improvement of domestic remedies (Rec(2004)6), adopted at its 114th session on 12 May 2004.
[138] *Kudła* v. *Poland* (2002) 35 EHRR 198.
[139] Harmsen, 'ECtHR as Constitutional Court', 16–17.

Human Rights'.[140] Members of the Assembly may also ask oral questions of the President of the Ministers' Deputies, or submit written questions to the Committee of Ministers inquiring about the failure to execute certain judgments, which the Committee is required to answer in writing. The agenda of one of the Assembly's four annual sessions now includes an item about the execution of judgments. Following discussion, resolutions or recommendations are adopted and the national delegations of specific states may be contacted in writing to request that they urge their governments to execute judgments more promptly and comprehensively. In certain cases of particular concern to the Assembly, the Minister of Justice of the state in question may be invited to the Assembly to offer an explanation. The regular formal consultation which takes place between the Group of Rapporteurs of the meetings of the Committee of Ministers on Human Rights, and the Assembly's Committee on Legal Affairs and Human Rights, also enables national delegations to question their own governments. As Lambert-Abdelgawad puts it: 'The significance of the involvement of the Parliamentary Assembly lies in particular in the public nature of the denunciation of recalcitrant states', but 'it is too early to evaluate the true effectiveness of such measures . . .'[141]

The Protocol 14 debate was peppered with bland, but worthy injunctions to states about taking their responsibilities more seriously and proposals to strengthen the relevant bureaucratic enforcement processes. Although various modifications to the supervision process were canvassed, little of significance emerged. In contrast with the debate which preceded Protocol 11, it was not officially proposed that responsibility for supervising the execution of judgments should be transferred from the Committee of Ministers to the Court.[142] The CDDH concluded that, since it generally works well, the supervision process does not need to be replaced but merely improved, both to assist states with genuine compliance problems and to provide sanctions for the rare occasions when there is a wilful refusal to remedy a breach.[143] The most tangible, though nonetheless relatively marginal, modifications introduced by Protocol 14 concern the involvement of the Court in the supervision process through, what may be called (although neither

[140] Order No. 485 (1993) of the Parliamentary Assembly of the Council of Europe.

[141] Lambert-Abdelgawad, *Execution of Judgments*, p. 42.

[142] A. Lester, 'Merger of the European Commission and the European Court of Human Rights from the Perspective of Applicants and their Legal Representatives', *Human Rights Law Journal* **8** (1987), 34–41 at 39–41.

[143] 'Protocol No. 14 to Convention', para. 17.

of these terms is used in the Explanatory Report), 'infringement' and 'interpretation' proceedings, activated by a two-thirds majority vote of the Committee of Ministers. Where the supervision of the execution of a judgment of the Court is hindered by problems in determining what it means, the Court may be called upon to provide further clarification ('interpretation' proceedings).[144] But, as the Explanatory Report states, such difficulties are only encountered 'sometimes'.[145] Under the new 'infringement proceedings' the Grand Chamber may be required to determine, by further judgment, whether or not the respondent state has complied with the original judgment.[146] Under these arrangements, which the Explanatory Report anticipates will also only be invoked in 'exceptional circumstances', there will be no prospect of re-opening the original verdict nor of financial penalties.[147] Without offering any convincing reasons the Explanatory Report states: 'It is felt that the political pressure exerted by proceedings for non-compliance in the Grand Chamber and by the latter's judgment should suffice to secure execution of the Court's initial judgment by the State concerned', and that the 'procedure's mere existence, and the threat of using it, should act as an effective new incentive to execute the Court's judgments.'[148] But, if the compliance problem derives from one, or more, of the genuine difficulties highlighted by the CDDH and noted above, rather than from wilful obstruction, it is difficult to see how a further judgment will contribute to its resolution. While NGOs support infringement proceedings,[149] respondents in the Strasbourg interviews were generally opposed, as is the Court itself on account of a number of procedural difficulties – including determining what procedural rights the respondent state should have and who would represent the Committee of Ministers – and the blurring of the distinction between judicial and political decisions in the Convention process which such proceedings are deemed to represent.[150]

The Explanatory Report to Protocol 14 also recommends strengthening the department for the execution of judgments of the

[144] New Art. 46(3) (Art. 16, Protocol 14). [145] 'Protocol No. 14 to Convention', para. 96.

[146] New Art. 31(2)(b) (Art. 10, Protocol 14); New Art. 46(4) (Art. 16, Protocol 14). For an earlier debate on infringement proceedings see S. K. Martens, 'Commentary', in M. K. Bulterman and M. Kuijer, *Compliance With Judgments of International Courts: Proceedings of the Symposium Organized in Honour of Professor Henry G. Schermers by Mordenate College and the Department of International Public Law of Leiden University* (The Hague/Boston/London: Martinus Nijhoff, 1996).

[147] 'Protocol No. 14 to Convention', paras. 99 and 100. [148] *Ibid.*

[149] '(Updated) Joint Response', para. 6. [150] CDDH, 'Response of ECtHR', paras. 27–31.

General Secretariat of the Council of Europe, that optimum use be made of other existing Council of Europe institutions, mechanisms, and activities to promote effective execution, and that the Committee of Ministers should adopt a special procedure to give priority to the rapid execution of judgments revealing structural problems capable of generating a significant number of repetitive applications.[151] The CDDH also wisely decided against recommending that Protocol 14 include a provision imposing financial penalties on states for failure to comply with the Court's judgments, because this would require the introduction of other sanctions to enforce payment, raising similar problems to those fining was intended to solve.[152] Some respondents in the Strasbourg interviews thought that national compliance could be greatly enhanced by better dissemination of judgments in national languages, improved training of lawyers and judges in states with poor compliance records, and closer collaboration between national judges. Some also took the view that the European Commissioner for Human Rights could have a role in the enforcement process.

Disheartening though it may be, if the Council of Europe is to retain its character as an intergovernmental institution, it is doubtful if there is much more that can be done to the process by which the execution of judgments is supervised to enhance its effectiveness in raising the level of Convention compliance, particularly in states with the highest violation rates. And any change in the direction of becoming a supranational institution is extremely unlikely in the foreseeable future, not least because the enlarged EU, to which most Council of Europe states already belong or aspire to join, already possesses supranational characteristics. The challenge instead lies in further refinement of the individual applications process, considered in the remainder of this chapter, and in finding more effective ways of ensuring that decisions of the European Court of Human Rights receive the attention and

[151] 'Protocol No. 14 to Convention', paras. 16 and 19.

[152] The April 2003 report of the CDDH concluded that the payment of penalties would be 'preferable' to the daily fines the European Court of Justice can impose on states for failure to comply with its judgments, CDDH, 'Guaranteeing Long-Term Effectiveness', April 2003, p. 41. But this was abandoned in the November 2003 report in preference for the 'strong pressure' exerted upon states by the 'great symbolic value', and the 'moral and political consequences', of an adverse judgment in the new 'infringement' proceedings, CDDH, 'Guaranteeing Long-Term Effectiveness', November 2003, para. 44. Fining recalcitrant states appeals to the Parliamentary Assembly, see Opinion No. 251 (2004), para. 5.

respect they deserve in domestic legal systems, an issue considered further in Chapters 4, 5 and 6.

'INDIVIDUAL' OR 'CONSTITUTIONAL' JUSTICE?

If, as President Wildhaber thinks, Protocol 14 will not solve the Court's excessive workload problems, the question arises – what will? In its turn the answer hinges on a more fundamental issue, which underpinned the controversy over admissibility – should the Court be concerned with delivering 'individual' or 'constitutional' justice or both? Regrettably, none of the Strasbourg committees contributing to the pre-Protocol 14 debate adequately considered the matter. Some respondents in the Strasbourg interviews claimed that the Court itself was split over it, while others even doubted the utility of the distinction. Of the four principal official discussion papers to precede the April 2003 report of the CDDH, only that of the Evaluation Group raised the matter, and then only briefly. It argues that, in re-fashioning Convention procedure, it is 'vital' that 'judges are left with sufficient time to devote to what have been called "constitutional judgments", i.e. fully reasoned and authoritative judgements in cases which raise substantial or new and complex issues of human rights law, are of particular significance for the State concerned or involve allegations of serious human rights violations and which warrant a full process of considered adjudication'.[153] The April 2003 report of the CDDH states that, in modifying the Convention's 'control system', it does not believe, '. . . that the choice is one between two views that seem radically opposed: one under which the Court would deliver "individual justice"; the other under which the Court would deliver "quasi-constitutional justice". Both functions are legitimate functions for a European Court of Human Rights, and the proposals set out in this report seek to reconcile the two.'[154] Some respondents in the Strasbourg interviews effectively endorsed this view pointing out that 'constitutional' justice can only be delivered through the adjudication of individual complaints.

The April 2003 report of the CDDH adds that, while individual justice should be dispensed in the first instance by national courts, 'there will always be a need for the Court to act as a safety net in order to

[153] 'Report of Evaluation Group', para. 98.

[154] CDDH, 'Guaranteeing Long-Term Effectiveness', April 2003, p. 4, para. 11.

adjudicate cases that require individual justice even if they do not raise issues of "constitutional" significance'.[155] Yet, later it claims that '(u)ltimately the real measure of the effectiveness of the Convention system is not the quantity of judgments and decisions rendered every year, but the degree to which the Court is able to fulfil the role given to it under the Convention, namely to ensure the observance by the State Parties of the obligations they have contracted under the Convention',[156] which sounds more like 'constitutional' justice. The CDDH's November 2003 report states that 'in the current Convention system, defence of the general interest is not given the importance it deserves',[157] but the Explanatory Report to Protocol 14 does not mention the distinction between individual and constitutional justice at all, much less debating which should be the Court's priority.

Three questions relating to this issue need to be more fully considered. What do the terms 'individual' and 'constitutional justice', or 'judgment', mean? To what extent is each compatible with the underlying purposes of the Convention? And to what extent can each be realized given current, and likely, conditions? To begin with, two senses of the term 'individual justice' should be distinguished. First, it can mean, in a narrow sense that, since the only viable vehicle through which any judicial objective under the Convention system can currently be achieved is by judgments delivered in response to individual applications, the Court is inescapably committed to the delivery of 'individual justice' no matter what other goals it might have. However, it can also mean, secondly, the attempt by the Convention system to ensure that every genuine victim of a violation receives a judgment in their favour from the Court however slight the injury, whatever the bureaucratic cost, whether or not compensation is awarded, and whatever the likely impact of the judgment on the conduct or practice in question (call this 'the systematic delivery of individual justice'). The pursuit of 'constitutional justice', on the other hand, is the attempt by the Convention system to ensure that cases are both selected and adjudicated by the Court in a manner which contributes most effectively to the identification, condemnation, and resolution of violations, particularly those which are serious for the applicant, for the respondent state (because, for example, they are built into the structure or modus operandi of its public institutions), or for Europe as a whole (because,

[155] *Ibid.*, p. 5, para. 13. [156] *Ibid.*, p. 6, para. 19.
[157] CDDH, 'Guaranteeing Long-Term Effectiveness', November 2003, para. 22.

for example, they may be prevalent in more than one state). In an ideal world the Court would effortlessly dispense justice in every possible sense. But the environment is far from ideal. Given that nobody disputes that the delivery of 'individual justice' in the first, narrow, sense of the term is inescapable, the real debate is therefore about which of the other two alternatives should have priority given current and foreseeable conditions.

The Case for the Systematic Delivery of Individual Justice

The Court has affirmed that while 'the primary purpose of the Convention system is to provide individual relief, its mission is also to determine issues on public policy grounds in the common interest'.[158] Nevertheless, in spite of this ordering of priorities, a full and coherent argument that the systematic delivery of individual justice should be the key objective, has yet to be articulated. Instead, it tends to take the form of blunt and largely unsupported assertions, or largely inexplicit assumptions held by those who regard any departure from the pre-Protocol 14 admissibility tests as a threat to the right of individual petition. And some very influential contributors to the debate – including the Parliamentary Assembly, NGOs, academic commentators, some respondents in the Strasbourg interviews, and the delegations of certain states – have either stated or implied that they take this view.[159] For example, experts from German-speaking countries and observers

[158] *Karner* v. *Austria* (2004) 38 EHRR 528 at para. 26.

[159] See, e.g., M.-B. Dembour, '"Finishing Off" Cases: The Radical Solution to the Problem of the Expanding ECtHR Caseload', *European Human Rights Law Review* (2002), 604–623 at 604, 612, 622; Beernaert, 'Protocol 14', 553 at 556; J. Wadham and T. Said, 'What Price the Right of Individual Petition: Report of the Evaluation Group to the Committee of Ministers on the European Court of Human Rights', *European Human Rights Law Review* (2002), 169–174. The Parliamentary Assembly has described the new admissibility criterion as 'vague, subjective and liable to do the applicant a serious injustice', Opinion No. 251 (2004), para. 11. Four judges of the European Court of Human Rights have strongly supported the right of individual petition, F. Tulkens, M. Fischbach, J. Casadevall and W. Thomassen, 'Pour le Droit de Recours Individuel' preprinted as Annex 3 in G. Cohen-Jonathan and C. Pettiti (eds.), *La Réforme de la Cour Européene des Droits de L'homme* (Brussels: Bruylant, 2003), cited by Harmsen, 'ECtHR as Constitutional Court'. Harmsen also cites some leading French and Dutch supporters of the right of individual petition – F. Benoît-Rohmer, 'Il faut sauver le recoure individuel…' *Recueil Dalloz* **38** (2003), 2584–2590 and T. Barkhuysen and M. L. van Emmerick, 'De Toekomst van het EHRM: Meer middelen voor effectievere rechtserscherming', *NJCM-Bulletin* **28** (2003), 299.

from other jurisdictions meeting in Graz (Austria) in February 2003 to discuss the future of the European Court of Human Rights concluded, among other things, that there is 'no necessary contradiction in the two aims of protecting human rights at a general level ("the constitutional role") and protecting them in individual cases'. They added that 'if at some time in the future a choice had to be made, ... preference should be given to the aim of protecting rights in individual cases'.[160] The short English language report of these proceedings gives no indication of why this is the appropriate priority, why the issue is merely hypothetical rather than an urgent contemporary problem, nor of how the Court could ever be equipped to deliver individual justice systematically.

The closest to a sustained, and a remarkably widely endorsed, public articulation of the case for the systematic delivery of individual justice can be found in the robust defence of the admissibility criteria contained in a response to the draft Protocol 14, signed in April 2004 by 114 NGOs and other bodies throughout Europe.[161] The NGOs stated that 'amending the admissibility criteria is wrong in principle', that it will 'be seen as an erosion of the protection of human rights' by member states, that it will 'have the effect of severely curtailing the right of individual petition ... leaving more victims of human rights violations without a remedy', and that it will not contribute to weeding out the 90 per cent of applications which are inadmissible under the existing tests, nor to improving the processing of the 'manifestly well founded' cases which make up some 60 per cent of the Court's judgments on the merits. On the contrary, it is claimed the admissibility process will become more complex and time-consuming because the criteria permitting applications to be rejected where the applicant has not suffered a 'significant disadvantage', and where 'respect for human rights does not require an examination', are 'objectionable, vague and may be interpreted differently with respect to different states'. The NGOs also argue that '*all* violations of human rights are "significant" and that the individual victim, members of the community, and the integrity of the authorities suffer "disadvantage" when violations of human rights go without redress' (italics in original). The new admissibility test would also, it is said, result in some repetitive cases being ruled inadmissible with the result that victims would be left without remedy and an 'inappropriate

[160] A. Rodger, 'The Future of the European Court of Human Rights: Symposium at the University of Graz', *Human Rights Law Journal* **24** (2003), 149–151 at 150.

[161] '(Updated) Joint Response', paras. 26–31.

message' would be sent to the offending state. Amnesty International, one of the signatories to this common position, adds: 'The right of individuals to submit an application directly to the European Court of Human Rights lies at the heart of the European regional system for the protection of human rights. The essence of this right is the right of individuals to receive a binding determination from the European Court of Human Rights of whether the facts presented constitute a violation of the rights secured in the European Convention.'[162]

The Case for 'Constitutional' Justice

The case for constitutional justice, powerfully advanced in their personal capacities by the President of the Court, Luzius Wildhaber, the former President, Rolv Ryssdall, and the former Registrar Mr Paul Mahoney among others, rests on the observations that it is logistically impossible for the Court to deliver individual justice systematically, and that the only other viable alternative, constitutional justice, has consistently been the priority of the judicial institutions of the Convention system since its foundation.[163] It could, and should, be added that the role of Constitutional Court for Europe is one which the Court has not yet fully realized.

Given the sheer scale of the individual application rate, discussed in Chapter 1 and earlier in this chapter, there is no realistic prospect that

[162] Amnesty International, 'Comments', para. 5.

[163] L. Wildhaber, 'Role of ECtHR' and 'A Constitutional Future for the European Court of Human Rights?' *Human Rights Law Journal* **23** (2002), 161–165; P. Mahoney, 'New Challenges' and 'Insider's View'. See also F. J. Bruinsma and S. Parmentier, 'Interview with Mr Luzius Wildhaber, President of the ECHR', *Netherlands Quarterly of Human Rights* **21** (2003), 185–201; R. Ryssdall, 'On the Road to a European Constitutional Court', Winston Churchill Lecture on the Council of Europe, Florence, 21 June 1991, quoted in E. A. Alkema, 'The European Convention as a constitution and its Court as a constitutional court' in P. Mahoney, F. Matscher, H. Petzold and L. Wildhaber (eds.), *Protecting Human Rights: The European Perspective – Studies in Memory of Rolv Ryssdall* (Cologne/Berlin/Bonn/Munich: Carl Heymans, 2000) 41–63. Leading French and Dutch academic contributors to the debate – J.-F. Flauss, 'La Cour Européen des Droits de L'homme est-elle une Cour Constitutionelle?', *Revue Française de Droit Constitutionel* (1999) 36, 711–728 and R. Lawson, 'De Mythe van het Moeten: Het Europees Hof voor de Recheten van de Mens en 800 miljoen klagers', *NJCM-Bulletin* (2003) 28, 12–130 – are cited in Harmsen, 'ECtHR as Constitutional Court', 4 and 7.

every applicant with a legitimate complaint about a Convention violation will receive judicial redress at Strasbourg. At the risk of labouring the point, it is worth repeating some of the key facts and figures. According to the figures for 2005, the Court's capacity for judgment on the merits has increased to 1,039 judgments a year.[164] But with jurisdiction over more than 800 million people, any given citizen of a Council of Europe state has, on the bare statistics, about one in a million chance of having their complaint adjudicated or resolved by friendly settlement. While an annual average of around 40,000 apply to the Court, only between 1 and 2 per cent are likely to have their cases adjudicated on the merits. In spite of being available from the beginning, the right of individual application did not become compulsory until 1998, although by then it had been accepted by all member states.[165] But, neither becoming compulsory nor becoming virtually the exclusive mode for the judicial enforcement of Convention obligations, have themselves changed the original strategic and constitutional functions of the Convention system discussed in Chapter 1: to contribute to the prevention of another war between western European states; to provide a statement of common values contrasting sharply with Soviet-style communism capable of serving as a Cold War totem; to re-enforce a sense of common identity and purpose should the Cold War turn 'hot'; and to establish an early warning device by which a drift towards authoritarianism in any member state could be detected and dealt with by complaints to an independent trans-national judicial tribunal.[166]

Nevertheless, as Chapter 1 also pointed out, by the end of the twentieth century the entire original raison d'être for the Convention had undergone subtle, yet fundamental, transformation.[167] No longer does it express the identity of western European liberal democracy in

[164] This figure is a summation of 'judgments finding at least one violation' (994) and 'judgments finding no violation' (45), and excludes 'friendly settlements/striking out judgments' (55) and 'other judgments' (13), ECtHR, 'Violations by Article and by Country' issued at the Annual Press Conference by President Luzius Wildhaber, 'Brighter Prospects for the European Court of Human Rights', European Court of Human Rights Press Release – 034(2006).

[165] S. C. Prebensen, 'Inter-State Complaints Under Treaty Provisions – The Experience Under the European Convention on Human Rights', *Human Rights Law Journal* **20** (1999) 446, 449.

[166] Mahoney, 'Insider's View', 1–3.

[167] Mahoney, 'Speculating on Future', 1 and 4.

contrast with the rival communist model of central and eastern Europe; it now provides an 'abstract constitutional identity' for the entire continent, especially for the former communist states recently received into membership. Its most important current role is, therefore, to provide national institutions, and particularly national courts, with a clear indication of the constitutional limits provided by Convention rights upon the exercise of national public power. This involves generating a case law embodying shared European values, identifying structural problems with the exercise of power by national public bodies, and scrutinizing plausible allegations of serious human rights abuse even where these are not systemic in nature, which, in its turn, promotes convergence in the way institutions at every level of governance operate in Europe.[168] As President Wildhaber has pointed out, the granting of individual relief is of secondary importance to the 'primary aim of raising the general standard of human rights protection and extending human rights jurisprudence throughout the community of Convention States'.[169] This is because, as already noted in this Chapter, the Court is restricted to declaring whether or not the Convention has been violated – with the choice of remedial action left to the respondent state under the supervision of the Committee of Ministers – and because the award of 'just satisfaction' to the aggrieved applicant is discretionary. Individual applications are, therefore, the 'magnifying glass which reveals the imperfections in national legal systems ... the thermometer which tests the democratic temperature'[170] of states and the means by which 'defects in national protection of human rights are detected with a view to correcting them and thus raising the general standard of protection of human rights'.[171] As President Wildhaber also asks: 'Once the Court has established the existence of a structural violation or an administrative practice, is the general purpose of raising the level of human rights protection in the state concerned really served by continuing to issue judgments establishing the same violation?'[172] And as Paul Mahoney, the former Registrar also writing in a personal capacity notes, it was

[168] Mahoney, 'Insider's View', 3.
[169] Wildhaber, 'Constitutional Future', 163.
[170] *Ibid.*, p. 164. [171] *Ibid.*, p. 162.
[172] Wildhaber, 'Role of ECtHR', 26.

never intended that the Court should become a 'small claims' tribunal.[173]

The question of what constitutes a 'constitution' has been much debated.[174] In its broadest sense it can mean how any entity, for example the human body, is constituted, while in its narrowest it refers only to the fundamental laws of the modern sovereign nation state as declared in a single formal document. A conception which lies somewhere in between takes a 'constitution' to refer to the terms upon which any human association – from a university stamp collectors' club to the United Nations – is based, particularly those associations which have been deliberately and consciously created by their founding members. In this sense, constitutions do not have to be contained in a single document, or to be entirely free from dispute, even over fundamentals, although the clearer and less contentious they are the better. Employing a narrow but largely implicit conception, Alkema states that the 'Convention's framework is not a constitution' and that 'analogies between the Convention system and a constitution are problematic and delicate'. Nevertheless, he admits that some comparisons between the two are possible, 'at least as a mental exercise'.[175] The view taken in this study, and explored more fully in the following chapter, is that the Convention contains 'an abstract constitution' which seeks to structure the relationship between various national and trans-national institutions and attempts to constrain the exercise of public power within a framework of, what are effectively, constitutional rights. President Wildhaber maintains that the question of whether the Court is, or is not, a 'constitutional court' is largely a matter of semantics since it could, quite properly, be called a 'quasi-Constitutional Court sui generis' albeit subsidiary to national supreme, or constitutional, courts.[176] The reputed fears of some member states, that to characterize it in this way would

[173] Mahoney, 'Insider's View', 2. One respondent in the Strasbourg interviews complained about applicants regarding the Court as a 'cash machine' and claimed that 60 per cent of applications to the Grand Chamber concerned disputes about the adequacy of the award of damages.

[174] For a recent review of the debate about whether, in spite of the lack of a formal constitutional document, the EU has a constitution, see A. Dyevre, 'The Constitutionalization of the European Union: Discourse, Present, Future and Facts', *European Law Review* **30** (2005), 165–189 at 168–176. Dyevre takes the 'narrow' view that the EU does not have a constitution because it lacks a key element – being an autonomous legal order, 172.

[175] Alkema, 'European Convention as Constitution', 62 and 45.

[176] Wildhaber, 'Constitutional Future', 161.

be to risk encouraging a drift towards federalism in the Council of Europe, are therefore completely without foundation. It is already the 'Constitutional Court for Europe' in the sense that it is the final authoritative judicial tribunal in the only fully pan-European constitutional system there is. The real question is how effectively it fulfils this mission.

Finally, the case for constitutional justice is bolstered by several specific flaws in the position outlined by the NGOs. Take first the assertion of Amnesty International that 'the right of individuals to submit an application directly to the European Court of Human Rights lies at the heart of the European regional system for the protection of human rights' and that 'the essence of this right is the right of individuals to receive a binding determination from the European Court of Human Rights of whether the facts presented constitute a violation of the rights secured in the European Convention'.[177] While few could disagree with the first part, the second, which underpins the entire case for the systematic delivery of individual justice, rests on a misconception. Everyone under the jurisdiction of a member state has a right to *petition* the Court alleging a breach of their Convention rights, and to *receive a response* from it. But only those whose cases are admissible, a tiny fraction of those who apply, have a right to *receive a 'binding determination'*.[178] And the question of which cases should be admissible cannot be divorced from the Court's overriding mission, the delivery of constitutional justice. Regrettably this misconception is widely shared by advocates of the systematic delivery of individual justice. For example, Beernaert argues that, so far 'the Convention system has been able to fulfill two key roles: to provide an avenue of redress for every individual with human rights complaints and to function as a (quasi-) constitutional instrument of European public order'.[179] However, it was never intended, and has never come close, to fulfilling the first of these objectives because its jurisdiction is limited to a relatively narrow category of human rights and it can only provide an 'avenue of redress' for a tiny fraction of those with a complaint that one of these has been violated. Similarly, ignoring the fact that the Convention was originally conceived as almost entirely an inter-state judicial process, Dembour poses the rhetorical question: 'It is all very well for the Court to say that

[177] Amnesty International, 'Comment', para. 5.
[178] 'Protocol No. 14 to Convention', para. 10; Mahoney, 'Insider's View', 4.
[179] Beernaert, 'Protocol 14', 556.

it has too many applicants, but surely this is exactly why it was created in the first place.'[180]

There are also several critical flaws in the NGOs' joint paper. First, as discussed in the account of the substantive admissibility tests earlier in this chapter, it is debatable whether the 'manifestly ill-founded' criterion is any more objective than the extra new test provided by Protocol 14. Arguably, the only 'certainties' offered applicants and their advisers is that there is only a 2 per cent chance, at best, of the complaint being adjudicated, a 94 per cent chance of winning should this happen, but not much chance of securing what any applicant is likely to regard as sufficient compensation. Second, it is a mistake to assume that victims of repetitive violations currently receive adequate redress, and that an apparently endless series of judgments on different aspects of a structural compliance problem – as with, for example, delays in the judicial process in Italy – is an effective way of improving Convention compliance. Finally, whether all Convention violations are 'significant' is debatable. But they are clearly not all equally serious for two reasons. First, breaches of any given Convention provision can vary in severity. For example, being interned without charge or trial for years is a much more serious violation of Article 5(3) than a short delay which, nevertheless, results in not being brought 'promptly' before a judicial authority. Second, the Convention contains not a list, but an implicit hierarchy of rights, with some, particularly the non-derogable ones, clearly singled out as more fundamental than the others. A violation of the right not to be tortured (Article 3) is, for example, patently a more serious violation of the Convention than an unjustified interception of communication which violates the right to respect for correspondence (Article 8), especially when the latter causes the victim no other harm.

ENHANCING THE COURT'S CONSTITUTIONAL MISSION

It is difficult to contest, therefore, that one of the key tasks for the Council of Europe in the near future is to improve the procedures governing the processes by which individual applications are made, and the execution of judgments supervised, in order better to fulfill

[180] Dembour, 'Finishing Off Cases', 622,

the Court's constitutional mission.[181] In the remainder of this chapter an attempt will be made to assess what contribution, if any, might be made by expanding the Court's advisory jurisdiction, and what lessons, if any, might be learned from the EU's judicial system, and from the US Supreme Court and the German Federal Constitutional Court.

Expanding the Court's Advisory Jurisdiction

Although some commentators have called for an extension of the Court's advisory jurisdiction,[182] Protocol 14 makes no mention of it, nor did it feature prominently in the preceding debate. For three related reasons, advisory opinions are by their nature incapable of contributing significantly to the delivery of constitutional justice, to the resolution of structural compliance problems in specific states, nor to anything of significance for the Convention's future. First, although the Court has the power under Article 47(1) of the Convention to 'give advisory opinions on legal questions concerning the interpretation of the Convention and the protocols thereto', at the request of a majority of the Committee of Ministers, this is severely circumscribed by Article 47(2) which excludes 'any question relating to the content or scope of the rights and freedoms defined in Section 1 of the Convention and the Protocols thereto', and 'any other question which the Court or the Committee of Ministers might have to consider in consequence of any such proceedings as could be instituted in accordance with the Convention'. Although it is for the Court to decide if a request for an advisory opinion is within its competence, it is difficult to imagine any substantial issue of interpretation arising under the first paragraph which would not simultaneously be excluded by the second paragraph. Second, since they can be prompted only by hypothetical issues – albeit ones potentially related to concrete problems – advisory opinions must necessarily be expressed in vague and general terms and are, therefore, unlikely to add anything of substance to how the Convention is understood. It would, thirdly, be a breach of the rule of law if an advisory opinion were to impose extra obligations on states not already apparent from the terms of the Convention and protocols themselves,

181 Mahoney, 'Insider's View', 4.

182 See, for example, van Dijk and van Hoof, *Theory and Practice*, p. 265 and D. J. Harris, M. O'Boyle and C. Warbrick, *Law of the European Convention on Human Rights* (London/Dublin/Edinburgh: Butterworths, 1995), p. 690.

without states being given an opportunity for this to be contested before the Court.

Courts of First Instance and Preliminary Rulings – Lessons from the European Court of Justice

In spite of some fleeting references to it, little attention was paid in the Protocol 14 debate to the lessons the European Court of Human Rights might learn from the practice and procedures of the European Court of Justice of the European Union (the ECJ). However, as it turns out, the two systems are so different that there is little which can, in fact, be derived from the latter of benefit to the procedure of the former. While it has never been seriously suggested that a single Court of First Instance should be added to the Convention process – as one has been to the judicial process of the EU – the two main objections to 'regional human rights courts of first instance', which some have advocated, are that such an innovation would be prohibitively expensive and bureaucratically cumbersome and that it would create a two-speed system running counter to the goal of establishing a uniform pan-European judicial human rights protection process.[183] Such a proposal also assumes, in essence, the model of the systematic delivery of individual justice – more courts and more judges to settle more individual complaints – which would divert the European Court of Human Rights from the much more pressing need to concentrate upon the delivery of thoroughly reasoned and authoritative judgments, as discussed in the following Chapter.

There was also little discussion in the Protocol 14 debate about the pros and cons of creating a process under the Convention similar to the 'preliminary ruling' procedure by which national courts of member states of the European Union can request guidance on points of Community law from the Community courts in Luxembourg. Having decided not to discuss it further because the majority of its members were against it, the CDDH nevertheless left open the possibility of returning to it 'at a later stage, in the light of all the decisions which have been taken'.[184]

[183] Mahoney, 'New Challenges', 107.

[184] CDDH, *Interim Report of the CDDH to be submitted to the Committee of Ministers – 'Guaranteeing the Long-Term Effectiveness of the European Court of Human Rights'*, CDDH(2002)016 Addendum, 14 October 2002, p. 8, para. 14.

The preliminary ruling procedure under Article 234 of the EC Treaty occupies a central place in the judicial system of the European Union and currently accounts for about two thirds of cases brought before the ECJ, a dramatic increase from 4 per cent in 1961.[185] References for preliminary rulings may be mandatory or discretionary depending on the circumstances. Certain EU law issues must be referred to the ECJ where there is no domestic judicial remedy against the decision of the national court or tribunal – principally those relating to the interpretation of the European Community Treaty, to the interpretation of the statutes of bodies established by the Council of the European Union (where the statute itself so provides), and to the validity and interpretation of acts of the institutions of the Community and the European Central Bank. However, this obligation does not arise if the point of law at issue has already been decided by the ECJ, or if the correct application of Community law would be so obvious to the court of any member state, or to the ECJ itself, that there is no reasonable doubt about how the matter should be resolved (the acte clair doctrine). At the instigation of either of the parties or the judge, any national court or tribunal may also make a preliminary reference to the ECJ if it considers the ECJ's decision is necessary to enable judgment to be given at the national level. Resort to the preliminary rulings procedure may therefore save time and money by involving the ECJ early in litigation when it would otherwise be difficult to avoid its intervention later.

The ECJ may decline jurisdiction in a preliminary reference where the national court has failed to define adequately the legal and factual background to the dispute, where the question referred is general or hypothetical, or where it bears no relation to the actual nature of the case or to the subject matter of the main action.[186] But where the application passes this admissibility test, written and oral observations may be submitted by the parties to the national litigation, and, in certain circumstances, by Member States, the Commission and/or Council of the European Union, the European Central Bank, and the European Parliament. Since preliminary references are not appeals against decisions of domestic courts, the ECJ does not consider the specific issues raised in the national litigation. But rulings by the ECJ

[185] Tridimas, 'Knocking on Heaven's Door', pp. 16 and 47.
[186] *Ibid.*, p. 22.

under Article 234 are binding on national courts both in the instant case and in subsequent proceedings, and may require conflicting provisions of national law to be ruled unlawful, impuned acts to be treated as void, and damage remedied. Arnull *et al.* maintain that the proper functioning of the preliminary rulings procedure depends to a large extent on the way national judges exercise their discretion,[187] and that the ECJ needs to be aware of the risk of compounding the national dilemma about whether to make a reference or not by being 'alert to the danger of discouraging references in cases where its guidance is genuinely needed'.[188]

The relationship between national courts and the ECJ in preliminary ruling proceedings is 'cooperative rather than hierarchical in nature' and may be regarded as a 'form of dialogue'[189] which promotes the integration of national and trans-national approaches to the adjudication of Community law issues. Of considerable relevance to the central theme in this study, Tridimas argues that preliminary rulings have contributed significantly to the process of constitutionalization in the EU in several ways. First, they have enabled the ECJ to 'lay down fundamental principles of the Community legal system', and second to 'develop constitutional doctrine'. Third, in combination with the principles of primacy and direct effect, preliminary rulings have also 'redefined constitutionalism at European level'.[190] Fourth, Article 234 has been 'more than any other jurisdictional clause, the procedural facilitator of constitutional change'.[191] This has, fifth, re-allocated powers on three levels: from governments of Member States to the institutions of the Community, from national executives and legislatures to national judiciaries, and from the highest to the lowest national courts. Sixth, the acte clair doctrine has promoted the 'federalization' of the Community's legal order and has, seventh, 'internalized' Community law in the legal systems of Member States. But the success of the ECJ in constitutionalizing the Treaties through the preliminary reference procedure also 'owes much to the approval, encouragement, and cooperation of national courts'.[192]

187 A.M. Arnull, A.A. Dashwood, M.G. Ross, and D.A. Wyatt, *Wyatt and Dashwood's European Union Law*, 4th edn. (London: Sweet & Maxwell, 2000), p. 270.

188 *Ibid.* pp. 270 and 272. 189 *Ibid.*, p. 269.

190 Tridimas, 'Knocking on Heaven's Door', p. 10.

191 *Ibid.*, p. 11. 192 *Ibid.* p. 37.

There is no technical reason preventing the introduction of a preliminary ruling procedure to the legal process of the European Convention on Human Rights. But there are arguments for and against doing so.[193] On the positive side, it could have a constitutionalizing effect in the Convention system, similar, at least in some respects, to that achieved in the Community legal order. As the previous chapter suggested and as Chapter 6 will seek to show, ways of promoting constitutional change in member states are urgently needed in order to address structural Convention violation more effectively. Second, preliminary rulings would also empower the European Court of Human Rights to assist national courts in fashioning effective domestic judicial remedies before the domestic litigation is resolved (without compromising the principle of subsidiarity). In their turn, judgments by national courts incorporating the authoritative interpretation of the Convention by the European Court of Human Rights could help prevent what might otherwise be a flood of applications to Strasbourg arising from structural compliance problems. Third, a preliminary reference procedure could promote the harmonization of Convention interpretation at both national and trans-national levels. Finally, although the European Court of Human Rights would have to consider which preliminary references to hear, this might be a less time-consuming activity than the current admissibility process for individual applications.

But there are three principal problems. First, the potential case management saving provided by preliminary references could be offset by other workload-related effects. The fact that the preliminary reference procedure has greatly added to the burden of the ECJ – with recourse to it increasing by 85 per cent between 1992 and 1998[194] – is not encouraging, even if under the Convention applicants, in cases which had been the subject of a preliminary reference, were precluded from petitioning Strasbourg any further.

193 The case in favour is put, for example, by: A. Drzemczewski, *European Human Rights Convention in Domestic Law: A Comparative Study* (Oxford: Clarendon Press, 1983), pp. 330–341; L. Betten and J. Korte, 'Procedure for Preliminary Rulings in the Context of Merger', *Human Rights Law Journal* **8** (1987), 75–80; R. St. J. MacDonald, 'The Luxembourg Preliminary Ruling Procedure and its Possible Application in Strasbourg' in Anon (ed.), *Mélanges en Hommage à Louis Edmond Pettiti* (Bruxelles: Bruyant, 1998), pp. 593–603.

194 Tridimas, 'Knocking on Heaven's Door', 16. See also A. Stone Sweet, *The Judicial Construction of Europe* (Oxford: Oxford University Press, 2004), pp. 98–106.

Indeed, a preliminary reference procedure could even increase the workload of the European Court of Human Rights, because a refusal by national courts to utilize it could add to an applicant's sense of grievance, and therefore to their determination to seek redress at Strasbourg. Second, rates of application for preliminary references vary considerably between member states of the EU with some courts, for example those in England, operating on the maxim 'if in doubt decide yourself', while others, for example in Austria, take the view 'if in doubt, refer'.[195] If this approach were to be replicated in a preliminary reference procedure introduced to the Convention there would be no guarantee that cases would be referred to Strasbourg by the national courts of those states which have the highest rates of Convention violation and, therefore, which arguably need them most.[196]

But the third, and most serious, problem is that introducing a preliminary reference process to the Convention would not alter the dependence of the Convention's judicial process on sporadic complaints about violation brought by aggrieved individual applicants, the systemic impact of which, at the national level, depends on how the respondent state reacts. This is not true of the legal order of the EU for three significant reasons. First, Community law, as interpreted by the ECJ, is directly effective in domestic law and takes precedence over conflicting national law. Second, a third of the cases heard by the ECJ are brought by the European Commission or by one member state against another. This means that the judicial processes of the EU can be initiated for *strategic* reasons, with Community-wide implications, without the need to wait for aggrieved individual applicants to embark upon litigation for their own private motives. Third, strategic legal objectives can also be pursued in the EU through the legislative activity of the Council and Commission, a function unparalleled in the Council of Europe. The constitutionalizing effects of the EU's preliminary reference procedure, therefore, occur in a constitutional environment not only fundamentally different from that which applies to the Convention and to the Council of Europe, but also one which is fundamentally different from any in which the latter are likely to operate for the foreseeable future.

[195] Tridimas, 'Knocking on Heaven's Door', 38.

[196] This is also true in the EU context, Stone Sweet, *Judicial Construction*, pp. 98–106.

Lessons from the US Supreme Court and the German Federal Constitutional Court

If, as this study seeks to argue, the European Court of Human Rights is effectively a Constitutional Court for Europe, much could potentially be learned from national constitutional courts. While a great deal more comparative research may be necessary in order to reap the maximum benefits, some useful insights can, nevertheless, be obtained from a more limited comparison with the experience of the US Supreme Court and the German Federal Constitutional Court (the Bundesverfassungsgericht), two of the most mature democratic constitutional courts in the world, each of which also enjoys a high public prestige, greater indeed than that of other political institutions in the respective jurisdictions.[197] Some respondents in the Strasbourg interviews expressed concern that prioritizing constitutional, over the systematic delivery of individual, justice would reduce applicants to mere means for the refinement of national legal and administrative systems. However, the main lessons to be learned from the experiences of the US Supreme Court and the German Federal Constitutional Court are that modern constitutional courts are, typically, more concerned with addressing structural failures to respect constitutional rights in the exercise of public power than they are with ensuring that every applicant with a legitimate complaint is provided with a judicial remedy, and that they manage what would otherwise be overwhelming case loads by delegating responsibility for the elimination of all but a few percent of the applications they receive to the discretion of 'junior' judicial or legal officials.

Some differences in 'jurisdictional scale' between these two courts and the European Court of Human Rights ought to be noted first. There are, to begin with, nearly twice as many judges on the German Federal Constitutional Court (sixteen in two eight-judge Chambers) as on the US Supreme Court (nine). In its turn the European

[197] R. Rogowski and T. Gawron, 'Constitutional Litigation as Dispute Processing: Comparing the U.S. Supreme Court and the German Federal Constitutional Court' in R. Rogowski and T. Gawron (eds.), *Constitutional Courts in Comparison: The US Supreme Court and the German Federal Constitutional Court* (New York and Oxford: Berghahn Books, 2002), pp. 1–21 at 7. See also G. Kleijkamp, 'Comparing the Application and Interpretation of the United States Constitution and the European Convention on Human Rights', *Transnational Law and Contemporary Problems* **12** (2002), 307–334.

Court of Human Rights (with forty-six) has almost three times as many as the German Federal Constitutional Court, and five times as many as the US Supreme Court. Second, the professional and cultural backgrounds of the judges on the European Court of Human Rights are much more diverse than those of their US and German counterparts. These two factors are likely to complicate, although not necessarily render impossible, the formulation of judicial policy by the European Court of Human Rights, a key feature of a successful constitutional court. Third, the 9 judges of the US Supreme Court exercise jurisdiction over a population of 290 million, and receive around 9,000 applications a year (1,000 applications per judge and one application for every 30,000 or so inhabitants), while the 16 judges of the German Federal Constitutional Court exercise jurisdiction over a population of 82 million and receive about 5,000 applications a year, substantially fewer per head of population (1 for every 16,000 or so inhabitants) and many fewer per judge (about 300 each). With its 46 judges exercising jurisdiction over a population of 800 million, and receiving over 40,000 applications a year (870 applications per judge and 1 application for every 20,000 inhabitants), the European Court of Human Rights lies in between the US Supreme Court and the German Federal Constitutional Court on these criteria. Fourth, and most significantly, unlike the European Court of Human Rights, the US Supreme Court and the German Federal Constitutional Court sit at the apex of integrated national judicial systems structured by federal legislation and written constitutions. A persistent failure by the US or German governments to respond positively to a judgment of, respectively, the US Supreme Court or the German Federal Constitutional Court is therefore likely to provoke a national constitutional crisis. The lack of a comparable 'polity' in the Council of Europe, and the unavoidable limitations in the process by which the execution of judgments is supervised, means that the judgments of the European Court of Human Rights are limited, at best, to exerting international pressure on respondent states and to contributing to whatever domestic political and legal debate surrounds the particular non-compliance issue. But the success of each of these levers depends upon national political and legal forces being interested in the issue in question, taking notice of what the Court has said about it, being concerned about avoiding a negative reputation internationally, and pursuing the matter in the domestic political and judicial arenas. Over this, neither the Court nor the Council of Europe has much control.

Yet in spite of these differences the US Supreme Court and the German Federal Constitutional Court share a number of features highly germane to the debate about how cases should be selected for hearing before the European Court of Human Rights. First, a 'constitutional mission' on the part of the European Court of Human Rights is wholly consistent with the function of contemporary constitutional courts. As Stone Sweet states: 'The protection of human rights is a central purpose of modern European constitutionalism, and constitutional judges are the agents of that purpose.'[198] Second, notwithstanding a much wider formal jurisdiction, 99 per cent of the docket of the modern US Supreme Court concerns discretionary review of petitions for writs of certiorari to quash allegedly unlawful administrative or judicial decisions.[199] Although the German Federal Constitutional Court has jurisdiction over four main areas, constitutional complaints lodged by individuals against an alleged infringement of their constitutional rights (Verfassungsbeschwerde), accounted for 99.4 per cent of its case load between 1992 and 2000,[200] a figure comparable with its Spanish counterpart.[201] While strictly not an appeal court, the requirement to exhaust all other remedies means that most litigation to the German Federal Constitutional Court concerns decisions of lower courts.[202] Third, since the Second World War both the US Supreme Court and the German Federal Constitutional Court have experienced a dramatic rise in the application rate, especially in the 1990s.[203]

Fourth, only 1 to 2 per cent of applications submitted to either the US Supreme Court or to the German Federal Constitutional Court are

198 A. Stone Sweet, *Governing with Judges: Constitutional Politics in Europe* (Oxford: Oxford University Press, 2000), p. 29.

199 D. M. O'Brien, *Storm Center: The Supreme Court in American Politics*, 6th edn. (New York and London: W.W. Norton and Co., 2002), p. 169.

200 The other three are: disputes involving the highest federal bodies (Organklage); abstract constitutional review of statutes at the instigation of, on the one hand, political parties and groups within Parliament, or, on the other, the highest organs or branches of the Federal Republic (abstrakte Normencontrolle); and 'concrete norm control' or 'preliminary rulings' on the constitutionality of statutes at issue in litigation referred by other courts prior to making their own decisions (konkrete Normenkontrolle), E. Blankenburg, 'Mobilization of the German Federal Constitutional Court' in Rogowski and Gawron (eds.), *Constitutional Courts*, 157–172 at 158.

201 J. Bell, 'Reflections on continental European Supreme Courts', *Legal Studies* **24** (2004), 156–168 at 163.

202 W. Heun, 'Access to the German Federal Constitutional Court' in Rogowski and Gawron (eds.), *Constitutional Courts*, pp. 125–156 at 143.

203 Rogowski and Gawron, 'Constitutional Litigation', Table 0.1, p. 7.

accepted for decision on the merits, a characteristic which is strikingly similar to the experience of the European Court of Human Rights.[204] Given ideological differences on the US Supreme Court, and the fact that the selection of cases often involves political negotiations between justices,[205] unanimity is remarkably high with, for example, 88 per cent of applications being rejected unanimously in the 1990–1 term.[206] Although there is some debate about what the rejection of an application signifies, reasons are rarely given, and, since the Court has not formally considered the arguments, of itself this cannot constitute an adverse decision on the merits. Rejection merely implies that at its discretion the Court does not think the decision of the lower court ought to be reviewed.[207] Between a quarter and half of complaints fail even to be registered for an admissibility decision by the German Federal Constitutional Court and 85 per cent of decisions against admissibility are also made without either reasons being given or criteria cited.[208]

Fifth, while each Court has formal grounds for determining which cases are selected for a decision on the merits, much of the responsibility for preliminary screening has been delegated to court officials who exercise a wide discretion. Although each justice of the US Supreme Court receives copies of all petitions, 90 per cent of these are eliminated by their teams of four clerks (five for the Chief Justice) in the preliminary screening before the composite 'discuss list' of all justices is drawn up by the Chief Justice from what is left.[209] Between 70 and 80 per cent of applications listed are then rejected without discussion, as are most of those scheduled for consideration.[210] There are three stages to the admission of a constitutional complaint to the German Federal Constitutional Court: registration, admission by a three judge Chamber (formerly known as a 'committee'), and formal acceptance for decision by a Senate.[211] Several changes have been introduced over the years in an attempt to lighten the Court's work load, which mirrors the increasing work load of all German courts and which has been the subject of concerns since 1956, a mere five years after the Court was first

[204] *Ibid.*, p. 9. [205] *Ibid.*, p. 10.
[206] O'Brien, *Storm Center*, p. 207.
[207] *Ibid.*, pp. 214–218.
[208] Heun, 'Access', 135; Blankenburg, 'Mobilization', 168.
[209] O'Brien, *Storm Center*, p. 192; Rogowski and Gawron, 'Constitutional Litigation', 12.
[210] O'Brien, *Storm Center*, p. 199.
[211] Heun, 'Access', 134–137.

established, when 686 constitutional complaints were received.[212] In 1956 the three-judge committees of the Court were empowered to reject constitutional complaints which were 'not admissible or if for other reasons the likelihood of success ... (was) ... not sufficient',[213] a responsibility now discharged by three-judge Chambers whose unanimous decisions against admissibility are unchallengeable.[214] As in the US, a key role is played by 'legal assistants', three of whom (mostly experienced judges of lower courts themselves)[215] are assigned to each judge, to prepare 'routine' cases and to pre-screen petitions or constitutional complaints for discussion in chambers.[216] Since 1985 chambers have also been able to decide on the merits where the complaint is obviously well-founded because the Court has already settled the relevant constitutional questions.[217] There are, therefore, national parallels for the creation of a separate filtering institution in the individual applications process under the Convention, staffed, as suggested by the European Court of Human Rights and the former Registrar, Mr Paul Mahoney (in his personal capacity), by a distinct cadre of judges/assessors and Registry officials who would apply clear, objective, and non-discretionary admissibility tests for the disposal of the vast bulk of inadmissible applications.[218] Such a proposal is therefore worthy of further consideration, notwithstanding that there may be problems, for example in meeting the likely demand that the judicial staff of the new filtering institution were recruited proportionately from all member states, that its introduction could paradoxically result in a short-term reduction in productivity while new appointees were trained, and that it is an open question whether the 'manifestly ill founded' criterion is an appropriate standard as it is arguably more discretionary than is officially admitted.

Sixth, a powerful factor determining whether any given application is selected for adjudication by either the German or American court is

[212] Blankenburg, 'Mobilization', 161–163.
[213] Heun, 'Access', 135.
[214] *Ibid.*, p. 136. Since 1985, Chambers have also been able to decide on the merits where the complaint is obviously well-founded because the Court has already settled the relevant constitutional questions, *ibid.*, pp. 135–136; Rogowski and Gawron, 'Constitutional Adjudication', 12.
[215] Blankenburg, 'Mobilization', 168.
[216] Rogowski and Gawron, 'Constitutional Litigation', p. 12.
[217] *Ibid.*; Heun, 'Access', 135–136.
[218] CDDH, 'Response of ECtHR', para. 5; Mahoney, 'Insider's View', 12–14; Mahoney, 'New Challenges', 108–109.

whether admitting it is likely to produce beneficial effects for the respective legal and constitutional systems as a whole, a consideration which can take precedence over whether or not the applicant has a deserving case. According to William Taft, one-time Chief Justice of the US Supreme Court: 'No litigant is entitled to more than two chances, namely, to the original trial and to a review, and the intermediate courts of review are provided for that purpose. When a case goes beyond that, it is not primarily to preserve the rights of the litigants. The Supreme Court's function is for the purpose of expounding and stabilizing principles of law for the benefit of the people of the country, passing upon constitutional questions and other important questions of law for the public benefit.'[219] As Rogowski and Gawron state: 'The practice of acceptance and rejection reveals the strong concern of both courts to protect themselves from case load overflow. Selection is thus a mechanism for case load management. Furthermore, through the selection process, cases are excluded that are not deemed relevant for the development of the law. ... Through the selection of cases ... (these courts) ... set their agenda'.[220]

The US Supreme Court may reject an application, without a hearing on the merits, on one or more of five formal grounds.[221] First, the applicant lacks 'standing to sue', i.e. there is no proof of a real rather than a speculative injury to a legally protected right. However, while petitioners must generally show a personal stake in the outcome, even if this is shared with society as a whole, the Court now 'directly and indirectly encourages interest groups and the government to litigate issues of public policy'.[222] As Chief Justice Vinson put it, since the Court selects and decides 'only those cases which present questions whose resolution will have immediate importance far beyond the particular facts and parties involved', attorneys in such cases 'are, in a sense, prosecuting or defending class actions'.[223] This is less true of the German Federal Constitutional Court which is not generally seen as

[219] W. H. Taft, testimony, in *Hearings before the House Committee on the Judiciary*, 67th Cong., 2nd sess. p. 2 (Washington, D.C., 1922) quoted in O'Brien, *Storm Center*, p. 165.

[220] Rogowski and Gawron, 'Constitutional Litigation', 10.

[221] O'Brien, *Storm Center*, pp. 164–182, presented here in a different order.

[222] Interest groups may also enter litigation as third parties by filing partisan amicus curiae briefs, *ibid.*, pp. 222 and 225.

[223] *Ibid.*, p. 222 quoting F. Vinson, 'Address before the American Bar Association', 7 September 1949, reprinted in 69 S.Ct. vi (1949).

a platform for advancing causes pursued by social movements.[224] One possible implication for the Convention system, considered more fully in Chapter 6, is that the victim test should be expanded to enable the European Commissioner for Human Rights, and possibly National Human Rights Institutions, to bring test cases to the European Court of Human Rights.

A petition to the US Supreme Court may be rejected, second, because it 'lacks adverseness' (which means the Court will not consider hypothetical disputes or deliver advisory opinions), third, because it raises issues which are 'unripe' (because, for example the injury has not yet occurred or other remedies have not yet been exhausted), or, fourth, because the issues are 'moot' (since, for example, the pertinent facts or law have changed). It may also be rejected, fifth, because it concerns 'political' issues deemed the responsibility of other branches of government. But distinguishing between what lies within the province of the executive and the legislature, and what is justiciable, is not easy because the cases heard by the US Supreme Court are by their very nature also political. As O'Brien points out: 'The power to decide what to decide ... enables the Court to set its own agenda', and permits it to function 'like a roving commission, or legislative body, in responding to social forces',[225] no longer functioning 'to correct errors in particular cases, but rather to resolve only controversies of nationwide importance'.[226] 'Cues' in the filings are said to elicit the Court's interest, the most important being civil liberties issues, a disagreement in the lower court, and the fact that the federal government is the petitioner, with some studies indicating that the latter is the most important factor in ensuring a hearing.[227]

Blankenburg claims that, 'relative to the case load of regular courts', criminal and civil cases are underrepresented among constitutional complaints to the German Federal Constitutional Court, with administrative cases over represented only because of asylum claims.[228] Heun says the opposite – that '(c)ivil and criminal decisions dominate those of administrative courts'.[229] However, each agree that between 1990 and 1995 45 per cent of complaints concerned violations of due

224 Rogowski and Gawron, 'Constitutional Litigation', 8–9.
225 O'Brien, *Storm Center*, p. 165.
226 *Ibid.*, p. 231. 227 *Ibid.*, p. 226.
228 Blankenburg, 'Mobilization', 163.
229 Heun, 'Access', 148.

process,[230] and 41 per cent violations of due process combined with another complaint.[231] About half of complaints are said to be made by prison inmates or defendants complaining about a violation of one of their rights under Article 103 of the Basic Law (the rights to a judicial hearing, to non-retrospective punishment, and to be protected from 'double jeopardy'), with comparatively few complaints referring to the classic freedoms.[232] Nevertheless, the criteria for admission for hearing by the German Federal Constitutional Court – 'constitutional relevance', 'intensity of the violation of basic rights', etc. – are deliberately vague, allowing the Court legitimately, and swiftly, to reject cases and to select applications in accordance with its own general agenda.[233]

Complaints which have crossed the admissibility threshold are received for judgment on the merits by one of the two eight-judge Senates of the German Federal Constitutional Court, if at least three judges believe that adjudication will lead to the clarification of a constitutional question, or if denial will cause the petitioner severe and unavoidable disadvantage.[234] Further amendments in 1993 mandated the Court to accept constitutional complaints of general constitutional importance, or when necessary for the protection of basic rights.[235] However, from an early stage in its history the Court has 'emphasized the dual function of constitutional complaints'; that they should 'not only maintain the individual protection of basic rights but, above and beyond this, should safeguard and develop the objective constitutional law' with, in some cases, the 'objective' aspect pushing the 'subjective' element into the background.[236] As Blankenburg states: 'As a matter of course, a Supreme Court cannot satisfy all the demands of rectifying justice in individual cases ... In place of guarding individual justice, it has to select a few leading cases and use them to further the policy it deems relevant to protect the constitutionality and consistency of the entire legal system.'[237]

[230] Blankenburg, 'Mobilization', 164; Heun, 'Access', 149.
[231] Blankenburg, 'Mobilization', 164.
[232] Heun, 'Access', 149–150.
[233] Rogowski and Gawron, 'Constitutional Litigation', 10.
[234] Heun, 'Access', 136. [235] *Ibid.* [236] *Ibid.*, 137.
[237] Blankenburg, 'Mobilization', 168.

Finally, although the admissibility processes of both the US Supreme Court and the German Federal Constitutional Court have been criticized by lawyers in both jurisdictions on the grounds that they lack transparency, certainty, and predictability[238] – a further resemblance with the debate about the European Court of Human Rights – logistical constraints make it extremely unlikely that they will be replaced by anything more palatable to their critics.

CONCLUSION

Although it may not solve the current case overload crisis, Protocol 14 has, nevertheless, probably bought extra time for further reflection on the Court's future. Respondents in the Strasbourg interviews doubted if the draft protocol would achieve significant reductions in workload, but none thought the long-term prospects for either the Court or the Convention system were particularly bleak. Subject to a few criticisms, the provisions regarding the Court's composition, and the terms of judicial office, have been generally well-received. The new summary procedure for well-founded applications has also been welcomed as an appropriate response to repetitive complaints stemming from structural compliance problems, although there has been some disappointment that the 'pilot judgment' proposal has not been more formally adopted. Concerns have also been expressed about the discretion of committees to include the judge elected in respect of the respondent state where recourse to the summary process is contested. Although the Committee of Ministers approved extra resources for the Registry and for the Council of Europe's Secretariat involved in execution of the Court's judgments for the period 2003–5 following submission of the report of the Evaluation Group in September 2001,[239] the debate about the adequacy of resources is likely to continue. Respondents in the Strasbourg and London interviews also stressed the need for the Court's productivity to be monitored with much greater scientific rigour and openness than hitherto, for example by a dedicated research department in the Registry. Opinions also differ over the propriety of further

[238] Heun, 'Access', 137; Rogowski and T. Gawron, 'Constitutional Litigation', 9. It has even been claimed that the entire process of constitutional litigation in the German Federal Constitutional Court is, itself, unconstitutional, Heun, 'Access', 137.

[239] 'Protocol No. 14 to Convention', para. 23.

adjudication on the execution of judgments, over how useful such a process will prove to be, and whether the European Commissioner for Human Rights should be empowered to take cases on his own initiative in order to draw the Court's attention to serious structural violations in one or more states. In spite of attempts to find a satisfactory compromise, admissibility remains a highly contentious issue, and solving the problem of structurally non-compliant states through individual applications is as elusive as ever.

The debate about the Court's future, and about its evolving character as the Constitutional Court for Europe, must therefore continue. It cannot be denied that it is already a constitutional, or 'quasi-constitutional' court, in the sense of being the final authoritative judicial tribunal for a specific constitutional system designed to ensure that the exercise of public power throughout Europe is constitution-compliant, the constitution in this case being the European Convention on Human Rights. It is trite to assert that it ought to dispense both individual and constitutional justice since every judgment in an individual application delivers 'individual' justice in the narrow sense. But the consistent and systematic delivery of individual justice is simply beyond the Court's capacity, and dispensing small amounts of compensation to a tiny percentage of individual applicants for what may or may not be substantial Convention violations inhibits the fulfilment of its constitutional mission. As Mahoney puts it, having 'successfully assumed the mantle of a quasi-constitutional court for Western Europe, the European Court of Human Rights has as its future task to become an effective one for the whole of Europe'.[240] The 'significant disadvantage' element to the new admissibility test, which resembles the German equivalent, may have made this a more likely prospect. But there is a risk that this gain could be undermined by the increased complexity of the admissibility test and the possibility that valuable judicial time will be taken up considering whether the applicant has suffered such a disadvantage, or whether the complaint has been 'duly considered by a domestic tribunal'.[241]

As already indicated, some commentators and the Court itself, argue that continuing pressure from the inexorably rising tide of applications is likely, in the not-too-distant future, to require the creation of a separate judicial filtering institution. However, certain

[240] Mahoney, 'Speculating on Future', 4.
[241] Beernaert, 'Protocol 14', 556.

problems, for example the proportionate recruitment of its staff from all member states, would have to be addressed. But whether the Court should also be granted greater discretion over which applications then receive full adjudication, remains the most contentious issue in the procedural debate. The former Registrar and the Court itself are in favour,[242] and the three-stage admissibility procedure of the German Federal Constitutional Court provides a viable precedent. However, those who advocate the systematic delivery of individual justice strongly object. But not all contributions from this perspective are wholly consistent. Dembour, for example, welcomes the Court taking on a more consistently constitutional role yet, strangely, regards giving it more discretionary control over its own docket – a function routinely discharged by national constitutional courts – as 'a drastic, regrettable, and possibly dangerous transformation' which she hopes 'will be resisted successfully'.[243]

Ironically, greater discretionary control should mean both narrowing and broadening the grounds for admissibility. As far as broadening is concerned, the victim test may need to be widened to enable test cases to be brought by the European Commissioner for Human Rights and by National Human Rights Institutions. This is considered more fully in Chapter 6. As for narrowing, a radical solution would be to collapse all grounds for rejecting an application, except the purely formal non-discretionary ones – anonymity, failure to satisfy the (expanded) 'victim' test, failure to exhaust domestic remedies, breach of the six-months rule, abuse of process, and incompatibility – into a single inadmissibility criterion: 'the application does not raise an allegation of a Convention violation which, in the opinion of the Court, is sufficiently serious for the applicant, the respondent state, and/or for Europe as a whole to warrant adjudication on the merits'. While a 'serious' violation may, of course, entail, at the Court's discretion, any mixture of elements from the old and new admissibility criteria, plus others besides, it could be argued that it would unduly restrict the Court's discretion for this to be formally specified.

However, increasing the number of judges, creating regional human rights courts, extending the Court's advisory jurisdiction, or introducing a preliminary reference procedure have found little favour and would

242 CDDH, 'Response of ECtHR', para. 5; Mahoney, 'Insider's View'; Mahoney. New Challenges', 110–113.

243 Dembour, 'Finishing Off Cases', 622–623.

deliver few benefits. There are costs and coherence arguments against doubling the number of judges and creating regional courts, and since advisory opinions can only be expressed in vague and general terms, they are unlikely to add anything of substance to the future of the Convention system. Prima facie, the experience of the European Union suggests that a preliminary reference procedure might strengthen the Court's constitutional role by encouraging the more careful articulation of fundamental principles, clarifying the allocation of responsibility between the Court and national executive, legislative, and judicial institutions, developing constitutional doctrine, and promoting constitutional change in member states. But, regrettably, this process has compounded the workload problems of the ECJ, adjudication by the ECJ is less dependent upon litigation initiated by aggrieved individual applicants than its Convention counterpart, and it also takes place in a context where problems of systemic non-compliance with EU law can be addressed dynamically and strategically through the legislative activity of the Commission and Council of Ministers, a dimension both the Convention and the Council of Europe completely lack. While preliminary references may help reduce the time the European Court of Human Rights currently devotes to admissibility decisions, choices would still have to be made about which references deserved a hearing. It would also be difficult to foreclose access to the Court in cases where national courts had declined to make a preliminary reference, and the very fact that a preliminary reference was available but not used, might, in itself, exacerbate applicants' sense of grievance and thereby increase the individual application rate. There is also no guarantee that the courts of states with the worst records of Convention violation would be more likely to use a preliminary reference procedure than states with better records. In short it would be more bother than it is worth.

4

The Method of Adjudication

INTRODUCTION

Harmsen claims the Court has tended to adopt an 'excessively conservative' and casuistic method lacking principled coherence,[1] and President Wildhaber argues that ways need to be found for it 'to concentrate its efforts on decisions of "principle", decisions which create jurisprudence'.[2] However, the building blocks of a more coherent approach are already available, already partly employed, and merely need to be applied with greater consistency in order effectively to address core constitutional problems in the Convention which are also familiar in some form in all contemporary democratic constitutional systems – the division of responsibility between judicial and non-judicial bodies, how 'activist', 'restrained', or 'deferential' courts should be in scrutinizing the exercise of non-judicial public power, and the relative responsibilities of institutions at different levels of a constitutional system, in this case national and pan-European ones. The core thesis of this chapter is that the key to the more effective delivery of constitutional justice lies in the Court being more formally committed to the distinction between primary and secondary constitutional principles already inherent in the Convention.[3]

Since the Convention's provisions are abstract and sparse, the key to resolving individual complaints ultimately lies in how the text is interpreted.[4] In addition to the guidance provided by the precise terms

[1] R. Harmsen, 'The European Convention on Human Rights after Enlargement', *International Journal of Human Rights* **5** (2001), 18–43 at 32, 33, 35 and 38, note 53.

[2] L. Wildhaber, 'The Role of the European Court of Human Rights: An Evaluation', *Mediterranean Journal of Human Rights* **8** (2004), 9–32 at 28.

[3] This was first advanced in outline in, S. Greer, 'Constitutionalizing Adjudication under the European Convention on Human Rights', *Oxford Journal of Legal Studies* **23** (2003), 405–433.

[4] C. Gearty, 'The European Court of Human Rights and the Protection of Civil Liberties: An Overview', *Cambridge Law Journal* **52** (1993), 89–127 at 95.

of particular provisions, which often specify limits to rights, the process of interpretation is said to be governed by the application of a dozen or so 'interpretive principles'. Some of these are explicit in the text, while others have been inferred by the Strasbourg institutions. Some are sharply distinct from each other, while others are closely linked. The role they play in determining, directly or indirectly, the outcome of litigation has increasingly been recognized in recent years. The process by which legal texts are, and should be, interpreted has also been much debated, with a particularly rich literature on constitutional interpretation, especially in the US.[5] However, the relevant debate in the Convention context lacks depth and theoretical rigour. While the principles of interpretation can be distinguished and classified in a variety of ways,[6] the universally held view is that they fall into no particular order.[7] As Simor and Emmerson put it, they should not be 'viewed in isolation, or as a hierarchical system, but as part of a single complex exercise intended to ensure that the purpose and object of the Convention is fulfilled'.[8]

It is strange, however, that such an unstructured approach should have become so widely and uncritically accepted because some of the interpretive principles (for example, *democracy, effective protection* and *legality*) are obviously more intimately connected with the Convention's core purpose than are others (for example, the *margin of appreciation*, or *evolutive* and *autonomous* interpretation). This, in itself, suggests a more formal and hierarchical structure than has yet been acknowledged. But what form does this take? The first step in finding an answer lies in recognizing that the principles of interpretation address three distinct and quintessentially constitutional questions: the 'normative

[5] For a useful recent review see P. de Marneffe, 'Popular Sovereignty, Original Meaning, and Common Law Constitutionalism', *Law and Philosophy* **23** (2004), 223–260.

[6] Particularly useful accounts have been provided by J. Simor and B. Emmerson Q.C. (eds.), *Human Rights Practice* (London: Sweet & Maxwell, 2000), Ch. 1, and by B. Emmerson, Q.C. and A. Ashworth Q.C., *Human Rights and Criminal Justice* (London: Sweet & Maxwell, 2001), Ch. 2.

[7] Simor and Emmerson (eds.), *Human Rights Practice*, paras. 1.026–1.089. See also F. Ost, 'The Original Canons of Interpretation of the European Court of Human Rights' in M. Delmas-Marty and C. Chodkiewicz (eds.), *The European Convention for the Protection of Human Rights: International Protection Versus National Restrictions* (Dordrecht/Boston/London: Martinus Nijhoff, 1992), 283–318; F. Matscher, 'Methods of Interpretation of the Convention' in R. St. J. Macdonald, F. Matscher and H. Petzold (eds.), *The European System for the Protection of Human Rights* (Dordrecht/Boston/London: Martinus Nijhoff, 1993), 63–81.

[8] Simor and Emmerson (eds.), *Human Rights Practice*, para. 1.026.

question' of *what* a given Convention right means including its relationship with other rights and with collective interests; the 'institutional question' of *which* institutions (judicial/non-judicial, national/European) should be responsible for providing the answer; and the 'adjudicative question' of *how*, i.e. by which judicial method the normative question should be addressed.

PRIMARY CONSTITUTIONAL PRINCIPLES

The sheet anchor of the Convention's principles of interpretation is the *teleological* principle. Deriving from Articles 31–33 of the Vienna Convention on the Law of Treaties 1969, this requires the text to be interpreted in good faith according to the ordinary meaning of its terms in context – unless any special meaning was intended by the parties – and in the light of its overall object and purpose. Preparatory work, any subsequent practice or agreement between the parties regarding interpretation, and the circumstances in which the Convention was drafted, may be taken into account where the meaning of the text is ambiguous or obscure or where it would otherwise lead to a manifestly absurd or unreasonable result.[9] But unlike most international treaties, which are merely reciprocal agreements between states, the Convention is a 'constitutional instrument of European public order in the field of human rights', creating a 'network of mutual bilateral undertakings (and) objective obligations'.[10] As observed in Chapter 1, like national constitutions and much national legislation the Convention is the product of compromise and happenstance and does not obviously reflect a carefully articulated and theoretically grounded design. It would nevertheless be difficult to deny that its primary purpose is the protection of certain designated individual rights from violation by contracting states in the context of the core Council of Europe ideals

[9] See I. Brownlie, *Principles of Public International Law* (Oxford: Oxford University Press, 6th edn., 2003), pp. 602–607; H. Golsong, 'Interpreting the European Convention on Human Rights Beyond the Confines of the Vienna Convention on the Law of Treaties?' in R. St. J. Macdonald *et al.* (eds.), *European System*, pp. 147–162. The Court has endorsed this approach as a central element in the interpretation of the Convention, *Lithgow* v. *United Kingdom* (1986) 8 EHRR 329 at paras. 114–119; *Golder* v. *United Kingdom* (1979) 1 EHRR 524 at paras. 29–30.

[10] *Ireland* v. *United Kingdom* (1980) 2 EHRR 25 at para. 239; *Austria* v. *Italy* (1961) Y. B. 116 at 138.

of democracy and the rule of law.[11] It is not therefore an international treaty for the protection of democracy in the context of human rights and the rule of law, nor a treaty for the protection of the rule of law in the context of democracy and human rights, an observation which has important implications for the argument developed below.

The central constitutional issue raised by the Convention is how its basic purpose, identified by the teleological principle, can be realized institutionally. In other words how can responsibility for rights protection and the democratic pursuit of the public interest be distributed between judicial and non-judicial institutions each acting in accordance with the rule of law? This is more fundamental than the distribution of competence between national institutions, on the one hand, and the European Court of Human Rights on the other, because the function of national non-judicial bodies is different under the Convention from that of both national courts and the European Court of Human Rights which together share similar, though not identical, responsibilities. The teleological principle, therefore, suggests a re-arrangement of the primordial soup of principles of interpretation, and a re-structuring, but not a substantive revision, of the orthodox principle of *effective protection of human rights*, and the principles of *legality/rule of law* and *democracy*, to produce three primary constitutional principles, each exercised according to the principle of legality/procedural fairness/rule of law, to which the remaining principles of interpretation are subordinate. The 'rights' principle holds that in a democratic society Convention rights should be protected by national courts and by the European Court of Human Rights through the medium of law. The 'democracy' principle maintains that in a democratic society collective goods/public interests should be pursued by democratically accountable national non-judicial public bodies within a framework of law. The principle of 'priority to rights' mediates the relationship between the other two by emphasizing that Convention rights take procedural and evidential, but not conclusive substantive, priority over the democratic pursuit of the public interest, according to the terms of given Convention provisions. It should be observed that each of these three primary constitutional principles

[11] The Court has recognized the Preamble to the Convention as part of the context of the substantive text and indicative of its object and purpose, *Golder* v. *United Kingdom* (1979) 1 EHRR 524 at para. 34.

incorporates, what might otherwise be regarded as a fourth, the principle of 'legality/rule of law'. However, providing the role of the principle of legality is recognized as being integral to the other three, little of consequence results from counting them one way or the other.

The Rights Principle

The principle of *effective protection of Convention rights*, which is inherent rather than explicit in the text, holds that the Convention 'is intended to guarantee not rights that are theoretical and illusory but rights that are practical and effective'.[12] The reality of the applicant's position rather than its formal status is therefore what matters most.[13] The Court has also expressed this idea in other terms, for example the Convention should not be interpreted in a manner which leads to unreasonable or absurd consequences.[14]

The principles of *implied rights* and *implied limitations*, and the principles of *non-abuse of rights* and *non-abuse of limitations*, are closely related to the principle of effective protection. While some Convention provisions are stated in bald, and apparently absolute terms, seemingly subject to no exceptions at all – for example the right not to be tortured or inhumanly or degradingly treated or punished – others are limited in a variety of different ways by other rights or by public interests such as 'national security', 'the prevention of disorder or crime', or the 'economic well-being of the country'. However, according to Simpson, there is no obvious coherent rationale for the different forms the limitations take.[15] Most Convention rights can also be suspended in 'time of war or other public emergency threatening the life of the nation . . . to the extent strictly required by the exigencies of the situation'.[16] Although the Court has held that subsequent practice by the parties to the Convention cannot 'create new rights

[12] *Peltier* v. *France* (2003) 37 EHRR 197 at para. 36; *Soering* v. *United Kingdom* (1989) 11 EHRR 439 at para. 87.

[13] *Welch* v. *United Kingdom* (1995) 20 EHRR 247 at para. 27; *Deweer* v. *Belgium* (1980) 2 EHRR 439 at para. 44.

[14] Ost, 'Original Canons', 304.

[15] A. W. B. Simpson, *Human Rights and the End of Empire – Britain and the Genesis of the European Convention* (Oxford: Oxford University Press, 2001), p. 715.

[16] Art. 15(1).

and obligations which were not included in the Convention at the outset',[17] the principles of implied rights and implied limitations allow rights to be extended or restricted in limited ways not expressly found in the text provided the rights are interpreted broadly and the exceptions narrowly,[18] and provided the restrictions do not undermine the 'very essence'[19] of the right in question. As the following chapter will show, the right of access to a court, the right to have a judgment enforced, and the right to be represented by a competent lawyer, have for example been read into the right to a fair trial in Article 6, while a right not to be extradited to a state where there is a risk of being tortured, inhumanly or degradingly treated or punished has been derived from Article 3. Reliance on an exception to a Convention right must also be justified in every case according to its specific circumstances.[20] The line between reading implied rights into the Convention and creating new rights which the contracting parties did not intend is a fine one which the Court has not always drawn carefully.[21] But it has refused to imply rights into one Convention provision which would neutralize the effect of another provision – for example, by regarding the death penalty as a form of inhuman and degrading punishment – since to do so would be inconsistent with Article 2.[22] The principles of non-abuse of rights and non-abuse of limitations found in Articles 17 and 18 also derive from the principle of effective protection since they prohibit states and others from undermining the protection of rights by abusing either the rights themselves or their limitations. For example, forms of expression intended to incite racial hatred are beyond the protection of Article 10 since they undermine the rights of minorities.[23]

[17] *Cruz Varas* v. *Sweden* (1992) 14 EHRR 1 at para. 100.

[18] See P. van Dijk and G. J. H. van Hoof, *Theory and Practice of the European Convention on Human Rights*, 3rd edn. (The Hague/London/Boston: Kluwer, 1998), pp. 74–76.

[19] See, for example, *Ernst* v. *Belgium* (2004) 39 EHRR 724 at para. 56; E. Brems, 'The Margin of Appreciation Doctrine in the Case-Law of the European Court of Human Rights', *Zeitschrift für Auslandisches Offentliches Recht und Volkrecht* **56** (1996), 240–314 at 289–290.

[20] *Sunday Times* v. *United Kingdom* (1980) 2 EHRR 245 at para. 65.

[21] Simor and Emmerson (eds.), *Human Rights Practice* at para. 1.050.

[22] *Soering* v. *United Kingdom* (1989) 11 EHRR 439 at para. 101. The death penalty is now outlawed, even in time of war, by optional Protocol No. 6, which has not yet been signed by all Council of Europe states.

[23] *Glimmerveen and HagenBeek* v. *Netherlands* (1980) 18 D. R. 187 at 195–196.

The Democracy Principle

The idea of democracy appears in the text of the Convention in three different forms:[24] as a pervasive principle contained in the Preamble which states that human rights and fundamental freedoms are 'best maintained on the one hand by an effective political democracy and on the other by a common understanding and observance of the human rights upon which they depend'; as a right to participate in the democratic process found in Article 3 of Protocol No. 1; and as an express limitation upon the scope of specific rights, particularly those in Articles 8–11, usually incorporating a legality test and a requirement that the interference is in pursuit of a 'legitimate aim' proportionate to a pressing social need.

Marks maintains that, while the conception of democracy found in the early jurisprudence of the Convention organs was 'a starkly drawn contrast with "totalitarianism"', this was later more subtly contrasted with the 'absence of adequate safeguards against arbitrary exercises of power even by the more benign welfare state', which included such notions as the separation of powers and the principle of accountability.[25] The Court has also repeatedly declared that 'democracy appears to be the only political model contemplated by the Convention and, accordingly, the only one compatible with it'.[26] Both Court and Commission have also attempted to identify those Convention rights which are most central to democratic society, particularly in the context of litigation on Articles 8–11. Freedom of expression has consistently been singled out as particularly vital. But, as Marks points out, others have included the right of peaceful assembly, freedom to form and join professional associations, freedom from state indoctrination in education, the right to a fair trial, the right to personal liberty and security, freedom from arbitrary detention, and freedom of political association. It has also been held that the essential features of democratic society include pluralism, tolerance, and broadmindedness, that democracy

[24] See C. Gearty, 'Democracy and Human Rights in the European Court of Human Rights: A Critical Appraisal', *Northern Ireland Legal Quarterly* **51** (2000), 381–396; A. Mowbray, 'The Role of the European Court of Human Rights in the Promotion of Democracy', *Public Law* (1999), 703–725; S. Marks, 'The European Convention on Human Rights and its "Democratic Society"', *British Yearbook of International Law* **66** (1995), 209–238.

[25] Marks, 'ECHR and "Democratic Society"', 211–212.

[26] *Ždanoka* v. *Latvia* (2005) 41 EHRR 659 at para. 78; *United Communist Party of Turkey* v. *Turkey* (1998) 26 EHRR 121 at para. 45.

does not simply mean that the views of a majority must always prevail, but that a balance must be achieved which ensures the fair and proper treatment of minorities and avoids the abuse of a dominant position.[27]

While the Strasbourg institutions have made little attempt to articulate a clear theory, Marks describes the model found in Convention jurisprudence as a 'thin' conception of 'representative democracy'. It is 'thin' because it has not been extended beyond the state to include civil society, and because even within the state context it is limited to largely formalistic and minimalist requirements. It is 'representative' because it assumes that sovereignty belongs to the people but is vested in representatives, and that the essence of the democratic process is free elections supported by those rights and freedoms which most ensure electoral competition and the accountability of representatives to electors, i.e. the classic democratic rights of freedom of expression, association, assembly, fair trial, and freedom from arbitrary arrest and detention. However, according to Harvey, the democratization of central and eastern Europe and the rise of Islamism are challenging the Court's Cold War model and forcing it to identify a more substantive, but not as yet an entirely clear, alternative.[28] In central and eastern Europe, the Court has endorsed post-Soviet restrictions on the political activities of Communists and upon their access to positions in the police and civil service, but only until the transition has been effectively consolidated in the states concerned. But a second, yet to be litigated, problem in the region concerns restrictions on political activity by some of these states which, as Chapter 2 pointed out, appear to be consolidating their own political identity around a hybrid of democracy and authoritarianism rather than proceeding to full democratization. Like other commentators, Harvey also criticizes the decision to uphold the ban on the Islamic Refah Partisi (Welfare Party), for lack of sufficient evidence that it constituted a genuine threat to Turkish democracy. However, on the evidence which was available, the question of whether the party could properly be characterized as a threat to democracy, or merely radical and unorthodox but not inherently anti-democratic, was very finely balanced, and the decision could not obviously be said to have been wrong whichever way it had gone.

[27] Marks, 'ECHR and "Democratic Society"', 212–214.

[28] P. Harvey, 'Militant Democracy and the European Convention on Human Rights', *European Law Review* **29** (2004), 407–420.

The Principles of Legality, Procedural Fairness, and the Rule of Law

Pervasive in the Convention are the closely related principles of *legality, the rule of law* and *procedural fairness*, which seek to subject the exercise of public power to effective, formal legal constraints in order to avoid arbitrariness. For example, Article 2(1) provides that 'everyone's right to life shall be protected by law', while the right to liberty and security of the person enshrined in Article 5 is subject to a series of limited exceptions provided these are 'in accordance with a procedure prescribed by law'. The right to a fair trial in Article 6 refers to adjudication by 'an independent and impartial tribunal established by law', and Article 7 prohibits conviction and punishment without law. Restrictions on the rights to respect for private and family life, home and correspondence, freedom of thought, conscience and religion, freedom of expression, and freedom of assembly and association found in the second paragraphs of Articles 8–11 are also contingent upon being 'prescribed by' or 'in accordance with law' and 'necessary in a democratic society'. Article 12 provides a 'right to marry and found a family according to the national laws governing the exercise of this right'. Indeed Gearty maintains that 'due process' is the 'core unifying concept in the Convention and its case law'.[29] President Wildhaber points out that the principle of subsidiarity ensures that the Convention has a 'strong procedural bias' because the Court's responsibility is largely limited to satisfying itself that adequate domestic procedures, permitting all relevant considerations to be properly considered, are not only available, but have been properly applied.[30] Closely linked to the principles of legality and procedural fairness is the right, provided by Article 13 of the Convention, to an effective remedy for Convention violations. As Chapter 2 argued, a strong case can be made for this to be 'upgraded' to a right to a judicial remedy.

In a series of cases on Articles 8–11, but extending beyond these provisions, the Strasbourg institutions have developed a four-fold test determining what 'law' means for this purpose.[31] First, does the national legal system sanction the infraction? What counts as domestic 'law' may vary between states, and, on the grounds that national authorities are

29 Gearty, 'ECtHR and Civil Liberties', 125.

30 Wildhaber, 'Role of ECtHR', 9.

31 *Enhorn* v. *Sweden* (2005) 41 EHRR 633 at para. 36; *Maestri* v. *Italy* (2004) 39 EHRR 832 at para. 30.

best placed to judge, the Court permits a broad national discretion in interpreting domestic law and in determining whether or not national law-making procedures have been followed.[32] Second, is the relevant legal provision accessible to the citizen? In the *Sunday Times* case the Court held that this means that the citizen 'must be able to have an indication that is adequate in the circumstances of the legal rules applicable to a given case'.[33] Third, is the legal provision sufficiently precise to enable the citizen reasonably to foresee the legal consequences of their conduct? The Court has consistently recognized that many laws are framed in general terms the interpretation and application of which are matters of practice and judicial interpretation.[34] It has also been held that the degree of precision necessary depends upon the particular subject matter,[35] and that the predictability of consequences may require expert advice.[36] Laws which confer discretion must indicate its scope, although this need not be found in the legal text itself.[37] For example, laws permitting tapping and other forms of official interference with telephone conversations must be particularly precise because of the seriousness of the interference with private life, the lack of public scrutiny, and the risk of the abuse of power, especially since the relevant technology is rapidly becoming more sophisticated.[38]

Fourth, does the law provide adequate safeguards against arbitrary interference with the respective substantive rights? In *Malone* the Court stated that the phrase 'in accordance with the law' implies that there must be a 'measure of legal protection in domestic law against arbitrary interferences by public authorities with the rights safeguarded by', in this case, Art. 8(1), and that 'the law must indicate the scope of any such discretion conferred on the competent authorities and the manner of its exercise with sufficient clarity, having regard to the legitimate aim of the measure in question, to give the individual adequate protection

[32] *Chorherr* v. *Austria* (1994) 17 EHRR 358 at para. 26; *Kokkinakis* v. *Greece* (1994) 17 EHRR 397 at para. 40.

[33] *Sunday Times* v. *United Kingdom* (1980) 2 EHRR 245 at para. 49.

[34] *Şahin* v. *Turkey* (2005) 41 EHRR 109 at para. 77; *Goodwin* v. *United Kingdom* (1996) 22 EHRR 123 at paras. 31–34; *Silver* v. *United Kingdom* (1983) 5 EHRR 347 at para. 88.

[35] *Vögt* v. *Germany* (1996) 21 EHRR 205 at para. 48; *Malone* v. *United Kingdom* (1985) 7 EHRR 14 at para. 68.

[36] *Groppera Radio AG* v. *Switzerland* (1990) 12 EHRR 321 at para. 68.

[37] *Herczegfalvy* v. *Austria* (1993) 15 EHRR 437 at para. 89; *Malone* v. *United Kingdom* (1985) 7 EHRR 14 at para. 68.

[38] *Doerga* v. *Netherlands* (2005) 41 EHRR 45 at paras. 44–54; *Kruslin* v. *France* (1990) 12 EHRR 547 at para. 33.

against arbitrary interference'.[39] The Strasbourg organs have recognized that this is particularly necessary where a broad discretion is conferred upon the executive, especially where this is exercised in secret.[40]

'Balancing' and the Principle of 'Priority-to-Rights'

While no one could deny that the 'rights', 'democracy', and 'rule of law' principles lie at the heart of the Convention, the relationship between them is much more contentious. Indeed, since these values are at the core of every modern western constitution, their relationship has been much debated by political, legal, and constitutional theorists.[41] The central question is how conflicts between them should be resolved. Most judges and jurists take the view that competing constitutional, fundamental, or human rights should be 'balanced' against each other, and against conflicting democratically conceived public interests.[42] As the former President of the European Court of Human Rights, Rolv Ryssdall, put it: 'The theme that runs through the Convention and its case law is the need to strike a balance between the general interest of the community and the protection of the individual's fundamental rights'.[43] The German constitutional theorist, Robert Alexy confirms that, from a 'methodological point of view', balancing is also 'the central concept' in the adjudication of the German Federal Constitutional Court.[44]

Nevertheless, 'balancing' raises deep theoretical problems, debated by Habermas and Alexy, among other contemporary political and

[39] *Malone* v. *United Kingdom* (1985) 7 EHRR 14 at paras. 66–68.

[40] *Leander* v. *Sweden* (1987) 9 EHRR 433 at para. 51.

[41] For a useful review of the alternatives see M. Loughlin, 'Rights, Democracy, and Law' in T. Campbell, K. D. Ewing, and A. Tomkins (eds.), *Sceptical Essays on Human Rights* (Oxford: Oxford University Press, 2001), pp. 41–60.

[42] This is a pervasive theme in the debate about the impact of the Human Rights Act 1998 in the UK. See, e.g. Lord Irvine of Lairg, Q. C., 'The Impact of the Human Rights Act: Parliament, the Courts and the Executive', *Public Law* (2003), 308–325 at 310, 313–314, 316, 319, 323; F. Klug and K. Starmer, 'Incorporation Through the "Front Door": the First Year of the Human Rights Act', *Public Law* (2001) 654–665 at 664–665; F. Klug, 'Judicial Deference under the Human Rights Act 1998', *European Human Rights Law Review* (2003), 125–133; D. Feldman, 'The Human Rights Act 1998 and constitutional principles', *Legal Studies* **19** (1999), 165–206 at 173–178.

[43] R. Ryssdall, 'Opinion: The Coming Age of the European Convention on Human Rights', *European Human Rights Law Review* (1996), 18–29 at 23.

[44] R. Alexy, 'Constitutional Rights, Balancing, and Rationality', *Ratio Juris* **16** (2003), 131–140, at 134.

legal theorists. Several objections to balancing can be distinguished in Habermas's critique.[45] First, it reduces all debate about the relationship between rights, or between rights and the pursuit of collective goals, to policy arguments. This, secondly, robs constitutional rights of their 'strict *priority*' over other considerations.[46] In other words, the 'fire wall' separating the protection of rights from the pursuit of public policy collapses.[47] Third, since there is no rational standard by which judges can reconcile competing policy objectives, judicial decisions based on balancing are irrational. Policy arguments are, therefore, merely weighed 'either arbitrarily or unreflectively, according to customary standards and hierarchies'.[48] This means, fourthly, that balancing takes adjudication outside the realm of rule-governed behaviour and into the domain of unregulated judicial discretion. Finally, the results of litigation which hinge on balancing can no longer be justified as right or wrong but only as appropriate, or adequate, to varying degrees.[49]

Alexy, on the other hand, argues that the exercise of judgment in the adjudication of conflicts between rights, and between rights and collective interests, is inescapable, and that balancing, properly understood and applied, is both rational and legitimate and does not necessarily lead to the consequences Habermas fears.[50] This conclusion derives from the claim, based on a close analysis of the jurisprudence of the German Federal Constitutional Court, that both constitutional rights and collective goals 'have the character of principles' and that 'principles' are essentially 'optimization requirements', which means that the objectives they enshrine should be realized to the greatest extent possible given the legal and factual constraints.[51] According to Alexy, while optimizing any given constitutional principle entails its full

[45] These are neatly set out by Alexy, 'Constitutional Rights', 134–135. I have taken the liberty of distinguishing five points from the two Alexy attributes to Habermas.

[46] J. Habermas, *Between Facts and Norms*, trans. W. Rehg (Cambridge: Cambridge University Press, 1996), p. 256.

[47] *Ibid.*, p. 258. [48] *Ibid.*, p. 259.

[49] As Habermas states, although 'valid norms make up a flexible relational structure, in which the relations can shift from case to case ... *this* shifting is subject to the coherence proviso, which ensures that all the norms fit together into a unified system designed to admit exactly one right solution for each case' (italics in original), *ibid.*, p. 261.

[50] Alexy, 'Constitutional Rights'; R. Alexy, *A Theory of Constitutional Rights*, trans. J. Rivers (Oxford: Oxford University Press, 2002), pp. 44–110 and 388–425; R. Alexy, 'On Balancing and Subsumption. A Structural Comparison', *Ratio Juris* **16** (2003), 433–449.

[51] Alexy, *Theory of Constitutional Rights*, pp. 47–48 and 65–66.

implementation where no other countervailing principle pulls in a different direction, conflicts between principles can only rationally be resolved by balancing each against the other according to the 'principle of proportionality' which consists of three sub-principles: 'suitability', 'necessity', and 'proportionality in the narrow sense'.

The principle of suitability excludes the use of means to realize any given principle (P_1) which are factually incapable of doing so where this would interfere with the fulfilment of any other principle (P_x). The principle of necessity requires that if there are several suitable means (M_x) of realizing P_1, some of which may as a matter of fact and causation interfere with the realization of another principle P_2, the means (M_1) which least interferes with P_2 should be chosen. The principle of 'proportionality in the narrow sense' (otherwise known as the 'Law of Balancing') requires that, where the fulfilment of P_1 by M_1 interferes with the realization of P_2, the extent of the interference must be justified by the importance of satisfying P_1. According to the 'Second' or 'Epistemic' Law of Balancing, the greater the interference with a constitutional right, the more empirically certain must the successful realization of a collective goal be. The Law(s) of Balancing, therefore, produce 'indifference curves' on which a number of equally acceptable resolutions of the tension between two competing principles may be found. As Alexy maintains: 'The theory of principles . . . has always emphasized that balancing is not a procedure which leads necessarily to precisely one outcome in every case', but merely that 'one outcome can be rationally established' in enough cases 'to justify balancing as a method'.[52]

The implications of the Habermas-Alexy debate for the Convention will be explored in due course. But before doing so it can be observed that there are, prima facie, three alternative ways of resolving the conflict between the Convention's democracy and rights principles: the rights principle should take precedence over the democracy principle (the 'rights privileging' model); the democracy principle should take precedence over the rights principle (the 'democracy privileging' model); each principle should be balanced against the other with neither taking precedence until all relevant features of the particular conflict have been considered (the 'balancing' model). The 'democracy privileging' model, is clearly inappropriate for the Convention since it is

[52] *Ibid.*, p. 402.

manifestly inconsistent with its core purpose, the effective judicial protection of human rights. But, since the Convention permits collective goods to prevail over rights, providing certain conditions are met, the choice between the remaining two is not obvious. As Chapter 1 pointed out, a 'rights privileging' political morality prevailed in the Convention-drafting process in response to the political needs of post-war Europe rather than as a result of the application of a carefully articulated theory. However, it can be argued that in spite of this such a theory nevertheless underpins the Convention.

In a compelling analysis of Articles 8–11 of the Convention, McHarg argues that the relationship between rights and public interests depends upon how each is conceived.[53] According to the 'common interest' theory, the public interest can be understood as the interests people living together in fact hold in common independently of their individual or sectional interests, with rights as 'protected', but not privileged, social interests. Since both rights and collective goods are merely different kinds of, prima facie, equally important social interests, neither is presumed to take precedence over the other and each needs to be balanced in the specific context in which the conflict has arisen (model 1 or the 'balance' model). Alternatively, rights and collective goods can be seen as different manifestations of an integrated theory of political morality (the 'unitary theory') according to which there can be no genuine conflict between either once each is properly understood and defined. The relationship between rights and public interests is not therefore determined by weighing each against the other, but by rigorously defining the legitimate scope of both in terms of rules plus exceptions derived from the transcendent political morality (model 2 or the 'trumps' model).[54] McHarg argues that the central problem with the 'balance model' is that it suggests a weighing of rights and collective goods which, not only down-grades rights to mere interests, but requires judges – who are ill-equipped to decide

[53] A. McHarg, 'Reconciling Human Rights and the Public Interest: Conceptual Problems and Doctrinal Uncertainty in the Jurisprudence of the European Court of Human Rights', *Modern Law Review* **62** (1999), 671–696.

[54] The author considers a third conception of the public interest – preponderance or aggregative models – which take the public interest to consist of the summation of individual interests. This is rightly rejected as inappropriate for the Convention because of its intimate connection with utilitarianism which, at least in its classical Benthamite form, is hostile to the notion that rights should ever take precedence over the pursuit of the common good (*ibid.*, 674–675).

what is in the public interest – constantly to defer to non-judicial determinations of how the balance between the two should be struck. The net result is to undermine the attempt to entrench rights which is the fundamental purpose of rights documents such as the Convention.

According to McHarg, the problem with the 'trumps model' on the other hand is that a universally accepted objective theory of social and personal goods is, to put it mildly, difficult to find, and, even if one could be identified, it would be too abstract to serve as a viable judicial theory for interpreting the Convention or other rights treaties. This leaves judges to consider each right separately and to attempt to determine its scope according to the purposes it is deemed to serve. But this is also a difficult and contentious task since the 'true' purposes of rights will be difficult to infer from the abstract provisions of the rights document itself, there may be differences of judicial opinion as to how broadly or narrowly rights and public interests should be construed, and it may be unclear whether the rights document should be interpreted in a manner faithful to the 'framers' intent' or in ways more responsive to social change. Moreover, paradoxically, according to McHarg, this model offers *less* protection to rights than the balance model because where they decide that a collective good should prevail over a right, judges have effectively conceded that the protection conferred by the right has run out and there is no jurisdiction to limit interference by non-judicial authorities any further. Therefore, 'even where alleged gains to the public interest are trivial compared with their impact on individuals, courts must decline jurisdiction because no rights have been violated'.[55] McHarg concludes that the jurisprudence on Articles 8–11 of the Convention oscillates between these two models depending on whether the emphasis is upon the right itself, the 'factual necessity' of the exception, or a genuine attempt at balancing.[56] However, while advocating the adoption of one or other model she declines to indicate which is most appropriate for the Convention because of the formidable theoretical problems with each, and because the choice depends on 'one's view of the relative importance of protecting individual rights or allowing pursuit of collective goals and on one's preference for judicial neutrality or a commitment to substantive human rights standards'.[57]

[55] *Ibid.*, 682. [56] *Ibid.*, 693. [57] *Ibid.*, 695.

However, there are grounds in the Convention context for rejecting the 'balance' model, as thus described, in favour of a modified version of 'rights as trumps'. First, the distinction between the 'balance' and 'trumps' models, although undeniably valid and useful, masks other possible ways of arranging the relationship between rights and collective goods as a matter of political and legal theory. There are different kinds of balancing for a start. A distinction can, for example, be drawn between 'ad hoc' balancing, where the relationship between rights and public interests is assessed afresh on a case-by-case basis, and 'structured' balancing, such as that advocated by Alexy, which might involve setting the fulcrum of the scales towards either rights or collective goods for all cases. Second, it is clear that the relationship between rights and public interests arises in different forms with respect to provisions other than Articles 8–11. Third, the Convention's principles of interpretation, even in their orthodox haphazard form, address some of the problems McHarg identifies with the 'trumps' model. The principles of effective protection and non-abuse require rights to be interpreted broadly and the exceptions narrowly, while the principles of dynamic and evolutive interpretation indicate that the Convention should be interpreted in a manner which accommodates social change rather than remaining slavishly faithful to the framers' intent.

But most fundamentally of all, the Convention's constitutional principles supply precisely the kind of interpretive theory which enables a 'rights privileging' model to be viable without the need for judges to refer directly to political morality at all. This is because, together with the other two primary constitutional principles, the teleological principle suggests the principle of 'priority to rights', found in both strong and weak forms throughout the text and jurisprudence, which systematically accords rights greater procedural and evidential weight than collective goods. The constitutional theory presented here does not however conform exactly to the 'trumps model' because it does not assume, as some versions do, that rights are more intrinsically valuable than public interests, that they should always (or nearly always) prevail over considerations of the public interest, nor that their scope and their relationship with public interests should, or even can, be precisely defined in terms of rules and exceptions derived from a transcendent political morality. Indeed, several different 'rights-privileging' political moralities might be invoked to support it.[58] Instead, it merely suggests that rights should be 'prioritized' over collective goods in different ways according to the terms of given Convention provisions.

While the full implications for the case law are explored in the following chapter, the broad contours of this approach are as follows. A strong version of the priority-to-rights principle applies to the rights derived from the prohibitive principles in Articles 3, 4(1), and 7(1). These rights are often said to be 'absolute' because the principles from which they derive are without express restriction and the rights themselves cannot be suspended even in time of war or public emergency threatening the life of the nation. This is not, however, an appropriate designation because in interpreting these provisions the Strasbourg institutions have – although not always with good reason – resorted to the principle of implied restrictions. The relevant rights have therefore emerged subject to inherent public interest exceptions as a matter of definition. But the formal structure of these provisions, allied with the constitutional model presented here, means that the relationship between the rights and their implicit restrictions should not be achieved by 'ad hoc balancing', nor by directly applying the principle of proportionality, but first by ensuring that certain universal minimum standards are observed and next by permitting restrictions only at the margins.

Other strong versions of the priority-to-rights principle are found in Articles 2 and 15 which require, respectively, that the use of force which results in interferences with the right to life should be 'no more than absolutely necessary', and that derogations from all but the non-derogable rights should only occur in time of 'war or other public emergency threatening the life of the nation', and that even then only to 'the extent strictly required by the exigencies of the situation'. Here again the relationship between the rights concerned, and the public interests which may limit them, is not achieved by balancing, nor by applying the principle of proportionality, but by requiring justifications

[58] For example theories, like Dworkin's, which see constitutional rights as setting the boundaries between personal and public self-determination, R. Dworkin, *Freedom's Law: The Moral Reading of the American Constitution* (Cambridge, Mass.: Harvard University Press, 1996), pp. 15–26, and those of Ely and others which regard constitutional rights as specifying the conditions for deliberative democracy, J. H. Ely, *Democracy and Distrust: A Theory of Judicial Review* (Cambridge, Mass. Harvard University Press, 1980). See also the review of these theories in L. Sager, 'The Domain of Constitutional Justice', pp. 235–270 at 244–247 in L. Alexander (ed.), *Constitutionalism: Philosophical Foundations* (Cambridge: Cambridge University Press, 1998).

for interference to cross the high evidential threshold of 'absolute' or 'strict' necessity first.

The priority principle is weakest in relation to Article 1 of Protocol No. 1 which provides a right to the peaceful enjoyment of possessions limited by 'the public interest . . . subject to the conditions provided for by law and by the general principles of international law', and which also entitles states to 'control the use of property in accordance with the general interest'. But, prima facie, a version of 'intermediate strength' applies to Article 4(2) and (3), and to Articles 5 and 6 where the right not to be subject to forced or compulsory labour and the rights to liberty and to fair trial are more formally defined than any other Convention right and are subject, in the case of Article 4(2) and (3) and Article 5, to a series of narrowly conceived express restrictions. However, although the principle of implied restrictions has also affected the way in which these rights have been defined, the formal structure of these provisions, and the Convention's inherent constitution, require these rights to be given procedural and evidential precedence, though not as strong as in the context of Articles 3, 4(1) and 7(1).

Another version of the priority principle of 'intermediate strength' applies to Articles 8–11 where the rights in question take procedural and evidential priority over broadly expressed collective goods. Whether or not there has been an 'interference' is, for example, formally considered before the question of its justification, which is in turn filtered through a series of tests – 'prescribed by law', 'democratic necessity', pursuit of a specific 'legitimate purpose', and 'proportionality to a pressing social need'. While these may present less demanding thresholds than is the case with the strong versions of the priority principle, the structure of Articles 8–11, together with the Convention's primary and secondary constitutional principles, make clear that the respective rights are presumed to take precedence over collective goods unless a strong case can be made out otherwise. So, in spite of the language sometimes used by the Strasbourg institutions in these circumstances, rights and public interests are not prima facie equal variables to be weighed in a balance. The scales are loaded, but not conclusively, in favour of rights.[59] In order to navigate

[59] A similar view is taken by Emerson who argues that, in the US context, conflicts between constitutional rights and national security should be mediated with a presumption in favour of the constitutional right. The burden of proof should rest on the government to show a 'direct, immediate, grave, and specific' threat, courts should

these dangerous waters, the Court must adhere as scrupulously as possible to the formal conception of the burden and standard of proof suggested by the priority principle, considered more fully below.

Therefore, although there is merit in Habermas's insistence that rights have priority over the pursuit of the collective good, his objections to 'balancing' are, otherwise, not convincing in the Convention context for four main reasons. First, it could be argued that in some sense 'balancing' amounts to no more than an exercise in interpretation, common in some form or other to the proper understanding of any legal standard, including Convention norms and even to apparently crystal clear legal rules. Second, even when rights have effectively been accorded priority over the common good, the incommensurability of values and goals means that it is inappropriate to expect objectively right answers to be embedded in the Convention system merely awaiting excavation by the application of the 'correct' juridical method. Third, the distinction between rights and collective goods is clear and sustainable in the Convention and its jurisprudence even though it has not always been consistently drawn by the Strasbourg institutions when accommodations have had to be found between them. Finally, Habermas's critique is underpinned by an unfashionably formalistic model of the 'routine' adjudicative process in which the legitimacy of judicial decisions depends upon the extent to which they are governed by strict and predictable legal rules, while as already indicated Convention jurisprudence is characterized by the application of principles, rather than rules, to facts.

But Alexy's model of balancing cannot be applied to the Convention without substantial revision either. First, it is clear that in cases where Convention rights conflict with each other or with collective goods the European Court of Human Rights follows a formal sequence of questions different from that which he discerns in the jurisprudence of the German Federal Constitutional Court. In the particularly problematic context of Articles 8–11, for example, the interference must be prescribed by law, necessary in a democratic society in pursuit

view government claims with 'healthy skepticism' formulating and applying hard and fast rules rather than loose balancing tests, and, even where the government case is substantiated, rights should be restricted only to the narrowest extent, T. I. Emerson, 'National Security and Civil Liberties', *Yale Journal of World Public Order* **9** (1982), 78–112 at 85.

of one or more of the specified interests, and proportionate to a pressing social need. Second, in most cases which reach the European Court of Human Rights the principles of suitability and necessity will already have been answered in the affirmative, and Alexy's neat tripartite test will therefore have collapsed into a single 'balancing question': is M_1 factually capable of implementing P_1 while in the circumstances only infringing P_2 to the minimum degree tolerable by reference to broader considerations? Third, whereas Alexy treats constitutional rights and collective goods as competing principles capable of being balanced according to his formula, the Convention formally assigns priority to Convention rights. This means that the process by which the Court reconciles Convention rights with each other is subtly different from that by which it reconciles Convention rights with the 'common good', notwithstanding the fact that in both the key issue is how particular constitutional arrangements permit and regulate various kinds of discretion. Fourth, unlike national constitutional courts, the European Court of Human Rights lacks the constitutional authority in both these contexts – 'rights v. rights' and 'rights v. collective goals' – to set out the various relationships in terms of formal legal rules.

However, 'balancing' is not inappropriate in the Convention context provided the principle of priority-to-rights is observed and two subtly different scenarios are carefully distinguished. First, when two Convention rights are directly in conflict in the absence of any competing public interest, the Court has the ultimate constitutional responsibility for determining what each right means. As the following chapter will seek to show, whether this process is described as 'defining' vague rights more precisely, 'determining their scope', or 'balancing' one right against the other, matters less than the recognition that there is no scope for genuine domestic discretion concerning how the rights themselves should be understood, although there is on the question of whether or not the disputed conduct is compatible with them thus defined. Second, in seeking to reconcile a conflict between a Convention right and a collective goal, by contrast, the central issue is not about how the meaning of a given right should be determined, but about whether a clearly defined right should be overridden by a competing collective goal, the pursuit of which is deemed more compelling in the circumstances. This is, therefore, more obviously an exercise in 'structured' balancing than is the reconciliation of conflicts between Convention rights. The Court's key constitutional task here is to determine if in conducting their own balancing exercises national authorities have observed the Convention's constitutional principles, a critical element in which concerns the proper allocation of burdens of proof considered more fully below. This conclusion is not yet fully grasped by the European Court of Human Rights and, although under developed in Alexy's theory, is not wholly inconsistent with it.

SECONDARY CONSTITUTIONAL PRINCIPLES

The remaining principles of interpretation are subordinate to the 'rights', 'democracy', and 'priority' principles and provide a complex web of overlapping and not clearly distinguishable support. The principles of *subsidiarity, positive obligations*, and *non-discrimination* mediate between the 'rights', 'democracy', and 'priority' principles, although subsidiarity in relation to the 'rights' principle has the effect of making the role of the Court subsidiary only to that of national judicial organs. The principles of *proportionality* and *strict/absolute necessity* determine the strength of the 'priority' principle in different contexts, the principles of *review, commonality, evolutive, dynamic*, and *autonomous interpretation* derive from the 'rights' principle, while the *margin of appreciation doctrine* (strictly interpreted) derives from the 'democracy' principle.

Commonality, Autonomous and Evolutive/Dynamic Interpretation

Armed with the principle of *autonomous interpretation* the Court can define for itself some of the Convention's key terms either on the grounds that they do not have a common meaning in member states, or more frequently in order to prevent states conveniently re-defining their way around Convention obligations, for example by designating certain crimes as merely 'administrative infractions'.[60] However, in its turn this principle is constrained by the principle of 'commonality' which appears in four different forms in the Convention, the first three of which are found in the Preamble. The 'unity' principle states that 'the aim of the Council of Europe is the achievement of greater

[60] *Ezeh and Connors* v. *United Kingdom* (2004) 39 EHRR at paras. 82–89; *Engel* v. *Netherlands* (1979) 1 EHRR 647.

unity between its members' and that one of the methods by which this is to be achieved is 'the maintenance and further realization of human rights and fundamental freedoms'. The 'common understanding' principle maintains that one of the ways fundamental freedoms are best secured is through a 'common understanding and observance' of human rights. The 'common heritage' principle affirms that the Convention derives from the 'common heritage of political traditions, ideals, freedom, and the rule of law' of European countries. The principle of *evolutive*, or *dynamic, interpretation*, a principle the Court has developed for itself, facilitates the abandonment of out moded interpretations of the Convention when significant, durable, and pan-European changes in the climate of public opinion have occurred, for example that homosexuality and trans-sexualism are aspects of private life requiring respect from public authorities.[61] Prebensen distinguishes three uses of this principle: the majority of cases in which evolutive argument has supplemented other means of interpretation, typically where domestic approaches in member states are similar; cases where evolutive argument has been outweighed by primary means of interpretation, to prevent, for example, the emergence of new rights; and cases where evolutive argument has outweighed supplementary means of interpretation, because (as his analysis suggests although he does not make this point in these terms himself) the principle of effective protection of rights requires it.[62] Mahoney maintains that the principle of evolutive interpretation permits the appropriate degree of judicial activism, while the margin of appreciation (considered below) provides the appropriate degree of judicial restraint.[63] However, while these principles indisputably have such roles to play, their contribution can best be understood as means by which the Convention's primary constitutional principles are mediated and applied.

[61] I v. *United Kingdom* (2003) 36 EHRR 967; *Dudgeon* v. *United Kingdom* (1982) 4 EHRR 149.

[62] S.C. Prebensen, 'Evolutive interpretation of the European Convention on Human Rights' in P. Mahoney, F. Matscher, H. Petzold and L. Wildhaber (eds.), *Protecting Human Rights: The European Perspective – Studies in Memory of Rolv Ryssdal* (Cologne/Berlin/Bonn/Munich: Carl Heymans, 2000), pp. 1123–1137.

[63] P. Mahoney, 'Judicial Activism and Judicial Self-Restraint in the European Court of Human Rights: Two Sides of the Same Coin', *Human Rights Law Journal* **11** (1990), 57–88.

Positive Obligations

The principle of *positive obligations* allows the Court to interpret the Convention in a manner which, in addition to the negative obligation on states to refrain from violating Convention rights, also requires them actively to protect Convention rights by, for example, passing laws prohibiting citizens from violating the Convention rights of each other.[64] It is not however clear when a positive obligation arises. Some provisions expressly create them, for example the duties under Articles 2 and 13, respectively, to protect the right to life by law and to provide an effective national remedy for a Convention violation. However, by suggesting, though not stating, that in certain circumstances Convention rights cannot be effectively secured by negative obligations alone, the principle of effective protection, its sub-principles, and Article 1 – which requires states to secure Convention rights to everyone within their jurisdiction – provide sources from which other positive obligations have been derived.[65]

Nevertheless, even when a positive obligation has been officially recognized, its scope may be difficult to predict. According to Mowbray, the principal circumstances in which the Court has derived implicit positive obligations from Convention provisions, have included taking reasonable steps to protect individuals from infringement of their Convention rights by other private parties, the treatment of those detained under criminal justice processes, and conducting effective investigations into credible claims that serious violations of the Convention have occurred.[66] Citing relevant cases, Simor and Emmerson identify a number of factors conducive to the emergence of positive obligations: whether the right is narrowly or broadly defined, the importance of the interest at stake, whether fundamental values or core elements of a right are at issue, the extent of any burden that would be imposed on the state including whether or not it would involve a departure from its general approach in similar matters, the nature and extent of any prejudice suffered by the applicant, common European practice, the state's other international obligations, scientific advances,

[64] A. Mowbray, *The Development of Positive Obligations under the European Convention on Human Rights by the European Court of Human Rights* (Oxford/Portland: Hart, 2004). See e.g. Moreno, *Gómez* v. *Spain* (2005) 41 EHRR 899 at para. 55.

[65] Mowbray, *Development of Positive Obligations*, p. 221.

[66] *Ibid.*, pp. 225–227.

changing social attitudes, and the impact which the obligation in question would have on other Convention rights.[67]

Subsidiarity and Review

The twin principles of *subsidiarity* and *review* indicate that the role of the Court is subsidiary to that of member states and is limited to considering Convention-compliance rather than acting as final court of appeal or fourth instance.[68] Applicants are also required by Article 35 to exhaust domestic enforcement procedures before petitioning the Court, while Articles 1 and 13 respectively make it clear that primary responsibility for securing the rights and freedoms provided by the Convention lies with national authorities. The Convention provides minimum and non-exhaustive standards with states being at liberty to provide better protection, to safeguard additional rights, and, since they are in a better position to do so, to choose for themselves between a range of equally Convention-compliant alternatives.[69] The principle of review is found most clearly in Article 19 which provides that 'the observance of the engagements undertaken by the High Contracting Parties' shall be ensured by the European Court of Human Rights.

Proportionality and Strict/Absolute Necessity

In a study of the contribution of the European Court of Justice to the process of European integration Stone Sweet argues that, together with the development of a doctrine of precedent, and 'with the exception of the diffusion of the Court's constitutional doctrines ... the most transformative institutional innovation in the history of legal integration will be the emergence of proportionality balancing as a master technique of judicial governance ....'.[70] In the context of the

67 Simor and Emmerson (eds.), *Human Rights Practice*, para. 1.017.

68 H. Petzold, 'The Convention and the Principle of Subsidiarity', in R. St. J. Macdonald *et al.* (eds.), *European System*, pp. 41–62. According to the former President of the Court, Rolv Ryssdall, the principle of subsidiarity is 'probably the most important of the principles underlying the Convention', Ryssdall, 'Opinion', 24.

69 Petzold, 'Convention and Principle of Subsidiarity', 44 and 60.

70 A. Stone Sweet, *The Judicial Construction of Europe* (Oxford: Oxford University Press, 2004), p. 243. Although the European Court of Human Rights does not have as rigorous a notion of precedent as that found in the common law tradition, President Wildhaber argues that it nevertheless adheres to its previous judgments, L. Wildhaber, 'Precedent in the European Court of Human Rights' in Mahoney *et al.* (eds.), *The European Perspective*.

Convention, however, the central function of the principle of *proportionality* is to facilitate the consistent application of the 'democracy', 'rights' and 'priority-to-rights' principles.

While the concepts of strict and absolute necessity are expressly found in the text of certain Convention provisions, there is no mention of proportionality whatsoever. Yet it is difficult to deny that the principle of proportionality is an entirely legitimate judicial creation, closely linked to the margin of appreciation. The strict and absolute necessity criteria are, in effect, proportionality tests attached to strong versions of the priority-to-rights principle. The character of the proportionality principle and its application are at the heart of the debate about how conflicts between Convention rights – and between Convention rights and public interests – should be resolved. This has been conducted mainly in the context of the restrictions upon the rights found in Articles 8(2)–11(2), the anti-discrimination principle in Article 14, implied rights, and positive obligations.[71] However, proportionality has also featured in decisions relating to 'formally unqualified' rights – for example the right not to be tortured or inhumanly or degradingly treated or punished – although in this context it effectively becomes an implicit strict or absolute necessity test as the following chapter will seek to show.[72] Together with the margin of appreciation doctrine and the notion of 'legitimate aim', the principle of proportionality has also been read into the obligation undertaken by states in Article 3 of Protocol No. 1 to hold free elections.[73]

The proportionality test under the Convention is less formal than that found in other bills of rights. In Canada for example, several sub-elements are more sharply distinguished, the burden is on the state to prove that the objective in question was sufficiently important to justify overriding a constitutional right and if it was that the measure used to achieve it was not arbitrary, unfair, or irrational, and that the right was impaired as little as possible. However, these are flexible tests, and even where they have been fulfilled the right may still prevail

[71] See J. McBride, 'Proportionality and the European Convention on Human Rights' in E. Ellis (ed.), *The Principle of Proportionality in the Laws of Europe* (Oxford/Portland: Hart Publishing, 1999), pp. 23–35; M.-A.Eissen, 'The Principle of Proportionality in the Case-Law of the European Court of Human Rights' in R. St. J. Macdonald *et al.* (eds.), *European System*, pp. 125–146.

[72] See Simor and Emmerson (eds.), *Human Rights Practice*, para. 1.079.

[73] *Hirst* v. *United Kingdom (No. 2)* (2004) 38 EHRR 825 at para. 36; *Aziz* v. *Cyprus* (2005) 41 EHRR 164 at para. 25.

if the effect of interfering with it would be particularly serious for the group or individual concerned.[74] The Convention test, in its orthodox formulation, is much looser. In determining whether an interference with a right has been proportionate, it is said that there must be a real connection between the interference and the legitimate public policy being pursued. Important factors in determining if the orthodox proportionality test has been satisfied include the nature of the right in question, the extent of the interference in the circumstances, the strength of the public interest goal being pursued, the significance of local knowledge, the difficulty of weighing competing policy goals objectively, and the possibility that the same goal could have been achieved with a less intrusive impact on individual rights.[75]

However, although the principle of proportionality is vital to the resolution of disputes about Convention rights, there are two critical problems with the way in which the Court currently understands and applies it. First, because the Court has not consistently acknowledged the priority to rights principle, there is uncertainty about whether the applicant or the respondent state has the burden of proving that the interference in question has, or has not been, proportionate.[76] Generally the conceptions of burden and standard of proof applicable in Convention litigation are less strict and less formal than those found in the adversarial tradition. As Simor and Emmerson argue, some frequently used phrases support the view that 'the burden of establishing that an interference is proportionate lies on the government'.[77] For example, the grounds for interfering with a Convention right, or at least certain Convention rights in certain circumstances, must be 'relevant and sufficient',[78] the necessity for a restriction must be 'convincingly established'[79] or 'convincing and

[74] Simor and Emmerson (eds.), *Human Rights Practice*, para. 1.080.

[75] *Ibid.*, paras. 1.070–1.076.

[76] For a review of the approach under the Convention to the proof of facts at issue see U. Erdal, 'Burden and standard of proof under the European Convention', *European Law Review Human Rights Survey* **26** (2001), HR/68-HR/85.

[77] Simor and Emmerson (eds.), *Human Rights Practice*, para. 1.071.

[78] *Ernst* v. *Belgium* (2004) 39 EHRR 724 at para. 104; *Krone Verlag GmbH & Co KG (No. 2)* v. *Austria* (2004) 39 EHRR 906 at para. 42; *Nikula* v. *Finland* (2004) 38 EHRR 944 at para. 44.

[79] *Société Colas Est* v. *France* (2004) 39 EHRR 373 at para. 47; *Tele 1 Privatfernsehgesellschaft MBH* v. *Austria* (2002) 34 EHRR 181 at para. 34; *Autronic AG* v. *Switzerland* (1990) 12 EHRR 485 at para. 61; *Weber* v. *Switzerland* (1990) 12 EHRR 508 at para. 47.

compelling',[80] the exceptions should be narrowly construed,[81] the interference must be justified by a 'pressing social need',[82] and public policy should be pursued in the 'least onerous way as regards human rights'.[83] However, some confusion has also been created by other decisions which have opted instead for a 'fair balance' being struck between Convention rights and the 'general interests of the community' without offering any particular formula as to how this should occur.[84]

Jurists in the common law tradition have distinguished two principal senses of the burden of proof: the obligation to show there is sufficient evidence to make a contentious fact an issue in the trial (the 'evidential burden' or the 'burden of adducing evidence') and the obligation to prove what needs to be proven to the satisfaction of the court (the 'persuasive burden').[85] A party bearing the evidential burden need not also bear the persuasive burden. The standard of evidence required to discharge each type of burden also varies. Evidence which, 'if believed and if left un-contradicted and unexplained',[86] may be sufficient to discharge the burden of adducing evidence. In criminal cases the standard of evidence necessary to discharge the persuasive burden is 'proof of guilt beyond reasonable doubt', and in civil cases, 'proof on a balance of probabilities', or 'on a preponderance of the evidence'. Acknowledging that there are degrees of probability, the law of the United States distinguishes an intermediate standard between 'probably true' and 'proof beyond reasonable doubt'– proof by 'clear, strong and cogent' evidence, or, in constitutional litigation, 'clear and convincing evidence'.[87] English law

[80] *Refah Partisi (Welfare) Party* v. *Turkey* (2003) 37 EHRR 1 at para. 135; *ÖZDEP* v. *Turkey* (2001) 31 EHRR 674 at para. 44.

[81] *Société Colas Est* v. *France* (2004) 39 EHRR 373 at para. 47; *Sunday Times* v. *United Kingdom* (1980) 2 EHRR 245 at para. 65.

[82] *The Observer and The Guardian* v. *United Kingdom* (1992) 14 EHRR 153 at para. 71.

[83] *Hatton* v. *United Kingdom* (2002) 34 EHRR 1 at para. 97 (Chamber judgment).

[84] *Grande Oriente d'Italia di Palazzo* v. *Italy* (2002) 34 EHRR 629 at para. 25; *Piermont* v. *France* (1995) 20 EHRR 301 at para. 77; *Klass* v. *Germany* (1994) 18 EHRR 305 at para. 59; *Barfod* v. *Denmark* (1991) 13 EHRR 493 at para. 29; *Gaskin* v. *United Kingdom* (1990) 12 EHRR 36 at para. 40.

[85] See, C. Tapper, *Cross and Tapper on Evidence*, 10th edn. (London: Butterworths, 2004), Ch. 3.

[86] *Jayasena* v. *R* [1970] AC 618 at 624, per Lord Devlin.

[87] Tapper, *Evidence*, pp. 184–185; J. Kokott, *The Burden of Proof in Comparative and International Human Rights Law: Civil and Common Law Approaches with Special Reference to the American and German Legal Systems* (The Hague/London/Boston: Kluwer Law International, 1998), pp. 128–135.

also recognizes that certain allegations in civil cases, for example professional misconduct, may need to be proven to a standard higher than merely probable.[88] In her comparative study of the burden of proof in international human rights law, Kokott argues that international tribunals do not always clearly distinguish between the evaluation of evidence, the degree of persuasion required, and the burden of proof. However, she maintains that 'essential individual liberties' can only be legitimately infringed if the state establishes the case for lawful restriction beyond reasonable doubt, while the individual applicant may have the burden in relation to 'fringe values'. Although wide national margins of appreciation, and extenuating circumstances such as war, may reduce the state's persuasive burden or even shift it to the individual applicant, Kokott argues that allocating the burden of proof may not be reduced to mere ad hoc balancing between the consequences of two possible decisions.[89] The implications of this analysis for the Convention will be explored more fully in the following chapter.

The second problem is that the Court uses the doctrine of the margin of appreciation and the principle of proportionality to resolve conflicts between Convention rights when the task is more properly one of definition. While this may appear to an overly subtle distinction it is, on the contrary, one with enormous juridical and political implications for the whole Convention system. The difference between 'defining' Convention rights to resolve conflicts between them, and 'balancing' them against each other according to the margin of appreciation doctrine and the principle of proportionality, is that under the former there is no real scope for discretion on the part of national non-judicial authorities. The full implications of this conclusion will be explored in the following chapter.

Non-Discrimination

The anti-discrimination provision found in Article 14 of the Convention[90] can be regarded as either a principle, which mediates

[88] Tapper, *Evidence*, p. 185.
[89] Kokott, *Burden of Proof*, pp. 234, 136–137.
[90] Art. 5 of Protocol No. 7 also provides a right of equality between spouses in private law matters, subject to the overriding interests of children.

between the primary constitutional principles, or a right itself.[91] It is a 'principle' in the sense that it governs how the other rights and freedoms in the Convention are applied, that is to say, in a non-discriminatory way. It is a 'right' in the sense that its breach constitutes a violation of the Convention even though no other Convention right at issue may also have been violated. Protocol 12 provides much wider protection by prohibiting discrimination in relation to the 'enjoyment of any right set forth by law'.[92] In the seminal *Belgian Linguistics* case the Court defined discrimination under Article 14 as a difference between categories of person in the exercise of Convention rights which has 'no objective and reasonable justification',[93] giving rise to a distinction between 'different' treatment, which can be justified under the Convention, and 'discrimination', which would violate Article 14.[94] In a series of decisions four factors have been identified as guidelines for drawing the line.

First, the applicant must show that the treatment in question was less favourable than that received by other comparable groups, the identity of which will usually be determined objectively by the complaint itself. For example, if the alleged discrimination is based on gender, the comparator will be members of the opposite sex not suffering the same alleged disadvantage. Second, it is then for the state to show, as a matter of fact supported by evidence, that the practice is reasonable and rational. This will require reference to the policy goals which it is said to facilitate.[95] Third, the effects of the treatment must be

[91] See R. Wintemute, '"Within the Ambit": How Big is the "Gap" in Article 14 European Convention on Human Rights? Part 1', *European Human Rights Law Review* (2004), 366–382 and 'Filling the Article 14 "Gap": Government Ratification and Judicial Control of Protocol No. 12 ECHR: Part 2', *European Human Rights Law Review* (2004), 484–499; O.M. Arnardóttir, *Equality and Non-Discrimination under the European Convention on Human Rights* (The Hague/London/New York: Martinus Nijhoff, 2003); J. Schokkenbroek, 'The Prohibition of Discrimination in Article 14 of the Convention and the Margin of Appreciation', *Human Rights Law Journal* **19** (1998), 20–23; S. Livingstone, 'Article 14 and the Prevention of Discrimination in the European Convention on Human Rights', *European Human Rights Law Review* (1997), 25–34.

[92] N. Grief, 'Non Discrimination under the European Convention on Human Rights: A Critique of the United Kingdom Government's Refusal to Sign and Ratify Protocol 12', *European Law Review* **27** (2002), 3–18.

[93] *Belgian Linguistics Case* (No. 2) (1979) 1 EHRR 252 at para. 10.

[94] See, e.g. *Swedish Engine Drivers Union v. Sweden* (1979) 1 EHRR 617 at para. 44–48.

[95] *Abdulaziz, Cabales, Balkandali* v. *United Kingdom* (1985) 7 EHRR 471 at paras. 74–83.

disproportionate to the pursuit of the policy objective and must fail to strike 'a just balance between the protection of the general interest of the community and the respect due to fundamental human rights while attaching particular importance to the latter'.[96] The second and third factors have provided the basis for variable margins of appreciation, and a fourth factor – whether the practice in question is regarded as non-discriminatory in other democratic states – has been 'of major relevance' in determining their scope.[97] Since drawing the line between difference and discrimination involves matters of social policy, the width of the margin of appreciation 'will vary according to the circumstances, the subject matter and its background'.[98] The policy issue can, however, cut both ways. As Schokkenbroek points out, the Court has assumed certain kinds of differential treatment to be prima facie discriminatory – for example those based on sex, religion, illegitimacy, nationality – on the express or implicit grounds that they run counter to major priorities of European social policy. The same is arguably true of race, but the matter has yet to be fully litigated.[99]

The Margin of Appreciation

The *margin of appreciation*, typically described as a 'doctrine' rather than a principle, refers to the room for manoeuvre the Strasbourg institutions are prepared to accord national authorities in fulfilling their Convention obligations. However, the term is not found in the text of the Convention itself, nor in the travaux préparatoires.[100] It first appeared in 1949 in the European Movement's proposals,[101] and was adopted officially for the first time by the Commission in its 1958 report in the case brought by Greece against the UK over alleged human rights violations in counter-insurgency operations in Cyprus.[102] By the end of the 1990s it had been endorsed by numerous other Commission

96 *Belgian Linguistics Case* (1979) 1 EHRR 252 at para. 5.
97 Schokkenbroek, 'Prohibition of Discrimination', 21.
98 *Rasmussen* v. *Denmark* (1985) 7 EHRR 371 at para. 40.
99 Schokkenbroek, 'Prohibition of Discrimination', 22.
100 H. C. Yourow, *The Margin of Appreciation Doctrine in the Dynamics of European Human Rights Jurisprudence* (The Hague/Boston/London: Kluwer, 1996), p. 14.
101 Simpson, *Human Rights*, pp. 676–677.
102 *Greece* v. *United Kingdom* (1956–57) 2 Y.B. 174.

decisions and by over 700 judgments of the Court.[103] As Kokott points out, the principled management of national margins of appreciation has become one of the most important and difficult tasks, not only under the Convention, but in every mature system for the protection of human rights.[104] The margin of appreciation doctrine has also inspired a vast literature in the Convention context, much more extensive than that relating to any other principle of interpretation and indeed probably greater than that on any other single aspect of the Convention.[105] Most of this is devoted to describing its complex contours in the Convention landscape and to identifying fields of application and factors regulating its 'bandwidth'.

There is universal acknowledgment of when the doctrine made its first official appearance and broad consensus on several other core issues. All commentators agree that no simple formula can describe how it works and that, in spite of the mountain of jurisprudence and analysis, its most striking characteristic remains its casuistic, uneven, and largely unpredictable nature. Most also recognize the following features. First, that in addition to Article 15, the margin of appreciation

[103] Editors' note, 'The Doctrine of the Margin of Appreciation under the European Convention on Human Rights: Its Legitimacy in Theory and Application in Practice', *Human Rights Law Journal* **19** (1998), 1.

[104] Kokott, *Burden of Proof*, p. 234.

[105] The most comprehensive are Y. Arai-Takahashi, *The Margin of Appreciation Doctrine and the Principle of Proportionality in the Jurisprudence of the ECHR* (Antwerp/Oxford/New York: Intersentia, 2002) and Yourow, *Margin of Appreciation*. Those published in the past ten years or so include J. A. Sweeney, 'Margins of Appreciation: Cultural Relativity and the European Court of Human Rights in the Post-Cold War Era', *International and Comparative Law Quarterly* **54** (2005), 459–474; S. Greer, *The Margin of Appreciation: Interpretation and Discretion Under the European Convention on Human Rights* (Strasbourg: Council of Europe Publishing, Human Rights Files No. 17, 2000); M. R. Hutchinson, 'The Margin of Appreciation Doctrine in the European Court of Human Rights', *International and Comparative Law Quarterly* **48** (1999), 638–650; P. Mahoney, J. Callewaert, C. Ovey, S. C. Prebensen, Y. Winisdoerffer, J. Schokkenbroek and M. O'Boyle (Council of Europe internal seminar), 'The Doctrine of the Margin of Appreciation under the European Convention on Human Rights: Its Legitimacy in Theory and Application in Practice', *Human Rights Law Journal* **19** (1998), 1–36; N. Lavender, 'The Problem of the Margin of Appreciation', *European Human Rights Law Review* (1997), 380–390; E. Brems, 'The Margin of Appreciation Doctrine in the Case-Law of the European Court of Human Rights', *Zeitschrift für Auslandisches Offentliches Recht und Volkrecht* **56** (1996), 240–314; T. H. Jones, 'The Devaluation of Human Rights Under the European Convention', *Public Law* (1995), 430–449.

has had a high profile in litigation relating to certain Convention rights – the right to peaceful enjoyment of possessions in Article 1 of Protocol No. 1, the anti-discrimination provision of Article 14, and the personal freedoms enshrined in Articles 8–11 – but a lower profile with respect to others. Second, that drawing lines between Convention rights and legitimate public interest limitations will involve weighing difficult and controversial political, rather than judicial, questions. Third, national authorities are in a better position to obtain and to assess local knowledge, which the Court may either not have, or the significance of which it may misjudge. Fourth, there may be a range of equally defensible places where such lines could be drawn each of which may attract support from sections of public opinion in the state concerned, and some of which may be more appropriate in some member states than in others. For the Court to substitute its own conception of what is appropriate might therefore result in it taking sides in the resolution of genuine human rights/public interest dilemmas which are not amenable to any straightforward legal solution. Fifth, as Simor and Emmerson show, the width of the margin of appreciation will vary according to 'such factors as the nature of the Convention right in issue, the importance of the right for the individual, the nature of the activity involved, the extent of the interference, and the nature of the state's justification'. Sixth, intensity of review will vary from 'extreme deference on issues such as social and economic policy and national security', to a more intense review in cases involving 'criminal procedure, intimate aspects of private life, or political debate on matters of public interest'.[106] Finally, the extent to which there may be a pan-European consensus on the relationship between a particular Convention right and public interest may also govern the scope accorded the margin of appreciation.

However, opinion is also divided over a range of other issues. Commentators disagree, for example, over whether the doctrine embraces every kind of discretion by national institutions under the Convention, or relates only to certain types. This is linked to the question of whether it pervades the entire Convention or is restricted to specific provisions. Macdonald, for instance, maintains that 'in theory there is no limit to the articles of the Convention to which the margin of

[106] Simor and Emmerson (eds.), *Human Rights Practice*, para. 1.084.

appreciation could be applied for the Court has never imposed a limit'.[107] However, others have pointed out that it has never been invoked in respect of Article 2 (the right to life), Article 3 (the right not to be subjected to torture or to inhuman or degrading treatment or punishment), or Article 4 (the right not to be held in slavery or servitude, or subject to forced or compulsory labour),[108] and that it has had a very limited role in relation to Articles 5 and 6.[109] While some have argued for the elimination of the doctrine altogether,[110] most maintain that greater clarity, coherence, and consistency in its application are required. But few have ventured to suggest how this might be achieved.

It is not the purpose of this chapter to add another detailed account of the role of the margin of appreciation to those which already dominate the literature. Instead it makes a much simpler claim: the key to understanding the margin of appreciation lies in recognizing that it is subordinate to the Convention's primary constitutional principles which discipline it in two ways. First, the primary constitutional principles suggest that there is no genuine margin of appreciation at all on the part of national non-judicial institutions as far as the definition of Convention rights and their interface with each other is concerned, although there may be some 'implementation' discretion, for example on the mechanics of trial processes, and over how such adjectives and adverbs such as 'reasonable' and 'promptly' are applied. This is not to say that national legislative, executive, and administrative bodies should renounce the attempt to understand what a Convention right means, or refuse to delineate the boundaries between Convention rights, since these tasks are clearly and

107 R. St. J. Macdonald, 'The Margin of Appreciation in the Jurisprudence of the European Court of Human Rights', in Anon (ed.), *International Law at the Time of its Codification, Essays in Honour of Judge Roberto Ago* (Milan: Giuffrè, 1987), pp. 187–208 at 192.

108 J. Callewaert, 'Is there a Margin of Appreciation in the Application of Articles 2, 3 and 4 of the Convention?', *Human Rights Law Journal* **19** (1998), 6–9.

109 J. Schokkenbroek, 'The Basis, Nature and Application of the Margin-of-Appreciation Doctrine in the Case Law of the European Court of Human Rights', *Human Rights Law Journal* **19** (1998), 30–36, 34; Arai, *Margin of Appreciation*, pp. 28 and 49.

110 For example, in a partly dissenting opinion, Judge De Meyer stated that it was 'high time for the Court to banish that concept from its reasoning' because 'where human rights are concerned there is no room for a margin of appreciation which would enable the states to decide what is acceptable and what is not', *Z* v. *Finland* (1998) 25 EHRR 371 at para. III.

inescapably not only part of their daily functions, but also encompassed by the democracy principle. What it does mean is that, where the definition of Convention rights is in dispute, the matter must be resolved authoritatively by national courts, and ultimately by the European Court of Human Rights, with no genuine margin of appreciation accorded national non-judicial bodies. Secondly, where the exercise of a Convention right and a public interest conflict, the Court's main responsibility is not merely to permit a national balancing exercise, but to ensure that the priority-to-rights principle has been properly observed by national judicial and non-judicial authorities, according to the terms of the Convention provision(s) at issue. As already indicated, this is quite a different kind of 'balancing' from that which is usually conceived in the literature. Constrained in this way the margin of appreciation legitimately permits different resolutions of the tension between Convention rights and the collective good in different contexts in different states. The implications of this analysis will be considered more fully in the following chapter.

CONCLUSION

If it is to dispense constitutional justice, the Court must first solve the deepest and most intractable problems of constitutional interpretation inherent in the Convention, the most debated of which, and yet still the most elusive, is the margin of appreciation doctrine. This task requires in the first place a more formal recognition that the Convention contains primary and secondary constitutional principles derived from the bedrock teleological principle. A better understanding of these principles would alter the Court's adjudicative method in two significant ways. First, it would provide a justification for the Court taking much more responsibility than hitherto for the authoritative definition of, and the resolution of conflicts between, Convention rights where no public interest considerations capable of being assessed by national non-judicial authorities arise. Two initial objections to this suggestion can swiftly be dealt with. First, although many conflicts between Convention rights involve hidden public interests, some do not, apart that is from the public interest in the conflict being resolved properly and authoritatively by a court which, by definition, is not the kind of public interest which can be settled by national non-judicial authorities. Second, the absence of genuine public interests does not mean that national non-judicial bodies, particularly legislatures, should not make an attempt either to define Convention rights or to determine their relationship with each other and with collective goods. It merely means that these decisions remain provisional until approved in contentious cases by the European Court of Human Rights, and that in the absence of genuine public interests the Court has the ultimate authority of deciding these matters for itself. The second change in adjudicative method suggested by a more formal distinction between primary and secondary constitutional principles, would be the more consistent recognition by the Court that the exercise of genuine public-interest-related discretion on the part of national non-judicial bodies can, and should be, more formally regulated by the Convention's constitutional principles than is currently the case.

This interpretation of the Convention – and in particular the priority to rights principle which it yields – is subtly different both from Alexy's, and from the 'trumps' and 'balance' models described above. In most cases to come before the Court Alexy's neat tripartite test will have dissolved into a single 'balancing question' – is M_1 factually capable of implementing P_1 while in the circumstances only infringing P_2 to the minimum degree tolerable? And because, unlike Alexy's model, the Convention formally assigns priority-to-rights, the formal process by which it reconciles Convention rights with each other should be different from that by which it reconciles Convention rights and competing public interests. However, unlike 'trumps', this model does not imply that Convention rights are inherently more important than public interests, nor that the Court should apply a transcendent political morality delineating the boundary between them in terms of sharply defined rules and exceptions. But conversely, unlike the 'balance' model, it insists that in weighing rights and public interests the fulcrum should be comprehensively set closer to the 'public interest' than 'rights' so that much stronger leverage is required from considerations of the collective good in order to tilt the scales. What this means, and in particular how strong the priority to rights principle should be and how the proportionality test should be applied, will depend upon the construction of the particular Convention provision at issue, a matter pursued at greater length in the following chapter. Therefore, while it is not inappropriate for the Court and others to use the balance metaphor when considering, or referring to, the resolution of conflicts between Convention rights and the collective good, a much clearer understanding is needed of the different ways in which the Convention requires priority to be given to rights in reaching an appropriate result.

The distinction drawn between primary and secondary constitutional principles, and its implications, may be greeted with scepticism by some on the grounds that it is too formalistic, there is no evidence that it was intended by those who drafted the Convention, it has not been endorsed by the Court or by other commentators, it is too academic, too theoretical, and too prescriptive, and it overlooks the practical realities of adjudication at Strasbourg. But these are not the key issues. The fundamental questions are whether the distinction is sustainable in the context of the overall purpose and objectives of the Convention, and whether it contributes to a positive future for the Court and Convention system. As with the case for individual justice, the debate can be turned on its head. The questions then become: how can the Court deliver constitutional justice effectively without addressing the unresolved constitutional issues at the core of its adjudicative method more coherently? And how can it do this if it continues to approach the text of the Convention in such a haphazard manner, if it continues to regard the Convention's constitutional principles as of equal status, and in particular if the principle of priority to rights remains, at best, inconsistently recognized? In spite of the received wisdom, there is no clearly articulated argument in the literature that the Convention's principles of interpretation are, or should be regarded, as non-hierarchical. It is, however, difficult to deny that some derive from other principles, that they give these other principles greater specificity, and that, without reference to the principles from which they derive, the derivative principles would have little or no meaning. The principles of autonomous and evolutive/dynamic interpretation are, for example, essentially principles of exegesis which seek to give the rights principle greater substance. Similarly, the principle of positive obligations only makes sense as an expression of the rights principle and, unless grounded in it, the Court could impose much more onerous obligations on states than those which they believed they had undertaken. The principles of subsidiarity, review, and the margin of appreciation seek to distribute responsibility between national authorities and the Court for the supervision of the discharge of Convention obligations.

But authority for this distribution, and for the scope of these responsibilities, derives from the deeper rights, democracy, and priority principles. The principle of non-discrimination is also parasitic on a web of other values, principles, and rights.

While there can be no denying that constitutionalization is 'theoretical' and 'academic' in the sense that it concerns matters of deep purpose and value, there is no escaping issues of this kind in any legal system. The only choice is between keeping them buried and hidden, or making them as explicit and visible as possible. The more explicit they are, and the more adequately understood and structured, the more coherent and authoritative adjudication is likely to be. The constitutional model presented here offers a framework within which the Convention's core systemic interpretive and constitutional problems can be addressed, but not a set of off-the-peg solutions themselves. It provides a means by which the current confusion about the role of national non-judicial authorities in defining what specific Convention rights mean and conflicts between them can be approached by indicating that both tasks are ultimately matters for the Court to resolve with universal application in all member states and that national non-judicial authorities have no genuine margin of appreciation. On the other hand the presence of an identifiable public interest, competing with a given Convention right, opens up the possibility of divergence between states provided the Court is convinced that the priority principle, the strength of which is to be determined by the formal characteristics of the particular Convention right, has been observed.

One final possible criticism deserves a response. It could be argued that, if the Court's mission is the *systemic* protection of Convention rights, Convention rights are merely a species of public interest, and therefore both the distinction between rights and public interests and the entire analysis of this chapter and the next collapses. This is however misconceived. Even if Convention rights are regarded as particular types of public interest, this does not mean they have the same status under the Convention as any other public interest not expressed as a Convention right. In other words, the Convention privileges only certain specific interests as rights, according to the terms of given provisions, against encroachment from every other kind of public interest not expressed as a Convention right. For example, while the Convention recognizes the 'prevention of crime' as a public interest which may legitimately compete with, or even prevail over, the rights found in Articles 8, 10, and 11, there is no Convention *right* as such to be protected from crime. The distinction between the rights and democracy principles is therefore not only sound, but fundamental to the Convention's constitutional arrangements.

5

The Jurisprudence

INTRODUCTION

The purpose of this chapter is to assess the extent to which the Strasbourg case law adequately implements the constitutional principles discussed in the previous chapter, particularly the principle of 'priority-to-rights'. However, some provisions have been ignored because their application is relatively uncontroversial, because they do not raise sharp constitutional questions, or because they have simply not yet generated enough judgments to warrant inclusion. Bearing in mind that the Strasbourg case law does not establish 'authorities' for 'propositions of law' in anything like the same sense as judicial decisions in common law systems, cases relating to those provisions which are discussed here were selected because they illustrate how well, or how badly, the Strasbourg institutions have applied the Convention's inherent constitution. Other examples could just as readily have been used for the same purpose.

The framework for the following discussion is based on the formally distinct clusters of Convention provisions, derived from the priority principle, which were distinguished in the previous chapter. But these categories are not hermetically sealed. For example, on account of the formal characteristics of Article 4(2) and (3), the right not to be required to perform forced or compulsory labour could be regarded as a 'negatively defined' right (as it was in Chapter 4), although it is, in effect, a 'specially protected' right like those in Articles 3, 4(1) and 7(1), hence its inclusion in this section here. Similarly, the rights derived from the obligation under Article 2(1) to protect the right to life by law, are 'adjectivally' limited like those in Articles 5 and 6, albeit implicitly rather than expressly, and in spite of the fact that the formal structure of Article 2(1) differs from that of Articles 5 and 6. Article 2(1) could therefore have been included in the section on Articles 5 and 6. But in the interests of greater clarity it has been given its own section.

Some readers may be concerned that an exercise of this kind risks ascribing more significance to the formal structure of the Convention than those who drafted it intended, or is appropriate whatever their intentions, and that splitting any given Convention right into different formal categories may distort how it should be understood in its totality. However, the view taken here is that the lack of coherence and authority in the case law, which many commentators have criticized, stems in no small measure from a failure by the Strasbourg institutions to take the formal characteristics of the Convention seriously enough. A greater appreciation of the Convention's formal features offers a more robust and consistent structure within which judgment can be more effectively exercised. But, as already indicated in the previous chapter, it is not suggested in what follows that 'logically necessary' solutions to disputes about Convention rights are deeply embedded in the text merely awaiting discovery by application of the 'correct' juridical method. The challenge for critics is instead to suggest how a more coherent and authoritative case law could be constructed if the approach taken here, or something like it, is rejected.

ARTICLES 3, 4 AND 7(1)

Although the substance of Articles 3, 4(1), and 7(1) is different, they share the same form.[1] First, these provisions contain, not rights as such, but unqualified negative (or prohibitive) principles (or imperatives). However, second, these principles suggest rights, and little of consequence follows from expressing the underlying value in this rather than in an alternative format, such as – '*everyone* has the right *not* be tortured/held in slavery etc.'.[2] What matters is that no restrictions or

[1] Some of the provisions found in the Protocols also take the form of unqualified prohibitions, for example on: deprivation of liberty merely because of inability to fulfil a contractual obligation (Art. 1 of Protocol No. 4); the expulsion of nationals from, or refusal of entry to, their national state (Art. 3 of Protocol No. 4); the collective expulsion of aliens (Art. 4 of Protocol No. 4); and the death penalty (Art. 1 of Protocol No. 13). But not all Council of Europe states have agreed to be bound by these Protocols and there is very little case law on any.

[2] As Evans and Morgan record, the precise format of Article 3 'provoked little controversy' in the drafting process and, although there were different draft texts, all appear to have been expressed as 'unqualified prohibitive principles', M. D. Evans and R. Morgan, *Preventing Torture: A Study of the European Convention for the Prevention of Torture and Inhuman or Degrading Treatment or Punishment* (Oxford: Clarendon Press, 1998), p. 70.

exceptions are formally specified. Third, the most critical aspect of these rights is what constitutes the prohibited conduct. The primary task for the Court, therefore, is the appropriate identification of the basic values these provisions seek to protect, largely determined by the Convention's 'rights' principle. Fourth, while the principles in question are unqualified, and apparently absolute, the rights they suggest need not be because 'torture', 'slavery' etc., may be defined in ways which excludes certain conduct in certain circumstances. However, fifth, although not absolute themselves, these rights deserve a 'specially protected status' not conferred on other Convention rights, because they derive from formally unqualified prohibitive principles and because they cannot be suspended under Article 15 even in war or states of emergency, a manifestation of a particularly strong version of the 'priority-to-rights' principle.[3] While the commitment of the Court, and others, to the notion that these rights are 'absolute' may stem from a reluctance to accept the possibility of hidden implicit exceptions which could lead to their gradual erosion, it would, nevertheless, be clearer to avoid the term 'absolute' altogether. Sixth, in spite of dicta to the contrary, there is no scope for 'balancing' these rights, either against other Convention rights or countervailing public interests. Indeed, if the prohibited conduct is properly understood such conflicts will not even arise.[4]

[3] M.K. Addo and N. Grief, 'Does Article 3 of the European Convention on Human Rights Enshrine Absolute Rights?', *European Journal of International Law* **9** (1998), 510–524; Y. Arai-Taskahashi, 'Uneven, But in the Direction of Enhanced Effectiveness – A Critical Analysis of "Anticipatory Ill-treatment" under Article 3 ECHR', *Netherlands Quarterly of Human Rights* **20** (2002), 5–27. The right to freedom of thought, conscience and religion, and the right to change one's religion or belief under Art. 9(1) are also commonly said to be 'absolute' rights on the grounds that it is only the manifestation of religion or belief which is subject to express restriction under Art. 9(2), see e.g. P.W. Edge, 'The European Court of Human Rights and Religious Rights', *International and Comparative Law Quarterly* **47** (1998), 680–687 at 680; G. Moon and R. Allen, Q.C., 'Substantive Rights and Equal Treatment in Respect of Religion and Belief: Towards a Better Understanding of the Rights, and their Implications', *European Human Rights Law Review* (2000), 580–601 at 582. Although these might qualify as further 'specially protected' rights there is nothing in the formal construction of this provision – 'Everyone has the right to freedom of thought, conscience and religion; this right includes freedom to change his religion or belief and freedom, . . .' – to exclude implicit exceptions.

[4] As Simor and Emmerson observe, the Court sometimes uses the language of proportionality in respect of these rights to determine whether the treatment was sufficiently serious to fall within the ambit of the prohibition, J. Simor and B. Emmerson, Q.C. (eds.), *Human Rights Practice* (London: Sweet & Maxwell, 2000), para. 1.079.

The Rights not to be Tortured, or to be Inhumanly or Degradingly Treated or Punished: Article 3

The case law on Article 3 is more extensive than that on Articles 4(1) and 7(1). Much of it is concerned, quite properly, with how torture, inhuman or degrading treatment or punishment, are to be understood and distinguished.[5] But there is also a lot of confusion over the role of subjective and public interest factors. It is not uncommon, for example, to find assertions in the Strasbourg case law that the rights in question are 'absolute', followed in the next sentence or paragraph, by claims that subjective factors and the wider public interest may also have to be considered.[6] For example, in *Selmouni* v. *France* it was held that changes in public opinion may result in acts being reclassified as torture which in the past would have been regarded merely as inhuman or degrading.[7] In *Soering* v. *United Kingdom* the Court held that, while Article 3 contains an absolute prohibition on torture, inhuman or degrading treatment or punishment, what amounts to inhuman or degrading treatment or punishment will depend on all the circumstances including striking 'a fair balance between the demands of the general interest of the community and the requirements of the protection of the individual's fundamental rights'.[8] But the Court has also held in several expulsion and extradition cases that the 'absolute nature of the protection' afforded by Article 3 is such that, in determining whether the issue of state responsibility arises, there is no room for 'balancing the risk of ill-treatment against the reasons for expulsion'.[9]

[5] See J. Vorhaus, 'On Degradation. Part One. Article 3 of the European Convention on Human Rights', *Common Law World Review* **31** (2002), 374–399 and 'On Degradation. Part Two. Degrading Treatment and Punishment', *Common Law World Review* **32** (2003), 65–92; Evans and Morgan, *Preventing Torture*, pp. 79–105. As Evans argues, for the Court, this is less about finding 'definitions' than developing an 'approach', M. D. Evans, 'Getting to Grips With Torture', *International and Comparative Law Quarterly* **51** (2002), 365–383 at 368–369.

[6] *Veznedaroglu* v. *Turkey* (2001) 33 EHRR 1412 at paras. 28 and 29; *Tekin* v. *Turkey* (2001) 31 EHRR 95 at paras. 52 and 53; *Soering* v. *United Kingdom* (1989) 11 EHRR 439 at paras. 88 and 89; *Tyrer* v. *United Kingdom* (1980) 2 EHRR 1 at paras. 38 and 39.

[7] (2000) 29 EHRR 403 at para. 101.

[8] (1989) 11 EHRR 439 at para. 89.

[9] For example, in *Chahal* v. *United Kingdom* the Court rejected the United Kingdom government's argument that, in determining whether expulsion would constitute a violation of Article 3 the risk the applicant posed to national security if he was not expelled had to be weighed against the treatment he might receive in the state to which he was expelled (1997) 23 EHRR 413 at para. 81; *Ahmed* v. *Austria* (1997) 24 EHRR 278 at paras. 38–41; *D* v. *United Kingdom* (1997) 24 EHRR 423 at para. 47.

There can be no doubt that 'ill-treatment must attain a minimum level of severity if it is to fall within Article 3' and that determining whether this threshold has been crossed or not is 'relative' and will depend on 'all the circumstances of the case such as the duration of the treatment, its physical or mental effects and, in some cases, the sex, age and state of health of the victim etc.'.[10] But, other than dangerousness, the subjective characteristics of victims should reduce rather than raise the threshold. For example, while handcuffing a suspect to a radiator for three hours in a police station, as in *M-AV* v. *France*,[11] may not constitute a violation of Article 3 in most circumstances, it might if the suspect were elderly, in poor health, or unusually vulnerable for some other reason.[12] But taking the subjective characteristics of the particular victim into account is quite different from allowing wider social attitudes in a particular state, or the public interests in crime control or counter-terrorism, to influence what is to count as torture, inhuman or degrading treatment or punishment. The only public interests capable of affecting how the terms 'torture, inhuman or degrading treatment or punishment' are defined, are the risks to the stability of the prison regime and to the outside world presented by the escape of particularly dangerous prisoners, and these should alter what counts as tolerable treatment of prisoners only to the extent strictly required by the circumstances.[13]

In *Kröcher and Möller* v. *Switzerland*,[14] for example, the two applicants, each terrorist suspects, were arrested on a charge of attempted murder in December 1977 not far from the Franco-Swiss border following an exchange of gunfire with customs officials. They claimed that the regime under which they were remanded in custody, although progressively modified as a result of legal challenges, the intervention of prison doctors and their own hunger strike, amounted

[10] *Ireland* v. *United Kingdom* (1980) 2 EHRR 25 at para. 162.

[11] (1994) 79-B D.R. 54 at 58. See also *Henaf* v. *France* (2005) 40 EHRR 990.

[12] Indeed the very fact of detention may amount to inhuman and degrading treatment where the detainee is in poor health – *Mouisel* v. *France* (2004) 38 EHRR 735.

[13] It was held in *Dankevich* v. *Ukraine* (2004) 38 EHRR 542 at para. 144, that 'lack of resources cannot in principle justify prison conditions which are so poor as to reach the threshold of treatment contrary to Art. 3 of the Convention', while in *Kalashnikov* v. *Russia* (2003) 36 EHRR 587 the Court held, at para. 93, that harsh prison conditions, which the government admitted were common in Russia, amounted to degrading treatment.

[14] (1982) 34 D.R. 24. See also *Öcalan* v. *Turkey* (2005) 41 EHRR 985 at paras. 179–196; *Van der Ven* v. *Netherlands* (2004) 38 EHRR 967.

to a violation of Article 3. The most striking characteristics of this regime, according to the European Commission of Human Rights, were the facts that the applicants were accommodated in non-adjacent cells on a floor not occupied by any other prisoner, the lack of any opening on to the outside world, illumination by constant artificial light, permanent surveillance by closed-circuit television, denial of access to newspapers and radio, and a lack of physical exercise. But, citing some of its previous decisions, the Commission concluded by a majority that, while total isolation coupled with complete sensory deprivation could not be justified on any grounds, this particular regime did not amount to a violation of Article 3 because its objectives were the security of both the prison and the applicants themselves, given that they were undoubtedly violent and dangerous and that prison suicide had been part of the 'climate of terrorism' at the time.[15]

The confusion surrounding the role of subjective and public interest factors in adjudication on Article 3 can, therefore, best be resolved first by the recognition that the 'special character' of these rights means that the Court should identify a set of universal minimum standards subject to no exceptions whatever the competing public policy goals or the subjective characteristics of alleged victims. Second, whether a standard higher than the minimum is appropriate, and whether it has been violated, will depend upon how these rights and others with which they may be in conflict are defined. Third, departures from all but the minimum standards must be strictly necessary. 'Balancing' one of these rights against others, or against any wider public interest is therefore not appropriate, except that more secure and restrictive custodial regimes will not be inhuman with respect to those who pose a particularly serious danger to others or a serious threat to the security or stability of the place of detention unless adequately restrained. The extent of restriction must not, however, exceed that which is strictly necessary to meet legitimate, and well-founded, security concerns.[16] Fourth, the discretion of potential violators should also be strictly limited. Fifth, the Court should scrutinize the alleged limits to these provisions with particular thoroughness and require the same of national judicial authorities.[17] Finally, although the standard

[15] *Kröcher and Möller* v. *Switzerland* (1982) 34 D.R. 24 at para. 78.

[16] *Ibid.*, at paras. 63 and 64.

[17] A. Mowbray, 'Duties of Investigation under the European Convention on Human Rights', *International and Comparative Law Quarterly* **51** (2002), 437–448 at 443–446.

of proof in relation to violations of Article 3 is 'beyond reasonable doubt', where an applicant is taken into official custody in good health but emerges injured, the onus of proof shifts to the state to show that the injuries in question were caused in ways which did not amount to the prohibited conduct.[18] Effective action must also have been taken to reduce the risk of violation,[19] and an effective investigation, capable of identifying those responsible, conducted into the allegations.[20]

The Right not to be Held in Slavery or Servitude: Article 4(1)

The few cases on Article 4(1) have hinged upon how the Strasbourg institutions have defined the proscribed conduct, a manifestation of the primacy of the rights principle over other constitutional principles. Not surprisingly Article 4(1) has been held inapplicable to prisoners complaining that compulsory prison work amounts to 'slavery or servitude', the main source of alleged violations, since such work is expressly excluded by Article 4(3)(a) from the less onerous category of 'forced or compulsory labour'.[21] In *Van Droogenbroek* v. *Belgium*, it was held, for example, that the ten-year order served on the applicant, a recidivist, to remain 'at the government's disposal', including semi-custodial care, attending vocational courses, and working to earn 12,000 Belgian Francs, did not amount to 'servitude'. His detention complied with Article 5 of the Convention and the work he was required to do was for a limited term. It was also intended to facilitate his rehabilitation, and comparable arrangements could be found in other member states.[22] In *Siliadin* v. *France* the Court held that the conditions under which a teenage girl from Togo worked as a domestic servant amounted

[18] *Öcalan* v. *Turkey* (2005) 41 EHRR 985 at para. 180; *Yüksel* v. *Turkey* (2005) 41 EHRR 316 at paras. 25 and 26. See Addo and Grief, 'Article 3', 524 and C. Warbrick, 'The Principles of the European Convention on Human Rights and the Response of States to Terrorism', *European Human Rights Law Review* (2002), 287–314 at 296.

[19] *E* v. *United Kingdom* (2003) 36 EHRR 519.

[20] *Krastanov* v. *Bulgaria* (2005) 41 EHRR 1137 at para. 57; *Yüksel* v. *Turkey* (2005) 41 EHRR 316 at para. 36.

[21] P. van Dijk and G. J. H. van Hoof, *Theory and Practice of the European Convention on Human Rights* (The Hague, London & Boston: Kluwer, 1998), p. 334.

[22] (1982) 4 EHRR 443.

to servitude and that, by failing effectively to criminalize such practices, France was in violation of Article 4(1).[23]

The Right not to be Required to Perform Forced or Compulsory Labour: Article 4(2)&(3)

Article 4(2) provides that '(n)o one shall be required to perform forced or compulsory labour', while Article 4(3) provides a series of limited exceptions, for example military service and prison or community work. Unlike the rights derived from Article 4(1) these rights are derogable. However, although broadly expressed, the exceptions have been narrowly interpreted leaving little scope for a domestic margin of appreciation, or for balancing with the right in Article 4(2) itself. The little litigation there has been on these provisions has been dominated by mostly unsuccessful attempts by dentists, physicians, and lawyers to evade discharging limited public service obligations as part of their professional responsibilities.[24] Relying on the principles of proportionality, commonality, legality, and non-discrimination the Strasbourg institutions have, therefore, defined 'normal civic responsibilities' in Article 4(3)(d) to mean: permitted by domestic law or professional codes, encompassing a foreseeable possibility of joining the profession in the country concerned, common amongst member states, applied without discrimination or arbitrariness, and not excessively burdensome considering time spent, connection with normal professional duties, remuneration received, and service rendered. Therefore, in spite of its different format the right not to be subjected to forced or compulsory labour is a strongly protected right with a universal European character, similar to those in Articles 3, 4(1) and 7(1).

For example, in *Van der Mussele* v. *Belgium* the applicant complained of a breach of Article 4(2) in that as a trainee lawyer he had not been entitled to refuse to represent a defendant in criminal proceedings when instructed to do so by the Legal Advice and Defence Office of the Antwerp Bar, nor to receive remuneration for the seventeen to eighteen hours work spent on the case. Noting the lack of any guidance on what constituted 'forced and compulsory labour' from Council of Europe

[23] Judgement of 26 July 2005 at paras. 129 and 148. See V. Mantouvalou, 'Servitude and Forced Labour in the 21st Century: the Human Rights of Domestic Workers', forthcoming in *Industrial Law Journal.*

[24] *Van der Mussele* v. *Belgium* (1984) 6 EHRR 163; *Reitmayr* v. *Austria* (1995) 20 EHRR C.D. 89.

documents, the Court took as its starting point the International Labour Organization's definition of 'forced or compulsory labour' as 'all work or service which is exacted from any person under the menace of any penalty and for which the said person has not offered himself voluntarily'.[25] But it added that, in determining whether this requirement had been fulfilled, all relevant facts had to be considered, including the underlying objectives of Article 4, and whether the burden imposed was excessive or disproportionate considering the rewards received upon full admission to the career in question. Although the threat of being de-barred in the event of a refusal to accept the contentious brief constituted 'the menace of a penalty',[26] the Court concluded that it could be assumed that the applicant entered the Belgian legal profession knowing of its long-standing tradition of such pro bono work. Moreover, this contributed to his professional training, the expenses incurred were small, the obligation could not be regarded as unreasonable or disproportionate since the hours involved left plenty of time for remunerated work, and it was increasingly common for other member states to have similar arrangements.[27]

The Right not to be Punished Without Law: Article 7(1)

Article 7(1), which prohibits both retrospective criminalization and the retrospective imposition of heavier penalties, derives from the rule of law principle which, among other things, requires that crimes and penalties are defined only by law, and that 'the criminal law must not be extensively construed to an accused's detriment'.[28] Article 7(2) provides that '(t)his article shall not prejudice the trial and punishment of any person for any act or omission which, at the time when it was committed, was criminal according to the general principles of law recognized by civilized nations.' The few cases on Article 7(1) have also been almost entirely concerned with determining what the prohibition entails.[29] Exercising the principle of autonomous interpretation derived from the 'rights' principle, the Strasbourg institutions have

[25] (1984) 6 EHRR 163 at para. 32.

[26] *Ibid.*, at para. 35. [27] *Ibid.*, at paras. 39 and 40.

[28] *Veeber* v. *Estonia (No. 2)* (2004) 39 EHRR 125 at paras. 30 and 31; *Kokkinakis* v. *Greece* (1994) 17 EHRR 397 at para. 52.

[29] E.g. *Ecer and Zeyrek* v. *Turkey* (2002) 35 EHRR 672; *SW and CR* v. *United Kingdom* (1996) 21 EHRR 363.

chosen to define 'criminal offence' and 'penalty' entirely for themselves.[30] But, unlike the key concepts in Articles 3 and 4(1), there is less scope here for context-specific variability. In *SW & CR* v. *United Kingdom*, for example, the applicants complained that their convictions for raping their wives violated their right under Article 7(1) not to have their behaviour retrospectively criminalized because marital rape was not an offence under national law when the conduct in question occurred.[31] Applying the 'rights' principle, and the primacy this gives to matters of definition, the Court concluded that there had been no violation since the object and purpose of Article 7 was to provide effective safeguards against arbitrary prosecution, conviction, and punishment, a requirement which is satisfied when a court's interpretation of certain acts and omissions as giving rise to criminal liability can reasonably be foreseen.[32] The conviction of a husband for raping his wife was held not to be an inconsistent, nor an unforeseeable, judicial extension of the relevant common law offence, since UK courts had been developing the law in this direction for some time. While this might have disposed of the matter, the Court bolstered its decision by reference to two other factors: the physical integrity and dignity of a wife, which would be damaged by non-consensual sex with her husband, and the character of modern marriage which no longer regards a wife as a husband's chattel. Although the Convention does not expressly provide wives with the right not to be forced to have sex with their husbands against their consent, such a right is well within the implicit scope of Articles 3, 5 and 8. However, of particular importance to the present analysis, the central issue in this case was not settled by 'balancing' the wife's implicit right not to have sex with her husband against her consent, with the husband's putative right not to be punished without law provided by Article 7(1). Nor was the right provided by Article 7(1) 'balanced' against the public interest represented by the modern conception of marriage. Instead the Court itself *defined* the scope of each right by identifying, through reference to contemporary standards, the underlying interests and values most at stake.

[30] *Engel* v. *Netherlands (No. 1)* (1979) 1 EHRR 647 at para. 82; *Welsh* v. *United Kingdom* (1995) 20 EHRR 247 at paras. 27–35.

[31] (1996) 21 EHRR 363.

[32] *Ibid.*, at para. 43/41; *Radio France* v. *France* (2005) 40 EHRR 706 at para. 20.

ARTICLES 2(2) AND 15

Articles 2(2) and 15 require respectively that the use of force which results in interferences with the right to life should be 'no more than absolutely necessary' in pursuit of a number of specific law enforcement objectives, and that derogations from all but the non-derogable rights should only occur in time of 'war or other public emergency threatening the life of the nation', and even then only to 'the extent strictly required by the exigencies of the situation'. Here again the relationship between the rights concerned, and the public interests which may affect their scope, is not achieved by balancing, nor strictly speaking by applying the principle of proportionality, but by requiring justifications for interference to cross the high evidential threshold of 'absolute' or 'strict' necessity first.

The Right not to be Unlawfully Deprived of Life: Article 2(2)

Article 2, which is permeated by the rule of law principle discussed in Chapter 4, is in the form of two imperatives which create two distinct obligations on the part of member states – the positive obligation in the first sentence of Article 2(1) to protect everyone's right to life through law (considered separately below), and the negative obligation in the second sentence of Article 2(1) and in Article 2(2) not to deprive anyone of their life except by using no more force than is absolutely necessary in defence of any person from unlawful violence, in order to effect a lawful arrest or to prevent the escape of a person lawfully detained, or lawfully to quell a riot or insurrection.

The negative obligation not to deprive anyone of their life requires both appropriate legal arrangements and appropriate conduct on the part of those for whom the state is responsible. To defend oneself, or others, from unlawful violence by killing raises potential conflicts between several Convention rights. There is the obvious conflict between two instances of the right to life. But there is also a conflict between the right to life of the assailant, on the one hand, and their would-be victim's right not to be subjected to torture or to inhuman treatment on the other. But since the criterion is 'unlawful' rather than 'lethal' violence it may not be a violation of Article 2(2) to kill an assailant who threatens serious harm, for example rape, even though the threat may not be to the victim's life. Defending oneself or others from unlawful violence by wounding the assailant raises a potential conflict between, on the one hand, the rights to life, security of the person, and freedom from inhuman treatment, of the person(s) thereby protected, and on the other the offender's rights to security of the person and freedom from inhuman treatment. However, killing in pursuit of a lawful arrest, preventing the escape of a person lawfully detained, and the lawful quelling of a riot or insurrection raises a potential conflict between the right to life and these specific public interests.[33] The right to life cannot, however, be 'balanced' either against other rights or against the lawful pursuit of these law enforcement goals because it is strongly prioritized by the 'absolute necessity' test.[34] As the Court held in *McCann* v. *United Kingdom*: 'The use of the term "absolutely necessary" ... indicates that a stricter and more compelling test of necessity must be employed from that normally applicable when determining whether State action is "necessary in a democratic society" under paragraph 2 of Articles 8 to 11 of the Convention. In particular the force used must be strictly proportionate to the achievement of the aims set out in subparagraphs 2(a), (b), and (c) of Article 2.'[35]

The provisions of Article 2(2) must, therefore, be 'strictly construed'[36] and are limited only by the 'exhaustive and ... narrowly interpreted'[37] objectives listed. The lethal force must be no more than the minimum necessary depending upon 'the nature of the aim pursued, the dangers to life and limb inherent in the situation and the degree of the risk that the force employed might result in loss of life ... (with) due regard to all the relevant circumstances',[38] 'including such matters as the planning and control of the actions under examination'.[39]

The tension between the right to life and the public interest is particularly apparent where lethal force has been used by law enforcement

[33] The concept of legality at issue here is the Convention standard and not merely the national legal standard, *McCann* v. *United Kingdom* (1996) 21 EHRR 97 at paras. 153–155.

[34] However, the Court still finds it hard to avoid using the balance metaphor even when it immediately qualifies it by reference to the principle of absolute necessity, see *Isayeva* v. *Russia* (2005) 41 EHRR 791 at para. 181.

[35] (1995) 21 EHRR 97 at para. 149. See also *McShane* v. *United Kingdom* (2002) 35 EHRR 593 at para. 93; *Ogur* v. *Turkey* (2001) 31 EHRR 912 at para. 78.

[36] *Isayeva* v. *Russia* (2005) 41 EHRR 791 at para. 172; *Andronicou and Constantinou* v. *Cyprus* (1997) 25 EHRR 491 at para. 171; *McCann* v. *United Kingdom* (1996) 21 EHRR 97 at para. 147.

[37] *Stewart* v. *United Kingdom* (1984) 39 D.R. 162 at para. 13.

[38] *Ibid.*, p. 171.

[39] *Isayeva* v. *Russia* (2005) 41 EHRR 791 at paras. 174–176; *Nachova* v. *Bulgaria* (2004) 39 EHRR 793 at para. 95; *McCann* v. *United Kingdom* (1996) 21 EHRR 97 at para. 150.

personnel. According to Ní Aoláin, in spite of a slow start the Court is increasingly applying in this context, what this study has identified as the Convention's constitutional principles. Judgments from *McCann* onwards have elevated the right not to be unlawfully deprived of life to the status of a specially protected right subject to no margin of appreciation at all.[40] The Court also expects such cases will be effectively investigated by the defendant state itself,[41] and it may conclude that the manner in which an operation resulting in the use of potentially lethal force was conceived, planned and executed, makes the force itself excessive, even where those who used it had an honest though mistaken belief that it was no more than absolutely necessary in pursuit of the legitimate objectives specified in Article 2(2).[42] Prior to the judgment in *McCann*, several decisions arising from the conflict in Northern Ireland were criticized for being overly deferential to the official version of events and their justification.[43] For example, in *Stewart* v. *United Kingdom* the European Commission of Human Rights concluded that the death of a 13-year-old boy from injuries received by a plastic bullet discharged by a soldier, did not constitute a breach of Article 2(2) because, on the evidence, this was an unintentional consequence of a lawful attempt to control a riot.[44] And in *Kelly* v. *United Kingdom* the Commission held that Article 2(2) had not been violated by the shooting of a 'joy-rider' travelling with others in a stolen car which failed to stop at a military check-point in Belfast because the Commission accepted that believing the occupants were terrorists, the soldier concerned had acted to effect a lawful arrest.[45] However, in *McCann* v. *United Kingdom* the Court concluded that it was not absolutely necessary in all the circumstances to kill three IRA suspects in order to prevent the detonation of a bomb in Gibraltar, which British security forces mistakenly believed they were carrying and which, had this been true, would have

[40] F. Ní Aoláin, 'The Evolving Jurisprudence of the European Convention Concerning the Right to Life', *Netherlands Quarterly of Human Rights* **19** (2001), 21–42 at 31.

[41] *Isayeva* v. *Russia* (2005) 41 EHRR 791 at paras. 209–24; *Tepe* v. *Turkey* (2004) 39 EHRR 584.

[42] *McCann* v. *United Kingdom* (1996) 21 EHRR 97 at paras. 150, 200–201.

[43] Ní Aoláin, 'Evolving Jurisprudence', 26–28; S. Joseph, 'Denouement of the Deaths on the Rock: the Right to Life of Terrorists', *Netherlands Quarterly of Human Rights* **14** (1996), 5 at 9; D. J. Harris, 'The Right to Life under the European Convention on Human Rights', *Maastricht Journal of European and Comparative Law* (1994), 122–138 at 136.

[44] (1984) 39 D.R. 162. [45] (1993) 74 D.R. 139.

killed many when it exploded. The three suspects, although on a bombing mission, were not, in fact, in possession of a bomb at the time they were shot, and the Court held they could have been arrested as they crossed the Spanish frontier into the British territory.[46]

Derogations Under Article 15

Article 15 is based on a presumption that the public interest in the preservation of 'the life of the nation' should take precedence over the protection of all but a handful of non-derogable rights whenever this is 'threatened' by 'war or other public emergency'.[47] This embodies the 'priority' principle in two ways. First, states seeking to derogate must show that the life of the nation is genuinely threatened by a real rather than imagined emergency and, second, that each derogation from a specific provision of the Convention is 'strictly required by the exigencies of the situation'.[48] The Convention does not, therefore, contemplate the direct balancing of rights against the public interest in preserving the life of the nation because, even in these circumstances, there is an assumption that Convention rights apply unless a compelling case can be made that they do not.

In *Lawless* v. *Ireland* the applicant claimed his rights under Articles 5, 6, and 7 of the Convention had been violated by his detention without trial under emergency powers in the Republic of Ireland because of his suspected involvement with the IRA, then actively engaged in terrorist activities in border areas of Northern Ireland.[49] Prior to his detention the Irish government had notified the Secretary General of the Council of Europe that it wished to derogate from the Convention

46 *McCann* v. *United Kingdom* (1996) 21 EHRR 97. One of the few other cases on killing in self defence is *Diaz Ruano* v. *Spain* (1995) 19 EHRR 542 where it was held on the facts, at para. 50, that the fatal shooting of a prisoner by a police officer amounted to legitimate self defence.

47 J. Hedigan, 'The European Convention on Human Rights and Counter-Terrorism', *Fordham International Law Journal* **28** (2005), 392–431; A. Mokhtar, 'Human Rights Obligations v. Derogations: Article 15 of the European Convention on Human Rights', *International Journal of Human Rights* **8** (2004), 65–87; Warbrick, 'ECHR and Response to Terrorism'.

48 *Denmark, Norway, Sweden and the Netherlands* v. *Greece (The Greek Case)* (1969) 12 Y.B. at paras. 153–165; see J. Oraá, *Human Rights in States of Emergency in International Law* (Oxford: Clarendon Press, 1992), pp. 144–152.

49 (1979) 1 EHRR 15.

under Article 15 although the precise provisions were not specified. The Court upheld the derogation on the grounds that 'the life of the nation' was threatened by the IRA, a secret army engaged in unconstitutional activities determined to use violence to achieve its objectives both inside and outside the national territory and actively engaged in an escalating terrorist campaign in Northern Ireland in 1956 and 1957. Having considered the legal context, the internment of the applicant was also deemed proportionate in the circumstances. The willingness of the Court to accept that the 'life of the nation' was under threat is not wholly convincing, however, since although the IRA may have posed a nascent but not imminent threat to the Irish state, this threat had existed for decades and the border campaign of the mid-1950s was directed against Northern Ireland, part of the United Kingdom.

The decision in *Lawless* contrasts with *The Greek Case.* Following a coup d'état in Greece in 1967, the military government suspended certain constitutional guarantees and notified the Secretary General of the Council of Europe that it wished to derogate from certain provisions of the Convention under Article 15. In an inter-state application lodged by Denmark, Norway, Sweden, and the Netherlands, the Commission held that, although both constitutional and revolutionary governments enjoy a margin of appreciation in relation to Article 15, the burden in the present case lay with the Greek military government to prove that derogation was justified.[50] Having carefully considered the evidence, the majority was not satisfied that the two-year period of political instability preceding the coup was so serious that it threatened the life of the nation. Nor was it convinced that disorder following the coup could not have been adequately handled by ordinary measures.

In 1976 Ireland applied to the Court complaining that the UK was in breach of Articles 3, 5, 6, 14, and 15 of the Convention in having instituted an anti-terrorist regime of internment without trial which, it was alleged, operated in a discriminatory manner and which had resulted in the ill-treatment of some detainees.[51] Although the existence of an emergency justifying a derogation under Article 15 was not in dispute, the Court confirmed that a wide margin of appreciation was applicable on the grounds that '(b)y reason of their direct and continuous contact with the pressing needs of the moment, the national

[50] *Denmark, Norway, Sweden and the Netherlands* v. *Greece* (1969) 12 Y.B. at para. 154.
[51] *Ireland* v. *United Kingdom* (1980) 2 EHRR 25.

authorities are in principle in a better position than the international judge to decide both on the presence of such an emergency and on the nature and scope of derogations necessary to avert it'.[52] However, it added that this discretion was subject to review at Strasbourg according to the criterion that states must not exceed what is 'strictly required by the exigencies' of the situation. On the substantive issue the Court held that 'five techniques' of sensory deprivation to which some of the detainees had been subjected, amounted to inhuman and degrading treatment, but, contrary to the Commission's view, did not constitute torture. In *Brannigan and McBride* v. *United Kingdom* the applicants were detained and questioned under the UK's anti-terrorist legislation for periods of six days fourteen hours, and four days six hours respectively.[53] The UK government relied on its derogation of 23 December 1988 to defend a complaint by the applicants that their right under Article 5(3) to be brought promptly before a judicial authority had been violated. The Court affirmed the existence of a wide margin of appreciation, both in relation to the decision to derogate and the measures taken as a result, justified by the 'better position rationale' and subject to European supervision where appropriate weight would be given to such relevant factors as the nature of the rights affected, the circumstances, and the duration of the emergency.[54] But it held that it was not its role to substitute its own view as to what measures were most appropriate or expedient since the Government has direct responsibility for striking the proper balance between taking effective action and respecting individual rights.

As already indicated in the previous chapter, for several reasons the Convention's 'democratic' principle implies a genuine margin of appreciation in the exercise, by national executive institutions, of the derogation power under Article 15, subject to review at Strasbourg. First, a genuine public order emergency creates a dilemma between the observance of normal Convention obligations and their suspension to preserve 'the life of the nation'. Judging when these conditions have arisen may not be easy and may involve weighing conflicting public interests in, on the one hand, a flourishing rights regime, and

[52] *Ibid.*, at para. 207.
[53] *Brannigan and McBride* v. *United Kingdom* (1994) 17 EHRR 539.
[54] *Ibid.*, at para. 43.

on the other a minimum level of stability and order upon which such a regime depends. Second, national non-judicial authorities are closer to the 'coal face' and therefore in principle better placed to make the appropriate assessment (the 'better position rationale'). Third, the choice is by nature political rather than judicial and may be highly controversial in the state in question. Finally, different responses may be justified in different emergencies in different states. While the jurisprudence on Article 15 has so far stemmed from the terrorism of militant nationalism and the extreme left and right, there are no grounds yet for believing that contemporary Islamic fundamentalist terrorism poses greater challenges for the Convention system, in spite of its potentially more lethal capability than anything seen in Europe before. One indicator is that, five years on from 9/11, and in spite of the Madrid and London bombings of 2004 and 2005, the UK is as yet the only member of the Council of Europe to derogate from the Convention on account of this threat. This may however be attributable neither to the UK's unique vulnerability to attack, nor to a lower level of official respect for Convention rights compared with other European governments, but to a lack of the kind of extended, judicially supervised, detention arrangements which are common place in the regular criminal justice systems of most other European countries.

There are, however, two particular constitutional problems with the case law on Article 15. First, the older cases make no explicit attempt to link the scope of the margin of appreciation available to national executive institutions with different types of state, for example established democracy, fledgling democracy, revolutionary, or repressive regime.[55] This is difficult to square with the democracy principle, and would be unlikely to be endorsed by the Court if the issue were tested today, since the key element in legitimizing the margin of appreciation in this context lies in the plausibility of the evidence that the democratic integrity of the state in question is genuinely threatened, and not merely that its survival is at risk irrespective of its political complexion.[56]

55 M. O'Boyle, 'The Margin of Appreciation and Derogation under Article 15: Ritual Incantation or Principle?', *Human Rights Law Journal* **19** (1998), 23–29 at 26.

56 See also *United Communist Party of Turkey* v. *Turkey* where it was held that democracy 'appears to be the only political model contemplated by the Convention and, accordingly, the only one compatible with it' (1998) 26 EHRR 121 at para. 45.

Second, although the evidential standard for derogation is formally high there are grounds for believing that the Court has not exercised its powers of review with sufficient vigour, particularly with respect to assessing the efficacy of particular emergency measures, and in relation to prolonged emergencies.[57]

ARTICLES 5 AND 6

In spite of their different subject matter, Articles 4(2) and (3), 5 and 6 are expressed in a common format with a general statement of a right, or injunctive principle, followed by a series of 'negative' and/or 'positive' definitions providing further specification of what the right means, some of which refer to matters of the public interest.[58] However, as already indicated, on closer inspection Article 4(2) and (3) turn out in spite of this format to be a 'specially protected' right, hence their inclusion in a previous section. President Wildhaber claims that '(t)he search for a balance between competing interests may be relevant even to the due process guarantees' in Articles 5 and 6.[59] But, as Ashworth states, although the jurisprudence is uneven, the Strasbourg approach in respect of these provisions is 'predominantly in favour of resisting arguments that public interest considerations should be allowed to outweigh these strong rights'.[60]

[57] See O. Gross and F. Ní Aoláin, 'From Discretion to Scrutiny: Revisiting the Application of the Margin of Appreciation Doctrine in the Context of Article 15 of the European Convention on Human Rights', *Human Rights Quarterly* **23** (2001), 623–649 at 634–6; O. Gross, '"Once More unto the Breach": The Systematic Failure of Applying the European Convention on Human Rights to Entrenched Emergencies', *Yale Journal of International Law* **23** (1998), 437–502; R. St. J. Macdonald, 'Derogations under Article 15 of the European Convention on Human Rights', *Columbia Journal of Transnational Law* **36** (1997), 225–268.

[58] Most of the rights in Protocol No. 7, which have generated very little case law, are in a similar format: the rights of aliens to procedural safeguards in expulsion proceedings (Art. 1); the right of appeal in criminal matters (Art. 2); the right to compensation for wrongful conviction (Art. 3); the right not to be tried or punished twice for the same offence (Art. 4).

[59] L. Wildhaber, 'The Role of the European Court of Human Rights: An Evaluation', (2004) 8 '*Mediterranean Journal of Human Rights*' 9–32 at 13.

[60] A. Ashworth, *Human Rights, Serious Crime and Criminal Procedure* (London: Hamlyn Lectures, 53rd Series, Sweet & Maxwell, 2002), p. 69.

Freedom from Arbitrary Arrest and Detention: Article 5

Article 5 embodies the principle that no one should be 'dispossessed of liberty in an arbitrary fashion'.[61] An exhaustive and narrowly construed list of what may be termed 'formal definitional restrictions' specify a series of discrete circumstances in which loss of liberty is not arbitrary, provided it is 'in accordance with a procedure prescribed by law'.[62] Each is also specifically linked further to the Convention's principle of legality,[63] most are related to formal stages of the legal process, and all are matters of public interest.

The key issue raised by Article 5 is how the right to freedom from arbitrary arrest and detention, and its associated procedural guarantees, are to be defined. The 'rights' and 'priority' principles dominate the jurisprudence with the result that, although the 'balance' metaphor is sometimes used, the right to liberty is effectively presumed to prevail unless the case for its restriction derives from one of the express limitations and is based on persuasive evidence.[64] For example, in *Enhorn* v. *Sweden* the Court held that although the compulsory detention of someone infected with the HIV virus could be justified under Article 5(1)(e) – 'the lawful detention of persons for the prevention of the spreading of infectious diseases' – the respondent state had not shown that the applicant's detention was the last resort, nor had it 'provided any examples of less severe measures which might have been considered' but were 'found to be insufficient to safeguard the public interest'.[65] Two more common areas in which the public interest can impinge powerfully upon the right to liberty are: decisions regarding the release or detention of an accused prior to trial and the detention of

[61] *İ Bilgin* v. *Turkey* (2002) 35 EHRR 1291 at para. 149; *Engel* v. *Netherlands* (1979) 1 EHRR 647 at para. 58. See R. Kolb, 'The Jurisprudence of the European Court of Human Rights on Detention and Fair Trial in Criminal Matters from 1992 to the End of 1998', *Human Rights Law Journal* **21** (2000), 348–373.

[62] *Assanidze* v. *Georgia* (2004) 39 EHRR 653 at para. 170; *Čonka* v. *Belgium* (2002) 34 EHRR 1298 at para. 42; *Ireland* v. *United Kingdom* (1980) 2 EHRR 25 at para. 194.

[63] *Dougoz* v. *Greece* (2002) 34 EHRR 1480 at para. 61; *Chahal* v. *United Kingdom* (1997) 23 EHRR 413 at para. 127.

[64] *Murray* v. *United Kingdom* (1995) 19 EHRR 193 at paras. 61–63; *Fox, Campbell and Hartley* v. *United Kingdom* (1990) 13 EHRR 157 at para. 34. Kolb, however, maintains that, 'by it's very nature', the Court is 'under a diffuse and hidden – but not less tangible – danger' of giving too much weight to the rights and freedoms of the individual in this context, Kolb, 'Jurisprudence', 373.

[65] (2005) 41 EHRR 633 at paras. 46, 49, 55.

particularly dangerous offenders. Each typically involves an assessment of the risks posed to the prevention of crime and/or the administration of justice, including absconding, if the accused or offender were to be set free. Yet these public interests are not simply balanced against the right to liberty. The scales are loaded in favour of liberty because the defendant state has the burden of providing adequate reasons to justify detention. The Strasbourg institutions also require such decisions to be taken by courts rather than by national non-judicial bodies, and for the reasons in favour of, and those against, release to be clearly stated.[66] For example, as the Court held in *Kudła* v. *Poland*, re-stating a dictum repeated in several earlier cases: 'Continued detention can be justified in a given case only if there are specific indications of a genuine requirement of public interest which, notwithstanding the presumption of innocence, outweigh the rule of respect for individual liberty laid down in Article 5 of the Convention.' The persistence of a reasonable suspicion that the person arrested has committed an offence is a necessary condition for continued detention to be lawful. But after a 'certain lapse of time it no longer suffices'. At this point the Court must determine if other grounds provided by the judicial authorities are capable of providing adequate justification. But even where such grounds are 'relevant' and 'sufficient' the Court must also be satisfied that the national authorities displayed 'special diligence', and, since the applicant in this case had already been held in detention for a year, 'only very compelling reasons would persuade the Court that his further detention for two years and four months was justified under Article 5(3)'.[67] In other cases it has been held that release must also be ordered if sufficient guarantees can be obtained.[68] Where the only reason for continued pre-trial detention is the fear that the accused will abscond, this must be evidenced by factors beyond the mere opportunity to do so, such as the severity of the sentence, the attitude of the accused towards serving it, and their social connections in the detaining state.[69]

Article 5 therefore permits little scope for a 'domestic margin of appreciation' in the strict sense of a discretion available to national non-judicial bodies in determining how conflicts should be settled between

[66] *Smirnova* v. *Russia* (2004) 39 EHRR 450 at para. 62; *Klamecki* v. *Poland (No. 2)* (2004) 39 EHRR 137 at para. 118.

[67] (2002) 35 EHRR 198 at paras. 110–114.

[68] *Wemhoff* v. *Germany* (1979) 1 EHRR 55 at para. 15.

[69] *Stögmüller* v. *Austria* (1979) 1 EHRR 155 at para. 15.

permitting the right to liberty to be exercised or interfering with it in pursuit of the collective good. However, there is room for more limited kinds of 'adjectival discretion' in determining for example if an individual is of 'unsound mind' for the purpose of Article 5(1)(e), and in complying with the 'reasonableness' and 'promptness' requirements in Article 5(1)(c), 5(2), and 5(3).[70] Since these terms cannot be conclusively defined, a range of alternatives may be deemed to satisfy them which national non-judicial authorities may be capable of judging at least as well as the European Court of Human Rights. But this must be within strict limits. For example, applying the principle of effective protection in *Brogan* v. *United Kingdom* the Court held that, while the struggle against terrorism could legitimately prolong the period of detention before terrorist suspects are brought before a judge, the 'promptness' criterion should not be so flexible as to impair the 'very essence' of the right to liberty. In its view even the shortest period of detention experienced by the four applicants, four days and six hours, was excessive.[71]

The Right to a Fair Trial: Article 6

In considering compliance with the right to a fair trial under Article 6, the Strasbourg institutions have principally been concerned with procedural fairness rather than with either the merits of decisions or with trial machinery.[72] States, therefore, have been permitted a wide discretion concerning the formalities of trial processes, provided the trials themselves are deemed to fulfil Convention requirements. An 'implementation discretion' such as this suggests quite a different kind of 'margin of appreciation' from that applied in the context of Articles 8–11. But the distinction between this and other types of margin of appreciation is not carefully drawn in either the jurisprudence or the literature.

Fairness is clearly a variable standard and, in relation to trials, may depend upon technical procedural issues and wider circumstances including considerations of the public interest. The matter is

[70] *Winterwerp* v. *Netherlands* (1980) 2 EHRR 387 at paras. 42 and 49; *Stogmüller* v. *Austria* (1979) 1 EHRR 155.

[71] (1989) 11 EHRR 117 at para. 62.

[72] D. J. Harris, M. O'Boyle and C. Warbrick, *Law of the European Convention on Human Rights* (London: Butterworths, 1995), p. 164.

complicated further by the fact that a 'fair trial' is both a right available to the accused and itself a general public interest.[73] Similarly, the expression – 'the proper administration of justice' – refers simultaneously to both normative standards and to administrative necessity.[74] The 'priority to rights' principle operates differently in civil/administrative proceedings on the one hand, and in criminal trials on the other. Article 6(1) expressly provides that civil/administrative trials should be fair, held in public, subject to the exceptions already mentioned, and conducted within a reasonable time by an independent and impartial tribunal established by law. The Court has held that this implies a right to equality of arms,[75] and a right of access to courts, the latter of which can be limited, according to a national margin of appreciation, provided a legitimate aim is pursued, the principle of proportionality is observed, and the very essence of the right itself is not impaired.[76] Prima facie, therefore, Article 6 provides ample scope for balancing the content of the right to a fair civil/administrative trial with competing public interests such as the costs of delivering civil and administrative justice. But the 'priority' principle operates here through the exacting requirement that tribunals should be independent and impartial.[77] It was held, for example, in *Kostovski* v. *Netherlands* that 'the right to a fair administration of justice holds so prominent a place in a democratic society that it cannot be sacrificed to expediency'[78] (although this was a criminal case the principle was expressed in a universal form) and in *Perez* v. *France*, a civil case, the Court concluded that 'there can be no justification for interpreting Article 6(1) restrictively'.[79] Therefore, although what counts as an independent and impartial tribunal may be open to interpretation, and while there may be some trade-offs between public interests and certain civil and administrative justice procedures, Article 6 provides no scope for diluting the impartiality or the independence of tribunals in order to accommodate competing collective goals such as costs and administrative convenience.

[73] Kolb, 'Jurisprudence', 361. [74] *Ibid.*, p. 363.

[75] *Steel and Morris* v. *United Kingdom* (2005) 41 EHRR 403; *Yvon* v. *France* (2005) 40 EHRR 938; *Ernst* v. *Belgium* (2004) 39 EHRR 724 at para. 60.

[76] *Steel and Morris* v. *United Kingdom* (2005) 41 EHRR 403 at para. 62; *Aćimović* v. *Croatia* (2005) 40 EHRR 584 at para. 29; *Ernst* v. *Belgium* (2004) 39 EHRR 724 at para. 48.

[77] *Whitfield* v. *United Kingdom* (2005) 41 EHRR 967 at para. 43.

[78] (1990) 12 EHRR 434 at para. 44. [79] (2005) 40 EHRR 909 at para. 64.

The standard of fairness for criminal trials embraces the same general Article 6(1) criteria as apply in civil proceedings, but also includes the more detailed specifications found in Article 6(2) and (3).[80] Article 6(2) imposes an obligation on states to ensure that criminal justice processes presume those charged with criminal offences are innocent until proven guilty according to law, from which a right to the same effect can be derived. Article 6(3) provides the right to be informed promptly of the accusation in a language the accused understands, the right to adequate time and facilities to prepare a defence, the right to defend oneself in person or to state-funded legal assistance, the right to call and examine witnesses, and the right to an interpreter. These are all manifestations of the 'priority' principle. Because every viable democratic criminal justice system must compromise between the competing aims of effective crime control and the highest conceivable standards of due process, 'fairness' in criminal trials cannot realistically mean procedures which guarantee absolute certainty of guilt as a condition for conviction. But Article 6 requires that whatever balancing occurs greater weight should be placed upon rights than upon competing public interests.[81] For example, in *Rowe and Davis* v. *United Kingdom* the applicants complained that their right to a fair trial under Article 6(1) and 6(3) had been breached by the prosecution withholding, on public interest grounds, certain evidence from the defence without notifying the trial judge. Deciding that there had been a violation, the Court held that the right of defendants to disclosure of relevant evidence is not absolute and may be limited by the competing right to protect witnesses at risk of reprisals and public interests such as national security or keeping police investigative methods secret. But it added that 'only such measures restricting the rights of the defence which are strictly necessary are permissible under Article 6(1)' and that 'in order to ensure that the accused receives a fair trial, any difficulties caused to the defence by a limitation on its rights must be sufficiently counterbalanced by the procedures followed by the judicial authorities'.[82] The Court also took the view that while it is primarily for national courts to determine whether or not non-disclosure on public interest grounds is strictly necessary, it is for the European Court of Human Rights to ascertain whether the decision-making procedure applied in such cases complies, as far

[80] *Barberà, Messegué and Jabardo* v. *Spain* (1989) 11 EHRR 360 at para. 67.

[81] See Ashworth, *Human Rights*, pp. 56–64.

[82] (2000) 30 EHRR 1 at para. 61.

as possible, with the requirements of adversarial proceedings and equality of arms, and incorporates adequate safeguards to protect the interests of the accused. In this case it held that the decision by the prosecution to withhold relevant evidence from the accused on public interest grounds violated the defendants' right to a fair trial mainly because the trial judge had not been notified.[83]

In *Doorson* v. *Netherlands*, to take another example, the applicant complained that his right to a fair trial under Article 6(1) and 6(3)(d) had been violated by his conviction for drug trafficking on the evidence of witnesses who had not been heard in his presence, and whom he had not had the opportunity to question. The Court recognized that a balance may have to be struck between the unimpeded right to call and examine witnesses and the need, in certain cases, to protect their anonymity both for their own protection and to ensure the proper administration of justice.[84] In this case there was no suggestion that the applicant had sought to put pressure on any witnesses, although on previous occasions one of the witnesses concerned had suffered in precisely this way, while the other had been threatened. The Court held that the decision to grant the witnesses in question anonymity could not be regarded as unreasonable given that drug dealers frequently resort to threats or actual violence against those who give evidence against them, but that in such circumstances other procedural protections must be available to secure the defendant's right to a fair trial. For example, in this case, the defendant's lawyer had been permitted, in the absence of the accused, to question and to receive answers from the witnesses, apart from those concerning their identity, and there were arrangements to ensure that a conviction could not be based either solely or to a decisive extent on such anonymous statements.[85]

Article 6(1) also provides that the right to a public trial may be wholly or partly restricted 'in the interests of morals, public order or national security in a democratic society, where the interests of juveniles or the protection of the private life of the parties so require, or to the extent strictly necessary in the opinion of the court in special circumstances where publicity would prejudice the interests of justice'. However, the case law clearly embodies the 'priority' principle because the Strasbourg

[83] *Ibid.*, at paras. 62 and 66. [84] (1996) 22 EHRR 330 at para. 70.

[85] *Ibid.*, at paras. 72–73, 76. See also *Van Mechelen* v. *Netherlands* (1998) 25 EHRR 647 at paras. 54 and 55.

institutions have insisted that in camera proceedings 'must be strictly required by the circumstances'[86] and are 'exceptional'.[87]

ARTICLE 2(1)

The positive obligation under Article 2(1) is to protect everyone's *right to life* through law, but not to provide legal protection for everyone's *life* through law. This is because, paradoxically, and unlike any other interest protected by the Convention, life necessarily embraces its own negation, death. It follows, therefore, that death as such does not constitute an interference with the right to life and that states do not have to justify the deaths of their citizens as they are required, for example, to justify restrictions upon liberty. In *Pretty* v. *United Kingdom* the Court also held that the obligation to protect everyone's right to life through law does not entail an obligation to permit (or to prohibit) assisted suicide by mentally competent persons enduring great suffering who cannot end their lives themselves.[88]

The obligation to 'protect the right to life by law' implies, at a minimum, an entitlement to legally regulated processes concerning the criminalization, proper investigation, and legal sanctioning of culpable killing.[89] For example in *Sabuktekin* v. *Turkey* the applicant claimed that her husband had been killed by the security forces because of his involvement with a pro-Kurdish political party and that there had been no adequate and effective official investigation. The Court found that although there was insufficient evidence to show that the deceased had died in this way, the obligation to protect the right to life under Article 2 of the Convention, read in conjunction with the State's general duty under Article 1 to 'secure to everyone within ... (its) ... jurisdiction the rights and freedoms defined in ... (the) ... Convention', required 'by implication' some form of effective official investigation into deaths occasioned by lethal force of which the authorities

[86] *Diennet* v. *France* (1995) 21 EHRR 554 at para. 34.

[87] *Stallinger and Kuso* v. *Austria* (1998) 26 EHRR 81 at para. 51.

[88] *Pretty* v. *United Kingdom* (2002) 35 EHRR 1 at paras. 39–41. See A. Pedain, 'The Human Rights Dimension of the *Diane Pretty* Case', *Cambridge Law Journal* **62** (2003), 181–206.

[89] *Sabuktekin* v. *Turkey* (2003) 36 EHRR 314 at paras. 97 and 98; *Osman* v. *United Kingdom* (1998) 29 EHRR 245 at para. 115; *McCann* v. *United Kingdom* (1996) 21 EHRR 97 at para 161.

were aware, whether or not the deaths in question had been caused by agents of the state.[90] Although the 'priority' principle requires that these rights cannot be balanced against competing public interests, such as, for example the costs and administrative convenience of such investigations, there is, however, scope for broadly the same kind of 'adjectival discretion' on the part of national non-judicial institutions as in the case of Articles 5 and 6, because determining if some of the essential ingredients have been satisfied – for example, whether a particular death is 'suspicious' – may require the exercise of judgment based on inconclusive evidence.

Abortion presents a particularly contentious issue under Article 2, not fully resolved by the Strasbourg institutions. Although the Commission heard several cases in the 1980s and 1990s[91] it was not until 2004 that the Court considered the matter. In *Vo* v. *France* a pregnancy of between 20 and 24 weeks was terminated following medical negligence. The mother complained of a breach of Article 2 on the grounds that the doctor, though negligent, was acquitted by the French courts of the crime of causing unintentional injury because the foetus was not deemed to be a human person by that stage of the pregnancy. A majority of the Grand Chamber of the European Court of Human Rights ruled that there had been no violation of Article 2 because the domestic legal protection afforded the applicant was adequate and the requisite procedural requirements had been fulfilled, particularly since it was open to her to bring civil and/or administrative proceedings in respect of the accident. The majority observed that the Convention is silent as to when human life attracting the protection of Article 2 begins. It also concluded that there is, at best, a consensus in Europe that embryos and foetuses are part of the human race with the potential to develop into persons with full legal rights. But, because there is no consensus on when, legally and scientifically, human life begins, member states must be permitted a margin of appreciation in finding their own answers to this question. The majority therefore, declined to judge whether the foetus in this case was a person or not. Nor, given that the interests of

[90] (2003) 36 EHRR 314 at para. 97.

[91] *H* v. *Norway* (1992) 73 D.R. 155; *Paton* v. *United Kingdom* (1981) 3 EHRR 408; *Brüggemann and Scheuten* v. *Germany* (1981) 3 EHRR 244. G. Hogan, 'The Right to Life and the Abortion Question under the European Convention on Human Rights' in L. Heffernan with J. Kingston (eds.), *Human Rights: A European Perspective* (Blackrock: Round Hall Press, 1994), pp. 104–116.

the foetus and the mother coincided in this case, was there any need to speculate on possible conflicts between their respective rights.[92] Because, as the Court noted, the Convention does not clearly determine when the right to life is acquired, there is no fixed point in pregnancy when it could conclusively be said that the Convention's constitutional 'rights' principle comes into operation. It follows, then, that, provided the 'democracy' principle is also respected, the Convention permits abortion up to the point of viability of a foetus outside the womb but does not mandate it. Therefore, so long as the abortion laws of any member state are the result of a genuine democratic debate, their content may vary from state to state and still be Convention-compliant.[93]

It remains unclear to what extent the obligation to provide legal protection for the right to life implies a right to be legally protected from the risk of death arising from social and natural hazards, such as accidents, environmental pollution, and ill-health. But the democracy principle suggests that national democratic processes should determine the degree, manner, precise form, and content of the protection national law offers against such risks. States, therefore, have wide margins of appreciation in this respect, and the degree of protection offered the right to life beyond the minimum rights discussed in the first paragraph of this subsection may also therefore legitimately vary from state to state.[94]

ARTICLES 8–11

Articles 8–11 provide a series of rights covering respect for private and family life, home and correspondence, freedom of thought, conscience and religion, freedom of expression, and freedom of association and assembly. Each is subject to restriction for a number of 'legitimate purposes' found, although not uniformly, in the second paragraphs. These include the protection of the 'rights of others', and a range of

92 (2005) 40 EHRR 259. A further five judges agreed with the majority's decision but disputed the application of Art. 2, two others agreed with the majority verdict in spite of concluding that Art. 2 did apply, while three judges dissented from the majority (two of whom delivered a joint opinion) on the grounds that Art. 2 had been violated.

93 *H* v. *Norway* (1992) 73 D.R. 155 at p. 168.

94 *Öneryildiz* v. *Turkey* (2005) 41 EHRR 325; *Edwards* v. *United Kingdom* (2002) 35 EHRR 487 at paras. 54 and 55.

express public interests such as 'public safety'. Decisions involving these exceptions are formally filtered through the 'prescribed by law' and the 'democratic necessity' tests, and rely heavily on the margin of appreciation doctrine and the principle of 'proportionality to a pressing social need'.[95] Prima facie, some of the 'legitimate purposes' – for example 'national security', 'the economic well-being of the country', 'territorial integrity' – are 'pure' public interests which people can only benefit from collectively and from which they cannot separate out their individual share. On the other hand, although there is some element of ambiguity, the phrases, 'the rights and freedoms of others' and 'the protection of the reputation or rights of others', suggest individual rights and freedoms of *specific* others. Other restrictions on the rights found in these provisions, such as 'health' and 'morals', can plausibly be either public interests or individual rights according to the circumstances.[96] Although the Convention does not expressly provide individual rights to morals or health as such, certain moral and health rights may be derived from other express Convention rights. For example, in *Hatton* v. *United Kingdom*, discussed below, a 'right to sleep' was derived from the right to respect for private and family life, home and correspondence found in Article 8.

Although various patterns have been identified in the case law on Articles 8–11, most commentators agree that the 'legitimate purposes' are fluid and are not underpinned by any clear or coherent rationale.[97] As already indicated in Chapter 4, this is largely attributable to a less than adequate appreciation of the Convention's constitutional principles, and in particular the loose and unprincipled use of the margin of appreciation doctrine together with confusion about which party has

95 Art. 2 of Protocol No. 4 provides rights to freedom of movement, choice of residence and departure from any country, subject to a general 'public interest' exception, plus specific public interest restrictions similar to those found in Arts. 8–11, and the rights and freedoms of others. However, it has been the subject of very few judgments.

96 Nowlin argues that referencing 'morality' to a de facto public morality threatens to undermine the kind of 'liberal, pluralistic, constitutional morality' which, he maintains, the European Court of Human Rights should be asserting, C. Nowlin, 'The Protection of Morals Under the European Convention for the Protection of Human Rights and Fundamental Freedoms', *Human Rights Quarterly* **24** (2002), 264–286, at 279, 284–285.

97 See W. B. Simpson, *Human Rights and the End of Empire – Britain and the Genesis of the European Convention* (Oxford: Oxford University Press, 2001), p. 715; A. McHarg, 'Reconciling Human Rights and the Public Interest: Conceptual Problems and Doctrinal Uncertainty in the Jurisprudence of the European Court of Human Rights',

the burden of proving that a specific interference was proportionate. In what follows an attempt will be made to illustrate how a clearer appreciation of the Convention's constitutional principles could assist in the reconciliation of conflicts between these Convention rights and, respectively, competing public interests and other Convention rights.

Reconciling Rights and Public Interests

As Chapter 4 argued, the solution to much of the confusion and indeterminacy which surrounds the relationship between the rights in Articles 8–11 and competing public interests, lies in a much greater commitment to the 'priority' principle, already clear in the structure of these provisions and in much of the jurisprudence, but too readily abandoned in favour of the margin of appreciation and an exercise in ad hoc balancing. In the final analysis this amounts to a requirement on the defendant state to discharge a much more formal burden of proving, upon credible and convincing grounds supported by reliable evidence, that interfering with the right in pursuit of the specific public interest in question is proportionate to a pressing social need. As also already indicated, the problem with the balance metaphor is not the notion that Convention rights and competing social interests have to be weighed, but the implication that, prima facie, each has equal value. The idea of 'proportionality to a pressing social need', on the other hand, implies a presumption that the right should be upheld unless there are compelling grounds for interfering with it in pursuit of a legitimate and specific public interest, which may well be worth pursuing, but only by the most effective and least intrusive means given the costs involved.

Modern Law Review, **62** (1999), 671–696 at 685–95; S. Greer, *The Exceptions to Articles 8 to 11 of the European Convention on Human Rights* (Strasbourg: Council of Europe Publishing, Human Rights Files No. 15, 1997), pp. 42–44; F. G. Jacobs, 'The "Limitation Clauses" of the European Convention on Human Rights' in A. de Mestral, S. Birks, M. Bothe, I. Cotler, D. Klinck and A. Morel (eds.), *The Limitation of Human Rights in Comparative Constitutional Law* (Cowansville: Les Éditions Yvon Blais Inc., 1986), pp. 21–40; B. Hovius, 'The Limitation Clauses of the European Convention on Human Rights: A Guide for the Application of Section 1 of the Charter?', *Ottowa Law Review* **17** (1985) 213–261. For a discussion of limitation clauses in rights documents generally see M. E. Badar, 'Basic Principles Governing Limitations on Individual Rights and Freedoms in Human Rights Instruments', *International Journal of Human Rights*, **7** (2003), 63–92.

The case of *Hatton* v. *United Kingdom* provides a particularly useful illustration. The applicants complained that their right to respect for home, private, and family life under Article 8(1) of the Convention had been violated by sleep deprivation caused by the increase in noise levels from night flights at Heathrow airport under a new quota scheme introduced in 1993.[98] Each type of aircraft was given a 'quota count' with Heathrow allotted a certain number of quota points. Aircraft operators could then choose whether to operate a greater number of quieter aircraft, or fewer noisier ones, up to their noise quota. During the 'night' (11.00 pm–7.00 am) noisier types of aircraft were prohibited entirely, while during the 'night quota period' (11.30 pm–6.00 am) there was a noise quota, which varied between the summer and winter seasons, plus restrictions on aircraft movements. The UK argued that night flights were justified under Article 8(2) as necessary for the 'economic well-being of the country' since they formed an integral part of the global network of air services impacting directly upon the demand for day-time flights due to such operational constraints as geography, journey length time, number of time zones, direction of flight, turn-around time, and efficient utilization of aircraft. In written comments British Airways plc (BA), which indicated that its comments were also endorsed by the British Air Transport Association (BATA), stated that the loss of only some of its night flights at Heathrow would have a serious and disproportionate effect on its competitiveness due both to the damage to the network and to the scheduling difficulties entailed, particularly for long-haul arrivals. It was claimed, for example, that if BA flights scheduled to arrive before 7.15 am in 1999 had not been permitted to operate at Heathrow, a loss of 49 per cent of the company's long haul flight output at its main airport base would have been sustained because these flights could not have been re-scheduled for day time due to lack of spare terminal and runway capacity. A report by Berkeley Hanover Consulting, submitted by the applicants, challenged the validity of these claims. The government also claimed that the night flight regime at all three London airports, including Heathrow, was more restrictive than that at any other principal European hub airport, for example, Paris Charles de Gaul, Amsterdam Schiphol and Frankfurt, and if it were to become more restrictive still, UK airlines would

[98] (2002) 34 EHRR 1 (Chamber judgment); (2003) 37 EHRR 611 (Grand Chamber judgment).

be placed at a significant competitive disadvantage. However, the applicants submitted that many of the 'world's leading business centres (for example Berlin, Zurich, Munich, Hamburg, and Tokyo) have full night-time passenger curfews of between seven and eight hours'.[99] In July 1996, in an action for judicial review brought by the local authorities for the areas around the three main London airports, the Court of Appeal for England and Wales decided that the Secretary of State had given adequate reasons and sufficient justification for his conclusion that it was reasonable, on balance, to run the risk of increasing to some extent the possibility of sleep disruption to local residents because of other countervailing considerations, and that the 1993 regime could not be said to be irrational. In November 1996 the House of Lords declined leave for appeal against this decision.

On 7 November 2000, by a majority of five to two, a Chamber of the Court's Third Section found in the applicants' favour. It was also held, by a majority of six to one, that there had been a breach of Article 13 (the right to an effective domestic remedy) on the grounds that the judicial review conducted by the domestic courts did not extend to considering whether the increase in night flights under the 1993 scheme represented a justifiable limitation on the Article 8 rights of those living within the vicinity of Heathrow airport. The majority began its judgment by recognizing that since neither Heathrow nor the aircraft operating there were owned by the government, the question was whether the UK was in breach of a positive obligation to take reasonable and appropriate measures to ensure that the applicants' rights under Article 8 were respected. This hinged upon whether it could be said that a 'fair balance' had been struck between the interests of the individual and the community as a whole, a matter which, it was held, was subject to a 'certain margin of appreciation'.[100] However, the Court added that, in 'the particularly sensitive field of environmental protection' states are required to minimize interference with Article 8 rights by pursuing legitimate policy objectives in ways which have the 'least onerous' impact upon human rights.[101] This required finding the best possible solution by conducting a complete and proper investigation into the matter prior to proceeding with the project in question. While the government had acquired some relevant information derived from

[99] (2003) 37 EHRR 611 at para. 114. [100] (2002) 34 EHRR 1 at para. 96.
[101] *Ibid.*, at para. 97.

the research of others, there was no evidence that it had conducted any research itself into the precise economic benefits of night flights. Although there was also some official research into the problem of sleep disturbance caused by such flights, this had not included the subtly different problem of sleep prevention, i.e. the difficulty of being unable to return to sleep having been woken. The Consultation Paper which preceded the introduction of the 1993 regime indicated that the government had not attempted to quantify the aviation and economic benefits of night flights in monetary terms because of the difficulties of obtaining reliable and impartial data, some of which were commercially sensitive, and the challenge of modelling these complex interactions. Nevertheless the Court concluded that although it was likely that night flights contributed to the economic well-being of the country, in the absence of officially-sponsored research which quantified these benefits, it could not be said that a fair balance had been struck between the interests in question. Consequently, there had been a violation of Article 8.

Judge Greve dissented on Article 8 (though not on Article 13) on the grounds that the majority's decision was inconsistent with the wide margin of appreciation accorded states in other planning cases, and that there were no major shortcomings either in the State's inquiry into the noise created by night flights, or in relevant UK decision-making processes. Judge Sir Brian Kerr dissented on both Articles 8 and 13. As for Article 8 he thought that it had not been established that there was a 'significant interference'[102] with the applicants' right to private life (especially since the applicants' opportunities to move elsewhere remained unaffected because aircraft noise had not resulted in a decrease in house prices) and that, by conducting a 'substantial'[103] amount of research into the night noise problem and by introducing a series of noise abatement and mitigation measures in addition to restrictions on night flights the government had shown concern that the right to respect for private life should not be unduly interfered with. It was also 'beyond plausible dispute' that night flights contributed to the national economic interest.[104] To require specific research into the extent of the obvious placed a 'very substantial and retroactive burden on the Government'.[105] According to Sir Brian, the rights of

[102] *Ibid.*, at para. O-III7. [103] *Ibid.*, at para. O-III9. [104] *Ibid.*, at para. O-III11
[105] *Ibid.*, at para. O-III16.

air carriers and of passengers also had to be brought into the equation. The majority's 'minimum interference' test, he held, was also unprecedented in Convention case law and incompatible with the principles of subsidiarity and the margin of appreciation. Given that so many factors weighed against the applicants and so few in their favour, and that a macro-economic issue was at stake which should more appropriately be dealt with in the political than in the judicial sphere, Sir Brian stated that he could not subscribe to the conclusion that the balance required by Article 8 had been struck inappropriately. Unlike Judge Greve, he also dissented from the majority decision on Article 13 on the grounds that the obligation to provide a domestic remedy is limited to grievances which are 'arguable' under the Convention, whereas, in this case, there was no arguable Article 8 case at all.

On 8 July 2003, on a reference from the government of the UK, a majority of twelve to five of the Grand Chamber reversed the Chamber's decision on Article 8, but by a majority of sixteen to one upheld its decision that the limitations on judicial review in domestic law constituted a violation of Article 13.[106] Two of the judges in the Chamber – Judge Costa and Sir Brian Kerr – also sat on the Grand Chamber, with each maintaining the views they had taken as members of the Chamber panel. The minority of the Grand Chamber largely agreed with the majority of the Chamber that, apart from merely relying on evidence provided by the aviation industry, the UK had failed to demonstrate that it had adequately discharged its positive duty to protect the right to sleep derived from the broader right to environmental protection under Article 8, which since it was increasingly important under international and Convention law also narrowed its margin of appreciation. The majority of the Grand Chamber agreed with the majority of the Chamber that the central question was whether, taking the state's margin of appreciation into account, the implementation of the 1993 regime struck a 'fair balance' between the competing interests of the individuals affected by aircraft noise at night and the economic interests of the national community as a whole.

[106] For a critique of the Grand Chamber's decision, which argues that the Court misunderstood the role of the margin of appreciation and failed properly to weigh all the alleged consequences of the night flight regime, see J. Hyam, '*Hatton* v. *United Kingdom* in the Grand Chamber: One Step Forward, Two Steps Back?', *European Human Rights Law Review* (2003), 631–40.

However, unlike the majority of the Chamber the majority of the Grand Chamber concluded that, while the state is required to give due consideration to the particular interests it is obliged to respect under Article 8, 'it must, in principle, be left a choice between different ways and means of meeting this obligation'.[107] Since the supervisory function of the European Court of Human Rights is of a subsidiary nature, 'it is limited to reviewing whether or not the particular solution adopted can be regarded as striking a fair balance'.[108] Because the interference complained of did not intrude into private life in a manner comparable to the threat of criminal sanctions in *Dudgeon* v. *United Kingdom*, the margin of appreciation could not be considered particularly narrow, nor were there adequate grounds for elevating the rights in question to a special status merely because they were environmental in nature.

Assuming that a 'fair balance' depends upon the relative weight assigned to each of these competing interests, the majority of the Grand Chamber accepted that the national authorities were entitled to conclude, relying on statistical data on the average perception of noise disturbance provided by a study conducted in 1992, that sleep disturbance caused by aircraft noise was comparatively rare and, therefore, although it could not be ignored it could be treated as negligible in comparison with the average disturbance caused. The Grand Chamber also noted that, unlike previous cases in which respondent states had been found in breach of the Convention in respect of inadequate environmental protection, there was no question here of any failure by domestic authorities to comply with national regulations. Further factors in assessing if the correct balance had been struck included the fact that measures had been introduced to mitigate the effects of aircraft noise generally, including night noise – for example, aircraft noise certification, compulsory phasing out of older, noisier jet aircraft, noise preferential routes and minimum climb gradients for aircraft taking off, noise-related airport charges etc. – and the fact that the applicants could have moved house since adverse noise levels had not affected property prices in the area. The Grand Chamber held that, while the relevant governmental decision-making processes, as in the present case, must necessarily involve appropriate investigations and studies, this does not mean that valid decisions can only be taken if

[107] (2003) 37 EHRR 611 at para. 123. [108] *Ibid.*

comprehensive and measurable data are available in relation to each and every particular. The 1993 regime was the result of a series of investigations and studies spanning three decades and was itself preceded by the publication of a Consultation Paper to which the public had access and which included the results of recent research into both aircraft noise and sleep disturbance. Each new night flight regime lasted only five years in order, among other things, to take account of developments in research, including into sleep patterns.

The key controversy in *Hatton*, therefore, is how the substantive issue is to be approached procedurally. There is a fine line separating legitimate *interference* with Convention rights in pursuit of specific collective goals – which is consistent with the Convention – from *violating* individual rights in order to secure this objective, which is not. Therefore, the Court must adhere as scrupulously as possible to the formal conception of the burden and standard of proof suggested by the 'priority' principle as discussed in the previous chapter. The notion of an intermediate standard of proof is particularly appropriate for Convention cases such as *Hatton*, chiming, as it does, with some, though not all, of the dicta of the European Court of Human Rights in litigation calling for a resolution of conflicts between Convention rights and the pursuit of the public interest. While the applicants could be said to have had the 'evidential burden' of sustaining a prima facie case that their rights under Article 8 had been interfered with, the 'priority' principle suggests that the government of the UK should then have the 'persuasive burden' of proving, by 'clear, strong and cogent' evidence, that the interference was justified in pursuit of the economic well-being of the country. While evidence that the night flight regime at Heathrow was in the commercial interests of airlines may be deemed to have discharged the burden of proof 'on a balance of probabilities', more concrete evidence about how this may have contributed to the economic well-being of the country would be required to reach the standard of 'clear, strong and cogent' evidence. Hence, although the Chamber's verdict would be difficult to defend if the relevant interests were merely to be balanced against each other according to the standard of 'proof on a preponderance of the evidence', it is more faithful to the allocation of the burden of proof, and the 'intermediate' standard of proof, suggested by the Convention's primary constitutional principles, than is the Grand Chamber's decision.

Reconciling Competing Rights

The only rights which can legitimately limit express or implicit Convention rights are other express or implicit Convention rights. If it were otherwise, the privileged position of Convention rights would be undermined by rights which those who drafted the Convention chose not to include. However, 'pure' conflicts between Convention rights are uncommon in the Strasbourg case law because most conflicts between Convention rights also often involve a public interest exception. Like other human rights treaties, the Convention neither formally ranks rights in a hierarchical order, nor prescribes any particular method of resolving conflicts between them. Where clashes occur, the Court has therefore largely sought to balance one Convention right against another in the context of the litigation, according to the principle of proportionality and the margin of appreciation doctrine.[109] But the Convention's primary constitutional principles indicate that reconciling conflicts between Convention rights is quintessentially a judicial task, permitting no genuine margin of appreciation to national non-judicial institutions at all. As already indicated, these difficulties may arise in relation to various Convention provisions, for example the right to life under Article 2 (especially abortion and killing in defence from unlawful violence), in Article 6(1), and as considered here, in respect of the complex relationship between the rights found in the first paragraphs of Articles 8–11 and the 'rights and freedoms of others' exception found in the second paragraphs.[110] However, particularly sharp clashes occur between the right to freedom of expression, under Article 10, and other Convention rights, for example the right to respect for private and family life, home and correspondence, under Article 8, and the right to freedom of thought, conscience and religion, under Article 9.

Two examples illustrate these problems particularly well. In *Otto-Preminger-Institut* v. *Austria*, the applicant, a private, non-profit making arts cinema in Innsbruck, complained that its freedom of expression under Article 10 of the Convention had been violated by the official seizure and confiscation of a film, Das Liebeskonzil (Council in Heaven)

109 *Kutzner* v. *Germany* (2002) 35 EHRR 653 at paras. 64–82; *Kokkinakis* v. *Greece* (1994) 17 EHRR 397 at paras. 47–50; *Sigurjónsson* v. *Iceland* (1993) 16 EHRR 462 at paras. 39–41.

110 For a thoughtful contribution to the debate see E. Brems, 'Conflicting Human Rights: An Exploration in the Context of the Right to a Fair Trial in the European Convention on Human Rights', *Human Rights Quarterly* **27** (2005), 294–326.

which depicted God, Christ, and the Virgin Mary in an unflattering, and sometimes obscene manner, and portrayed them conspiring with the Devil to infect the human race with syphilis as punishment for immorality.[111] Screenings of the film were open to members of the public over seventeen years of age, and the cinema's advertising indicated that the film caricatured the Christian creed and explored 'the relationship between religious beliefs and worldly mechanisms of oppression'. The seizure and confiscation were instigated at the request of the Innsbruck diocese of the Catholic church and were based on the offence of 'disparaging religious doctrines' under s. 188 of the Austrian Penal Code.

A majority of the Court (six out of nine) held that the cinema's right to freedom of expression had not been violated, while the minority held that it had. All, however, agreed that the seizure and forfeiture of the film constituted an interference with the right to freedom of expression, and that this was in accordance with both Austrian law and the Convention principle of legality. There was also a high level of consensus about the relevant principles, viz. that freedom of expression is one of the foundations of democratic society characterized by tolerance and broadmindedness, that its exercise carries obligations including not to cause gratuitous offence to others, and that since there is no uniform conception of the importance of religion in member states there can be no comprehensive definition of what constitutes permissible interference with the exercise of freedom of expression where it is directed against religious sensibilities. National authorities therefore have a 'certain margin of appreciation', which goes hand in hand with Convention supervision, in assessing the necessity and the extent of such interference which must be convincingly established.

While both majority and minority agreed that the interference was in pursuit of the legitimate aim of protecting the right to freedom of thought, conscience and religion of others under Article 10(2), the majority also thought it could be justified by the need to prevent disorder and crime. But the main difference of opinion was over whether or not the seizure and forfeiture were 'necessary in a democratic society'. The majority held that the state's margin of appreciation had not been exceeded because the overwhelming majority (87 per cent) of the population in the Tyrol region were Catholic and in seizing the film

[111] (1995) 19 EHRR 34.

the Austrian authorities had acted to prevent an offensive attack upon their religious beliefs and to ensure the public peace. The minority, on the other hand, decided that while it may be necessary to prohibit violent and abusive criticism of religious groups – since tolerance works both ways and the democratic character of society may be damaged by such criticisms – prohibiting such conduct must be proportionate and this will not be the case if a less restrictive solution was available but not used. The minority thought a complete ban on expression would only be acceptable if the behaviour concerned reached such a high level of abuse, and came so close to a denial of the freedom of religion of others, as itself to forfeit the right to be tolerated by society. Since the film was to be shown to paying audiences over age seventeen at an art cinema, which had acted responsibly in notifying the public that the screening was critical of the Catholic faith, the minority took the view that there was little likelihood of any religiously sensitive person being confronted with it unwittingly.

The central issue in this case can, therefore, be characterized in three different ways. Although neither majority nor minority considered this possibility, it can be seen, first, as a clash between two manifestations of the right to freedom of association and assembly on the part of the cinema and those who wanted to see the film, and the right of outraged Christians to demonstrate against it outside. But only if there were reasonable grounds for believing that screening the film would have presented a serious risk to public order could it legitimately have been banned under the 'prevention of disorder' exception to Article 11.

It can also be seen, second, as a clash between the cinema's right to freedom of expression and the public interest in the prevention of disorder, which the majority considered and dropped, but later resurrected without adequate justification to support its conclusion. Viewed in these terms, the Austrian legislature, police and prosecuting authorities have a margin of appreciation in deciding how to resolve the matter. However, the 'priority-to-rights' principle requires that the prevention of disorder defence (a public interest) is supported by cogent, credible and concrete evidence of the risk of disorder, and no evidence whatever to this effect is offered in the entire report of the Court's decision. Therefore, without such evidence defining the issue in terms of a clash between the right to freedom of expression and the prevention of disorder cannot be defended.

Finally, it can be characterized in terms of a clash between two Convention rights, the right to freedom of expression and the right to freedom of thought, conscience, and religion. The key issue then becomes how these rights are to be defined, a matter for the Austrian courts and for the European Court of Human Rights to resolve through the application of the subordinate principles related to the rights principle, namely legality, effective protection, subsidiarity (to national judicial institutions), non-abuse of rights and exceptions, evolutive, dynamic and autonomous interpretation, review, and positive obligations. These point to the need carefully to define what each right means in the context in question. But there can be no legitimate consideration of the demographic characteristics of a particular locality for three reasons. First, if the scope of the right to freedom of expression depends upon the tolerance threshold of those criticized it becomes progressively more limited the less tolerant they are. Second, factoring the demographics of a particular locality into the equation makes the right to freedom of expression contingent upon the will of a majority, a utilitarian consideration at variance with the rights-privileging character of the Convention. Third, where there is no public interest for national authorities to determine, the term 'democratic society' must refer to the character of European, and not to national much less to local, society. The scope of the right to freedom of expression in European democratic society can therefore be defined as including the freedom to criticize religious beliefs, but not to be abusive or gratuitously offensive towards those who hold them. Conversely, and by necessary implication, the scope of the right to freedom of thought, conscience, and religion in a democratic society does not include the right to be free from criticism, but does include the right to be free from gratuitously offensive criticism. Whether this line has or has not been crossed is a question of fact to be decided by relevant national non-judicial public authorities subject to review by domestic courts and ultimately to the European Court of Human Rights at Strasbourg, according to an objective European standard with no reference to local demography. Only in this narrow sense, therefore, is there a margin of appreciation on the part of national non-judicial institutions. But where, as here, a particular form of expression is borderline acceptable/unacceptable, the case for permitting it is stronger if viable ways of limiting its impact upon those likely to be offended can be found short of banning it entirely. Since there were other alternatives, the minority decision is, therefore, more consistent with the Convention's constitutional principles than the majority's.

Wingrove v. *United Kingdom* provides a rare example of a 'pure' conflict between Convention rights with no competing public interest.[112] The applicant, a film director, complained that his right to freedom of expression under Article 10 of the Convention had been violated by the decision of the British Board of Film Classification (the 'Board') – upheld on appeal by the Video Appeals Committee – to refuse a classification certificate for his video, Visions of Ecstasy, on the grounds that it was blasphemous under the common law. The applicant was also unwilling to edit the video in a manner which would have ensured it received the certificate required for lawful distribution. The director claimed the eighteen-minute film derived from the life and writings of St Teresa of Avila, a sixteenth-century Carmelite nun who experienced powerful ecstatic visions of Christ. To the accompaniment of rock music and with no dialogue, it showed a youthful actress, among other things, stabbing her own hand with a large nail, spreading the blood over her naked breasts, and exchanging passionate kisses with another near-naked young woman, said to represent her psyche, while writhing in 'exquisite erotic sensation'.[113] She then straddled the horizontal body of the crucified Christ still fastened to the cross, 'moving in a motion reflecting intense erotic arousal', kissing his lips, and entwining her fingers with his, activities to which Christ himself appeared briefly to respond.[114]

In its report of 10 January 1995 the European Commission of Human Rights concluded by a majority of fourteen to two in the applicant's favour. Twelve[115] of those in the majority held that prior censorship based on speculation that a section of the public might be outraged, requires 'particularly compelling reasons'[116] which were absent here because, as a short video with a necessarily limited distribution, it was unlikely that anyone likely to be offended would see it, given the title, the proposed warning on the box, and the availability of an '18' classification. According to the Commission, the fact that some Christians might be outraged merely by the knowledge that such

[112] (1997) 24 EHRR 1. Another example of a pure conflict between Convention rights, involving gay adoption, is *Fretté* v. *France* (2004) 38 EHRR 438.

[113] (1997) 24 EHRR 1 at para. 9. [114] *Ibid.*

[115] Two other judges agreed with the majority decision but on different grounds. Mr Schermers thought the film contributed to public debate on the notion of 'ecstasy', while Mr Loucaides thought the film portrayed the human problems of St Teresa rather than projecting an offending or degrading image of Christ.

[116] (1997) 24 EHRR 1 at para. 65.

a video was legally in circulation would not be a sufficiently compelling reason to deny it lawful distribution. The refusal to award the certificate, therefore, did not correspond to a pressing social need, was disproportionate to the aim pursued, and could not be considered necessary in a democratic society within the meaning of Article 10(2) of the Convention. The dissentients, Mr Soyer and Mr Weitzel, thought that the domestic authorities had acted within their wide margin of appreciation and concluded that a prohibition upon distribution was necessary in order to protect the right of believers not to be subjected to such 'sacrilegious images' and 'deliberate blasphemy'.[117]

However, on 25 November 1996 seven of the nine judges on the panel of the European Court of Human Rights came to the opposite conclusion, deciding that the applicant's right to freedom of expression had not been violated because the certificate had been legitimately refused under Article 10(2) in order to protect the rights of others, namely the right of Christians not to have their religious feelings insulted. One of the two dissentients on the Court, Judge De Meyer, was opposed in principle to the prior restraint of publications, while the other, Judge Lõhmus, thought that banning the video on the assumption that Christians would be offended, but before any had the opportunity of complaining, could not qualify as a 'pressing social need', particularly since the English law of blasphemy only protects the Christian religion.[118] Judges Bernhardt and Pettiti delivered judgments concurring with the majority. The former stated that, while he was not personally convinced that the video should have been banned, he nonetheless accepted that the domestic authorities had acted within their considerable domestic margin of appreciation. The latter expressed the view that the same result could have been reached on the grounds that, in addition to blasphemy, the video constituted a seriously profane attack on the religious or secular ideals of others.

The verdict of the remaining five judges on the Court was reached by addressing a sequence of issues familiar in cases where one or more limitation found in the second paragraph of the provisions in Articles 8–11 is invoked to justify an interference with a right provided by the first paragraph. First, it was decided that the refusal to

[117] *Ibid.*, p. 24.

[118] The applicant argued, without objection from the respondent, that there is no uniform law of blasphemy in the United Kingdom, *ibid.*, at para. 16.

grant the applicant a certificate constituted an interference with the applicant's freedom of expression and that this was 'prescribed by law' in that it lay within the legal powers of the Board and was motivated by the desire to prevent the reasonably clear common law offence of blasphemy. This conclusion was supported by the fact that the applicant had decided not to seek judicial review having received counsel's opinion that the formulation of the offence of blasphemy upon which the domestic authorities relied was accurate. The majority of the Court noted that Article 10(2) recognizes that, although freedom of expression is 'one of the essential foundations of democratic society', its exercise carries certain duties and responsibilities and that the English law of blasphemy does not outlaw all hostile criticism of the Christian faith which its adherents might find offensive. The decision therefore turned on whether refusing the certificate, particularly since it involved prior restraint, was 'necessary in a democratic society' in pursuit of the 'legitimate aim' of protecting the right of Christians not to suffer an insult to their religious sentiments likely to be caused by the 'contemptuous', 'reviling', 'scurrilous', or 'ludicrous' treatment of a sacred subject – in particular God, Christ, the Bible, or the Church of England as established by law – whether or not this was the effect intended.[119]

The majority of the Court held that, for a particular restriction to satisfy this test it must correspond to a 'pressing social need' and be proportionate to the legitimate aim pursued. In determining if this were the case, national authorities – who are better placed than an international court to judge what is appropriate in all the circumstances – have a 'margin of appreciation', subject to review at Strasbourg, wider with respect to the regulation of forms of expression liable to offend intimate personal moral or religious convictions, than in relation to political speech or to debate on matters of public interest. The Court's task was, therefore, to determine whether the reasons relied on by the national authorities to justify the measures in question were 'relevant and sufficient' for the purposes of Article 10(2), a test which it found had been fulfilled.[120] Having considered the ease with which videos can be copied, lent, sold, and viewed by different viewers, the majority concluded that the decision of the national

[119] The terms, 'contemptuous', 'reviling', 'scurrilous', or 'ludicrous' are derived from the domestic law of blasphemy in the United Kingdom, *ibid.*, at para. 60.

[120] *Ibid.*, paras. 59–65.

authorities to refuse the certificate on the grounds that it was more focused on the erotic feelings of the audience than on the sexuality of the central character, and that it was blasphemous, could not be regarded as arbitrary or excessive. The applicant admitted to Midweek magazine that the film could also have been entitled 'Gay Nuns in Bondage',[121] and unless the viewer read the cast list, which appeared on the screen for a few seconds, he or she would have had no means of knowing that the central character was supposed to be St Teresa, that the other actress was portraying her psyche, or that the historical St Teresa was a nun who experienced religious ecstasy. St Teresa was also considerably older, at the age of 39, than the main actress when she had her visions, and there is no evidence in her writings, or from other reliable sources, that she ever injured her hands, had lesbian fantasies, or imagined herself in physical contact with Christ. Had it simply been a video showing a young woman apparently having sex with a crucified figure not obviously Christ it should not have been especially offensive to Christians, although it may have been highly distasteful to many.[122] Had it been a sequence in a longer, and more thoughtful, exploration of the issues of religious and sexual ecstasy in the life of St Teresa the offence to Christians, which it might nonetheless still have caused, may also have been more tolerable. The Board also claimed that had the video portrayed the Prophet Mohammed, or the Buddha, in a similar way its decision would have been the same.

As in *Otto-Preminger*, the two key issues in *Wingrove* are, first, how two competing Convention rights should be defined and, secondly, whether thus defined the conduct in question constitutes a realization of one involving no violation of the other, or a violation of one which cannot therefore be supported by any Convention right. Following the discussion of *Otto-Preminger* above, the right to freedom of expression can be defined as excluding the right to cause gratuitous insult to deeply held sentiments and the right to freedom of thought, conscience, and religion can be defined as limited to protection only from forms of expression which are gratuitously offensive. The key question in *Wingrove*, therefore, is whether granting a certificate

[121] *Ibid.*, para. 15.

[122] As the Board pointed out in its letter to the applicant notifying him of the rejection of his application for a certificate and recommending cuts which would circumvent the problem, *ibid.*, para. 13.

to Visions of Ecstasy would amount to permitting gratuitous insult to religious sensibilities. As in *Otto-Preminger*, it can be argued that, since *Wingrove* is also a borderline case, this turns, not only on the character of the form of expression, but also on whether other viable ways could be found of limiting the possible offence without banning distribution entirely. Although this is a matter of judicial discretion, it is not an exercise in 'balancing' as such. However, in view of the high evidential threshold on the prior restraint of publications, and given the fact that the video could have been released with an '18' certificate and a warning on the box, the decision of the majority of the Commission could be regarded as more faithful to the Convention's constitutional principles than the lower evidential threshold required by the majority of the Court.

ARTICLE 1 OF PROTOCOL NO. 1

The weakest form of the 'priority' principle applies to the right to the peaceful enjoyment of possessions under Article 1 of Protocol No. 1, which provides that '(e)very natural or legal person is entitled to the peaceful enjoyment of his possessions', that '(n)o one shall be deprived of his possessions except in the public interest and subject to the conditions provided for by law and by the general principles of international law', and that the State is entitled to control the use of property by law in accordance with, amongst other things, the 'general interest'.[123] Some rights found in other protocols could also arguably be included in this category because of the broad public interest constraints to which they are implicitly subject.[124] In litigation under Article 1 of Protocol No. 1 the Court has often used the balance metaphor and has granted states wide margins of appreciation. But a weak version of the 'priority' principle nonetheless applies in this context since it has also been held that the principle of proportionality must be observed, that arbitrariness is avoided, that other alternatives for achieving the aim in question have been properly considered, that

[123] The 'public interest in a democratic society' also provides an explicit justification for restricting the right of everyone lawfully within a territory to leave, to liberty of movement, and to freedom to choose residence, Article 2(4), Protocol No. 4.

[124] For example, the rights to education and to free elections in Arts. 2 and 3 of Protocol No. 1.

appropriate procedural safeguards are available, that due regard has been paid to the consequences of the interference for those affected by it, and most importantly of all, that interferences are adequately compensated.[125]

For example in *Sporrong and Lönnroth* v. *Sweden*, the applicants complained that the length of the periods during which their property in Stockholm had been subject to expropriation permits (twenty-three years in Sporrong's case and eight in Lönnroth's) accompanied by prohibitions on construction (twenty-five years in Sporrong's case and twelve in Lönnroth's) infringed their rights under Article 1 of Protocol No. 1.[126] The Court held that, although technically the permits had not 'deprived' the owners of their property, their capacity to use and dispose of it had been significantly reduced in practice. While the prohibitions on construction were deemed to constitute measures relating to the control of property within the second paragraph of Article 1, the expropriation permits were regarded as constituting an interference with the peaceful enjoyment of property under the first paragraph. A majority of ten to nine held that, taking both measures together in the context of planning and re-development of Sweden's capital city, a fair balance had not been struck between the interests of the community and the rights of the applicants because the latter 'bore an individual and excessive burden which could have been rendered legitimate only if they had had the possibility of seeking a reduction of the time-limits or of claiming compensation'.[127] Applying the same test as that used by the majority, eight of the nine dissentients concluded that, given the wide margin of appreciation available in such cases, there had been no violation. In contrast, in *Phocas* v. *France* the applicant complained that his right to peaceful enjoyment of his property had been violated by the duration of restrictions imposed from 31 July 1965 to 22 January 1982 in respect of a road improvement scheme.[128] The Court decided that there had been no violation of Article 1 of Protocol No. 1 because, although states enjoy a 'wide margin of appreciation in order to implement their town planning policy', a fair balance had been struck between the interests of the community and the rights of the individual.[129] The applicant had had the opportunity to sell his property to the local authority at a price

[125] Y. Windisdoerffer, 'Margin of Appreciation and Article 1 of Protocol No. 1', *Human Rights Law Journal* **19** (1998), 18–20.

[126] (1983) 5 EHRR 35. [127] *Ibid.*, para. 73. [128] (1997) 32 EHRR 221.

[129] *Ibid.*, paras. 53–57.

determined by an expropriations judge but had failed to do so within the specified time limit.[130]

CONCLUSION

The most significant implications of the constitutional model sketched in the previous chapter concern the effects of the 'priority' principle. Prima facie, the strongest versions are found in relation to Articles 3, 4(1), and 7(1), and in the 'strict' and 'absolute' necessity tests in Articles 2(2) and 15. A better appreciation of the role of the 'priority' principle in relation to Article 3 would help resolve some of the stark contradictions in the jurisprudence between the assertion that the principle prohibiting torture, inhuman or degrading treatment or punishment is absolute yet its application is not. The jurisprudence on Article 2(2) is now generally compliant with the Convention's constitutional principles, but that on Article 15 lacks a clear requirement that the democratic character of a given state must be threatened if derogation is to be justified and the Court can be criticized for having been too generous with national authorities seeking to invoke it. However, although formally a negatively defined right, the right not to be subjected to forced or compulsory labour under Article 4(2) and (3) turns out, on closer inspection, to be another specially protected right with a universal European character.

Less strong versions of the 'priority' principle are found in Articles 5 and 6, in respect of Article 2(1), in Articles 8–11, and in Article 1 of Protocol No. 1. The right not to be subject to arbitrary arrest and detention in Article 5 permits certain public interests to be taken into account in the process of defining what an arbitrary deprivation of liberty means, but with a clear presumption that the right prevails unless there are relevant and sufficient reasons in, for example bail applications, that it should not. Similarly, the public interests suggested by the concept of 'fairness' in Article 6 cannot be directly 'balanced' against the independence and impartiality of tribunals, and there is little scope for directly weighing them against the protections in Article 6(2) and (3) either. The rights to legally regulated processes derived from the obligation to protect the right to life by law under Article 2(1) are

130 More recent cases include *Wittek* v. *Germany* (2005) 41 EHRR 1060 and *Kjartan Ásmundsson* v. *Iceland* (2005) 41 EHRR 927.

also limited by (implicit) 'adjectival discretion' similar to those pertaining to Articles 5 and 6.

The case law on the relationship between Convention rights and collective goods in Articles 8–11 is unprincipled and confused largely because the Strasbourg institutions have not fully appreciated the need to give priority to rights and have too often sought refuge in the margin of appreciation and balancing as a substitute. The main effect of the 'priority' principle in this context is to require respondent states to discharge a more formal and exacting burden of proof, as illustrated by *Hatton* v. *United Kingdom*, in seeking to justify interference with these rights on public interest grounds, than is currently recognized to be the case. As *Otto-Preminger-Institut* and *Wingrove*, among other cases, illustrate, where conflicts between Convention rights have to be resolved, the key issues are how the rights in question are to be defined and whether, thus defined, the conduct in question constitutes their violation or realization. If the complaint concerns conduct lying on the boundary between a permissible and an impermissible expression of a Convention right, the case for permitting it is more persuasive if there are viable ways of limiting the impact on competing rights. For the reasons already given, the priority principle also applies, though least strongly, to the right to the peaceful enjoyment of possessions under Article 1 of Protocol No. 1.

6

Improving Compliance

INTRODUCTION

As things currently stand – apart from persuasion, suspension of voting rights on the Committee of Ministers, and expulsion – the Council of Europe lacks any direct means of inducing states to improve their Convention violation records. In many countries, as discussed in Chapter 2, systemic violations stem from problems which are simply too intractable to be dealt with by executive or legislative fiat, while in others the national and international legal and political costs of violation rank lower than those associated with making the necessary changes. Among other things Chapters 3 and 4 argued that these difficulties could be ameliorated by further development of the Court's currently cautious policy of identifying what needs to be done at the national level to correct the source of violations, and by refinements to the method of adjudication at Strasbourg. However, of themselves these are unlikely to be sufficient. The key question, therefore, is what more the Council of Europe can do to increase domestic compliance pressures. A key element concerns the effective delivery of information from member states to Strasbourg and vice versa. While improving the role of existing national and European institutions may provide part of the answer, this chapter argues that a case can also be made for the creation of a European Fair Trials Commission and for the development by the Council of Europe of a much more robust, coherent, and thorough policy with respect to National Human Rights Institutions and the European Commissioner for Human Rights. First, possible ways of increasing compliance pressures from domestic legal systems will be considered.

INCREASING COMPLIANCE PRESSURES FROM DOMESTIC LEGAL SYSTEMS

National legal systems are already a key site for the exertion of domestic pressure upon states to improve Convention compliance because, with the possible exception of Russia and some of the Caucasian republics discussed in Chapter 2, the rule of law is now sufficiently well established throughout Europe to ensure that a refusal, by a non-judicial public body, to abide by the clear decision of a national court will rapidly induce a national constitutional crisis which most governments will want to avoid in all but the most exceptional circumstances. However, several problems limit the domestic legal impact which the judgments of the European Court of Human Rights might otherwise have. First, there is 'no obligation arising out of the Convention to make judgments of the ECHR executable within the domestic legal system'[1] and, as already indicated in Chapter 2, many national courts do not accept that judgments of the European Court of Human Rights are binding on them, even when made against their own state. In 2002, for example, twenty-one European constitutional courts declared themselves not bound by rulings of the European Court of Human Rights, although a larger majority said they were influenced by them.[2]

Second, the orthodox view of Article 46(1) – which provides that the 'High Contracting Parties undertake to abide by the final judgment of the Court in any case to which they are parties' – is that any state is obliged to observe *only* those judgments made directly against it.[3] But others disagree.[4] In 1978 the Court held that its judgments serve not only to decide those cases brought before it

[1] G. Ress, 'The Effect of Decisions and Judgments of the European Court of Human Rights in the Domestic Legal Order,' *Texas International Law Journal* **40** (2005), 359–382 at 374.

[2] A. Alen and M. Melchior in collaboration with B. Renauld, F. Meersschaut and C. Courtoy, 'The Relations Between the Constitutional Courts and the Other National Courts, Including the Interference in this Area of the Action of the European Courts – XIIth Conference of the European Constitutional Courts, Brussels, 14–16 May 2002, General Report', *Human Rights Law Journal* **23** (2002), 304–330 at 327.

[3] D. J. Harris, M. O'Boyle and C. Warbrick, *Law of the European Convention on Human Rights* (London/Dublin/Edinburgh: Butterworths, 1995), p. 700.

[4] For example, the German scholar, J. A. Frowein, cited in A. Zimmermann, 'Germany' in R. Blackburn and J. Polakiewicz (eds.), *Fundamental Rights in Europe: The European*

but, 'more generally, to elucidate, safeguard and develop the rules instituted by the Convention, thereby contributing to the observance by the States of the engagements undertaken by them as Contracting Parties'.[5] Georg Ress, a former judge of the European Court of Human Rights, argues that although 'judgments of the Court do not have an erga omnes effect ... they have an orientation effect',[6] and the Parliamentary Assembly has stated that the 'principle of solidarity implies that the case law of the Court forms part of the Convention, thus extending the legally binding force of the Convention erga omnes (to all the other parties)'.[7] Although there may be room for debate about whether or not 'the principle of solidarity' is in fact embodied in the Convention, and whether or not it suggests an erga omnes effect, the Assembly's conclusion receives support from Article 1 which provides that '(t)he High Contracting Parties shall secure to everyone within their jurisdiction the rights and freedoms defined in Section I of this Convention'. Since the final, authoritative, interpretation of these rights and freedoms lies with the Court, if the Court finds a certain practice in a certain state to be contrary to the Convention, it would be very difficult for another state to argue that precisely the same practice did not constitute a breach of its obligations under Article 1 also. It is of course open to states to incorporate not only the Convention in national law, but the entire case law of the Strasbourg institutions as binding authority as well.[8] However, most seem to regard the Strasbourg case law as of only 'persuasive' authority, probably in order to avoid limiting the scope of national courts to interpret the Convention to meet national requirements.

Convention on Human Rights and its Member States, 1950–2000 (Oxford: Oxford University Press, 2001), p. 343; R. Ryssdall, 'The Enforcement System set up under the European Convention on Human Rights' in M. K. Bulterman and M. Kuijer (eds.), *Compliance With Judgments of International Courts: Proceedings of the Symposium Organized in Honour of Professor Henry G. Schermers by Mordenate College and the Department of International Public Law of Leiden University* (The Hague/Boston/London: Martinus Nijhoff, 1996), pp. 49–69 at 50 and 61; L. Wildhaber, 'The Role of the European Court of Human Rights: An Evaluation', *Mediterranean Journal of Human Rights* **8** (2004), 9–32 at 28.

[5] *Ireland* v. *UK* (1980) 2 EHRR 25 at para. 154; *Karner* v. *Austria* (2004) 38 EHRR 528 at para. 26.

[6] Ress, 'Effect of Decisions', 374.

[7] Parliamentary Assembly of the Council of Europe, 'Execution of Judgments of the European Court of Human Rights', Resolution 1226 (2000) adopted on 28 September 2000, para. 3.

[8] As recommended by the Parliamentary Assembly, *ibid.*, paras. 10.iii and 12.i.d.

While it is difficult to see how Convention compliance can be improved unless all member states regard the entire Convention case law as binding on their national courts, even full erga omnes effect, comprehensively acknowledged, has its limitations. For one thing, there is the enormous challenge of translating the entire Convention acquis into every official European language. Furthermore, even if this were universally achieved it is difficult if not impossible to identify concrete legal norms from the thinly reasoned Strasbourg jurisprudence. It is also very unlikely that the facts upon which any previous decision or judgment of the Strasbourg institutions is based will be repeated in all particulars in another state. As a result, there will virtually always be ample scope for lawyers to persuade national courts to refuse to follow a putatively relevant Strasbourg judgment on the grounds that, although binding authority, it does not cover the facts of the dispute at issue.

The third problem limiting the impact of the Court's judgments on domestic legal systems is that, in spite of the requirement in Article 13 of the Convention to provide effective remedies, and notwithstanding the fact that all member states have either incorporated the Convention into their domestic law – or have substantially the same standards in domestic constitutional bills of rights – not all states have equally effective means by which violations of Convention standards can be litigated in domestic courts. A case can, therefore, be made for Article 13 to be revised to require effective *judicial* remedies to be made available in all member states. This would involve granting jurisdiction to all domestic courts in each member state to consider complaints about the violation of Convention standards when adjudicating complaints against public authorities, and the provision of individual constitutional complaints processes to all national constitutional courts or their equivalents.

Two other ways in which the Council of Europe could improve awareness of Convention rights on the part of national courts deserve further consideration. First national lawyers and judges should receive better training in Convention law, including better contact with judges of the European Court of Human Rights. As the Committee of Ministers acknowledged in its recommendation accompanying the publication of Protocol 14 in May 2004, awareness of human rights generally, and of the Convention in particular, should be integral to the core curriculum for all branches of the legal profession throughout Europe. The Council of Europe already has several organizations relating to the legal profession – for example the Consultative Council of European Judges – and it also hosts regular meetings between the Presidents of Supreme Courts and between representatives of national bar associations. There are also a number of organizations and programmes concerned with education – for example the Higher Education and Research Steering Committee and the Division for Citizenship and Human Rights, the latter of which concentrates mostly upon schools. However, none of these gives the human rights element in both university law degrees, and in professional legal education, the profile it deserves. Several respondents in the Strasbourg interviews thought that national compliance with the Court's judgments could be greatly improved by better dissemination of judgments in national languages, better training of lawyers and judges in states with poor compliance records, and better collaboration between national judges. This could be included in the remit of the European Fair Trials Commission proposed below. Secondly, a commitment to uphold the Convention could be included in the professional oaths taken by national judges, particularly those serving on supreme and constitutional courts. Judges in member states typically take an oath of allegiance, either to the national constitution or, as in the UK, to the Crown. An oath to uphold the constitution will, necessarily, entail a commitment to uphold fundamental rights where the national constitution includes a bill of rights. Although a commitment to defend fundamental rights may be an implicit aspect of the judicial function in contemporary liberal democracy, even without a formal undertaking to this effect,[9] a formal judicial commitment to defend, either human rights generally or Convention rights more specifically, might make a modest contribution to making national judiciaries more sensitive to Convention rights.

TOWARDS A EUROPEAN FAIR TRIALS COMMISSION

Since, as already indicated in Chapter 2, the overwhelming majority of applications the Court adjudicates concern alleged violations of the right to a fair trial provided by Article 6 of the Convention, the majority of

[9] As, for example, Sir John Laws argues in 'Law and Democracy', *Public Law* (1995), 72–93.

these stemming from allegedly unreasonable length of legal proceedings, a strong case can be made for special measures to be introduced to address it more systematically than is currently the case. Once information relating to national trial processes has been compiled it could be used both by the Court in specifying more precisely to respondent states what needs to be done to correct a violation, and to the Committee of Ministers to assist it in ensuring that the judgment has been properly executed. Serious consideration should therefore be given to the establishment of a European Fair Trials Commission expressly designed for the purpose. Two possible models suggest themselves: a version of the regime established by the European Convention for the Prevention of Torture and Inhuman or Degrading Treatment or Punishment, and that of the Venice Commission. It is disappointing that the Council of Europe's Warsaw summit in May 2005 failed to consider this issue, especially given its decision to establish another democracy-promoting institution – the Forum for the Future of Democracy – which is in danger of duplicating the work of the Venice Commission.[10]

The European Convention for the Prevention of Torture and Inhuman or Degrading Treatment or Punishment

The European Convention for the Prevention of Torture and Inhuman or Degrading Treatment or Punishment (ECPT) – drafted in 1986, in force by 1989, and amended as from March 2002 – aims to 'strengthen by non-judicial means of a preventive nature',[11] the right of everyone detained by a public authority in a member state not to be subjected to torture or to inhuman or degrading treatment or punishment in their widest senses.[12] Unlike other human rights instruments, it does not establish any new norms, but instead provides a unique enforcement regime based on unannounced visits to places

[10] *Action Plan of the Council of Europe adopted by the Ministers' Deputies at the Warsaw summit*, CM(2005)80 Final, 17 May 2005, http://www.coe.int/dcr/summit/20050517_plan_action_en.asp

[11] Preamble to the ECPT.

[12] R. Morgan and M. Evans, *Combating Torture in Europe: The work and Standards of the European Committee for the Prevention of Torture* (Strasbourg: Council of Europe, 2001), p. 32–33. As Morgan and Evans show, at p. 153, although closely linked to the European Convention on Human Rights, the standards used by the CPT are 'very different from the well-known codes of custodial standards previously promulgated by the United Nations and the Council of Europe'.

of detention by the European Committee for the Prevention of Torture and Inhuman or Degrading Treatment or Punishment (CPT), whose findings and recommendations then form the basis of a constructive dialogue with the state concerned.[13] By the end of 2000, Belarus, Bosnia-Herzegovina, and Yugoslavia were the only European states west of the Urals not to have joined this regime, and over 2.5 million people had been brought squarely within its focus, with many more in its 'penumbra'.[14]

Members of the CPT are persons of high moral character known for their competence in human rights or their professional experience in the areas covered by the Convention. Elected by the Committee of Ministers from lists of names drawn up by the bureau of the Parliamentary Assembly, they meet in plenary session three times a year and serve part-time for periods of four years up to a maximum of twelve years. The number on the Committee – which is dominated by lawyers, medics, and men – is equal to the number of state parties to the ECPT.[15] The Committee's work is directed by a bureau consisting of the president and two vice presidents, supported by a nineteen-member Secretariat which arranges and prepares visits, accompanies, and provides administrative support to members when these take place, clerks meetings, and implements the Committee's decisions regarding dialogue with member states. Other experts may assist in a variety of ways, with two typically included in each five-member visiting delegation.[16] The CPT is obliged to inform states of its intention to conduct a visit, but not of the precise locations chosen for inspection. Although all states are subject to periodic visits, in principle once every four years, in practice the frequency varies according to demands on the CPT's time, resources, and priorities. Ad hoc visits are at the Committee's discretion and are prompted by concerns expressed by individuals, groups or other state parties that ill-treatment is occurring in a particular jurisdiction or at a particular place.[17] The CPT makes follow-up visits to assess progress in implementing recommendations made in a previous inspection.

[13] *Ibid.*, pp. 22 and 31. [14] *Ibid.*, p. 23 [15] *Ibid.*, p. 25. [16] *Ibid.*, p. 27.

[17] M. D. Evans and R. Morgan, *Preventing Torture: A Study of the European Convention for the Prevention of Torture and Inhuman or Degrading Treatment or Punishment* (Oxford: Clarendon Press, 1998), p. 168.

In 1999 and 2000 the CPT conducted 31 visits, 21 of which were periodic, lasting 311 days in total.[18]

The purpose of visits is to open up dialogue with the state concerned.[19] Missions end with a meeting at which members of the delegation convey their initial impressions to officials in the expectation of an official response to the subsequent report. Although confidential, reports can be published if the state concerned so requests. Publication has however become the rule rather than the exception,[20] and the Committee itself is empowered to 'make a public statement' if a state fails to cooperate or to improve defects in its compliance with the ECPT to which the CPT has drawn its attention. However, up to 2000 the CPT had only issued three such public statements, two with respect to Turkey in 1992 and 1996 respectively, and one regarding the Chechen Republic.[21] Confidential reports are also submitted to the Committee of Ministers of the Council of Europe. Aware of the practical difficulties facing states in implementing its recommendations, the CPT has also outlined three 'positive measures' for their assistance: 'enhanced interfacing' (improved communication and coordination) between the CPT and Council of Europe programmes for developing and consolidating democratic security in areas such as the training of law enforcement officials, prison officers and health care staff in prisons and psychiatric hospitals; developing channels for states to submit funding applications to international organizations where recommendations have substantial financial implications; and better arrangements for the delivery of emergency food or medical supplies to detainees which the CPT is not able to provide itself.[22] Although many CPT recommendations have been implemented others have not. However, various studies highlight the critical role played by national civil society, particularly NGOs, in pursuing domestically the agenda set by a CPT visit, a theme further considered below.[23] But, disappointingly, it is not clear if the imaginative regime established by the

[18] Morgan and Evans, *Combating Torture*, p. 29.

[19] *Ibid.* [20] *Ibid.*, p. 31. [21] *Ibid.*

[22] Evans and Morgan, however, caution against enmeshing the CPT in executive decisions to finance or implement change on the grounds that this would 'undermine its role as an impartial inspector setting and applying more or less universal standards', *Preventing Torture*, p. 166.

[23] *Ibid.*, p. 168.

ECPT has made any difference to preventing the torture or ill-treatment of those detained by public authorities in member states because, according to the most authoritative verdict, 'there are too many imponderables to be able to make a definitive assessment'.[24]

It is, however, extremely doubtful if the most innovative feature of the ECPT, ad hoc visits by the CPT, could be replicated with respect to the right to a fair trial. Violations of Article 6 – particularly alleged delays in the administration of justice – are likely to be much more varied, more complex, and less capable of being visually inspected than the detention facilities with which the CPT concerns itself. They are also more likely to hinge upon legal judgment than are instances of torture, inhuman or degrading treatment or punishment. While the CPT's other functions, periodic and follow-up visits, may be capable of being carried out with respect to the right to fair trial, this would also be a feature of a European Fair Trials Commission modelled on the Venice Commission, as considered in the following section.

The Venice Commission

The European Commission for Democracy through Law, better known as the 'Venice Commission', provides a more appropriate model for a European Fair Trials Commission than the ECPT.[25] Established in 1990 following the collapse of the Berlin Wall, it was charged with providing assistance and advice about constitutional matters to Council of Europe states. The right to fair trial, judicial independence, the rule of law, and democratization in the former communist bloc are among the many issues it has had to consider so far.[26] Each member state of the Council of Europe appoints an independent expert – often a law professor or judge.[27] Meeting four times a year in Venice, and supported by

[24] *Ibid.*, p. 159.

[25] See J. Jowell, Q.C., 'The Venice Commission: Disseminating Democracy Through Law', *Public Law* (2001), 675–683; G. Malinverni, 'The Contribution of the European Commission for Democracy Through Law (Venice Commission)', *International Studies in Human Rights* **67** (2001), 123–137; S. Bartole, 'Final Remarks: The Role of the Venice Commission', *Review of Central and East European Law* **26** (2000), 351–363.

[26] Jowell, 'Venice Commission', 676–680; Malinverni, 'Venice Commission', 135; Bartole, 'Final Remarks', 356–358.

a permanent office in Strasbourg, the activities of the Venice Commission span five main constitutional areas: providing advice and assistance about specific problems upon request; considering issues with trans-national dimensions; providing relevant training for government officials; promoting education in constitutional matters by hosting seminars and workshops; and providing a centre for documentation.

Typically a representative group of rapporteurs, with relevant expertise, will be appointed to study an issue, generally stemming from a request for assistance from a member state rather than from the Council of Europe's Parliamentary Assembly, Committee of Ministers, or Secretary General. Before submitting an opinion for the Commission's consideration, the country concerned will be visited and opinion canvassed. In making recommendations and monitoring their implementation the Commission attempts to be sensitive both to the universal characteristics of democratic constitutionalism and to the possibility of permissible national variation. Jowell reports that the Commission is also 'increasingly concerned to anticipate broader developments and to act proactively on what it calls "trans-national" issues by 'undertaking research designed to establish and guide constitutional values shared throughout Europe'.[28] To this end it has established standing committees on constitutional justice, federal and regional states, international law, protection of minorities, constitutional reform, democratic institutions, and emergency powers. Recent work by these committees includes surveys on the implementation of the decisions of constitutional courts (or their equivalent), how political parties are financed, constitutional referendums, and regional-central relations.[29] A permanent 'UniDem Campus' (Universities for Democracy) has also been established in Trieste for, among other things, training government officials from south-eastern Europe. The case law of constitutional courts and equivalent bodies is collected and disseminated by a Centre on Constitutional Justice, created

[27] It also has one associate member (Belarus) and nine observers – Argentina, Canada, the Holy See, Japan, Kazakhstan, Republic of Korea, Mexico, United States, and Uruguay. The European Commission, and South Africa, have 'special status'.

[28] Jowell, 'Venice Commission', 680.

[29] The Commission also receives requests for advice from beyond Europe and has established sub-committees on South Africa and Latin America in addition to those concerned with the Mediterranean Basin and south-eastern Europe, *ibid.*

in 1991, primarily through the Bulletin of Constitutional Case Law and the CODICES database, the latter of which makes some 20,000 pages of text available on CD ROM or via the Internet,[30] and contains the summaries published in the Bulletin and the Special Bulletin, plus the full text of nearly 3,500 decisions in several languages.

A European Fair Trials Commission could discharge several functions comparable to those of the Venice Commission, such as actively researching and promoting fair trial issues which affect more than one state, providing an archive for the collection of relevant documents, and monitoring a variety of sub-themes through subject-specific standing committees, in for example, legal education, civil justice, criminal justice, administrative justice, legal aid, the legal profession, the appeals process, the judiciary, the rule of law, and length of proceedings. However, since the latter is one of the most fertile sources of fair trial complaints this should be a top priority. The Commission should, in particular, seek to determine why certain states have the most expeditious trial processes, and why others have the most sluggish. Country-specific investigations could be commissioned by the Committee of Ministers and used in the supervision of the execution of judgments process. The Commission's reports, whether country-specific or thematic, could also be used by applicants, both in the domestic legal process and in making a complaint to the European Court of Human Rights. Although they would not be binding on it, such reports would also be useful in assisting the Court to identify the specific measures which ought to be introduced by the respondent state in order to correct the violation and to prevent it from recurring.

If properly funded and staffed a European Fair Trials Commission could play a major role in formulating Council of Europe policy in this area. However, welcome though this might be, in the final analysis it would suffer from the same defect as all other developments at this level: it is one thing for Europe collectively to decide what is appropriate at the national level – even if this is tailored to the specific requirements of particular countries – but quite another for European institutions to be able to ensure that their policies are effectively executed by states. Other mechanisms are therefore required to deliver these policy initiatives domestically with a potentially key role

[30] http://www.venice.coe.int/site/main/CODICES_E.asp

capable of being played by Human Rights Institutions on both the national and European dimensions.

THE ROLE OF HUMAN RIGHTS INSTITUTIONS

Prior to the Second World War it was widely assumed that the promotion and protection of human rights was the responsibility of governments, legislatures, and both national and international judicial systems, pressed to honour their commitments by intergovernmental and supranational organizations, NGOs, and civil society at all levels. However, since then the perception has grown that an intermediate institution – the independent, though publicly-funded and publicly-accountable, National Human Rights Institution (NHRI) – may also have a valuable role to play.[31] Earlier, and enduring, precursors have included ad hoc Commissions of Inquiry and ombudsmen, the latter of which remain difficult to distinguish from NHRIs in some contexts.[32] Indeed, about 50 per cent of the 110 national ombudsmen in the world have a human rights mandate.[33] Broadly speaking, however, the functions of ombudsmen are limited to the investigation of individual complaints about errors or wrongs in official decision-making, and seeking remedies through non-binding recommendations following negotiation and conciliation.[34] While NHRIs may also have this role, they usually perform a wide range of other tasks relating to the promotion and protection of human rights. The function of NHRIs has also been mirrored at the pan-European level by the creation in 2000 of the Council of Europe's European Commissioner for Human Rights, and by the

[31] For a thorough account of the historical background see B. Lindsnœs and L. Lindholt, 'National Human Rights Institutions: Standard-Setting and Achievements', *Human Rights in Development Yearbook* **1** (1998), 3–10.

[32] Although generally regarded as a Swedish innovation with roots in the eighteenth century 'Supreme Solicitor', one commentator claims that institutions providing the core function of the ombudsman, supervising the legality and fairness of public administration, can be traced to ancient Greece, Rome, Persia, and China, L. González Volio, 'The Ombudsman Institution: the Latin American Experience', Conference on the Effectiveness of National Human Rights Institutions, University of Notre Dame, London, 1 November 2003, p. 3. See also L. C. Reif, *The Ombudsman, Good Governance and the International Human Rights System* (Leiden/Boston: Martinus Nijhoff, 2004).

[33] Reif, *Ombudsman*, p. 393. [34] *Ibid.*, pp. 2–4.

establishment of the European Union's Fundamental Rights Agency (FRA) in 2004.

The roles of the European Commissioner for Human Rights and the FRA will be considered later. But before doing so four key questions about the possible contribution NHRIs might make to the protection of human rights in contemporary Europe should be considered. First, what can they do to increase the domestic political and legal costs of Convention violation? Second, given the uniquely homogenized constitutional, legal, and political landscape, should the Council of Europe require member states to ensure that their NHRIs conform to a much more carefully tailored common model than is the case anywhere else in the world? If so, third, what should that model be? Fourth, what relationship should European NHRIs have with the Strasbourg institutions? Before these questions can be addressed, however, the background to these world-wide developments and their efficacy need to be examined.

A Global Trend

When in 1946 the UN endorsed NHRIs, it was initially concerned to define and demarcate their boundaries and it saw their role as limited to supplementing the work of its own Commission on Human Rights.[35] Although the first NHRI was established in France in 1947,[36] Cardenas argues that the international pace quickened in the 1970s as the UN began to realize that NHRIs could share its expanding human rights activities and work load.[37] The idea also attracted a unique degree of support from states – irrespective of east-west and north-south differences – as a way of avoiding the creation of further international human rights institutions, protecting national sovereignty, and satisfying rising human rights demands. In 1993 the UN formalized these developments in the landmark

[35] United Nations, Economic and Social Council (ECOSOC) Resolution 9 (II), 21 June 1946, cited in S. Cardenas, 'Emerging Global Actors: The United Nations and National Human Rights Institutions', *Global Governance* **9** (2003), 23–42 at 28.

[36] B. Dickson, 'The Contribution of Human Rights Commissions to the Protection of Human Rights', *Public Law* (2003), 272–285 at 274.

[37] Cardenas, 'Emerging Global Actors', 28–29.

'Paris Principles', endorsed by the World Conference on Human Rights in Vienna the same year.[38]

The Paris Principles state that the mandate of NHRIs should be as broad as possible, and that their composition and role should be prescribed in national constitutions or statute. Their responsibilities should include submitting and publicizing human-rights related opinions, proposals, reports and recommendations raised by existing or proposed legislation or administrative practice (including judicial organization), to legislatures, government, and other competent authorities, either at their own instigation or having been prompted by others. They should be independent and pluralistic in membership and their functions should include liaising with other relevant national bodies, such as Ombudsmen and NGOs, and cooperating with relevant international and regional organizations. They should also be able to receive information, including documents, from any relevant source where necessary, to offer advice upon request, to raise human rights awareness, including through the media, and to contribute to relevant programmes of research, teaching, and training. The possibility of NHRIs exercising a quasi-judicial role, including the investigation and hearing of complaints and the settlement of disputes through conciliation or binding decision, is also envisaged.

Since 1993 the UN has established an International Coordinating Committee of National Institutions, published a comprehensive Handbook providing guidance on how to establish and strengthen NHRIs,[39] and created a Special Adviser on National Institutions, Regional

[38] Vienna Declaration and Programme of Action, Part 1, para. 36. 'Principles Relating to the Status of National Institutions', UN Commission on Human Rights resolution 1992/54 of 3 March 1992, Annex, UN doc. E/1992/22, chap. II, sect. A; *Principles Relating to the Status of National Institutions for the Promotion and Protection of Human Rights*, General Assembly Resolution 48/134 of 20 December 1993 (the 'Paris Principles').

[39] S. Spencer and I. Bynoe, *A Human Rights Commission: The Options for Britain and Northern Ireland* (London: IPPR, 1998), p. 47; United Nations, *National Human Rights Institutions: A Handbook on the Establishment and Strengthening of National Institutions for the Promotion and Protection of Human Rights*, UN Centre for Human Rights Professional Training Series No. 4, June 1995. The National Human Rights Institutions Forum, an organization funded by the Office of the UN High Commissioner for Human Rights and established through collaboration with the Danish Centre for Human Rights, also provides country-specific information on its website www.nrhi.net. See also Danish Centre for Human Rights, *The Work and Practice of Ombudsman and National Human Rights Institutions (articles and studies)* (Copenhagen: Danish Ministry of Foreign Affairs, 2002).

Arrangements, and Preventive Strategies based in the office of the High Commissioner for Human Rights, for whom NHRIs is a major policy priority.[40] Cardenas argues that 'rising UN support has facilitated the global diffusion of NHRIs, especially in areas lacking strong regional human rights mechanisms', and that without 'this web of UN activities, the global rise of NHRIs may not have been possible in the first place'.[41] Although the ending of the Cold War, the increasing global profile of human rights, and a resurgence of democratic governance provided a receptive environment in the 1990s, she maintains that the UN crucially 'defined and promoted the concept of an NHRI, provided states with the technical capacities needed to build these institutions, facilitated the networking of these new actors, and offered them the benefits of membership in international organizations'.[42] Most UN NHRI-related activity has occurred in Asia, southern Africa, Latin America, and Eastern Europe with less in the Middle East and in North Africa, a phenomenon which Cardenas explains in terms of 'relatively weak patterns of democratization rather than conventionally favoured explanations of cultural relativism'.[43] Human Rights Watch concludes that, although the performance of most African national human rights commissions (excluding Ombudsmen) has so far been 'disappointing',[44] they nevertheless still have 'the potential to contribute positively to strengthening a human rights culture and obtaining greater protection against abuses'.[45] Indeed, one of the features of the global rise of NHRIs has been their attractiveness to different types of state, including those making the transition to democracy, those with poor human rights records more interested in improving their image than in genuinely raising levels of compliance,[46] and those with generally good standards of compliance which are, nonetheless, keen to embrace innovation.[47] However, Human Rights Watch warns against unquestioning enthusiasm for

[40] Cardenas, 'Emerging Global Actors', 33; Human Rights Watch, *Protectors or Pretenders? Government Human Rights Commissions in Africa* (New York/Washington/London/Brussels: Human Rights Watch, 2001), p. 1.

[41] Cardenas, 'Emerging Global Actors', 32 and 36.

[42] *Ibid.*, p. 36. [43] *Ibid.*, p. 32.

[44] Human Rights Watch, *Protectors or Pretenders?*, pp. 1 and 4. [45] *Ibid.*, p. 5.

[46] As the Human Rights Watch, *Protectors or Pretenders?*, p. 2, states: 'Even some of the most repressive African governments appear to accept the international human rights discourse and an acknowledgment that human rights protection should be a part of their government portfolio.'

[47] Cardenas, 'Emerging Global Actors', 35.

NHRIs, and reprimands the UN High Commissioner for Human Rights for its reluctance publicly to identify and to criticize weak and officially compliant ones.[48]

As Cardenas points out, in fulfilling their main mission – implementing international human rights norms domestically – NHRIs typically have both 'regulative' and 'constitutive' functions.[49] The former spans three spheres: attempting to secure government compliance (by, for example, reviewing proposed legislation); relating with the judiciary (by participating in the legal enforcement of human rights violations); and independent activities (such as investigation, mediation, and issuing reports). 'Constitutive' activities are of two kinds: 'socialization' (i.e. the promotion of a culture of respect for rights through dissemination of information and education) and the cultivation of international cooperation, particularly through establishing links with other NHRIs. The Paris Principles permit considerable national variation in fulfilling this mission and, at the dawn of the twenty-first century, a wide range of alternative models can be found with sizes also ranging from a handful of officials, as in New Zealand, to the seventy-member Consultative Commission on Human Rights in France. Sticking close to the UN conception Cardenas identifies three types of NHRI: national commissions, about 100 altogether, which primarily address issues of human rights violations and discrimination whoever is responsible; national ombudsmen, of whom there are also about 100, with a remit limited to ensuring fairness and legality in public administration; and hybrids which combine elements of each. The International Council on Human Rights Policy distinguishes five types: multi-member national commissions on human rights with wide mandates likely to include the investigation of complaints, review legislation and promotional functions; multi-member national advisory commissions on human rights with no powers of investigation and, as the name suggests, a largely advisory function; national anti-discrimination commissions with many functions similar to those of national human rights commissions though confined to discrimination issues;

[48] Human Rights Watch, *Protectors or Pretenders?*, pp. 7–8.

[49] Cardenas, 'Emerging Global Actors', 25–27. Dickson, 'Human Rights Commissions', 275, regards this as their 'essential function'. But Spencer and Bynoe indicate that, while the mandate of some NHRIs refers to international standards, the mandate of others does not, *Human Rights Commission*, pp. 48 and 49

single-member ombudsman institutions likely to have a mandate limited to maladministration, or a particular kind of discrimination, in a system of interrelated institutions; Defensores del Pueblo usually covering the combined mandates of what might otherwise be several ombudsmen.[50] While the mandates of all NHRIs include civil and political rights, the jurisdictions of a few institutions also extend to social, economic and cultural rights with a particularly strong focus on non-discrimination, equal opportunities, and the rights of vulnerable groups, found in countries where these have been recognized as particularly significant historic problems.[51]

The Effectiveness of NHRIs

There are two initial problems in seeking to determine how effective NHRIs are in promoting and protecting human rights: even before any assessment of their contribution can be made, arriving at an appropriate notion of what 'effectiveness' or 'success' means is not straightforward, and as comparatively new actors on the world stage studies of their performance are in their infancy. As the International Council on Human Rights Policy points out, 'success' or 'effectiveness' will, to some extent, depend on the observer's point of view.[52] For individual complainants, for example, 'effectiveness' is likely to mean the resolution of complaints to their satisfaction which could in principle be measured by complainant surveys. But complainant satisfaction should not be confused with effectiveness, because not every complainant will have a meritorious case.

An NHRI could also be said to be effective if it has a 'transformative effect on the broader society' and is able to influence the behaviour of officials.[53] However, this will usually be very difficult to measure because it will generally be impossible to isolate the contribution made by an NHRI to the resolution, or amelioration, of any generic human rights problem from that made by other agencies – for example the legislature, the media, political parties, NGOs, interest groups, etc. Other factors in the wider context – for example the

[50] International Council on Human Rights Policy, *Performance & Legitimacy: National Human Rights Institutions* (Versoix, Switzerland: International Council on Human Rights Policy, 2000), p. 4.

[51] Lindsnœs and Lindholt, 'National Human Rights Institutions', 21.

[52] ICHRP, *Performance & Legitimacy*, p. 105. [53] *Ibid.*

presence or absence of a culture of official respect for human rights and the rule of law, a tradition of judicial independence etc. – may also have a strong influence. Dickson argues that NHRIs can 'add value' to the domestic protection of human rights by: influencing politicians and civil servants if appropriate mechanisms are in place; influencing courts as expert 'interveners' in proceedings brought by others, funding or representing litigants, or initiating litigation themselves; investigating alleged human rights abuses; and promoting public awareness and understanding of human rights.[54] Lindsnœs and Lindholt maintain that, while a focus on civil and political rights, non-discrimination, and equal opportunities for vulnerable groups 'show the most immediate results, for example in relation to the number of persons held legally responsible for human rights violations', achievements in relation to economic, social, and cultural rights so far are not impressive.[55]

Livingstone and Murray distinguish eighteen 'benchmarks' by which effectiveness could be assessed, lying on three dimensions: capacity, performance, and legitimacy.[56] The seven benchmarks related to capacity are: a clear legal foundation; independence; adequate political support at creation; independent and democratic state institutions; adequate powers and resources to fulfil a broadly defined mandate with clearly defined jurisdiction; the necessary financial resources; and clarity regarding the role of Commissioners and Chief Commissioner. Five factors are identified as being particularly important regarding performance: a clear strategic plan; full use of existing powers and resources; coherent management and operational efficiency; influence (being a catalyst for change); and dealing effectively and in a self-critical manner with problems. Other commentators have also stressed the importance of dynamism and courage on the part of Commissioners, particularly in the infancy of any given NHRI and in states undergoing democratization.[57] According to Livingstone and Murray, six factors are related to legitimacy: the perceived independence of the NHRI from

[54] Dickson, 'Human Rights Commissions', 278–284.

[55] Lindsnœs and Lindholt, 'National Human Rights Institutions', 32.

[56] S. Livingstone and R. Murray, 'The Effectiveness of National Human Rights Institutions', in S. Halliday and P. Schmidt, *Human Rights Brought Home: Socio-Legal Perspectives on Human Rights in the National Context* (Oxford and Portland Oregon: Hart Publishing, 2004), pp. 136–164 at 141–143.

[57] Human Rights Watch, *Protectors or Pretenders?*, p. 7; Reif, *Ombudsman*, p. 408.

government, and a perception that the former has a positive impact upon the latter; accountability to the legislature; close but independent relationships with NGOs and civil society; a role distinguishable from that of other statutory or constitutional bodies; accessibility; and a clear and coherent media and communications strategy. Human Rights Watch adds a seventh – 'transparency'.[58] Some of the Livingstone and Murray benchmarks could arguably have been listed under other categories. A 'media and communications strategy' might, for example, be considered part of 'coherent management' under 'Performance' as much as an aspect of 'Legitimacy'. And, with some rearrangement of the existing benchmarks, and the possible inclusion of others, four dimensions with different labels might be suggested instead – 'Context', 'Capacity', 'Management and Mission', and 'Reputation'. However, these minor criticisms aside, it is difficult to deny that these variables are each likely to have a bearing on the success of any given NHRI.

Some commentators attribute the success of NHRIs to a single, conclusive factor, but disagree over what it is. For example, according to the International Council on Human Rights Policy, the 'single most effective organizational step' in increasing both the accessibility and public legitimacy of NHRIs is a broad membership genuinely representative of the society they serve.[59] Reif claims that 'the level of positive response by ministers and government administration to an ombudsman's recommendations is the "key indicator" of the institution's effectiveness', but that this can often be hard to judge due to a lack of reliable information.[60] Other commentators have concluded that success or failure derives largely from the interaction between the kind of factors identified by Livingstone and Murray, in the specific national context, rather than to the universal effectiveness of any single variable or cluster of variables.[61] It follows from Cardenas's distinction between 'regulative' and 'constitutive'

58 Human Rights Watch, *Protectors or Pretenders?*, p. 16.

59 ICHRP, *Performance and Legitimacy*, p. 109.

60 Reif, *Ombudsman*, pp. 408–409.

61 ICHRP, *Performance and Legitimacy*, pp. 3, 6, 105–110; Human Rights Watch, *Protectors or Pretenders?*, pp. 14–26 and 83–91; Cardenas, 'Emerging Global Actors'; L. Reif, 'Building Democratic Institutions: the Role of National Human Rights Institutions in Good Governance and Human Rights Protection', *Harvard Human Rights Journal* **13** (2000), 1–58 at 1.

functions that any given NHRI may be more effective on one of these dimensions than it is on the other, and it may even be effective on some but not on other elements of the same dimension. Conformity with the Paris Principles is itself, however, no guarantee of success.[62] As the International Council on Human Rights Policy states, 'some institutions set up more or less in conformity with the Paris Principles have been completely ineffective, while others that had little independence and inadequate funding have made a positive impact on the human rights situation in their country'.[63] But as Cardenas maintains, '(a)ll evidence indicates that providing early international assistance to an NHRI can be critical for getting it off the ground and launching it in the right direction'.[64]

There is some dispute between commentators over whether the effectiveness of NHRIs depends upon there being mature democratic executive, legislative, and judicial institutions, or whether they can correct some of the deficiencies in the surrounding institutional environment. As Lindsnœs and Lindholt point out, NHRIs are unlikely to be effective and autonomous in societies 'with no traces of pluralistic governance and the rule of law', while another 'important condition ... is the existence of a vibrant civil society'.[65] Cardenas argues that NHRIs work most effectively as part of a functioning democratic framework, where the rule of law is generally accepted, and are ironically therefore likely to be most effective in states where respect for human rights is already well-established.[66] As the nongovernmental Asian Legal Resources Centre states: 'When a juridical system is fundamentally flawed national human rights institutions cannot do their work effectively'.[67] However, Reif claims in contrast that in 'newer democracies', where the legislature is relatively weak and courts are corrupt, politicized, or inefficient, classical or hybrid ombudsmen may

62 Human Rights Watch, *Protectors or Pretenders?*, p. 11.
63 ICHRP, *Performance and Legitimacy*, p. 3.
64 Cardenas, 'Emerging Global Actors', 30.
65 Lindsnœs and Lindholt, 'National Human Rights Institutions', 31.
66 Cardenas, 'Emerging Global Actors', 36–38; Reif, *Ombudsman*, p. 408.
67 Asian Legal Resources Centre, 'Effective Functioning of Human Rights Mechanisms: National Institutions and Regional Arrangements' Item 18(b) of the Provisional Agenda, United Nations Commission on Human Rights, 58th Session, March 2002, quoted in Cardenas, 'Emerging Global Actors', 37. See also C. R. Kumar, 'National Human Rights Institutions: Good Governance Perspectives on Institutionalization of Human Rights', *American University International Law Review* **19** (2003), 259–300 at 278 and 294; Reif, *Ombudsman*, p. 397.

have a 'stronger role to play in administrative oversight and the protection of human rights' than they have in established democracies, and that they can also 'serve as a more reliable complaint-handling mechanism'.[68] NHRIs and ombudsmen, she maintains, may provide a viable forum for the investigation and resolution of human rights complaints in democratizing states, and may also contribute to the democratization process by helping to develop a stronger human rights culture.[69] NHRIs are, however, generally powerless to address serious and systematic official abuses of human rights in politically sensitive contexts, which is arguably where their contribution would be most welcome.

The public legitimacy of NHRIs tends to be higher if their legal basis is provided by statute, or better still by the national constitution, and if they are able to develop links with institutions in civil society, especially NGOs who are often better situated to identify human rights grievances and to funnel complaints. As Cardenas argues, in the absence of concerted attention to several key factors – the particularities of the local context, organizational independence from government, clear rules delimiting the role of NHRIs from that of other actors, and an adequate base of sustainable resources – the introduction of NHRIs can have 'perverse' or counterproductive effects. An NHRI may not only be ineffective, it might even compound social tensions, or be introduced by cynical governments in order to co-opt human rights NGOs, and thereby to control and stifle the national human rights debate.[70]

Public expectations of what an NHRI can achieve are often too high and the general difficulty of enforcing their decisions can damage this further. In post-conflict societies their legitimacy may be eroded further by the lack of a sense of public ownership and a perception that they are the result of negotiations between warring parties, or a solution prescribed by the international community which lacks indigenous roots. Very few NHRIs receive the kind of funding envisaged by the Paris Principles, and they tend to suffer from failures to

[68] Reif, *Ombudsman*, 411.

[69] Reif, 'Building Democratic Institutions', 2; Reif, *Ombudsman*, pp. 398–399.

[70] Human Rights Watch, *Protectors or Pretenders?*, pp. 4 and 26. According to Lindsnœs and Lindholt, 'National Human Rights Institutions', 31, in the 1980s, representatives of state institutions which themselves had previously violated human rights became leading members of the human rights commissions in El Salvador and Guatemala.

evaluate their own performance and to develop coherent plans which can command the support of stakeholders.

Finally, opinion is divided over the contribution to effectiveness played by the successful investigation and the authoritative resolution of individual complaints. Lindsnœs and Lindholt state that: 'The main difference between the mandates of national institutions is whether or not they are mandated to handle individual complaints,' and that, in practice, only 'a few national institutions', such as the Danish and the French, lack this competence.[71] But there are major differences between the complaint-handling powers of those institutions which have them.[72] The minimum powers include investigation, conducting hearings, settling or deciding not to proceed with disputes, and conciliation. Various NHRIs also have the power to request any relevant information from state agencies, to summon witnesses, and to inspect public and private offices and places of detention including mental hospitals. Whether or not they can investigate or conduct inspections on their own initiative, or can only react to a formal complaint, also varies. But even those complaints-handling institutions vested with all these powers generally cannot make legally enforceable recommendations, although the majority of complaint-handling institutions have the power to refer complaints to tribunals or to the courts. Some NHRIs can issue administrative fines while others can recommend compensation. A small number can intervene in judicial proceedings.

Many commentators assume that NHRIs should have strong powers of investigation on the assumption that human rights cannot be adequately defended without them.[73] There is a wide consensus that these should include compulsory production of documents and

[71] Lindsnœs and Lindholt, 'National Human Rights Institutions', 18.

[72] *Ibid.*, 18–20. At least two Commissions, the Indian and Ugandan, have the power to make legally binding decisions.

[73] B. Dickson, 'The Investigative Powers of NHRIs', Conference on the Effectiveness of National Human Rights Institutions, Notre Dame University, London, 1 November 2003; Dickson, 'Human Rights Commissions', 282–283; Australian Human Rights Centre, Faculty of Law, University of New South Wales, Sydney, Australia & Human Rights Institute of the International Bar Association, London, UK, 'National Human Rights Institutions: An Overview of the Asia Pacific Region', *International Journal on Minority and Group Rights* **7** (2000), 207–277 at 268; Reif, *Ombudsman*, p. 403; J. Simor, 'Tackling Human Rights Abuses in Bosnia and Herzegovina: The Convention is up to it, are its institutions', *European Human Rights Law Review* **6** (1997), 644–662 at 662.

a legal obligation to appear at hearings and to answer questions. But some have proposed wider powers such as the granting of immunity from prosecution,[74] search and seizure, and citation for contempt.[75] Human Rights Watch states that 'the ability of a human rights commission to have a significant impact lies in its ability to address human rights protection activities: that is, to investigate human rights violations and to seek recourse or redress for victims'.[76] In a similar vein a study conducted by the Australian Human Rights Centre and the International Bar Association states: 'The power to make binding orders can strengthen the authority of a national human rights institution.'[77]

However, other commentators are more sceptical. For example, having acknowledged that '(a)lmost everyone outside national institutions whom we interviewed in the course of this study implicitly or explicitly used successful investigation and resolution of complaints as the touchstone of an effective and legitimate national institution', the International Council for Human Rights Policy, nevertheless, concludes that the 'principal focus' of the work of NHRIs should be less on the resolution of individual complaints as such, and more on using complaints as an indicator of broader systemic human rights issues.[78] In a similar vein, the Australian Human Rights Centre and International Bar Association states: 'Investigations of individual allegations of violations can be an important means of detecting widespread problems and/or revealing a pattern of bureaucratic conduct which violates the enjoyment of human rights.'[79] Savard also maintains that much of the work of the Canadian Human Rights Commission, and its provincial counterparts – which concern individual complaints of discrimination – have in recent years been managed by placing greater emphasis on the 'systematic' dimension where the 'focus is not on the circumstances of a particular individual' but on 'the discriminatory aspects of the broader social context'. As he adds: 'It is in the area of systematic discrimination, in fact, that human rights commissions may be

[74] AHRC and IBA, 'NHRIs: Asia Pacific', 268.
[75] Reif, *Ombudsman*, p. 403.
[76] Human Rights Watch, *Protectors or Pretenders?*, p. 20. See also pp. 15 and 84.
[77] AHRC and IBA, 'NHRIs: Asia Pacific', 270.
[78] ICHRP, *Performance and Legitimacy*, pp. 110 and 113.
[79] AHRC and IBA, 'NHRIs: Asia Pacific', 262.

most effective.'[80] Similarly, contributing to the (now resolved) debate about whether the UK should have a Human Rights Commission and what form it should take, Spencer and Bynoe argued that it should not – at least not initially – have the highly resource-intensive power to investigate individual complaints, but that it should be able to hold public inquiries. Nor, they maintained, should it have dispute-resolving functions, although it could play a key role in bringing test cases and ensuring access to justice.[81]

Reif argues that although the Paris Principles 'are lacking' because they do not mandate NHRIs to investigate complaints, 'ombudsman effectiveness does not always follow automatically from having stronger enforcement powers'. As she also points out most NHRIs do not have the power to make binding decisions and are limited to making non-binding recommendations, offering advice and submitting reports, plus sometimes being able to refer matters to tribunals for a legally binding decision. Only a minority have stronger powers, such as initiating prosecutions or launching court actions to determine the constitutionality of legislation. However, a 'growing number of ombudsmen', particularly in Europe and Latin America, now have the power to litigate human rights complaints or to seek legal clarification from constitutional courts.[82]

Towards a European model?

Writing in 2004 Reif claims that only eight of the (then) forty-five member states of the Council of Europe did not have a national ombudsman, four of which – Germany, Italy, Serbia and Montenegro, and Switzerland – had them at the sub-national level.[83] Northern and western European states tend to favour the classical type, limited to remedying maladministration in government decision-making,

[80] G. Savard, 'Complaint Handling at the Canadian Human Rights Commission' in V. Ayeni, L. Reif and H. Thomas, *Strengthening Ombudsman and Human Rights Institutions in Commonwealth Small and Island States – The Caribbean Experience* (London: Commonwealth Secretariat, 2000), pp. 132–137 at 135.

[81] S. Spencer and I. Bynoe, 'A Human Rights Commission for the United Kingdom – Some Options', *European Human Rights Law Review* (1997), 152–160 at 158–159; Spencer and Bynoe, *Human Rights Commission*, pp. 93–97 and 145–146. A Commission for Equality and Human Rights was established for the UK by the Equality Act 2006.

[82] Reif, *Ombudsman*, pp. 394, 403, and 404; Reif, 'Building Democratic Institutions', 28.

[83] Reif, *Ombudsman*, p. 127.

with southern Europe opting for the human rights ombudsman, whose jurisdiction usually covers not only a wider range of public authorities, but also encompasses the broader territory of human rights. However, nomenclature can be misleading, and the use of the term 'ombudsman' does not necessarily indicate the true character of a given institution.[84] Some states also have a range of ombudsmen, or complaint-handling institutions, either specializing in a particular branch of the public service, for example, health care, financial services, or policing, or a particular category of need or disadvantage, such as disability, race, or gender-based discrimination. Various kinds of NHRI have also been created in the processes of democratic transition/consolidation in central and eastern Europe. Some countries in the region have established a single institution, more closely based on the model of the human rights commission, while others have adopted commission-ombudsman hybrids. In addition to its more recently established Fundamental Rights Agency, the EU also has its own European Ombudsman, which follows the traditional model, although opinions differ as to its sensitivity to human rights.[85] However, in spite of all this, there are still only a handful of genuine human rights commissions anywhere in Europe.[86] As a result, it has been claimed that 'the European system of national institutions remains underdeveloped',[87] and that most European countries 'do not have a broadly based national institution to monitor and review human rights issues in a strategic and structured way'.[88] For some it may not even be a particularly high priority given other, more pressing, problems.

The impetus for the establishment of NHRIs in Europe appears to have come from indigenous national, or international, human rights movements inspired by the global trend, rather than from initiatives at the European level. Disappointingly, the Council of Europe has given only a

[84] Reif, 'Building Democratic Institutions', 38–39.

[85] Reif, *Ombudsman*, Ch. 11, claims it is sensitive to human rights, while Nowak states that '(i)n practice, human rights do not seem to play any significant role in the Ombudsman's activities', M. Nowak, 'The Agency and National Institutions for the Promotion and Protection of Human Rights' in P. Alston and O. de Schutter (eds.), *Monitoring Fundamental Rights in the EU: The Contribution of the Fundamental Rights Agency* (Oxford: Hart Publishing, 2005), pp. 91–107 at 102.

[86] Spencer and Bynoe, *Human Rights Commission*, p. 45.

[87] E. Decaux, 'Evolution and Perspectives for National Institutions for the Promotion and Protection of Human Rights: Their Contribution to the Prevention of Human Rights Violations,' *International Studies in Human Rights* **67** (2001), 233–243 at 241.

[88] Lindsnœs and Lindholt, 'National Human Rights Institutions', 18.

very equivocal lead. The Council of Europe's Steering Committee for Human Rights, the CDDH, began considering the matter in the early 1980s, abandoning it mid-decade, only to return to it again in the early 1990s.[89] By 1997 the most the Committee could bring itself to recommend was that governments should merely 'consider, taking account of the specific requirements of each member state, the possibility of establishing effective national human rights institutions, in particular human rights commissions which are pluralist in their membership, ombudsmen or comparable institutions'. It also recommended that member states should 'draw, as appropriate, on the experience acquired by existing national human rights commissions and other national human rights institutions', that they should have regard to the Paris Principles, that they should promote cooperation between such institutions and between them and the Council of Europe, and that they should ensure that its recommendation is distributed in civil society and, in particular, among NGOs.[90] The Explanatory Memorandum adds little of substance either to the recommendation or to the Paris Principles. For example, it states that the 'precise competence and function' of each NHRI 'will depend on the specific needs of each member state', and that they 'may' operate either in the general field of human rights, or in more specific fields. It adds that their functions 'could' include providing advice about human rights issues, promoting the provision of human rights information, education, and research, and 'dealing on a non-judicial basis with individual human rights complaints' and, 'where appropriate' making 'recommendations to the competent authorities'.[91] There are also the usual injunctions about establishment by law, independence, impartiality, competence, pluralist membership, the provision of adequate resources, and cooperation with other relevant agencies.

[89] *Explanatory memorandum to Recommendation No. R (97) 14 of the Committee of Ministers to Member States on the Establishment of Independent National Institutions for the Promotion and Protection of Human Rights*, 30 September 1997, paras. 1–4.

[90] *Recommendation No. R (97) 14 of the Committee of Ministers of the Council of Europe to Member States on the Establishment of Independent National Human Rights Institutions* adopted on 30 September 1997 at the 602nd meeting of Ministers' Deputies, para. a. Another resolution passed on the same day deals with cooperation between national institutions, *Resolution (97) 11 on Cooperation Between Member States' National Institutions for the Promotion and Protection of Human Rights, and Between Them and the Council of Europe.* The African Commission on Human and Peoples' Rights increasingly encourages states to create NHRIs, Human Rights Watch, *Protectors or Pretenders?*, p. 6.

[91] 'Explanatory memorandum to Recommendation No. R (97) 14', paras. 8–13.

Apart from the recently established Northern Ireland Human Rights Commission, whose activities have been both controversial and closely studied,[92] there is very little literature on the effectiveness of European NHRIs, and none of a comparative kind to match that conducted on the global plane to which reference has already been made. However, one of the most striking features in relation to national Convention compliance concerns another twist in the 'French paradox' discussed in Chapter 2. In spite of the fact that in 1947 France was the first country in the world to establish an NHRI, it nevertheless had the second worst official Convention violation rate in the period 1960–2000 and the third worst from 1999–2005. Three key characteristics of the French institution appear to have hampered its efficacy. First, it had no competence over domestic human rights issues until 1986 and, in spite of this, a great deal of its attention continues to be focused abroad as well as at home. Second, since it has no mandate to handle individual complaints, its connection with grass roots concerns about human rights is indirect and mediated by other agencies, for example state institutions, NGOs, and the media. Having organized the meeting in 1993 out of which the Paris Principles emerged, the French Consultative Commission on Human Rights was thereafter formally re-established in an attempt to bring it into line with the new international consensus. However, third, in spite of this its independence remains significantly compromised by its close association with the Prime Minister's office. Its legal basis rests on Prime Ministerial decree, its seventy members are not only appointed by the Prime Minister but an unspecified number officially represent the Prime Minister and other government ministers (albeit without voting rights), and it is funded by and directly attached to the Prime Minister's office.[93] Although the French Commission's website states that the scrutiny of the European Court of Human Rights is 'essential to the evaluation of laws and policies and in making them progress',[94] France's official violation rate indicates a lack of effective institutional commitment to realizing this objective. However, Lindsnœs and Lindholt claim that according to the comparative material independence is more seriously compromised by the lack of detachment

[92] See, e.g. Livingstone and Murray, 'Effectiveness of NHRIs'.

[93] Information obtained from the official website of the French Consultative Commission on Human Rights, http://www.commission-droits-homme.fr/

[94] *Ibid.*, 'The three assets of the National Consultative Commission of Human Rights'.

from politics than by the channelling of funds through a government ministry.[95] While there is clearly scope for more research on the French paradox one lesson is clear: if European NHRIs are to contribute effectively to improving national Convention compliance, the French model is not one to follow.

But apart from the key element of independence and the competence to receive individual complaints what other features should European NHRIs have if they are to assist states to honour their Convention obligations? There can be little controversy about the promotional, monitoring, advising, and educational functions of NHRIs in contemporary Europe, particularly regarding the domestic implementation of the European Convention on Human Rights, a function which classical and human rights ombudsmen in Europe already seek to discharge.[96] But two critical questions concern how extensive their powers of investigation should be, and whether or not they should be able to resolve disputes with binding effect upon the parties. While many of the Paris Principles are mandatory, some are merely permissive. For example, paragraph A.1. states that a 'national institution shall be given as broad a mandate as possible', while paragraph C.2. requires that 'within the framework of its operation, the national institution shall hear any person and obtain any information and any documents necessary for assessing situations falling within its competence'. However, in order for any given NHRI to avoid violating human rights itself, this principle must be subject to an implied requirement of respect for due process and the rule of law. On the other hand, the preamble to paragraph D states that a 'national commission may be authorized to hear and consider complaints and petitions concerning individual situations', while under paragraph D.1., its powers 'may' include 'seeking an amicable settlement through conciliation or, within the limits prescribed by law, through binding decisions . . .'.[97]

Most commentators take the view that the Paris Principles constitute minimum standards and that much more can, and should, be expected of most NHRIs in most circumstances. However, some are aware of the potential conflict of interest which can arise from an NHRI

[95] Lindsnœs and Lindholt, 'National Human Rights Institutions', 32.
[96] Reif, *Ombudsman*, pp. 168–169.
[97] UN, 'Paris Principles', Fact sheet 19, http://www.unhchr.ch/

being both prosecutor and judge.[98] Reif, for example, states that '(t)he ombudsman must also ensure that the procedures used by her own office are procedurally fair – for complainants and for the administrative authorities under scrutiny',[99] while Dickson argues that 'to avoid committing a human rights violation itself, the NHRI would need to have justifiable criteria' for initiating investigations, particularly intrusive ones, and that the power to compel answers to questions should be subject both to the right not to incriminate oneself and the right not to have answers used in later legal proceedings.[100] However, few of those who advocate strong investigative powers acknowledge that the stronger these are, the more they need to be offset by countervailing due process guarantees, and the more formal, rule-governed, lawyer-dominated, and contentious the investigation is likely to become. The powers used in investigations conducted in the UK by bodies with narrower remits than full-blooded Human Rights Commissions – such as the UK's Commission for Racial Equality, the Police Ombudsman for Northern Ireland, the Saville Inquiry into the Bloody Sunday shootings in Northern Ireland, and the Stephen Lawrence inquiry – provide ample illustration.[101] Dickson also remarks on two parallel trends: the erosion of the 'traditional view' that fair trial rights under Article 6 of the European Convention on Human Rights only apply to formal 'trials' or 'hearings', and the expansion of the scope of the privacy-related rights in Article 8 into newer territories.[102] However, even the mere existence of an NHRI's power to compel the production of information may produce the desired result without it having to be exercised. Some NHRIs which have such a power choose not to exercise it, and those which lack it can usually secure cooperation because those from whom they seek information believe they are legally obliged to provide it even though this is not the case.[103]

There are even greater problems with the aspiration that NHRIs should be able to resolve disputes by binding decision. Many assume this to be desirable on the basis of two, apparently parallel,

[98] Spencer and Bynoe, *Human Rights Commission*, pp. 95–96.
[99] Reif, *Ombudsman*, p. 403, quoting M. Zacks, 'Administrative Fairness in the Investigative Process' in L. Reif, M. Marshall and C. Ferris (eds.), *The Ombudsman: Diversity and Development* (Edmonton: International Ombudsman Institute, 1992) pp. 229, 234–235.
[100] Dickson, 'Investigative Powers', para. 1.
[101] *Ibid.*, para. 4. [102] *Ibid.*, para. 5. [103] *Ibid.*, para. 2.

developments: first, the global trend towards the diversion of disputes from the formal legal system, with its associated costs and procedural and normative complexities, into prompt, inexpensive, non-technical, and informal conciliation or mediation processes (Alternative Dispute Resolution); and, second, that dispute resolution functions have long been exercised by ombudsmen.[104] But, the issue is more complicated than this. First, ADR tends to be limited to civil disputes between consenting private parties – such as matrimonial or commercial disagreements involving relatively small sums of money – which have few, if any, implications for anyone other than those involved. While some human rights disputes may have this character, they are much more likely to involve the relationship between the individual and the state, and will therefore have much wider implications than those which are limited to a particular complainant.

Second, while there may be little objection to adding a human rights dimension to whatever the specific jurisdiction of any given ombudsman might be – as, in 1985, the Committee of Ministers recommended states to consider[105] – extending the ombudsman's jurisdiction to embrace the full panoply of human rights in respect of any, and every, public authority raises several due process concerns. Without adequate fair trial safeguards, an ombudsman/NHRI with a wide remit and a binding dispute-resolving function, supported by strong investigative powers, would be in danger of becoming a 'human rights inquisition', itself ironically a threat to the rule of law and human rights. However, if in its quasi-judicial capacity an NHRI is provided with adequate due process safeguards it will become increasingly difficult to distinguish from a human rights tribunal in the

104 Lindsnœs and Lindholt, 'National Human Rights Institutions', 19 and 32; AHRC & IBA, 'NHRIs: Asia Pacific', 267, para. v; Council of Europe Directorate of Human Rights, *Non-Judicial Means for the Protection of Human Rights at the National Level* (unpublished) (Strasbourg: Council of Europe, 1998), p. 5; V. O. Ayeni, 'The Ombudsman Around the World: Essential Elements, Evolution and Contemporary Issues' in Ayeni, Reif and Thomas, *Strengthening Ombudsman*, pp. 1–19 at 7; S. Beckett and I. Clyde, 'A Human Rights Commission for the United Kingdom: the Australian Experience', *European Human Rights Law Review* (2000), 131–146 at 144–5; Lord Woolf, *Review of the Working Methods of the European Court of Human Rights* (Strasbourg: Council of Europe, 2005), pp. 31–34.

105 *Recommendation No. R (85) 13 of the Committee of Ministers to member states on the institution of the ombudsman*, adopted at the 388th meeting of the Ministers' Deputies on 23 September 1985, paras. b and c.

regular hierarchical court system. In New Zealand, for example, those disputes not closed for lack of substance by the Human Rights Commission, are resolved by compulsory and binding conciliation, subject to review by a judicial tribunal.[106] But, unlike most tribunals or courts, which only have judicial powers, the judicial function of such an NHRI may be compromised by its promotional, advocacy, education, advising, and monitoring functions. However, a key question is: why devolve the binding resolution of human rights disputes to NHRIs with a wide range of administrative plus quasi-judicial responsibilities – when the latter will, in any case, be subject to review by the courts – rather than restrict their dispute-resolving functions to non-binding 'friendly settlement' coupled with powers to lodge prima facie well-founded complaints with a court, particularly when such complaints can be lodged as class actions?[107]

There are two further problems with granting NHRIs binding dispute-resolving powers. First, as already indicated, NHRIs tend paradoxically to be most effective where human rights, democracy, and the rule of law are already well-respected by executive, legislative, and judicial institutions. Their principal role in such places is, therefore, to bring human rights violations to the attention of legislatures and courts which are more constitutionally capable of correcting the systemic problems they represent. The comparative evidence suggests that to expect NHRIs themselves to remedy deficiencies in institutional commitment to democracy or the rule of law is to expect too much. Second, empowering NHRIs thoroughly to investigate and to resolve individual human rights complaints risks raising public expectations beyond what they can reasonably deliver and the comparative evidence suggests this is likely to damage their other functions. The New Zealand Human Rights Commission, for example, receives between 12–15,000 inquiries per annum, but only 250–300 (2 per cent) of these are within its jurisdiction, which among other things excludes complaints for which there is another available form of redress.[108] About 4 per cent of the annual number of inquiries to the Canadian Human Rights Commission (2,000 out of 50,000),

[106] AHRC and IBA, 'NHRIs: Asia Pacific', 223–224.

[107] Although committed to the dispute resolution model, AHRC and IBA, 'NHRIs: Asia Pacific', 275, nevertheless recognizes that 'a national institution can only ever complement the judiciary and final jurisdiction will lie with the courts'. See also ICHRP, *Performance and Legitimacy*, p. 113.

[108] AHRC and IBA, 'NHRIs: Asia Pacific', 224–225.

come under the Commission's jurisdiction and only 2 per cent of complaints are referred to a human rights tribunal,[109] while some 80 per cent of complaints made to the South African Human Rights Commission are also either rejected or referred to other bodies.[110] The effect of such low admissibility rates on public opinion does not appear to have been measured in any of these jurisdictions. But, if these facts were widely known, it would be surprising if the respective human rights commissions received enthusiastic public endorsement. The low admissibility rate also raises, for these institutions, substantially the same individual-constitutional justice dilemma as the parallel phenomenon, at the core of this study, does for the European Court of Human Rights.

At the very least there are, therefore, reasons to be cautious about seeking, as a matter of pan-European policy, to equip NHRIs with strong investigative and dispute-resolving powers. However, whatever other differences may be justified between European NHRIs, they should all have sufficiently similar characteristics in order to have the same relationship with, and to discharge the same functions vis-à-vis the Strasbourg institutions. The most obvious connection lies with the European Commissioner for Human Rights, an office established by the Council of Europe in 2000 with responsibilities for: promoting education in, and awareness of, human rights in member states; identifying possible shortcomings in the law and practice of member states with regard to human rights compliance; promoting the effective observance and full enjoyment of human rights as embodied in the various Council of Europe documents; and providing advice and information on the prevention of human rights violations including encouraging the establishment of national 'human rights structures'.[111] While the Commissioner is capable of receiving individual complaints, as a non-judicial officer, he or she cannot present them before any national or international court or administrative

[109] Savard, 'Complaint Handling', 134–135.

[110] R. Murray, 'Lessons from the South African Human Rights Commission: An Examination of a National Human Rights Institution' (unpublished and undated), p. 9.

[111] *Resolution (99) 50 of the Committee of Ministers on the Council of Europe Commissioner for Human Rights*, Art. 3.c. For a discussion of the background to the creation of this office see J. Schokkenbroek, 'The Preventive Role of the Commissioner for Human Rights of the Council of Europe', *International Studies in Human Rights* **67** (2001), 201–213; Reif, *Ombudsman*, pp. 356–357.

tribunal. Conclusions can however be drawn, and initiatives of a general nature taken on this basis. The Commissioner is also charged with encouraging action by, and working actively with, all national human rights bodies, national ombudsmen, and similar institutions, and cooperating with other international institutions in the promotion and protection of human rights. In performing these duties member states may be visited and governments, which are required to facilitate the effective and independent performance of these responsibilities, may be contacted directly. Given the intergovernmental character of the Council of Europe, the Commissioner does not have any investigative, much less binding dispute-resolution, powers.

Two critical aspects of the potential partnership between the European Commissioner for Human Rights and NHRIs can be distinguished. First, the 'top-down' aspect would involve the 'domestication' of the European human rights debate by the NHRI in each member state. Principally this would mean effectively transmitting information from Strasbourg to the national public via the national media and national public institutions, particularly concerning judgments of the European Court of Human Rights, especially in respect of the state concerned. Second, the 'bottom-up' aspect would involve NHRIs, authoritatively and dispassionately, providing information to the European Commissioner for Human Rights concerning national debates about alleged Convention non-compliance. This could occur through several channels, including for example annual reports, which could provide the basis for the Commissioner's own annual reports, which in their turn would be available to all other NHRIs and to other Strasbourg institutions.

The relationship between NHRIs and the European Court of Human Rights is, however, likely to be more contentious. First, if the test for the admissibility of individual complaints to the European Court of Human Rights were to become more discretionary – as Chapter 3 argues it should – the annual reports of NHRIs to the European Commissioner for Human Rights could be used by the Court as a guide to selecting cases for judgment. It is difficult to deny that the more authoritative information about national law and practice the Court has at its disposal, the better.[112] Second, without prejudice to the right of individual petition, NHRIs could be empowered to lodge complaints

[112] See, e.g., I. Cameron, *National Security and the European Convention on Human Rights* (The Hague/London/Boston: Kluwer Law International, 2000), p. 446.

with the European Court of Human Rights, fulfilling one of the two key determinants of successful compliance with EU law which, according to Zürn and Neyer are 'effective monitoring and the institutionalization of enforcement, such that the risks and costs for the complaining party are minimized'.[113] While the case overload implications of granting NHRIs the power to bring complaints would clearly have to be considered carefully, these might not be wholly negative since NHRIs could amalgamate individual complaints about the same grievance and bring them to the Court as class actions, thereby saving the Court's resources. It might also be worth considering making the submission of a complaint to an NHRI part of the process of exhausting domestic remedies. Protocol 14 enables the Commissioner to submit written comments in all cases before a Chamber or the Grand Chamber and to take part in hearings,[114] and as the Explanatory Report states: 'The Commissioner's experience may help enlighten the Court on certain questions, particularly in cases which highlight structural or systemic weaknesses in the respondent or other High Contracting Parties.'[115] Some have argued that the Commissioner should also be empowered to bring serious cases of a general nature directly to the Court at his/her own instigation,[116] a function which would merely mirror the power of an increasing number of ombudsmen/NHRIs to bring cases to their own national constitutional courts.[117] NHRIs could also assist in the enforcement of the Court's judgments by, for example, monitoring implementation and by seeking to identify to the Committee of Ministers the domestic legal and administrative changes necessary to increase the prospects of compliance.

[113] M. Zürn and J. Neyer, 'Conclusions – the Conditions of Compliance' in M. Zürn and C. Joerges (eds.), *Law and Governance in Postnational Europe: Compliance beyond the Nation-State* (Cambridge: Cambridge University Press, 2005), pp. 183–217 at 191.

[114] New Art. 36(3) (Art. 13, Protocol 14).

[115] *Protocol No. 14 to the Convention for the Protection of Human Rights and Fundamental Freedoms, Amending the Control System of the Convention, CETS No. 194, Explanatory Report as Adopted by the Committee of Ministers at its 114th Session on 12 May 2004*, para. 87.

[116] For example, (*Updated*) *Joint Response to Proposals to Ensure the Future Effectiveness of the European Court of Human Rights*, signed by 114 NGOs, April 2004, para. 32; Recommendation 1640(2004) of the Parliamentary Assembly of the Council of Europe adopted on 26 January 2004, para. 7(a). But this prospect divided respondents in the Strasbourg interviews (see Chapter 3).

[117] Reif, *Ombudsman*, p. 403; Reif, 'Building Democratic Institutions', 11, 40 and 43.

Finally, the prospects for the trans-national monitoring of human rights standards in Europe has also become more complex as a result of the creation in 2004 of a Fundamental Rights Agency by the EU.[118] According to de Búrca, 'even if – as the debate so far seems to indicate – a broadly informational model is chosen over one of the more powerful varieties with either decision-making, executive, monitoring, or dispute-resolution functions, this certainly would not of itself consign the agency to a marginal role' because 'a well-designed body with a clear data-gathering, information-providing, mainstreaming, advisory, and network-coordinating role can, if sufficiently well resourced and politically supported, play a powerful role in governing by information, advice, persuasion, and learning'.[119] In a similar vein, Nowak maintains that the FRA should 'not be a policy-making or policy-implementing body with enforcement powers, but rather a *think tank*' providing reliable, comparative, and properly analysed, data on human rights in the EU, in member states, and more widely. While accepting that the FRA should have promotional, educational, and awareness-raising functions – and that it should also be able to act in an advisory capacity either at the instigation of the EU or on its own initiative – he adds that the question of whether or not it should be able to mediate individual complaints in a judicial or quasi-judicial capacity requires further consideration.[120] However, Peers argues that an 'EU Human Rights Agency would have little or no impact if its tasks are essentially confined to the collection and presentation of statistical data', but neither should it be provided 'with anything like the full range of powers or scope of activities of "classic" national human rights institutions'. While it should monitor human rights compliance and contribute towards education, research, and publicity related to the EU's human rights functions, any other functions should 'be carefully adapted to its unique legal and political environment'.[121]

[118] Although the FRA has only just come into existence, there is already a rich literature debating its functions and potential, see, for example, Alston and de Schutter (eds.), *Monitoring Fundamental Rights.*

[119] G. de Búrca, 'New Modes of Governance and the Protection of Human Rights' in Alston and de Schutter (eds.), *Monitoring Fundamental Rights*, pp. 25–36 at 36.

[120] M. Nowak, 'Agency and National Institutions', 106–107 (italics in original).

[121] S. Peers, 'The Contribution of the EU Fundamental Rights Agency to Civil and Political Rights' in Alston and de Schutter (eds.), *Monitoring Fundamental Rights*, pp. 111–130 at 129–130.

CONCLUSION

If compliance with the Convention is to be improved by member states, and the EU if and when it joins, fresh initiatives, both within and outside the formal adjudication of individual complaints, and the process by which the Court's judgments are supervised by the Committee of Ministers need to be considered. Given its intergovernmental rather than supranational character, the key objective of the Council of Europe should be to find coherent and mutually supportive ways of contributing, if only indirectly, to raising the domestic political and legal costs of violations, particularly those of a systemic character. In its turn, this will involve strengthening the connection between Strasbourg and national constitutional and legal systems in a variety of ways, a critical component of which will include improving the quality and flow of information between Strasbourg and members about pan-European human rights standards and compliance problems.

Enhancing the Convention's profile in the education and training of judges and lawyers is essential, more so in some countries than in others. But the Court and the Council of Europe also needs to affirm that all the Court's judgments have an effect erga omnes, including in national legal systems. The Court's cautious policy, discussed in Chapter 3, of identifying what needs to be done at the national level for a given violation to be remedied, also needs to be developed further. But in order for this to happen, much more reliable information about national legal processes and national debates about Convention compliance issues will be necessary. Since the most pervasive difficulty concerns the right to a fair trial – and in particular delays in the administration of justice – there is a strong case for the establishment of a European Fair Trials Commission, on the Venice Commission model, to provide state-specific independent expert advice, referenced to best practice in Europe and elsewhere.

NHRIs could also play key roles, both in providing Strasbourg with country-specific information and in increasing the domestic political costs of persistent, structural violations. Several lessons can be learned from the global experience. First, NHRIs can have a genuinely beneficial impact upon national compliance with international human rights standards. Second, international organizations such as the UN or the Council of Europe can be instrumental in producing these results. But, third, an NHRI's effectiveness will depend upon the sensitive customization of the international model to specific national requirements, and an alertness to the risk that governments can co-opt and neutralize them, a fate which sadly has befallen some in other places.

Bearing this in mind, there is a strong case that the Council of Europe should develop its current policy of encouraging member states to establish NHRIs, to requiring them to do so, while permitting scope for national variation subject to the fulfilment of minimum specifications. For many states this would initially involve merely a reorganization of existing ombudsmen institutions. But the Paris Principles should only be used as a loose guide and should not be regarded as an unproblematic set of minimum standards. European NHRIs should have two principal roles. First, they would be pivotal in 'domesticating' the European debate about how effectively national institutions and processes protect Convention standards, thereby providing a form of nationally institutionalized pressure, particularly on executive institutions, to take more effective action to honour Convention obligations. Second, they would 'Europeanize' national human rights debates by providing the European Commissioner for Human Rights, the European Court of Human Rights, and the Committee of Ministers with reliable, comprehensive, and regular accounts of key domestic Convention-related issues and controversies. Their minimum specifications would include having a statutory (or better still a constitutional) foundation, effective legal guarantees of their independence, adequate state funding, and the duty to monitor national Convention compliance.

Although following the implications of the Paris Principles many human rights activists assume that NHRIs should have the most extensive range of powers imaginable – including those of investigation and the quasi-judicial resolution of disputes – there are several reasons why this should not be considered appropriate in the European context. First, given the increasingly homogenized constitutional environment, a key priority should be the promotion of dispute resolution by effective, independent courts since, as the Council of Europe has itself acknowledged, this is the 'classic' means of protecting human rights.[122] Secondly, particularly when coupled with the quasi-judicial power to resolve disputes and inadequate due process

[122] Council of Europe Directorate of Human Rights, *Non-Judicial Means*, p. 5.

safeguards, strong investigative powers tend to turn an NHRI into a human rights inquisition. Conversely, the provision of appropriate safeguards tends to turn them into courts of law in all but name. Therefore, in spite of what the Paris Principles permit, it would be more appropriate to limit the investigative and dispute-resolution powers of European NHRIs to those necessary to achieve settlement by conciliation. European NHRIs should however be able to refer the more intractable complaints they receive to national courts, particularly where they can be lodged as class actions representing systemic violations of human rights standards, and to initiate constitutional challenges to legislation. The European Commissioner for Human Rights should also be able to bring test cases to the European Court of Human Rights based on the information supplied by annual NHRI reports. Enabling NHRIs to bring cases to the European Court of Human Rights and requiring individual applicants to submit their complaints to their NHRI as part of the process of exhausting domestic remedies also deserve further consideration.

7

Conclusion

ACHIEVEMENTS AND PROBLEMS

In order to discover whether the European Convention on Human Rights has achieved anything more substantial than mere bureaucratic institutionalization in Strasbourg, the question of what it is for must be squarely addressed. The apparently obvious answer, and the one which underpins the approach of most jurists, maintains that, whatever it was intended to achieve over fifty years ago, its current primary purpose is to enable individuals to bring governments of member states before an international court for violations of their basic human rights – the model of 'individual justice'. Most who take this view would also add that the Convention has discharged this function very effectively, or at least that it has done so significantly more effectively than any comparable trans-national process in the world.

There are, however, several problems with this account of the system's rationale and this assessment of its success. The first is that although for some of its founding fathers the delivery of individual justice should have been a priority, this was not one of the Convention's original agreed objectives. As with many public institutions and official texts, the structure and content of the Convention were the result of compromise between competing visions. It emerged from the negotiations of the late 1940s primarily intended to contribute to the prevention of another war between western European states, to provide a statement of common values contrasting sharply with Soviet-style communism, to re-enforce a sense of common identity and purpose should the Cold War turn 'hot', and to establish an early warning device by which a drift towards authoritarianism in any member state could be detected and dealt with by complaints to an independent trans-national judicial tribunal. And even this 'early warning' function was also inextricably linked to the prevention of war because the experience of the slide towards the Second World War suggested that the rise of authoritarian regimes in Europe made the peace and security of the continent more precarious. But, those who designed the Convention agreed that its main modus operandi should be complaints made by states against each other, and not those made by individuals against their own governments. While some wanted the right of individual petition to be mandatory from the start, this did not become the case until 1998, although by then it had been voluntarily accepted by all signatory states.

Over the past half-century the Convention's surrounding environment has changed in several significant respects. First, not only have there been very few inter-state applications, they have also failed effectively to tackle authoritarianism in member states, and to prevent, or stop, gross or systematic Convention violations, largely because they rest on a contradiction – that litigious animosity between states will promote their greater unity, interdependence, and respect for shared values. Second, while the risk of a conflict between liberalism and authoritarianism over the 'ideological identity' of the state has diminished in most of Europe, the risk of conflict over its 'existential' identity has increased, particularly as ethnic and religious animosities stifled by communism can now be more easily re-asserted. Third, the identity which the Convention originally provided, and which was then limited only to western Europe, has now become an 'abstract constitutional identity' for the entire continent, linking EU with non-EU halves, and the European Court of Human Rights has become the European constitutional court. This constitutional identity is 'abstract' both in the sense of leaving considerable scope to national authorities in fashioning a range of equally Convention-compliant national norms, institutions and processes, and in providing the 'constitution' for a 'partial polity', that is to say one with executive and judicial, but no legislative, functions. Fourth, as the Constitutional Court for Europe, the European Court of Human Rights has become a vehicle for promoting national Convention compliance, which, in its turn, promotes greater convergence in the 'deep structure' of national constitutional, legal, and political (though less so economic) systems, around the 'contemporary European institutional model', characterized by the ideals of liberalism, democracy, the rule of law, human rights, welfarism, and the socially regulated market, albeit in different mixes in different states. Transforming the European Court of Human Rights into the Constitutional Court for Europe can now, rightly, be regarded as the Convention's greatest achievement. But the fact that this process is far from complete presents the greatest challenges for the future.

The second, and deeply ironic, problem with the model of individual justice is that the individual applications process is incapable of delivering individual justice. This is so, in the first place, for sheer logistical reasons. Given the current application rate, there is not the remotest prospect that every applicant with a legitimate complaint about a Convention violation will receive a judgment in their favour at Strasbourg. With one judge per member state (46 in total), the Court's capacity is limited to about 1,000 judgments a year. Currently about 98 per cent of the 40,000 or so who apply every year are turned away at the door without judgment on the merits, although about 94 per cent of those lucky enough to have their case adjudicated on the merits receive a judgment in their favour. While the summary process for well-founded complaints and the new admissibility test introduced by Protocol 14 may boost the Court's productivity and buy extra time for further reflection on its future, they are unlikely, of themselves, to solve the problem of case overload. Second, in spite of some recent developments, the Court remains reluctant, on account both of the principle of subsidiarity and a lack of information and expertise, to direct states on how to remedy violations, although it can, at its discretion, order victims to be compensated. It is, therefore, an open question if a mere declaration that the Convention has been violated, without a clear indication of what needs to be done to correct it, constitutes the delivery of 'justice' even to the tiny percentage of applicants who manage to receive judgment in their favour, let alone to the possibly numerous others who may also find themselves in a similar position in the state concerned. Third, even if these problems could be overcome, the vindication of all violations of all Convention rights would not amount to the delivery of 'individual justice', since 'individual justice' embraces a much wider range of rights, reflecting a more comprehensive picture of human well-being than those found in the Convention. However, there is no realistic prospect of the catalogue of Convention rights being extended to encompass any other class of right for the simple reason that the Convention system finds it almost impossible to cope with litigation on the rights it already has. Adjudication on whole new species of rights would further diminish the chances of adjudication on any of the current rights, and would also increase the risk of the judicial process grinding to a terminal standstill.

There can be no doubt that laws and practices in many member states have been changed as a result of successful litigation by individuals before the European Court of Human Rights. However, the third problem with the model of individual justice is that it is not clear that individual applications provide the most effective means of dealing with systemic or structural compliance problems – such as gross violations stemming either from an authoritarian culture in certain public institutions, struggles over the identity of the state, or intractable institutional problems such as those relating to delays in national judicial processes. Nor are individual applications obviously the best means for promoting better Convention compliance or increased national convergence around the contemporary European institutional model. One particular difficulty in assessing the effectiveness of the individual applications process is that, given the current state of knowledge, it is difficult to determine, even with the minimum degree of social scientific reliability, which states are most, and which least, Convention compliant. Plausible hypotheses, capable of being verified or falsified by more detailed national empirical studies yet to be conducted, will unfortunately have to do instead. While not providing a wholly unproblematic surrogate for national compliance, differential rates of official Convention violation invite explanation. There is little surprise in finding that, among western European states (leaving aside some of the micro-states with fewer than a million inhabitants), Denmark, Norway and Ireland, widely recognized as rights-sensitive democracies, have the lowest rates of official violation, and that Italy, with its notorious judicial problems, has the highest. The fact that France has the second highest official violation rate on the 1960–2000 figures, and the third highest between 1999 and 2005, is not, however, so easy to explain. The most plausible reason is a lack of opportunity in national judicial processes for the compatibility of French law and public policy to be effectively tested for compliance with Convention standards. The case of Turkey, third in the 1960–2000 table and second in 1999–2005, also graphically reveals the limits of the Council of Europe, the Convention, and the individual applications process in producing sustained respect for Convention standards where a member state is unwilling or unable to bring itself into line. In spite of having been a member of the Council of Europe since it was established, having permitted individual applications since January 1987, and having been at the receiving end of a string of adverse judgments by the Court, Turkey has had an appalling human rights record until the last few years. Tellingly, things only began to change for the better as a result of recent attempts by the Turkish government to join the EU, a fact not yet reflected in the Court's statistics.

The experience of the former communist states also provides little cause for satisfaction about the efficacy of the Convention system. First, while liberal democratic values played a critical role in the design of post-communist constitutions in the transition process, it is impossible to distinguish the contribution made by the Convention per se, from that made by the wider liberal democratic tradition of which it is merely one particular manifestation. Second, the liberal democratic tradition was itself only one of several influences in the constitutionalization process, and many post-communist constitutions were responsive to others, including the significant imprint of their socialist heritage. Third, the available, though incomplete, data suggest wide variation in the region between, on the one hand, the Baltic and central European states (including Slovenia) – where human rights are increasingly well protected – and, on the other, most of the former Soviet republics where a lot of progress still has to be made. Regrettably, in spite of having joined the Council of Europe and Convention systems, Russia and some Caucasian republics exhibit a unique mix of capitalism, nationalism, and 'authoritarian democracy'. It remains to be seen whether this is a half-way house on the road to greater conformity with the common European institutional model, or a transitional stage on a different road to more permanent divergence. And if it is the latter, it is difficult to predict how the Council of Europe will react. In the Balkans, in between these two categories, Croatia and Macedonia appear to be doing better than Albania, Bosnia-Herzegovina and Serbia-Montenegro. But it is, fourth, impossible to tell how much credit the Council of Europe, the Convention and the Court should receive for any of these developments. The same methodological problems which inhibit proper social scientific evaluation in western Europe apply even more powerfully in the former communist zone, and commentators are divided over the Convention's profile in constitutional adjudication in the process of democratic consolidation. The picture is, at best, uneven. The official violation rate is an even less satisfactory surrogate for assessing Convention compliance in central and eastern Europe than it is in the west, because many former communist states have not been in the system long enough for stable patterns to have emerged. The authors of comparative studies, cited in Chapter 2, conclude that constitutional adjudication in the former communist zone is almost exclusively referenced to national constitutions, with virtually no reference to external sources including the Convention. However, jurists commentating on specific states, also cited in Chapter 2, claim to have detected a more prominent role for the Convention, particularly in the Czech Republic, Hungary, Lithuania and Slovenia. But the problem with these studies is that they are dominated by the doctrinal tradition and make no attempt to calculate the Convention's domestic impact empirically.

Prima facie, better national records of Convention compliance appear, therefore, to be the result either of Convention values having been institutionalized at the national level before, even long before, the Convention itself was promulgated – as in the Scandinavian democracies, the low countries and Ireland – or an attempt to secure the long-term strategic goals associated with the successful assertion of a convincing European political, constitutional identity, as in the case of Germany, Spain, the Czech Republic, Poland, Hungary and the Baltic states. France and Italy are special cases for the reasons already explained, while, until the more exacting demands of acceding to the EU appeared on the horizon, Turkey's attempt to establish a European identity was compromised, not so much by its Islamic culture, but by its uniquely authoritarian, militaristic, secular and unitary process of modernization.

PROSPECTS

The Convention system, therefore, faces several challenges as the first decade of the twenty-first century draws to a close. One set concerns what needs to be done at the national level to improve compliance. Another requires the further improvement of the Convention's existing judicial process, while a third suggests the need for fresh institutional innovations. The key to the first set of challenges is the more thorough domestication of Convention values in national legal systems. Contrary to the received wisdom, this is less a matter of formal incorporation – the Convention has, after all, long been formally incorporated in those states with the highest official violation rates – and more a matter of effectively integrating it in national adjudication. One possible way of achieving this result would be to ensure that all judgments of the European Court on Human Rights are regarded as binding, and not merely persuasive authority (erga omnes), at least by the supreme and/or constitutional courts of all member states.

The core problem relating to the second set of challenges lies in determining how the Court's scarce judicial resources can be targeted most effectively on the most serious violations in Europe and how the tiny cluster of cases it is capable of subjecting to fully reasoned judgments can be settled with maximum authority and impact. Assuming the Council of Europe retains its intergovernmental nature – and there is no prospect of this changing in the foreseeable future – the process by which the execution of judgments is supervised by the Committee of Ministers is incapable of being altered to produce significant improvements in the promotion of levels of Convention compliance. Progress must, therefore, be sought elsewhere. In spite of its weaknesses it would be a mistake to terminate the individual applications process because it would be difficult to find a potentially more effective replacement and because, suitably altered, it may still be capable of facilitating the delivery of constitutional justice. However, individual applications should be selected for adjudication by the Court more because of their constitutional significance for the respondent state and for Europe as a whole, and less because of their implications for individual applicants. One consequence of this would be that cases from low-compliance/high-violation states should feature more prominently in the Court's docket than cases from high-compliance/low-violation states. Clearly finding out which states belong in each category should be another key Council of Europe objective and one which should be pursued with much greater scientific rigour than has been the case so far. The Council of Europe also needs a much clearer picture of which national factors are likely to produce high levels of Convention compliance/low levels of violation, particularly since there is much groundless assertion in the literature, especially about the importance of formal incorporation. The European Commissioner for Human Rights is uniquely well-placed to be able to provide such information, but only if the role of this office is properly mirrored by similar monitoring institutions in member states. Not surprisingly the availability of effective domestic judicial processes for the litigation of Convention rights, coupled with a positive official responsiveness to judicial correction, appear to be amongst the most significant factors in producing low levels of Convention violation.

The grounds for the admissibility of applications to the European Court of Human Rights also need to be both narrowed and broadened. While a separate quasi-judicial filtering agency may be required, this will not obviate the need for a more flexible admissibility test based on the seriousness criterion, bringing the admissibility process more into line with that of the German Federal Constitutional Court and the US Supreme Court, which are rightly regarded as amongst the most successful and mature constitutional courts in the world. But the 'victim test' also needs to be broadened to enable the European Commissioner for Human Rights and National Human Rights Institutions to bring systemic violations to the Court's attention. Extending the Court's advisory jurisdiction would deliver few benefits since they can only be expressed in vague and general terms, the application of which in any concrete dispute about Convention violation is likely to invite controversy. Although the preliminary reference procedure has enhanced the constitutional function of the European Court of Justice in the EU context, the structural differences between the two legal systems – not least the fact that the ECJ does not directly receive individual applications and the EU has legislative institutions by which it can effect systemic legal change – make its replication in the Convention's judicial process not only problematic but unattractive. It would, in the first place, be likely further to increase the Court's workload. Second, its implications for the right of individual petition are not clear, and there is, finally, no guarantee that it would be used by the courts of those states which need it most.

Another facet of the second set of challenges concerns how the method of adjudication could become much more constitutionally rigorous. The failure of the Court to develop a coherent constitutional model for interpreting the Convention has given its judgments a formulaic character, amounting in most areas to little more than 'decisions on the facts', and lacking the depth and authority they might otherwise possess. These problems are bedevilled by the 'margin of appreciation' doctrine, and by unstructured attempts to 'balance' conflicting rights either against each other or against competing public interests. Unless a more rigorous theory of interpretation is adopted, four other derivative constitutional problems are unlikely to be satisfactorily resolved: the appropriate division of labour in the protection of Convention rights between national courts, national public authorities, and the European Court of Human Rights; the relationship between Convention rights; the relationship between Convention rights and public interests; and the extent to which different accommodations between the same Convention standards can be permitted between member states. Although commentators increasingly recognize the importance of about a dozen 'principles of interpretation' these are said both to fall into no particular order and to operate in a single complex interpretive exercise. This is unsatisfactory for two main reasons. First, without a more structured approach to interpretation, the Convention's core constitutional questions will themselves remain beyond systematic resolution. Second, a more structured interpretation of the Convention is, in any case, already suggested by its own constitutional principles. This requires, in the first place, drawing a more formal distinction between primary constitutional principles – the 'rights' principle, the 'democracy' principle, and the principle of 'priority to rights' – and supportive secondary principles deriving from the Convention's overriding purpose, the judicial protection of designated human rights in the context of democracy and the rule of law.

If the Court followed this model two things in particular would become clearer. Where the nature and scope of Convention rights have to be defined in the absence of any public interest the matter should be settled authoritatively at Strasbourg, with universal application in member states. Describing this process as 'defining' vague rights more precisely, 'determining the scope' of rights, or 'balancing' one right against the other, matters less than the recognition that there is no genuine margin of appreciation on the part of domestic non-judicial bodies concerning how these rights should be understood, although there is on the question of whether or not the disputed conduct is compatible with them thus defined. Where, on the other hand, an interface between Convention rights and collective goods has to be addressed, the Court's main responsibility is not to balance these two elements against each other but to ensure that the 'priority' principle has been properly observed. Different resolutions of the tension between these factors may, therefore, be tolerable in different states. But, unlike the 'balance' metaphor, which is pervasive in the jurisprudence, the priority principle insists that, in weighing rights and public interests, the scales should be loaded, but not decisively, in favour of rights, with the 'extra weight' – or, to put it another way, the strength of the 'priority-to-rights' principle – depending upon the construction of the particular Convention provision at issue.

The strongest versions of the priority principle are found in relation to Articles 3, 4(1), and 7(1) and in the 'strict' and 'absolute' necessity tests in Articles 2(2) and 15. Although the rights under Article 3 not to be tortured, inhumanly or degradingly treated or punished are not absolute, the 'priority' principle indicates that they have a 'specially protected' status not conferred on any other Convention right.

This implies that certain minimum universal standards be identified and maintained and that any departures from these must be governed only by what is strictly necessary to prevent danger to the life and limb of others. The jurisprudence on Article 2(2) is now generally compliant with the priority principle elevating this right to a specially protected status but subject to limitation provided the absolute necessity requirement is fulfilled. On the other hand the jurisprudence on Article 15 lacks a clear requirement that the democratic character of a given state must be threatened if derogation is to be justified. Although formally a 'negatively defined' right, the right not to be subjected to forced or compulsory labour under Article 4(2) and (3) is also a specially protected right.

Less strong versions of the 'priority' principle are found in Articles 5 and 6, in respect of Article 2(1), in Articles 8–11, and in Article 1 of Protocol No. 1. The right not to be subject to arbitrary arrest and detention in Article 5 permits certain public interests to be taken into account in the process of defining what an arbitrary deprivation of liberty means, but with a clear presumption that the right prevails unless there are relevant and sufficient reasons in, for example bail applications, that it should not. Similarly, the public interests suggested by the concept of 'fairness' in Article 6 cannot be directly 'balanced' against the independence and impartiality of tribunals, and there is little scope for directly weighing them against the protections in Article 6(2) and (3) either. The rights to legally regulated processes derived from the obligation to protect the right to life by law under Article 2(1) are also limited by (implicit) 'adjectival discretion' similar to those pertaining to Articles 5 and 6. The case law on the relationship between Convention rights and collective goods in Articles 8–11 is unprincipled and confused largely because the Strasbourg institutions have not fully appreciated the need to give priority to rights and have too often sought refuge in the margin of appreciation and balancing as a substitute. The main effect of the 'priority' principle in this context would be to require respondent states to discharge a more formal and exacting burden of proof in seeking to justify interference with these rights on public interest grounds than is currently recognized to be the case. The priority principle also applies, though least strongly, to the right to the peaceful enjoyment of possessions under Article 1 of Protocol No. 1.

Finally, as far as fresh institutional initiatives are concerned, a European Fair Trials Commission should be established along the lines of the Venice Commission, and the Council of Europe should require, not merely recommend, member states to establish National Human Rights Institutions (NHRIs) as a condition of membership. For many this would involve the reorganization of existing ombudsmen or similar institutions rather than the construction of new institutions from scratch. Several lessons about the kind of NHRIs which might be appropriate for Europe can be learned from the global experience. European NHRIs would have two key roles. First, by domesticating the European debate about Convention rights, particularly that conducted by the European Court of Human Rights, they could become important sources of domestic political and legal pressure on governments to improve Convention compliance. Second, they would 'Europeanize' national human rights debates by providing Strasbourg and other institutions with reliable, comprehensive and regular information about key domestic Convention-compliance issues. Although they should be empowered to encourage the resolution of disputes by conciliation and to bring complaints to the attention of national courts and to the European Court of Human Rights, European NHRIs should have neither adjudicative nor investigative powers themselves, as this would compromise their information-providing role and the dispute-resolving function of national judicial institutions. Such powers would also threaten to turn them either into human rights inquisitions or fully fledged courts of law. The former would be wholly at variance with the fair trial provisions of the Convention itself, while the latter would add another unnecessary tier to existing national legal processes.

The accession of the EU to the Convention poses no significant problems and will probably take place by the end of the decade when a few technical difficulties have been solved. However, a more coherent set of pan-European norms, institutions and processes will soon be required to address the deepening incoherence which the further enlargement of the EU, and its increasing interest and activity in human rights, will inevitably cause. But another book-length study would be required to consider these issues properly.

Bibliography

Abdel-Monem, T., The European Court of Human Rights: Chechnya's Last Chance?, *Vermont Law Review* **28** (2004), 237–298.

Ackerman, B., The Rise of World Constitutionalism, *Virginia Law Review* **83** (1997), 771–797.

Addo, M. K., and Grief, N., Does Article 3 of the European Convention on Human Rights Enshrine Absolute Rights?, *European Journal of International Law* **9** (1998), 510–524.

Alen, A., and Melchior, M., in collaboration with Renauld, B., Meersschaut, F., and Courtoy, C., The Relations Between the Constitutional Courts, and the Other National Courts, Including the Interference in this Area of the Action of the European Courts – XIIth Conference of the European Constitutional Courts, Brussels, 14–16 May 2002: General Report, *Human Rights Law Journal* **23** (2002), 304–330.

Alexy, R., Constitutional Rights, Balancing, and Rationality, *Ratio Juris* **16** (2003), 131–140.

On Balancing and Subsumption. A Structural Comparison, *Ratio Juris* **16** (2003), 433–49.

A Theory of Constitutional Rights, trans. Rivers, J. (Oxford: Oxford University Press, 2002).

Alkema, E. A., The European Convention as a constitution and its Court as a constitutional court. In Mahoney, P., Matscher, F., Petzold, H., and Wildhaber, L. (eds.), *Protecting Human Rights: The European Perspective – Studies in Memory of Rolv Ryssdall* (Cologne/Berlin/Bonn/Munich: Carl Heymans, 2000), pp. 41–63.

Alston, P., and de Schutter, O. (eds.), *Monitoring Fundamental Rights in the EU: The Contribution of the Fundamental Rights Agency* (Oxford/Portland: Hart Publishing, 2005).

Alston, P., with Bustelo, M., and Heenan, J. (eds.), *The EU and Human Rights* (Oxford: Oxford University Press, 1999).

Amnesty International's Comments on the Interim Activity Report: Guaranteeing the Long-Term Effectiveness of the European Court of Human Rights, AI Index: IOR 61/005/2004, February 2004.

Anon (ed.), *The European Convention on Human Rights at 50,* Special Issue No. 50 of the Human Rights Information Bulletin (Strasbourg: Council of Europe, November 2000), 7.

'Tribute to Rolv Ryssdall, Ground-Breaking Reformer', *Human Rights Information Bulletin No. 50: The European Convention at 50* (Strasbourg: Council of Europe, 2000).

Arabadjiev, A., Bulgaria. In Blackburn R., and Polakiewicz, J. (eds.), *Fundamental Rights in Europe: The European Convention on Human Rights, and its Member States, 1950–2000* (Oxford: Oxford University Press, 2001), pp. 191–215.

Arai-Takahashi, Y., *The Margin of Appreciation Doctrine, and the Principle of Proportionality in the Jurisprudence of the ECHR* (Antwerp/Oxford/ New York: Intersentia, 2002).

Uneven, But in the Direction of Enhanced Effectiveness – A Critical Analysis of "Anticipatory Ill-treatment" under Article 3 ECHR, *Netherlands Quarterly of Human Rights* **20** (2002), 5–27.

Archer, C., *International Organizations* (London/New York: Routledge, 2nd edn., 1992).

Arikan, H., A Lost Opportunity? A Critique of the EU's Human Rights Policy Towards Turkey, *Mediterranean Politics* **7** (2002), 19–50.

Arnardóttir, O. M., *Equality and Non-Discrimination under the European Convention on Human Rights* (The Hague/London/New York: Martinus Nijhoff, 2003).

Arnull, A. M., Dashwood, A. A., Ross, M. G., and Wyatt, D. A., *Wyatt and Dashwood's European Union Law,* 4th edn. (London, Sweet and Maxwell, 2000).

Arnull, A., From Charter to Constitution and Beyond: Fundamental Rights in the New European Union, *Public Law* (2003), 774–793.

Ashiagbor, D., Economic and Social Rights in the European Charter of Fundamental Rights, *European Human Rights Law Review* (2004), 62–72.

Ashworth, A., *Human Rights, Serious Crime and Criminal Procedure* (London: Hamlyn Lectures, 53rd Series, Sweet and Maxwell, 2002).

Australian Human Rights Centre, Faculty of Law, University of New South Wales, Sydney, Australia and Human Rights Institute of the International Bar Association, London, UK, National Human Rights Institutions: An Overview of the Asia Pacific Region, *International Journal on Minority and Group Rights* **7** (2000), 207–277.

Ayeni, V., Reif, L., and Thomas, H. (eds.), *Strengthening Ombudsman and Human Rights Institutions in Commonwealth Small and Island States – The Caribbean Experience* (London: Commonwealth Secretariat, 2000).

Badar, M. E., Basic Principles Governing Limitations on Individual Rights, and Freedoms in Human Rights Instruments, *International Journal of Human Rights* **7** (2003), 63–92.

Barkhuysen, T., and van Emmerick, M. L., De Toekomst van het EHRM: Meer Middelen voor Effectievere Rechtserscherming, *Nederlands Juristen Comité voor de Mensenrechten-Bulletin* **28** (2003), 299.

Barry, D., Capital Punishment in Russia. In Feldbrugge, F., and Simons, W. B. (eds.), *Human Rights in Russia and Eastern Europe: Essays in Honor of Ger P. van den Berg* (The Hague/London/New York: Martinus Nijhoff, 2002), pp. 3–14.

Barsh, R. L., Measuring Human Rights: Problems of Methodology and Purpose, *Human Rights Quarterly* **15** (1993), 87–121.

Bartole, S., Final Remarks: The Role of the Venice Commission, *Review of Central and East European Law* **26** (2000), 351–363.

Beckett, S., and Clyde, I., A Human Rights Commission for the United Kingdom: the Australian Experience, *European Human Rights Law Review* 131–146 (2000), 144–145.

Beernaert, M. A., Protocol 14 and New Strasbourg Procedures: Towards Greater Efficiency? And At What Price?, *European Human Rights Law Review* (2005), 544–557.

Bell, J., Reflections on continental European Supreme Courts, *Legal Studies* **1 and 2** (2004), 156–168.

Bellamy, R., and Schönlau, J., The Normality of Constitutional Politics: An Analysis of the Drafting of the EU Charter of Fundamental Rights, *Constellations* **11** (2004), 412–433.

Benoît, F., and Klebes, H., *Council of Europe Law: Towards a pan-European Legal Area* (Strasbourg: Council of Europe Publishing, 2005).

Bentham, J., Anarchical Fallacies; Being an Examination of the Declaration of the Rights Issued During the French Revolution. In Schofield, P., Pease-Watkin, C., and Blamires, C. (eds.), *Jeremy Bentham – Rights, Representation, and Reform: Nonsense Upon Stilts and other Writings on the French Revolution* (Oxford: Clarendon Press, 2002).

Berglund, S., Ekman, J., and Aarebrot, F. H. (eds.), *The Handbook of Political Change in Eastern Europe*, 2nd edn. (Cheltenham, UK/Northampton, USA: E. Elgar, 2004).

Betten, L., and Korte, J., Procedure for Preliminary Rulings in the Context of Merger, *Human Rights Law Journal* **8** (1987), 75–80.

Birkinshaw, P., A Constitution for the European Union? – A Letter from Home, *European Public Law* **10** (2004), 57–84.

Blackburn, R., Current Developments, Assessment, and Prospects. In Blackburn, R., and Polakiewicz, J. (eds.), *Fundamental Rights in Europe: The European Convention on Human Rights, and its Member States, 1950–2000* (Oxford: Oxford University Press, 2001), pp. 77–100.

The Institutions and Processes of the Convention. In Blackburn, R., and Polakiewicz, J. (eds.), *Fundamental Rights in Europe: The European*

Convention on Human Rights and its Member States, 1950–2000 (Oxford: Oxford University Press, 2001), pp. 3–29.

Blankenburg, E., Mobilization of the German Federal Constitutional Court. In Ragowski, R., and Gawron, T. (eds.), *Constitutional Courts in Comparison: The US Supreme Court and the German Federal Constitutional Court* (New York and Oxford: Berghahn Books, 2002), pp. 157–172.

Blaško, M., Slovakia. In Blackburn, R., and Polakiewicz, J. (eds.), *Fundamental Rights in Europe: The European Convention on Human Rights and its Member States, 1950–2000* (Oxford: Oxford University Press, 2001), pp. 755–779.

Bloed, A., Leicht, L., Nowak, M., and Rosas, A., Introduction, p. xiv, and General conclusions and recommendations. In Bloed, A., Leicht, L., Nowak, M., and Rosas, A. (eds.), *Monitoring Human Rights in Europe: Comparing International Procedures and Mechanisms* (Dordrecht/Boston/London: Martinus Nijhoff, 1993).

Bobbio, N., *The Age of Rights*, trans. by Cameron, A. (Cambridge: Polity Press, 1996).

Bojkov, V. D., National Identity, Political Interest and Human Rights in Europe: The Charter of Fundamental Rights of the European Union, *Nationalities Papers* **32** (2004), 323–355.

Bokor-Szegö, H., and Weller, M., Hungary. In Blackburn, R., and Polakiewicz, J. (eds.), *Fundamental Rights in Europe: The European Convention on Human Rights and its Member States, 1950–2000* (Oxford: Oxford University Press, 2001), pp. 383–398.

Borghi, M., Switzerland. In Blackburn, R., and Polakiewicz, J. (eds.), *Fundamental Rights in Europe: The European Convention on Human Rights and its Member States, 1950–2000* (Oxford: Oxford University Press, 2001), pp. 855–878.

Bowring, B., Politics versus the Rule of Law in the Work of the Russian Constitutional Court. In Přibáň, J., and Young, J. (eds.), *The Rule of Law in Central Europe: The Reconstruction of Legality, Constitutionalism and Civil Society in the Post-Communist Countries* (Aldershot/Brookfield/Singapore/Sydney, 1999), pp. 257–277.

Politics, the Rule of Law and the Judiciary. In Robinson, N. (ed.), *Institutions and Political Change in Russia* (Basingstoke: Macmillan, 2000), pp. 69–84.

Russia's Accession to the Council of Europe and Human Rights: Compliance or Cross-Purposes, *European Human Rights Law Review* (1997), 628–643.

Russia's Accession to the Council of Europe and Human Rights: Four Years On, *European Human Rights Law Review* **4** (2000), 362–379.

Boyle, H., and Thompson, M., National Politics, and Resort to the European Commission on Human Rights, *Law and Society Review* **35** (2001), 321–344.

Brems, E., Conflicting Human Rights: An Exploration in the Context of the Right to a Fair Trial in the European Convention on Human Rights, *Human Rights Quarterly* **27** (2005), 294–326.

The Margin of Appreciation Doctrine in the Case Law of the European Court of Human Rights, *Zeitschrift für Auslandisches Offentliches Recht und Volkrecht* **56** (1996), 240–314.

Brett, R., Human Rights and the OSCE, *Human Rights Quarterly* **18** (1996), 668–693.

Brown, A., Political Culture and Democratization: The Russian Case in Comparative Perspective. In Pollack, D., Jacobs, J., Müller, O., and Pickel, G. (eds.), *Political Culture in Post-Communist Europe: Attitudes in new democracies* (Aldershot: Ashgate Publishing Ltd, 2003), pp. 17–27.

Brown, L. N., and Bell, J. S., *French Administrative Law*, 5th edn. (Oxford: Clarendon Press, 1998).

Brownlie, I., *Principles of Public International Law* (Oxford: Oxford University Press, 6th edn., 2003).

Bruinsma, F. J., and de Blois, M., Rules of Law from Westport to Wladiwostok. Separate Opinions in the European Court of Human Rights, *Netherlands Quarterly of Human Rights* **15** (1997), 175–186.

Bruinsma, F. J., and Parmentier, S., Interview with Mr Luzius Wildhaber, President of the ECHR, *Netherlands Quarterly of Human Rights* **21** (2003), 185–201.

Burke, E., Reflections on the Revolution in France. In McLoughlin, T.O., and Boulton, J. T. (eds.), *The Writings and Speeches of Edmund Burke* (Oxford: Clarendon Press, 1997).

Burskey, V., Times of Change – Can Turkey Make the Necessary Changes in its Human Rights Policies to be Admitted to the European Union?, *North Carolina Journal of International Law and Commercial Regulation* **29** (2004), 713–745.

Callewaert, J., Is there a Margin of Appreciation in the Application of Articles 2, 3 and 4 of the Convention?, *Human Rights Law Journal* **19** (1998), 6–9.

Cameron, I., Sweden. In Blackburn, R., and Polakiewicz, J. (eds.), *Fundamental Rights in Europe: The European Convention on Human Rights and its Member States, 1950–2000* (Oxford: Oxford University Press, 2001), pp. 833–853.

National Security and the European Convention on Human Rights (The Hague/London/Boston: Kluwer Law International, 2000).

Campbell, T., *The Left and Rights: A Conceptual Analysis of the Idea of Socialist Rights* (London/Boston/Melbourne/Henley: Routledge & Kegan Paul, 1983).

Canor, I., Primus Inter Pares: Who is the Ultimate Guardian of Human Rights in Europe?, *European Law Review* **25** (2000), 3–21.

Cardenas, S., Emerging Global Actors: The United Nations and National Human Rights Institutions, *Global Governance* **9** (2003), 23–42.

Carruthers, S., Beware of Lawyers Bearing Gifts: A Critical Evaluation of the Proposals on Fundamental Rights in the EU Constitutional Treaty, *European Human Rights Law Review* (2004), 424–435.

Cassel, D., Does International Human Rights Law Make a Difference?, *Yale Law Journal* **2** (2001), 121–135.

Churchill, R. R., and Young, J. R., Compliance with Judgments of the European Court of Human Rights and Decisions of the Committee of Ministers: the Experience of the United Kingdom, 1975–1987, *British Yearbook of International Law* **62** (1991), 283–346.

Claude, R. P., and Jabine, T. B., Exploring Human Rights Issues with Statistics. In Jabine, T. B., and Claude, R. P. (eds), *Human Rights and Statistics: Getting the Record Straight* (Philadelphia: University of Pennsylvania Press, 1992), pp. 5–34.

Clements, L., Striking the Right Balance: the New Rules of Procedure for the European Court of Human Rights, *European Human Rights Law Review* (1999), 266–272.

Coomber, A., Judicial Independence: Law and Practice of Appointments to the European Court of Human Rights, *European Human Rights Law Review* (2003), 486–500.

Danchin, P., and Cole, E. (eds.), *Protecting the Human Rights of Religious Minorities in Eastern Europe* (New York: Columbia University Press, 2002).

Danish Centre for Human Rights, *The Work, and Practice of Ombudsman and National Human Rights Institutions (Articles and Studies)* (Copenhagen: Danish Ministry of Foreign Affairs, 2002).

Darrow, M., and Alston, P., Bills of Rights in Comparative Perspective. In Alston, P. (ed.), *Promoting Human Rights Through Bills of Rights* (Oxford: Oxford University Press, 1999), pp. 465–524.

de Búrca, G., New Modes of Governance and the Protection of Human Rights. In Alston, P., and de Schutter, O. (eds.), *Monitoring Fundamental Rights in the EU: The Contribution of the Fundamental Rights Agency* (Oxford: Hart Publishing, 2005), pp. 25–36.

The Drafting of a Constitution for the European Union: Europe's Madisonian Moment or a Moment of Madness?, *Washington and Lee Law Review* **61** (2004), 555–586.

de Marneffe, P., Popular Sovereignty, Original Meaning, and Common Law Constitutionalism, *Law and Philosophy* **23** (2004), 223–260.

de Varennes, F., The Protection of Linguistic Minorities in Europe and Human Rights: Possible Solutions to Ethnic Conflicts?, *Columbia Journal of European Law* **2** (1996), 107–144.

Decaux, E., Evolution and Perspectives for National Institutions for the Promotion and Protection of Human Rights: Their Contribution to the Prevention of Human Rights Violations, *International Studies in Human Rights* **67** (2001), 233–243.

Dembour, M. B., "Finishing Off" Cases: The Radical Solution to the Problem of the Expanding ECtHR Caseload, *European Human Rights Law Review* (2002), 604–623.

Dembour, M. B., and Krzyżanowska-Mierzewska, M., Ten Years On: The Popularity of the Convention in Poland, *European Human Rights Law Review* (2004), 400–423.

Ten Years On: The Voluminous and Interesting Polish Case Law, *European Human Rights Law Review* (2004), 517–543.

Demitrova, A. L., The Council of Europe and the European Union and Their Roles in Democratization in Central and Eastern Europe: The Case of Bulgaria, Paper for the *Conference of JPSA/ECPR Project on Measuring Democratic Consolidation through inter-Regional Comparisons – Europe and East Asia*, 11–13 November 2001.

Dickson, B., The Contribution of Human Rights Commissions to the Protection of Human Rights, *Public Law* (2003), 272–285.

The Investigative Powers of NHRIs, unpublished paper to *Conference on the Effectiveness of National Human Rights Institutions*, Notre Dame University, London, 1 November 2003.

Dimitrijević, V., The Monitoring of Human Rights, and the Prevention of Human Rights Violations through Reporting Procedures. In Bloed, A., Leicht, L., Nowak, M., and Rosas, A. (eds.), *Monitoring Human Rights in Europe: Comparing International Procedures and Mechanisms* (Dordrecht/Boston/London: Martinus Nijhoff, 1993).

Dougan, M., The Convention's Draft Constitutional Treaty: Bringing Europe Closer to its Lawyers?, *European Law Review* **28** (2003), 763–793.

Douglas-Scott, S., The Charter of Fundamental Rights as a Constitutional Document, *European Human Rights Law Review* (2004), 37–50.

Douzinas, C., *The End of Human Rights: Critical Legal Thought at the Turn of the Century* (Oxford: Hart, 2000).

Drezemczewski, A., The Prevention of Human Rights Violations: Monitoring Mechanisms of the Council of Europe, *International Studies in Human Rights* **67** (2001), 139–177.

Ensuring Compatibility of Domestic Law with the European Convention on Human Rights Prior to Ratification: The Hungarian Model, *Human Rights Law Journal* **16** (1995), 241–260.

The Council of Europe's Cooperation and Assistance Programmes with Central and Eastern Europe in the Human Rights Field: 1990 to September 1993, *Human Rights Law Journal* **14** (1993), 229–248.

The European Human Rights Convention: A New Court of Human Rights in Strasbourg as of November 1, 1998, *Washington and Lee Law Review* **55** (1998), 697–736.

The European Human Rights Convention: Protocol No. 11 – Entry into Force and First Year of Application, *Human Rights Law Journal* **21** (2000), 1–17.

The Internal Organization of the European Court of Human Rights: the Composition of Chambers and the Grand Chamber, *European Human Rights Law Review* (2000), 233–245.

European Human Rights Convention in Domestic Law: A Comparative Study (Oxford: Clarendon Press, 1983).

Drzemczewski, A., and Nowicki, M. A., Poland. In Blackburn, R., and Polakiewicz, J. (eds.), *Fundamental Rights in Europe: The European Convention on Human Rights and its Member States, 1950–2000* (Oxford: Oxford University Press, 2001), pp. 657–679.

Drzemczewski, P., The Council of Europe's Position with Respect to the EU Charter of Fundamental Rights, *Human Rights Law Journal* **22** (2001), 14–31.

Dueck, J., HURIDOCS Standard Formats as a Tool in the Documentation of Human Rights Violations. In Jabine, T. B., and Claude, R. P. (eds.), *Human Rights and Statistics: Getting the Record Straight* (Philadelphia: University of Pennsylvania Press, 1992), pp. 127–158.

Dupré, C., France. In Blackburn, R., and Polakiewicz, J. (eds.), *Fundamental Rights in Europe: The European Convention on Human Rights and its Member States, 1950–2000* (Oxford: Oxford University Press, 2001), pp. 313–333.

Dworkin, R., *Freedom's Law: The Moral Reading of the American Constitution* (Cambridge, Mass.: Harvard University Press, 1996).

Taking Rights Seriously (London: Duckworth, 1977).

Dyevre, A., The Constitutionalisation of the European Union: Discourse, Present, Future and Facts, *European Law Review* **30** (2005), 165–189.

Edge, P. W., The European Court of Human Rights and Religious Rights, *International and Comparative Law Quarterly* **47** (1998), 680–687.

Editors' note, The Doctrine of the Margin of Appreciation under the European Convention on Human Rights: Its Legitimacy in Theory and Application in Practice, *Human Rights Law Journal* **19** (1998), 1.

Eissen, M. A., The Principle of Proportionality in the Case-Law of the European Court of Human Rights. In Macdonald, R. St. J., Matscher, F., and Petzold, H. (eds.), *The European System for the Protection of Human Rights* (Dordrecht/Boston/London: Martinus Nijhoff, 1993), pp. 125–146.

Ely, J. H., *Democracy and Distrust: A Theory of Judicial Review* (Cambridge, Mass.: Harvard University Press, 1980).

Emerson, T. I., National Security and Civil Liberties, *Yale Journal of World Public Order* **9** (1982), 78–112.

Emmerson, B., Q.C. and Ashworth, A., Q.C., *Human Rights and Criminal Justice* (London: Sweet & Maxwell, 2001).

Emmert, F., Editorial: The Independence of Judges – A Concept Often Misunderstood in Central and Eastern Europe, *European Journal of Law Reform* **3** (2002), 405–409.

Erdal, U., Burden and standard of proof under the European Convention, *European Law Review Human Rights Survey* **26** (2001) HR/68-HR/85.

Ergun, C. E., The EU Charter of Fundamental Rights: An Alternative to the European Convention on Human Rights?, *Mediterranean Journal of Human Rights* **8** (2004), 91–105.

Escobar Roca, G., Spain. In Blackburn, R., and Polakiewicz, J. (eds.), *Fundamental Rights in Europe: The European Convention on Human Rights and its Member States, 1950–2000* (Oxford: Oxford University Press, 2001), pp. 809–831.

European Convention on Human Rights, *Yearbooks of the European Convention on Human Rights Annuaire de la Convention Européenne des droits de l' homme (The Hague: Martinus Nijhoff, 1955–2004).*

European Court of Human Rights, *Statistics –2004.*
Survey of Activities 1999–2004.

Evans, M. D., Getting to Grips With Torture, *International and Comparative Law Quarterly* **51** (2002), 365–383.

Evans, M. D., and Morgan, R., *Preventing Torture: A Study of the European Convention for the Prevention of Torture and Inhuman or Degrading Treatment or Punishment (Oxford: Clarendon Press, 1998).*

Feingold, C. S., The Doctrine of Margin of Appreciation and the European Convention on Human Rights, *Notre Dame Lawyer* **53** (1977–78), 90–107.

Feldbrugge, F., Human Rights in Russian Legal History. In Feldbrugge, F., and Simons, W. B. (eds.), *Human Rights in Russia and Eastern Europe: Essays in Honor of Ger P. van den Berg* (The Hague/London/New York: Martinus Nijhoff, 2002), pp. 65–90.

Feldman, D., The Human Rights Act 1998 and constitutional principles, *Legal Studies* **19** (1999), 165–206.

Ferschtman, M., Russia. In Blackburn, R., and Polakiewicz, J. (eds.), *Fundamental Rights in Europe: The European Convention on Human Rights and its Member States, 1950–2000* (Oxford: Oxford University Press, 2001), pp. 731–754.

Fijalkowski, A., The Judiciary's Struggle towards the Rule of Law in Poland. In Přibáň, J., and Young, J., *The Rule of Law in Central Europe: The Reconstruction of Legality, Constitutionalism and Civil Society in the Post-Communist Countries* (Aldershot/Brookfield/Singapore/Sydney, 1999), pp. 242–253.

Freeman, M., *Human Rights: An Interdisciplinary Approach* (London: Polity Press, 2002).

Gearty, C., The European Court of Human Rights and the Protection of Civil Liberties: An Overview, *Cambridge Law Journal* **52** (1993), 89–127.

Democracy and Human Rights in the European Court of Human Rights: A Critical Appraisal, *Northern Ireland Legal Quarterly* **51** (2000), 381–396.

Germer, P., Denmark. In Blackburn, R., and Polakiewicz, J. (eds.), *Fundamental Rights in Europe: The European Convention on Human Rights and its Member States, 1950–2000* (Oxford: Oxford University Press, 2001), pp. 259–276.

Gewirth, A., *Human Rights: Essays on Justification and Applications* (Chicago/London: University of Chicago Press, 1982).

Gilbert, G., The Burgeoning Minority Rights Jurisprudence of the European Court of Human Rights, *Human Rights Quarterly* **24** (2002), 736–780.

Gilligan, E., *Defending Human Rights in Russia: Sergei Kovalyov, Dissident and Human Rights Commissioner, 1969–2003* (London/New York: Routledge Curzon, 2004).

Gil-Robles, A., *Opinion 2/2002 of the Commissioner for Human Rights, Mr Alvaro Gil-Robles on Certain Aspects of the Review of Powers of the Northern Ireland Human Rights Commission*, CommDH (2002)16 (Strasbourg: Council of Europe, Office of the Commissioner for Human Rights, 13 November 2002).

Report by Mr Alvaro Gil-Robles, Commissioner for Human Rights on the Effective Respect for Human Rights in France Following his Visit from 5–21 September 2005, CommDH (2006)2 (Strasbourg: Council of Europe, Office of the Commissioner for Human Rights, 15 February 2006).

Report by Mr Alvaro Gil-Robles, Commissioner for Human Rights on His Visit to Turkey, 11–12 June 2003, CommDH (2003)15 (Strasbourg: Council of Europe, Office of the Commissioner for Human Rights, 19 December 2003).

Report by Mr Alvaro Gil-Robles, Commissioner for Human Rights, on His Visits to the Russian Federation, 15 to 30 July 2004, 19 to 29 September 2004, for the attention of the Committee of Ministers and Parliamentary Assembly, CommDH (2005)2 (Strasbourg: Council of Europe, Office of the Commissioner for Human Rights, 20 April 2005).

Glendon, M. A., Knowing the Universal Declaration of Human Rights, *Notre Dame Law Review* **73** (1998), 1153–1190.

Rights Talk: The Impoverishment of Political Discourse (New York: Free Press, 1991).

Goldberg, M., EU Charter – the Baby in the Bathwater?, *Justice Bulletin* **6** (2005).

Goldie, M. (ed.), *John Locke: Two Treatises of Government* (London: Everyman, 1993).

Goldstein, R. J., The Limitations of Using Quantitative Data in Studying Human Rights Abuses. In Jabine, T. B., and Claude, R. P. (eds.), *Human Rights and Statistics: Getting the Record Straight* (Philadelphia: University of Pennsylvania Press, 1992), pp. 35–61.

Golsong, H., Interpreting the European Convention on Human Rights Beyond the Confines of the Vienna Convention on the Law of Treaties? In Macdonald, R. St. J., Matscher, F., and Petzold, H. (eds.), *The European System for the Protection of Human Rights* (Dordrecht/Boston/London: Martinus Nijhoff, 1993), pp. 147–162.

González Volio, L., The Ombudsman Institution: the Latin American Experience, paper to *Conference on the Effectiveness of National Human Rights Institutions*, University of Notre Dame, London, 1 November 2003.

Goodman, R., and Jinks, D., Measuring the Effects of Human Rights Treaties, *European Journal of International Law* **14** (2003), 171–183.

Green, M., What We Talk About When We Talk About Indicators: Current Approaches to Human Rights Measurement, *Human Rights Quarterly* **23** (2001), 1076–1084.

Greer, S., A Guide to the Human Rights Act 1998, *European Law Review* **24** (1999), 3–21.

Constitutionalizing Adjudication under the European Convention on Human Rights, *Oxford Journal of Legal Studies* (2003), 405–433.

Protocol 14 and the Future of the European Court of Human Rights, *Public Law* (2005), 83–106.

Reforming the European Convention on Human Rights: Towards Protocol 14, *Public Law* (2003), 663–673.

The Exceptions to Articles 8 to 11 of the European Convention on Human Rights (Strasbourg: Council of Europe Publishing, Human Rights Files No. 15, 1997).

The Margin of Appreciation: Interpretation and Discretion under the European Convention on Human Rights (Strasbourg: Council of Europe Publishing, Human Rights Files No. 17, 2000).

Grief, N., Non Discrimination under the European Convention on Human Rights: A Critique of the United Kingdom Government's Refusal to Sign and Ratify Protocol 12, *European Law Review* **27** (2002), 3–18.

Gross, A. M., Reinforcing the New Democracies: The European Convention on Human Rights and the Former Communist Countries – A Study of the Case Law, *European Journal of International Law* **7** (1996), 89–102.

Gross, O., and Ní Aoláin, F., From Discretion to Scrutiny: Revisiting the Application of the Margin of Appreciation Doctrine in the Context of

Article 15 of the European Convention on Human Rights, *Human Rights Quarterly* **23** (2001), 623–649.

"Once More unto the Breach": The Systematic Failure of Applying the European Convention on Human Rights to Entrenched Emergencies, *Yale Journal of International Law* **23** (1998), 437–502.

Gündüz, A., Human Rights and Turkey's Future in Europe, *Orbis-Philadelphia* **45** (2001), 15–30.

Habermas, J., *Between Facts and Norms*, trans. Rehg, W. (Cambridge: Cambridge University Press, 1996).

Hakyemez, Y. S., and Akgun, B., Limitations on Freedom of Political Parties in Turkey and the Jurisdiction of the European Court of Human Rights, *Mediterranean Politics* **7** (2002), 54–78.

Harmsen, R., National Responsibility for European Community Acts Under the European Convention on Human Rights: Recasting the Accession Debate, *European Public Law* **7** (2001), 625–649.

The European Convention on Human Rights after Enlargement, *International Journal of Human Rights* **5** (2001), 18–43.

The European Court of Human Rights as a 'Constitutional Court': Definitional Debates and the Dynamics of Reform, unpublished paper provided by author.

Harris, D. J., The Right to Life under the European Convention on Human Rights, *Maastricht Journal of European and Comparative Law* **1** (1994), 122–138.

Harris, D. J., O'Boyle, M., and Warbrick, C., *Law of the European Convention on Human Rights* (London/Dublin/Edinburgh: Butterworths, 1995).

Harrison, R. *Hobbes, Locke, and Confusion's Masterpiece: An Examination of Seventeenth-Century Political Philosophy* (Cambridge/New York: Cambridge University Press, 2003).

Harvey, C. J., Building a Human Rights Culture in a Political Democracy: The Role of the Northern Ireland Human Rights Commission. In Harvey, C. J. (ed.), *Human Rights, Equality and Democratic Renewal in Northern Ireland* (Oxford-Portland: Hart Publishing, 2001), pp. 113–130.

Harvey, C., and Livingstone, S., Protecting the Marginalised: The Role of the European Convention on Human Rights, *Northern Ireland Legal Quarterly* **51**, (2000), 445–465.

Harvey, P., Militant Democracy and the European Convention on Human Rights, *European Law Review* **29** (2004), 407–420.

Hathaway, O. A., Do Human Rights Treaties Make a Difference?, *Yale Law Journal* **111** (2002), 1935–2042.

Hedigan, J., The European Convention on Human Rights and Counter-Terrorism, *Fordham International Law Journal* **28** (2005), 392–431.

Helfer, L. R., and Slaughter, A. M., Towards a Theory of Effective Supranational Adjudication, *Yale Law Journal* **107** (1997), 273–391.

Helfer, L. R., Consensus, Coherence and the European Convention on Human Rights, *Cornell International Law Journal* **26** (1993), 133–165.

Henckaerts, J. M., and Van der Jeught, S., Human Rights Protection Under the New Constitutions of Central Europe, *Loyola of Los Angeles International and Comparative Law Review* **20** (1998), 475–506.

Hendley, K., Rewriting the Rules of the Game in Russia: the Neglected Issue of the Demand for Law. In Brown, A. (ed.), *Contemporary Russian Politics: A Reader* (Oxford: Oxford University Press, 2001), pp. 131–138.

Hendrych, D., Constitutionalism in the Czech Republic. In Přibáň, J., and Young, J., *The Rule of Law in Central Europe: The Reconstruction of Legality, Constitutionalism and Civil Society in the Post-Communist Countries* (Aldershot/Brookfield/Singapore/Sydney, 1999), pp. 13–28.

Heun, W., Access to the German Federal Constitutional Court. In Ragowski, R., and Gawron, T. (eds.), *Constitutional Courts in Comparison: The US Supreme Court and the German Federal Constitutional Court* (New York/ Oxford: Berghahn Books, 2002), pp. 125–156.

Heuschling, L., Comparative Law and the European Convention on Human Rights in French Human Rights Cases, *United Kingdom Comparative Law Series* **22** (2003), 23–61.

Hicks, N., Legislative Reform in Turkey and European Human Rights Mechanisms, *Human Rights Review* **3** (2001), 78–85.

Hoffmeister, F., Cyprus v. Turkey. App.No. 25781/94, *American Journal of International Law* **96** (2002), 445–452.

Hogan, G., The Right to Life and the Abortion Question under the European Convention on Human Rights. In L. Heffernan with J. Kingston (eds.), *Human Rights: A European Perspective* (Blackrock: Round Hall Press, 1994), pp. 104–116.

Honoré, T., *Ulpian: Pioneer of Human Rights* (Oxford: Oxford University Press, 2nd edn., 2002).

Horowitz, S., Human Rights in the Post-Communist World: The Roles of National Identity, Economic Development and Ethnic Conflict, *International Journal of Human Rights* **8** (2004), 325–343.

Hovius, B., The Limitation Clauses of the European Convention on Human Rights: A Guide for the Application of Section 1 of the Charter?, *Ottawa Law Review* **17** (1985), 213–261.

Huber, D., *A Decade Which Made History: The Council of Europe (1989–1999)* translated by Nash, V. (Strasbourg: Council of Europe, 1999).

Human Rights Watch, *Protectors or Pretenders? Government Human Rights Commissions in Africa* (New York/Washington/London/Brussels: Human Rights Watch, 2001).

Hunt, L., *The French Revolution and Human Rights: A Brief Documentary History* (Boston/New York: Bedford Books, 1996).

Hutchinson, M. R., The Margin of Appreciation Doctrine in the European Court of Human Rights, *International and Comparative Law Quarterly* **48** (1999), 638–650.

Hyam, J., *Hatton* v. *United Kingdom* in the Grand Chamber: One Step Forward, Two Steps Back?, *European Human Rights Law Review* (2003), 631–40.

International Council on Human Rights Policy, *Performance & Legitimacy: National Human Rights Institutions* (Versoix, Switzerland: International Council on Human Rights Policy, 2000).

Interview with President Luzius Wildhaber, The Reform is an Absolute Necessity, 21 April 2004, http://www.coe.int/t/e/com/files/interviews/20040421_interv_wildhabber (mis-spelling in original).

Ioannou, K., Greece. In Blackburn, R., and Polakiewicz, J. (eds.), *Fundamental Rights in Europe: The European Convention on Human Rights and its Member States, 1950–2000* (Oxford: Oxford University Press, 2001), pp. 355–381.

Jackson Preece, J., *Minority Rights* (Cambridge: Polity Press, 2005).

Jacobs, F. G., The "Limitation Clauses" of the European Convention on Human Rights. In de Mestral, A., Birks, S., Bothe, M., Cotler, I., Klinck, D., and Morel, A. (eds.), *The Limitation of Human Rights in Comparative Constitutional Law* (Cowansville: Les Éditions Yvon Blais Inc., 1986), pp. 21–40.

Janis, M. W., The Efficacy of Strasbourg Law, *Connecticut Journal of International Law* **15** (2000), 39–46.

Jílek, D., and Hofmann, M., Czech Republic. In Blackburn, R., and Polakiewicz, J. (eds.), *Fundamental Rights in Europe: The European Convention on Human Rights and its Member States, 1950–2000* (Oxford: Oxford University Press, 2001), pp. 241–258.

Jones, T. H., The Devaluation of Human Rights Under the European Convention, *Public Law* (1995), 430–449.

Jordan, P. A., Does Membership Have Its Privileges?: Entrance into the Council of Europe and Compliance with Human Rights Norms, *Human Rights Quarterly* **25** (2003), 660–688.

Russia's Accession to the Council of Europe and Compliance with Human Rights Norms, *Demokratizatsiya-Washington* **11** (2003), 281–296.

Joseph, S., Denouement of the Deaths on the Rock: the Right to Life of Terrorists, *Netherlands Quarterly of Human Rights* **14** (1996), 5–22.

Jowell, J., Q.C., The Venice Commission: disseminating democracy through law, *Public Law* (2001), 675–683.

Justice, *Annual Report* 2005.

Kahn, J., Russian Compliance with Articles Five and Six of the European Convention on Human Rights as a Barometer of Legal Reform and Human

Rights in Russia, *University of Michigan Journal of Law Reform* **35** (2002), 642–693.

Kamenka, E., The Anatomy of an Idea. In Kamenka, E., and Soon Tay, A. (eds.), *Human Rights* (London: Edward Arnold, 1978), 1–13.

Kamminga, M. T., Is the European Convention on Human Rights Sufficiently Equipped to Cope with Gross and Systematic Violations?, *Netherlands Quarterly of Human Rights* **12** (1994), 153–164.

Kańska, A. K., Towards Administrative Human Rights in the EU. Impact of the Charter of Fundamental Rights, *European Law Journal* **10** (2004), 296–326.

Keith, L. C., The United Nations International Covenant on Civil and Political Rights: Does it Make a Difference in Human Rights Behavior?, *Journal of Peace Research* **36** (1999), 95–118.

Kingdom, E., *What's Wrong with Rights? Problems for Feminist Politics of Law* (Edinburgh: Edinburgh University Press, 1991).

Kingsbury, B., The Concept of Compliance as a Function of Competing Conceptions of International Law, *Michigan Journal of International Law*, **19** (1998), 345–372.

Kleijkamp, G., Comparing the Application and Interpretation of the United States Constitution and the European Convention on Human Rights, *Transnational Law and Contemporary Problems* **12** (2002), 307–334.

Klerk, Y. S., Supervision of the Execution of the Judgments of the European Court of Human Rights – The Committee of Ministers' Role under Article 54 of the European Convention on Human Rights, *Netherlands International Law Review* **45** (1998), 65–86, 67.

Klug, F., Judicial Deference under the Human Rights Act 1998, *European Human Rights Law Review* (2003), 125–133.

Values for a Godless Age: The Story of the United Kingdom's New Bill of Rights (London: Penguin Books, 2000).

Klug, F., and Starmer, K., Incorporation Through the "Front Door": the First Year of the Human Rights Act, *Public Law* (2001), 654–665.

Klug, F., (with Singh, R., and M. Hunt), *Rights Brought Home: A Briefing on the Human Rights Bill*, Human Rights Incorporation Project, School of Law, King's College London, 1998.

Koçak, M., and Örücü, E., Dissolution of Political Parties in the Name of Democracy: Cases from Turkey and the European Court of Human Rights, *European Public Law* **9** (2003), 399–423.

Koh, H., Review Essay: Why Do Nations Obey International Law?, *Yale Law Journal* **106** (1997), 2599–2659.

Kokott, J., *The Burden of Proof in Comparative and International Human Rights Law: Civil and Common Law Approaches with Special Reference to the American and German Legal Systems* (The Hague/London/Boston: Kluwer Law International, 1998).

Kolb, R., The Jurisprudence of the European Court of Human Rights on Detention and Fair Trial in Criminal Matters from 1992 to the End of 1998, *Human Rights Law Journal* **21** (2000), 348–373.

Krüger, H. C., and Polakiewicz, J., Proposals for a Coherent Human Rights Protection System in Europe: the European Convention on Human Rights and the EU Charter of Fundamental Rights, *Human Rights Law Journal* **22** (2001), 1–13.

Krygier, M., and Czarnota, A., The Rule of Law after Communism: An Introduction. In Krygier, M., and Czarnota, A. (eds.), *The Rule of Law after Communism: Problems and Prospects in East-Central Europe* (Aldershot/ Brookfield/Singapore/Sidney: Ashgate/Dartmouth, 1999), pp. 1–18.

Kumar, C. R., National Human Rights Institutions: Good Governance Perspectives on Institutionalization of Human Rights, *American University International Law Review* **19** (2003), 259–300.

Kurczewski, J., The Rule of Law in Poland. In Přibáň, J., and Young, J., *The Rule of Law in Central Europe: The Reconstruction of Legality, Constitutionalism and Civil Society in the Post-Communist Countries* (Aldershot/Brookfield/ Singapore/Sydney, 1999), pp. 181–203.

Lacey, N., Feminist Legal Theory and the Rights of Women. In Knop, K. (ed.), *Gender and Human Rights* (Oxford: Oxford University Press, 2004).

Lambert-Abdelgawad, E., *The Execution of Judgments of the European Court of Human Rights* (Strasbourg: Council of Europe Publishing, Human Rights Files No. 19, 2002).

Landman, T., Measuring Human Rights: Principle, Practice and Policy, *Human Rights Quarterly* **26** (2004), 906–931.

Lanham, H. R., and Forsythe, D. P., Human Rights in the New Europe: A Balance Sheet. In Forsythe, D. P. (ed.), *Human Rights in the New Europe – Problems and Progress* (Lincoln/London: University of Nebraska Press, 1994), pp. 241–259.

Lavender, N., The Problem of the Margin of Appreciation, *European Human Rights Law Review* **4** (1997), 380–390.

Laws, Sir John, Law and Democracy, *Public Law* (1995), 72–93.

Leach, P., Beyond the Bug River – A New Dawn for Redress Before the European Court of Human Rights, *European Human Rights Law Review* (2005), 148–164.

The British Military in Iraq – the Applicability of the *Espace Juridique* Doctrine Under the European Convention on Human Rights, *Public Law* (2005), 448–458.

Lemmens, P., The Relation Between the Charter of Fundamental Rights of the European Union and the European Convention on Human Rights – Substantive Aspects, *Maastricht Journal of European and Comparative Law* **8** (2001), 49–67.

Lester, A., Merger of the European Commission and the European Court of Human Rights from the Perspective of Applicants and their Legal Representatives, *Human Rights Law Journal* **8** (1987), 34–41.

The Overseas Trade in the American Bill of Rights, *Columbia Law Review* **88** (1988), 537–561.

Lindsnœs, B., and Lindholt, L., National Human Rights Institutions: Standard-Setting and Achievements, *Human Rights in Development Yearbook* (1998), 3–10.

Livingstone, S., and Murray, R., The Effectiveness of National Human Rights Institutions. In Halliday, S., and Schmidt, P. (eds.), *Human Rights Brought Home: Socio-Legal Perspectives on Human Rights in the National Context* (Oxford/Portland: Hart Publishing, 2004), pp. 136–164.

Livingstone, S., Article 14 and the Prevention of Discrimination in the European Convention on Human Rights, *European Human Rights Law Review* (1997), 25–34.

Lopez, G. A., and Stohl, M., Problems of Concept and Measurement in the Study of Human Rights. In Jabine, T. B., and Claude, R. P. (eds.), *Human Rights and Statistics: Getting the Record Straight* (Philadelphia: University of Pennsylvania Press, 1992), pp. 216–234.

Lord Goldsmith, The Charter of Rights – A Brake Not an Accelerator, *European Human Rights Law Review* (2004), 473–478.

Lord Irvine of Lairg, Q.C., The Impact of the Human Rights Act: Parliament, the Courts and the Executive, *Public Law* (2003), 308–325.

Lord Steyn, 2000–2005: Laying the Foundations of Human Rights Law in the United Kingdom, *European Human Rights Law Review* (2005) 349–362.

Lord Woolf, *Review of the Working Methods of the European Court of Human Rights* (Strasbourg: Council of Europe, 2005).

Loucaides, L. G., The Judgment of the European Court of Human Rights in the Case of *Cyprus* v. *Turkey, Leiden Journal of International Law* **15** (2002), 225–236.

Loughlin, M., Rights, Democracy, and Law. In Campbell, T., Ewing, K. D., and Tomkins, A. (eds.), *Sceptical Essays on Human Rights* (Oxford: Oxford University Press, 2001), pp. 41–60.

Lukes, S., *Marxism and Morality* (Oxford: Clarendon Press, 1985).

Lundestad, A. G., *Empire by Integration: The United States and European Integration, 1945–1997* (Oxford: Oxford University Press, 1998).

Macdonald, R. St. J., Derogations Under Article 15 of the European Convention on Human Rights, *Columbia Journal of Transnational Law* **36** (1997), 225–268.

The Luxembourg Preliminary Ruling Procedure and its Possible Application in Strasbourg. In Anon (ed.), *Mélanges en Hommage à Louis Edmond Pettiti* (Bruxelles: Bruyant, 1998), pp. 593–603.

The Margin of Appreciation in the Jurisprudence of the European Court of Human Rights. In Clapham, A., and Emmert, F. (eds.), *Collected Courses of the Academy of European Law: Vol. II, Book 2 – The Protection of Human Rights in Europe* (Dordrecht/Boston/London: Martinus Nijhoff, 1990), pp. 99–161.

The Margin of Appreciation in the Jurisprudence of the European Court of Human Rights. In Anon (ed.), *International Law at the Time of its Codification, Essays in Honour of Judge Roberto Ago* (Milan: Giuffrè, 1987), pp. 187–208.

The Margin of Appreciation. In Macdonald, R. St. J., Matscher, F., and Petzold, H. (eds.), *The European System for the Protection of Human Rights* (Dordrecht/Boston/London: Martinus Nijhoff, 1993), pp. 83–124.

MacIntyre, A., *After Virtue* (London: Duckworth, 1981).

Madureira, J., Portugal. In Blackburn, R., and Polakiewicz, J. (eds.), *Fundamental Rights in Europe: The European Convention on Human Rights and its Member States, 1950–2000* (Oxford: Oxford University Press, 2001), pp. 681–709.

Mahoney, P., An Insider's View of the Reform Debate, paper presented at the *Symposium on the Reform of the European Court of Human Rights*, Strasbourg, 17 November 2003.

Judicial Activism and Judicial Self-Restraint in the European Court of Human Rights: Two Sides of the Same Coin, *Human Rights Law Journal* **11** (1990), 57–88.

New Challenges for the European Court of Human Rights Resulting from the Expanding Case Load and Membership, *Penn State International Law Review* **21** (2002), 101–114.

New Challenges for the European Court of Human Rights Resulting from Expanding Case Load and Membership, *Conference on Human Rights – Dynamic Dimension*, London, 27 April 2002.

Separation of powers in the Council of Europe: the Status of the European Court of Human Rights vis-à-vis the Authorities of the Council of Europe, *Human Rights Law Journal* **24** (2003), 152–161.

Short Commentary on the Rules of Court: Some of the Main Points, *Human Rights Law Journal* **19** (1998), 267–269.

Speculating on the Future of the Reformed European Court of Human Rights, *Human Rights Law Journal* **20** (1999), 1–4.

The Charter of Fundamental Rights of the European Union and the European Convention on Human Rights from the Perspective of the European Convention, *Human Rights Law Journal* **23** (2002), 300–303.

Mahoney, P., Callewaert, J., Ovey, C., Prebensen, S. C., Winisdoerffer, Y., Schokkenbroek, J., and O'Boyle, M. (Council of Europe internal seminar), The Doctrine of the Margin of Appreciation under the European

Convention on Human Rights: Its Legitimacy in Theory and Application in Practice, *Human Rights Law Journal* **19** (1998), 1–36.

Malinverni, G., The Contribution of the European Commission for Democracy Through Law (Venice Commission), *International Studies in Human Rights* **67** (2001), 123–137.

Malloy, T. E., *National Minority Rights in Europe* (Oxford: Oxford University Press, 2005).

Manas, J. E., The Council of Europe's Democracy Ideal and the Challenge of Ethno-National Strife. In Chayes, A., and Chayes, A. H. (eds.), *Preventing Conflict in the Post-Communist World – Mobilizing International and Regional Organizations* (Washington: Brookings Occasional Papers, Brookings Institution, 1996), pp. 99–144.

Mantouvalou, V., Servitude and Forced Labour in the 21st Century: the Human Rights of Domestic Workers forthcoming in *Industrial Law Journal.*

Marcus-Helmons, S., and Marcus-Helmons, P., Belgium. In Blackburn, R., and Polakiewicz, J. (eds.), *Fundamental Rights in Europe: The European Convention on Human Rights and its Member States, 1950–2000* (Oxford: Oxford University Press, 2001), pp. 167–190.

Marks, S., The European Convention on Human Rights and its "Democratic Society", *British Yearbook on International Law* **66** (1995), 209–238.

Marston, G., The United Kingdom's Part in the Preparation of the European Convention on Human Rights 1950, *International and Comparative Law Quarterly* **42** (1993), 796–826.

Martens, S. F., Individual Complaints under Article 53 of the European Convention on Human Rights. In Lawson, R., and de Bois, M. (eds.), *The Dynamics of the Protection of Human Rights in Europe: Essays in Honour of Henry G. Schermers*, Vol. III (Dordrecht: Martinus Nijhoff, 1994), pp. 253–292.

Martens, S.K., Commentary. In Bulterman, M. K., and Kuijer, M. (eds.), *Compliance With Judgments of International Courts: Proceedings of the Symposium Organized in Honour of Professor Henry G. Schermers by Mordenate College and the Department of International Public Law of Leiden University* (The Hague/Boston/London: Martinus Nijhoff, 1996).

Martínez-Torrón, J., The European Court of Human Rights, and Religion, *Current Legal Issues* (2001), 185–204.

Maruste, R., Estonia. In Blackburn, R., and Polakiewicz, J. (eds.), *Fundamental Rights in Europe: The European Convention on Human Rights and its Member States,* 1950–2000 (Oxford: Oxford University Press, 2001), pp. 277–287.

Matscher, F., Methods of Interpretation of the Convention. In Macdonald, R. St. J., Matscher, F., and Petzold, H. (eds.), *The European System for the Protection of Human Rights* (Dordrecht/Boston/London: Martinus Nijhoff, 1993), pp. 63–81.

Mavčič, A., Slovenia. In Blackburn, R., and Polakiewicz, J. (eds.), *Fundamental Rights in Europe: The European Convention on Human Rights and its Member States, 1950–2000* (Oxford: Oxford University Press, 2001), pp. 781–808.

McBride, J., Proportionality and the European Convention on Human Rights. In Ellis, E. (ed.), *The Principle of Proportionality in the Laws of Europe* (Oxford: Hart Publishing, 1999), pp. 23–35.

McHarg, A., Reconciling Human Rights and the Public Interest: Conceptual Problems and Doctrinal Uncertainty in the Jurisprudence of the European Court of Human Rights, *Modern Law Review* **62** (1999), 671–696.

Medda-Windischer, R., The European Court of Human Rights and Minority Rights, *European Integration* **25** (2003), 249–271.

Meriggiola, E., Italy. In Blackburn, R., and Polakiewicz, J. (eds.), *Fundamental Rights in Europe: The European Convention on Human Rights and its Member States, 1950–2000* (Oxford: Oxford University Press, 2001), pp. 475–501.

Meron, T., and Sloan, J. S., Democracy, Rule of Law and Admission to the Council of Europe, *Israel Yearbook on Human Rights* **26** (1996), 137–156.

Mill, J. S., *On Liberty* (London: Routledge, 1991).

Utilitarianism (Oxford: Oxford University Press, 1991).

Milton, J. R., and Milton, P. (eds.), John Locke: An Essay Concerning Toleration and Other Writings on Law and Politics, 1667–1683 (Oxford/New York: Clarendon Press, 2006).

Mokhtar, A., Human Rights Obligations v. Derogations: Article 15 of the European Convention on Human Rights, *International Journal of Human Rights* **8** (2004), 65–87.

Mole, N., *Issa v Turkey*: Delineating the Extra-Territorial Effect of the European Convention on Human Rights?, *European Human Rights Law Review* (2005), 86–91.

Moon, G., and Allen, R., Q.C., Substantive Rights and Equal Treatment in Respect of Religion and Belief: Towards a Better Understanding of the Rights, and their Implications, *European Human Rights Law Review* (2000), 580–601.

Moravcsik, A., The Origins of Human Rights Regimes: Democratic Delegation in Postwar Europe, *International Organisation* **54** (2000), 217–252.

Morgan, K., *Labour in Power* (Oxford: Clarendon Press, 1984).

Morgan, R., and Evans, M., *Combating Torture in Europe: the Work and Standards of the European Committee for the Prevention of Torture* (Strasbourg: Council of Europe, 2001).

Morozov, V., Human Rights and Foreign Policy Discourse in Today's Russia: Romantic Realism and Securitisation of Identity, *European Human Rights Review* **8** (2002), 143–198.

Resisting Entropy, Discarding Human Rights – Romantic Realism and Securitization of Identity in Russia, *Cooperation and Conflict* **37** (2002), 409–430.

Morrisson, C. C., Margin of Appreciation in European Human Rights Law, *Revue des Droits de l'Homme* **6** (1973), 263–286.

Møse, E., New rights for the new Court? In Mahoney, P., Matscher, F., Petzold, H., and Wildhaber, L. (eds.), *Protecting Human Rights: The European Perspective – Studies in Memory of Rolv Ryssdall* (Cologne/Berlin/Bonn/Munich: Carl Heymans, 2000), pp. 943–956.

Norway. In Blackburn, R., and Polakiewicz, J. (eds.), *Fundamental Rights in Europe: The European Convention on Human Rights and its Member States, 1950–2000* (Oxford: Oxford University Press, 2001), pp. 625–655.

Mowbray, A., Duties of Investigation under the European Convention on Human Rights, *International and Comparative Law Quarterly* **51** (2002), 437–448.

Proposals for reform of the European Court of Human Rights, *Public Law* (2002), 252–264.

The Composition and Operation of the New European Court of Human Rights, *Public Law* (1999), 219–231.

The Role of the European Court of Human Rights in the Promotion of Democracy, *Public Law* (1999), 703–725.

The Development of Positive Obligations under the European Convention on Human Rights by the European Court of Human Rights (Oxford/Portland: Hart, 2004).

Murray, R., Lessons from the South African Human Rights Commission: An Examination of a National Human Rights Institution, unpublished paper provided by author.

Ní Aoláin, F., The Evolving Jurisprudence of the European Convention Concerning the Right to Life, *Netherlands Quarterly of Human Rights* **19** (2001), 21–42.

Nicol, D., Original Intent and the European Convention on Human Rights, *Public Law* (2005), 152–172.

Novitz, T., Remedies for Violation of Social Rights within the Council of Europe: The Significant Absence of a Court. In Kilpatrick, C., Novitz, T., and Skidmore, P. (eds.), *The Future of Remedies in Europe* (Oxford: Hart, 2000), pp. 231–251.

Nowak, M., The Agency and National Institutions for the Promotion and Protection of Human Rights. In Alston, P., and de Schutter, O. (eds.), *Monitoring Fundamental Rights in the EU: The Contribution of the Fundamental Rights Agency* (Oxford: Hart Publishing, 2005), pp. 91–107.

Nowak, M., and von Hebel, H., A Statistical Analysis of Dutch Human Rights Case Law. In Jabine, T. B., and Claude, R. P. (eds.), *Human Rights and*

Statistics: Getting the Record Straight (Philadelphia: University of Pennsylvania Press, 1992), pp. 313–327.

Nowlin, C., The Protection of Morals Under the European Convention for the Protection of Human Rights and Fundamental Freedoms, *Human Rights Quarterly* **24** (2002), 264–286.

O'Boyle, The Margin of Appreciation and Derogation under Article 15: Ritual Incantation or Principle?, *Human Rights Law Journal* **19** (1998), 23–29.

O'Brien, D. M., *Storm Center: The Supreme Court in American Politics* (New York and London: W.W. Norton & Co., 6th edn., 2002).

O'Connell, D., Ireland. In Blackburn, R., and Polakiewicz, J. (eds.), *Fundamental Rights in Europe: The European Convention on Human Rights and its Member States, 1950–2000* (Oxford: Oxford University Press, 2001), pp. 423–473.

O'Donnell, T. A., The Margin of Appreciation Doctrine: Standards in the Jurisprudence of the European Court of Human Rights, *Human Rights Quarterly* **4** (1982), 474–496.

Olbourne, B., Case Anlaysis: Refah Partisi (The Welfare Party) v. Turkey, *European Human Rights Law Review* (2003), 437–444.

Oraá, J., *Human Rights in States of Emergency in International Law* (Oxford: Clarendon Press, 1992).

Orakhelashvili, A., Restrictive Interpretation of Human Rights Treaties in the Recent Jurisprudence of the European Court of Human Rights, *European Journal of International Law* **14** (2003), 529–568.

Orlov, O., Status of Human Rights in the Chechen Republic, Autumn 2000, *Russian Politics and Law* **39** (2001), 25–33.

Örücü, E., The Turkish Constitution Revamped?, *European Public Law* **8** (2002), 201–218.

Seven Packages towards Harmonisation with the European Union, *European Public Law* **10** (2004), 603–621.

Ost, F., The Original Canons of Interpretation of the European Court of Human Rights. In Delmas-Marty, M., and Chodkiewicz, C. (eds.), *The European Convention for the Protection of Human Rights: International Protection Versus National Restrictions* (Dordrecht/Boston/London: Martinus Nijhoff, 1992), pp. 238–318.

Ovey, C., and White, R. C. A., *Jacobs and White, The European Convention on Human Rights* (Oxford: Oxford University Press, 3rd edn., 2002).

Özdek, Y., and Karacaoğlu, E., Turkey. In Blackburn, R., and Polakiewicz, J. (eds.), *Fundamental Rights in Europe: The European Convention on Human Rights and its Member States, 1950–2000* (Oxford: Oxford University Press, 2001), pp. 879–914.

Paczolay, P., Traditional Elements in the Constitutions of Central and East European Democracies. In Krygier, M., and Czarnota, A. (eds.), *The Rule of Law after Communism: Problems and Prospects in East-Central*

Europe (Aldershot/Brookfield/Singapore/Sidney: Ashgate/Dartmouth, 1999), pp. 109–130.

Paine, T., *The Rights of Man* (London: Jordan, J. S., 1791).

Pasquino, P., Constitutional Adjudication and Democracy. Comparative Perspectives: USA, France, Italy, *Ratio Juris* **11** (1998), 38–50.

Peers, S., and Ward, A. (ed.), *The EU Charter of Fundamental Rights: Politics, Law and Policy* (Oxford: Hart Publishing, 2004).

The Contribution of the EU Fundamental Rights Agency to Civil and Political Rights. In Alston, P., and de Schutter, O. (eds.), *Monitoring Fundamental Rights in the EU: The Contribution of the Fundamental Rights Agency* (Oxford: Hart Publishing, 2005), pp. 111–130.

The European Court of Justice and the European Court of Human Rights: Comparative Approaches, *United Kingdom Comparative Law Series* **22** (2003), 107–128.

Petzold, H., The Convention and the Principle of Subsidiarity. In Macdonald, R. St. J., Matscher, F., and Petzold, H. (eds.), *The European System for the Protection of Human Rights* (Dordrecht/Boston/London: Martinus Nijhoff, 1993), pp. 41–62.

Pogany, I., (Re)Building the Rule of Law in Hungary: Jewish and Gypsy Perspectives. In Přibáň, J., and Young, J., *The Rule of Law in Central Europe: The Reconstruction of Legality, Constitutionalism and Civil Society in the Post-Communist Countries* (Aldershot/Brookfield/Singapore/Sydney, 1999), pp. 141–159.

Minority Rights and the Roma of Central and Eastern Europe, forthcoming in *International Journal of Human Rights* **11** (2007).

Post-Communist Legal Orders and the Roma: Some Implications for EU Enlargement. In Sadurski, W., Czarnota, A., and Krygier, M. (eds.), *Spreading Democracy And The Rule Of Law?* (New York: Springer Science, 2005), Ch. 15.

Righting Wrongs in Eastern Europe (Manchester: Manchester University Press, 1997).

Polakiewicz, J., The Application of the European Convention on Human Rights in Domestic Law, *European Human Rights Law Journal* **17** (1996), 405–411.

The Status of the Convention in National Law. In Blackburn, R., and Polakiewicz, J. (eds.), *Fundamental Rights in Europe: The European Convention on Human Rights and its Member States, 1950–2000* (Oxford: Oxford University Press, 2001), pp. 31–53.

Potapenko, V., and Pushkar, P., Ukraine. In Blackburn, R., and Polakiewicz, J. (eds.), *Fundamental Rights in Europe: The European Convention on Human Rights and its Member States, 1950–2000* (Oxford: Oxford University Press, 2001), pp. 915–934.

Prebensen, S. C., Evolutive interpretation of the European Convention on Human Rights. In Mahoney, P., Matscher, F., Petzold, H., and Wildhaber, L. (eds.), *Protecting Human Rights: The European Perspective – Studies in Memory of Rolv Ryssdall* (Cologne/Berlin/Bonn/Munich: Carl Heymans, 2000), pp. 1123–1137.

Inter-State Complaints under Treaty Provisions – The Experience under the European Convention on Human Rights, *Human Rights Law Journal* **20** (1999), 446–455.

Preece, J. J., *National Minorities and the European Nation-States System* (Oxford: Clarendon Press, 1998).

Přibáň, J., and Young, J., Central Europe in Transition: An Introduction. In Přibáň, J., and Young, J. (eds.), *The Rule of Law in Central Europe: The Reconstruction of Legality, Constitutionalism and Civil Society in the Post-Communist Countries* (Aldershot/Brookfield/Singapore/Sydney, 1999), pp. 1–10.

Pridham, G., *Democratization in Central and Eastern Europe: A Comparative Perspective* (Baskingstoke/New York: Palgrave MacMillan, 2003), pp. 269–289.

Protocol No. 14 to the Convention for the Protection of Human Rights and Fundamental Freedoms, Amending the Control System of the Convention, CETS No. 194, Explanatory Report as Adopted by the Committee of Ministers at its 114th Session on 12 May 2004.

Quinn, G., The European Union and the Council of Europe on the Issue of Human Rights: Twins Separated at Birth?, *McGill Law Journal* **46** (2001), 849–874.

Rawls, J., *A Theory of Justice* (London/Oxford/New York: Oxford University Press, 1972).

Raworth, K., Measuring Human Rights, *Ethics and International Affairs* **15** (2001), 111–131.

Reidy, A., Hampson, F., and Boyle, K., Gross Violations of Human Rights: Invoking the European Convention on Human Rights in the Case of Turkey, *Netherlands Quarterly of Human Rights* **15** (1997), 161–173.

Reif, L. C., *The Ombudsman, Good Governance and the International Human Rights System* (Leiden/Boston: Martinus Nijhoff, 2004).

Reif, L., Building Democratic Institutions: the Role of National Human Rights Institutions in Good Governance and Human Rights Protection, *Harvard Human Rights Journal* **13** (2000), 1–58.

Report of the Evaluation Group to the Committee of Ministers on the European Court of Human Rights, EG Court 1 (2001) 27 September 2001.

Response of the European Court of Human Rights to the CDDH Interim Activity Report Prepared Following the 46th Plenary Administrative Session, CDDH-GDR (2004)001, 10 February 2004.

Ress, G., The Effect of Decisions and Judgments of the European Court of Human Rights in the Domestic Legal Order, *Texas International Law Journal* **40** (2005), 359–382.

Risse, T., Ropp, S. C., and Sikkink, K. (eds.), *The Power of Human Rights: International Norms and Domestic Change* (Cambridge: Cambridge University Press, 1999).

Robertson, H., *The Council of Europe: Its Structure, Functions and Achievements* (London: Stevens & Sons, 2nd edn., 1961).

Rodger, A., The Future of the European Court of Human Rights: Symposium at the University of Graz, *Human Rights Law Journal* **24** (2003), 149–151.

Rogowski, R., and Gawron, T., Constitutional Litigation as Dispute Processing: Comparing the U.S. Supreme Court and the German Federal Constitutional Court. In Ragowski, R., and Gawron, T. (eds.), *Constitutional Courts in Comparison: The US Supreme Court and the German Federal Constitutional Court* (New York and Oxford: Berghahn Books, 2002), pp. 1–21.

Rosas, A., Finland. In Blackburn, R., and Polakiewicz, J. (eds.), *Fundamental Rights in Europe: The European Convention on Human Rights and its Member States, 1950–2000* (Oxford: Oxford University Press, 2001), pp. 289–312.

Rules adopted by the Committee of Ministers for the application of Article 46, paragraph 2, of the European Convention on Human Rights, text approved by the Committee of Ministers on 10 January 2001 at the 736th meeting of the Ministers' Deputies.

Rumford, C., Resisting Globalization? Turkey–EU Relations and Human and Political Rights in the Context of Cosmopolitan Democratization, *International Sociology* **18** (2003), 279–394.

Ryssdall, R., On the Road to a European Constitutional Court, Winston Churchill Lecture on the Council of Europe, Florence, 21 June 1991.

The Coming of Age of the European Convention on Human Rights, *European Human Rights Law Review* (1996), 18–29.

The Enforcement System set up under the European Convention on Human Rights. In Bulterman, M. K., and Kuijer, M. (eds.), *Compliance With Judgments of International Courts: Proceedings of the Symposium Organized in Honour of Professor Henry G. Schermers by Mordenate College and the Department of International Public Law of Leiden University* (The Hague/Boston/London: Martinus Nijhoff, 1996), pp. 49–69.

Sadurski, W., Rights and Freedoms under the new Polish Constitution. In Krygier, M., and Czarnota, A. (eds.), *The Rule of Law after Communism: Problems and Prospects in East-Central Europe* (Aldershot/Brookfield/Singapore/Sidney: Ashgate/Dartmouth, 1999), pp. 176–193.

Rights Before Courts – A Study of Constitutional Courts in Postcommunist States of Central and Eastern Europe (Dordrecht: Springer, 2005).

Sager, L., The Domain of Constitutional Justice. In Alexander, L. *Constitutionalism: Philosophical Foundations* (Cambridge: Cambridge University Press, 1998).

Salter, M., The Impossibility of Human Rights Within a Postmodern Account of Law and Justice, *Journal of Civil Liberties* 1 (1996), 29–66.

Sandel, M., *Liberalism and the Limits of Justice* (Cambridge, Cambridge University Press, 2nd edn., 1982).

Sardaro, P., *Jus Non Dicere* for Allegations of Serious Violations of Human Rights: Questionable Trends in Recent Case Law of the Strasbourg Court, *European Human Rights Law Review* (2003), 601–630.

Satter, D., *Darkness at Dawn: The Rise of the Russian Criminal State* (New Haven/London: Yale University Press, 2003).

Savard, G., Complaint Handling at the Canadian Human Rights Commission. In Ayeni, V., Reif, L., and Thomas, H. (eds.), *Strengthening Ombudsman and Human Rights Institutions in Commonwealth Small and Island States – The Caribbean Experience* (London: Commonwealth Secretariat, 2000), pp. 132–137.

Schokkenbroek, J., The Preventive Role of the Commissioner for Human Rights of the Council of Europe, *International Studies in Human Rights* **67** (2001), 201–213.

The Prohibition of Discrimination in Article 14 of the Convention and the Margin of Appreciation, *Human Rights Law Journal* **19** (1998), 20–23.

The Basis, Nature and Application of the Margin-of-Appreciation Doctrine in the Case-Law of the European Court of Human Rights, *Human Rights Law Journal* **19** (1998), 30–36.

Schwartz, H., *The Struggle for Constitutional Justice in Post-Communist Europe* (Chicago/London: University of Chicago Press, 2000).

Schwartz, R., The Paradox of Sovereignty, Regime Type and Human Rights Compliance, *International Journal of Human Rights* **8** (2004), 199–215.

Sera, J. M., The Case for Accession by the European Union to the European Convention for the Protection of Human Rights, *Boston University International Law Journal* **14** (1996), 151–186.

Service, R., *Russia – Experimenting With a People* (London: Macmillan, 2002).

Sikkink, K., The Power of Principled Ideas: Human Rights Policies in the United States and Western Europe. In Goldstein, J., and Keohane, R. O. (eds.), *Ideas and Foreign Policy: Beliefs, Institutions and Political Change* (New York: Cornell University Press, 1993), pp. 139–170.

Simor, J., Tackling Human Rights Abuses in Bosnia and Herzegovina: The Convention is up to it, are its institutions, *European Human Rights Law Review* **6** (1997), 644–662.

Simor, J., and Emmerson, B., Q.C. (eds.), *Human Rights Practice* (London: Sweet & Maxwell, 2000).

Simpson, A. W. B., Britain and the European Convention, *Cornell International Law Journal* **34** (2001), 523–554.

Hersch Lauterpacht and the Genesis of the Age of Human Rights, *Law Quarterly Review* (2004), 49–80.

Human Rights and the End of Empire – Britain and the Genesis of the European Convention (Oxford: Oxford University Press, 2001).

Skąpska, G., Between "Civil Society" and "Europe": Post-Classical Constitutionalism after the Collapse of Communism in a Socio-Legal Perspective. In Přibáň, J., and Young, J. (eds.), *The Rule of Law in Central Europe: The Reconstruction of Legality, Constitutionalism and Civil Society in the Post-Communist Countries* (Aldershot/Brookfield/Singapore/Sydney, 1999), pp. 204–222.

Paradigm Lost? The Constitutional Process in Poland and the Hope of a "Grass Roots Constitutionalism". In Krygier, M., and Czarnota, A. (eds.), *The Rule of Law after Communism: Problems and Prospects in East-Central Europe* (Aldershot/Brookfield/Singapore/Sidney: Ashgate/Dartmouth, 1999), pp. 149–175.

Sládeček, V., The Protection of Human Rights in the Czech Republic. In Přibáň, J., and Young, J., *The Rule of Law in Central Europe: The Reconstruction of Legality, Constitutionalism and Civil Society in the Post-Communist Countries* (Aldershot/Brookfield/Singapore/Sydney, 1999), pp. 82–98.

Smart, C., *Feminism and the Power of Law* (London: Routledge, 1989).

Sós, V., The Paradigm of Constitutionalism: The Hungarian Experience. In Krygier M., and Czarnota A. (eds.), *The Rule of Law after Communism: Problems and Prospects in East-Central Europe* (Aldershot/Brookfield/Singapore/Sidney: Ashgate/Dartmouth, 1999), pp. 131–148.

Spencer, S., and Bynoe, I., A Human Rights Commission for the United Kingdom – Some Options, *European Human Rights Law Review* (1997), 152–160.

A Human Rights Commission: The Options for Britain and Northern Ireland (London: Institute for Public Policy Research, 1998).

Spielmann, D., Human Rights Case Law in the Strasbourg and Luxembourg Courts: Conflicts, Inconsistencies and Complementarities. In Alston, P., with Bustelo, M., and Heenan, J. (eds.), *The EU and Human Rights* (Oxford: Oxford University Press, 1999), pp. 757–780.

Steering Committee for Human Rights (CDDH), *Activity Report of the Steering Committee for Human Rights and the Reflection Group on the Reinforcement of the Human Rights Protection Mechanism*, CDDH-GDR(2001)10, 15 June 2001.

Guaranteeing the Long-Term Effectiveness of the European Court of Human Rights – Implementation of the Declaration Adopted by the Committee of

Ministers at its 112th Session (14–15 May 2003) Interim Activity Report, CDDH(2003)026 Addendum I Final, 26 November 2003.

Guaranteeing the Long-Term Effectiveness of the Control System of the European Convention on Human Rights - Addendum to the Final Report Containing CDDH Proposals (Long Version), 9 April 2003, (CDDH(2003)006 Addendum final).

Interim Report of the CDDH to be Submitted to the Committee of Ministers – 'Guaranteeing the Long-Term Effectiveness of the European Court of Human Rights', CDDH(2002)016 Addendum, 14 October 2002.

Report of the Reflection Group on the Reinforcement of the Human Rights Protection Mechanism, CDDH-GDR(2002)012, 12 December 2002.

Study of Technical and Legal Issues of a Possible EC/EU Accession to the European Convention on Human Rights, Report adopted by the Steering Committee for Human Rights (CDDH) at its 53rd meeting (25–28 June 2002), Council of Europe DG-II(2002)006 CDDH(2002)010 Addendum.

Stone Sweet, A., *Governing with Judges: Constitutional Politics in Europe* (Oxford: Oxford University Press, 2000).

The Judicial Construction of Europe (Oxford: Oxford University Press, 2004).

Sweeney, J. A., Margins of Appreciation: Cultural Relativity and the European Court of Human Rights in the Post-Cold War Era, *International and Comparative Law Quarterly* **54** (2005), 459–474.

Swimelar, S., Approaches to Ethnic Conflict and the Protection of Human Rights in Post-Communist Europe: The Need for Preventive Diplomacy, *Nationalism and Ethnic Politics* **7** (2001), 98–126.

Tapper, C., *Cross and Tapper on Evidence*, 10th edn. (London: Butterworths, 2004).

Three Years Work for the Future, Final Report of the Working Party on the Working Methods of the European Court of Human Rights (Strasbourg: Council of Europe, 2002).

Tomkins, A., The Committee of Ministers: Its Roles under the European Convention on Human Rights, *European Human Rights Law Review* **1** (1995), 49–62.

Trechsel, S., Human rights and minority rights – Two Sides of the Same Coin? A Sketch. In Mahoney, P., Matscher, F., Petzold, H., and Wildhaber, L. (eds.), *Protecting Human Rights: The European Perspective – Studies in Memory of Rolv Ryssdall* (Cologne/Berlin/Bonn/Munich: Carl Heymans, 2000), pp. 1443–1453.

Tretter, H., Austria. In Blackburn, R., and Polakiewicz, J. (eds.), *Fundamental Rights in Europe: The European Convention on Human Rights and its Member States, 1950–2000* (Oxford: Oxford University Press, 2001), pp. 103–165.

Tridimas, T., Knocking on Heaven's Door: Fragmentation, Efficiency and Defiance in the Preliminary Reference Procedure, *Common Market Law Review* **40** (2003), 9–50.

Turner, C., Human Rights Protection in the European Community: Resolving Conflict and Overlap Between the European Court of Justice and the European Court of Human Rights, *European Public Law* **3** (1999), 453–470.

Uildriks, N., and van Reenen, P. (eds.), *Policing Post-Communist Societies: Police-Public Violence, Democratic Policing and Human Rights* (Antwerp: Intersentia, 2003).

Ulram, P. A., and Plasser, F., Political Culture in East-Central Europe: Empirical Findings 1990–2001. In Pollack, D., Jacobs, J., Müller, O., and Pickel, G. (eds.), *Political Culture in Post-Communist Europe: Attitudes in New Democracies* (Aldershot: Ashgate Publishing Ltd, 2003), pp. 31–46.

United Nations, Principles Relating to the Status of National Institutions, UN Commission on Human Rights resolution 1992/54 of 3 March 1992, Annex, UN doc. E/1992/22, chap. II, sect. A; *Principles Relating to the Status of National Institutions for the Promotion and Protection of Human Rights*, General Assembly Resolution 48/134 of 20 December 1993 (the 'Paris Principles').

(Updated) Joint Response to Proposals to Ensure the Future Effectiveness of the European Court of Human Rights, signed by 114 NGOs, April 2004.

Vadapalas, V., Lithuania. In Blackburn, R., and Polakiewicz, J. (eds.), *Fundamental Rights in Europe: The European Convention on Human Rights and its Member States, 1950–2000* (Oxford: Oxford University Press, 2001), pp. 503–529.

van Dijk, P., and van Hoof, G. J. H., *Theory and Practice of the European Convention on Human Rights*, 3rd edn. (The Hague/London/Boston: Kluwer, 1998).

Vincent, R. J., *Human Rights and International Relations* (Cambridge: Cambridge University Press, 1986).

von Beyme, K., Constitutional Engineering in Central and Eastern Europe. In White, S., Batt, J., and Lewis, P. G. (eds.), *Central and East European Politics III* (Basingstoke: Palgrave, 2003)

Vorhaus, J., On Degradation. Part One. Article 3 of the European Convention on Human Rights, *Common Law World Review* **31** (2002), 374–399.

On Degradation. Part Two. Degrading Treatment and Punishment, *Common Law World Review* **32** (2003), 65–92.

Wadham, J., and Said, T., What Price the Right of Individual Petition: Report of the Evaluation Group to the Committee of Ministers on the European Court of Human Rights, *European Human Rights Law Review* (2002), 169–174.

Waldron, J., A Right-Based Critique of Constitutional Rights, *Oxford Journal of Legal Studies* **13** (1993), 18–51.

Warbrick, C., The Principles of the European Convention on Human Rights and the Response of States to Terrorism, *European Human Rights Law Review* (2002), 287–314.

Weber, R., Romania. In Blackburn, R., and Polakiewicz, J. (eds.), *Fundamental Rights in Europe: The European Convention on Human Rights and its Member States, 1950–2000* (Oxford: Oxford University Press, 2001), pp. 711–730.

Weiler, J., *Human Rights in Russia: A Darker Side of Reform* (Boulder/London: Lynne Rienner, 2004).

Weller, M. (ed.), *The Rights of Minorities: A Commentary on the European Framework Convention for the Protection of National Minorities* (Oxford: Oxford University Press, 2005).

West, A., Desdevises, Y., Fenet, A., Gaurier, D., Heussaff, M-C., and Lévy, B., *The French Legal System*, 2nd edn. (London, Edinburgh, Dublin: Butterworths, 1998).

Wicks, E., The United Kingdom Governments Perceptions of the European Convention on Human Rights at the Time of Entry, *Public Law* (2000), 438–455.

Wildhaber, L., A Constitutional Future for the European Court of Human Rights?, *Human Rights Law Journal* **23** (2002), 161–165.

Precedent in the European Court of Human Rights. In Mahoney, P., Matscher, F., Petzold, H., and Wildhaber, L. (eds.), *Protecting Human Rights: The European Perspective – Studies in Memory of Rolv Ryssdall* (Cologne/Berlin/Bonn/Munich: Carl Heymans, 2000), pp. 1529–1545.

The Role of the European Court of Human Rights: An Evaluation, *Mediterranean Journal of Human Rights* **8** (2004), 9–32.

Williams, A., *EU Human Rights Policies: A Study in Irony* (Oxford: Oxford University Press, 2004).

Windisdoerffer, Y., Margin of Appreciation and Article 1 of Protocol No. 1, *Human Rights Law Journal* **18** (1998), 18–20.

Wintemute, R., "Within the Ambit": How Big is the "Gap" in Article 14 European Convention on Human Rights? Part 1, *European Human Rights Law Review* (2004), 366–382.

Filling the Article 14 "Gap": Government Ratification and Judicial Control of Protocol No. 12 ECHR: Part 2, *European Human Rights Law* (2004), 484–499.

Wolchover, L. E., What is the Rule of Law? Perspectives from Central Europe and the American Academy, *Washington Law Review* **78** (2003), 515–524.

Wolf, S., Trial Within a Reasonable Time: The Recent Reforms of the Italian Justice System in Response to the Conflict with Article 6(1) of the ECHR, *European Public Law* **9** (2003), 189–209.

Yourow, H. C., The Margin of Appreciation Doctrine in the Dynamics of European Human Rights Jurisprudence, *Connecticut Journal of International Law* **3** (1987), 111–159.

The Margin of Appreciation Doctrine in the Dynamics of European Human Rights Jurisprudence (The Hague/Boston/London: Kluwer, 1996).

Zacks, M., Administrative Fairness in the Investigative Process. In Reif, L., Marshall, M., and Ferris, C. (eds.), *The Ombudsman: Diversity and Development* (Edmonton: International Ombudsman Institute, 1992), pp. 229–237.

Zassorin, S., Human and Ethnic Minority Rights in the Context of an Emerging Political Culture in Russia, *Javnost-Ljubljana* **7** (2000), 41–54.

Zimmermann, A., Germany. In Blackburn, R., and Polakiewicz, J. (eds.), *Fundamental Rights in Europe: The European Convention on Human Rights and its Member States, 1950–2000* (Oxford: Oxford University Press, 2001), pp. 335–354.

Zürn, M., Introduction: Law and Compliance at different levels. In Zürn, M., and Joerges, C. (eds.), *Law and Governance in Postnational Europe: Compliance Beyond the Nation-State* (Cambridge: Cambridge University Press, 2005), pp. 1–39.

Zürn, M., and Neyer, J., Conclusions – the conditions of compliance. In Zürn, M., and Joerges, C. (eds.), *Law and Governance in Postnational Europe: Compliance Beyond the Nation-State* (Cambridge: Cambridge University Press, 2005), pp. 183–217.

Zwaak, L. F., Netherlands. In Blackburn, R., and Polakiewicz, J. (eds.), *Fundamental Rights in Europe: The European Convention on Human Rights and its Member States, 1950–2000* (Oxford: Oxford University Press, 2001), pp. 595–624.

INDEX